D1522560

Writing War

AARON WILLIAM MOORE

Writing War

SOLDIERS RECORD THE
JAPANESE EMPIRE

HARVARD UNIVERSITY PRESS   Cambridge, Massachusetts, and London, England
2013

Library of Congress Cataloging-in-Publication Data

Moore, Aaron William, 1977–
    Writing war : soldiers record the Japanese Empire / Aaron William
    Moore.—First edition.
        pages cm
    Includes bibliographical references and index.
    ISBN 978-0-674-05906-1 (alk. paper)
    1. World War, 1939–1945—Pacific Area—Diaries. 2. World War,
    1939–1945—Japan—Diaries. 3. World War, 1939–1945—China—Diaries.
    4. Soldiers' writings, American—History and criticism. 5. Soldiers'
    writings, Chinese—History and criticism. 6. Soldiers' writings, Japanese—
    History and criticism. I. Title.
    D767.M5755 2013
    940.53'52072—dc23   2012041384

Contents

Note to the Reader

East Asian names are given in the usual fashion: surnames precede given names. Thus, for Matsui Iwane, "Matsui" is the surname, and "Iwane" is the given name.

I use the *Hanyu pinyin* romanization system for all Chinese words and most names, with the exception of extremely well-known alternatives such as Chiang Kai-shek.

In some cases, I was able to gain access to personal documents only by agreeing to protect the privacy of the diarist through the use of a pseudonym. Whenever a pseudonym first appears, it will be marked with quotes in the notes (e.g., "Yamamoto Kenji").

Writing War

Introduction

World War, Diary Writing, and the Self

IN AN OBSCURE fairy tale novella called *The White Haired Acolyte* (Shiraga Kozō), surrealist fiction author Yumeno Kyūsaku painted a portrait of the brilliant princess Mirumi, an insomniac obsessed with finding new and exciting stories, and her discovery of a strange book at the foot of a ginko tree. Unable to suppress her desire for new fiction, she soon pours over the text, only to discover that it tells the story of her own life and that of a deaf and mute white-haired fool. The diary is the catalyst that causes parallel worlds to collide, ending in Mirumi, like the white-haired fool himself, having her identity compromised by a double—a doppelgänger. Kyūsaku quipped, "Everyone thought that this kind of ridiculous, mysterious tale could never really happen. Only the cleverest and the most foolish people in the world would accept it as truth." Truth and fiction became as unclear as the identities of the players themselves, until the characters realized that they were trapped in a dreamlike tale, and implored the princess to stop reading the diary. Kyūsaku's self-published novella arrived during the zenith of the Japanese public's fascination with dubious celebrity confessions (including many *shishōsetsu,* or "I-novels"), as well as popular travelogues, memoirs, and diaries. In fact, it was a cautionary tale that revealed the vulnerability of self to external subversion, as relevant to today's social media and blogging as it was to the last century's diarists. Taking Kyūsaku's warning to heart, this book aims to show how diaries in the modern era have become important tools in the construction of self in the modern era, with a potential to act for their authors but also for external forces, such as the government. A person's diary is a crucible wherein the author attempts to reconcile, through the medium of language, often silent individual desires with the articulate demands of society, media, and the state.

This is particularly important for studies of the Second World War, because postwar debates frequently revolve around personal and national responsibility for the horrors of the conflict.[1] Michel Foucault was profoundly skeptical of individualism and freedom, stating that "Discipline 'makes' individuals; it is the specific technique of a power that regards individuals both as objects and as instruments of its exercise."[2] For Foucault, then, individuality and what most consider "freedom" are constructs of modern institutions such as schools, hospitals, and barracks. If we accept that citizens in modern nations are products and producers of these institutions, including centers of mass media production (such as newspapers) and social organizations (such as youth groups), then it becomes extraordinarily difficult to meaningfully discuss the ethics of individual behavior. Conversely, if we assume that the private self is truly "free" from the power of social, state, and media organizations, we make ourselves even more vulnerable to their influence in our private lives. This book aims to acknowledge the power of disciplinary institutions but also to have a meaningful discussion concerning how much we control the process of defining who we are.

The raw materials for this consideration are war diaries written by soldiers in the modern era, with a particular focus on those who experienced combat during the Second World War in the Asia-Pacific Theater (1937–1945). Nevertheless, some discussion of the Meiji (1868–1912) and Taishō (1912–1925) periods in Japan and the early Republican (1911–1928) period in China, as well as some reference to historical precedent in the United States, is important to understand how these texts evolved. I have selected the war diaries of Japanese, Chinese Nationalist, and (Pacific Theater) American servicemen because the perceived cultural boundary between these combatants is often overstated and misleading. Most of the documents in the book have not been studied by scholars in any language, and certainly not as part of the same project. In addition to this, the conflict between Nationalist China and Japan (from July 1937 to August 1945), which Chiang Kai-shek referred to as a "total war" from the very beginning, is rarely included in the Anglophone history of the Second World War, or it is addressed inadequately, so every effort has been made to present the first-person accounts of this seldom studied conflict.[3]

This book therefore attempts to finally integrate social historical materials from the Asia-Pacific Theater into the larger narrative of the Second World War; as a consequence of reviewing the personal documents of men who fought in Asia and the Pacific, we must change the way "The War" is narrated. The book will show how important the war in China was for the entire global conflict and how diaries show us the way in which wartime states ultimately relied on the proactive support of their citizens to carry out the most brutal conflict in history. That support was not merely the product of institutional discipline but the cumulative effect of millions of decisions made by individuals. The diary is a historian's window into the process behind those decisions.

A NEW ORDER: TOWARD A GLOBAL HISTORY
OF THE SECOND WORLD WAR

In 1940, when Prime Minister Konoe Fumimaro pushed for a "New Order for East Asia," he was attempting to express an emerging political reality in the mid-twentieth-century world: the age of domination by the "West" had come to an end—that is to say, the colonies and empires of France, Great Britain, the Netherlands, and the United States were unsustainable. By 1942, the Japanese Empire would become one of the largest in world history, but more important was the change that had been occurring in the structure of national economies. Many major powers on the globe had abandoned liberal democracy for strong states, free trade for autarky, and, in a sense, free-market capitalism for state-led development;[4] contrary to neoliberal views, these economies grew more quickly and vigorously than their rivals such as Britain and the United States. This promise of a new world order inspired soldiers in both China and Japan, even as they killed each other. Once the Americans entered the fray, however, they too sought to recreate the world in their image. Common to all three countries' projects was the domestic development of new systems of social, political, and military organization that had a profound influence over how individual human beings thought about themselves, the enemy, and the world.

The Second World War was indeed a global event, but it has not always been treated as such by historians. First, total war in the Asia-Pacific Theater began not with Germany's invasion of Poland in 1939 but with Japan's invasion of China in 1937. Despite the fact that war was not officially declared, the Empire of Japan (including Japanese-controlled Taiwan, Korea, and northeastern China, or "Manchukuo") and China (at that time primarily controlled by the Nationalist Party, *Guomindang,* or GMD) were in a constant state of mobilization. It was in July and August 1937 that regional military clashes between local Chinese and Japanese army officers such as the Marco Polo Bridge Incident and the Ōyama Incident compelled Chiang Kai-shek, head of the GMD, to order troops into Shanghai, thereby expanding small-scale confrontations into a conflict that drew on the entirety of each nation's resources—a "total war."[5] Once Shanghai fell to the Japanese in November 1937, Nanjing (Nanking), the capital of the Nationalist government, was quickly taken by Japanese forces in mid-December. The GMD established a temporary center of operations in the western city of Wuhan until October 1938, but its official wartime capital following the fall of Nanjing was Chongqing (Chungking), in the more remote Sichuan (Szechuan) Province. From that point onward, GMD forces struggled to maintain supply routes through which the United States, Britain, and the Soviet Union supported their efforts against Japan. Well before Pearl Harbor, millions had died in East Asia, and civilians in both China and the Japanese Empire suffered under war rationing. The United States had already committed itself to the Chinese war effort by organizing various trade embargos against Japan. To suggest, then, that "The War" began with Hitler's invasion of Poland is a parochial view; to separate the 1941 attack on Pearl Harbor from the Japanese ambitions leading to the "China Quagmire,"[6] which brought the United States into the war (and thereby forever changed European modern history), would be a product of historical myopia and undermines the global nature of the "World War." Japan's and China's competing projects to recreate the world did indeed do so, with ramifications that affected not only Tokyo and Nanjing but also Berlin, London, Moscow, New York, and Paris.

The project to create a new world order predated Japan's aggressive imperialist expansion and has deep roots in anticolonial liberation discourse.[7]

The failure of the Qing Dynasty (1644–1911) to confront British military power in the Opium War (1839–1841) shocked the Japanese, but the arrival of Matthew Perry and his "gunboat diplomacy" (1853–1854) triggered a reevaluation of the relationship between military technology, social management, and national sovereignty that culminated in what Marius Jansen referred to as the "Meiji Revolution." From 1868, despite early Meiji reluctance to conduct major military expeditions abroad, emerging Japanese nationalist thinkers such as Tokutomi Sohō linked national strength to imperial expansion. Also, the Taiwan Expedition of 1874 demonstrated that imperial Japan was willing to engage in the sort of "mimetic imperialism" that might impress the foreign governments that were considering renegotiating "unequal treaties"; it also aimed to legitimize the new government in the eyes of a disenfranchised Japanese public that was increasingly demanding a voice in foreign affairs.[8] Still, Japanese public concern over "national prestige" went far beyond the defensive "rich nation, strong army" rhetoric that traditionally dominated Meiji politics.[9] At first, Japan was a "team player" in the imperial game: for example, Japan not only participated in the 1900 Eight Nation Alliance (following the Boxer Rebellion) and the 1918 Siberian Intervention (following the Bolshevik Revolution), the foreign ministry also formalized a critical alliance with Great Britain in 1902 to contain imperial Russia (achieved during the Russo-Japanese War in 1905) and signed agreements with the United States in 1905 (Taft-Katsura) and 1917 (Ishii-Lansing) to the mutual benefit of both colonial powers. Traditional Japanese fears of Russia, however, and the specter of an anti-Japanese nationalist movement in China since the May Fourth Movement (1919) pushed a more aggressive policy in the 1920s, which alarmed both the United States and the newly formed Soviet Union. In the end, carving a place for Japanese interests in the Asia-Pacific region required a vigorous expansion that would challenge "Western" hegemony; this, however, put the country on a collision course with new political movements emerging in China.

Like Japan, the Chinese Nationalist government also desired to dramatically restructure global politics in order to defeat the dominance of the "West." In fact, the Japanese government had sheltered and supported anti-Qing (Han Chinese) nationalist reformers such as Liang Qichao and Sun Yat-sen throughout the Meiji period under the banner of "Pan-Asianism." The modernization of China's armed forces was largely achieved in Japanese military academies—even Chiang Kai-shek studied in one. Both China and Japan "shared the same dream in different beds," as China sought to establish national sovereignty while Japan (particularly with the achievement of tariff autonomy in 1911) desired to become a major power in an era characterized by colonies and empires. Once Chiang Kai-shek had completed the Northern Expedition (1926–1928), Japanese imperialists, who had become accustomed to exploiting warlords and local officials, were faced with a stridently anti-imperialist movement that threatened their interests on the mainland. These interests were tied not simply to the development of China's vast natural resources but also to the Imperial Japanese Army's (IJA) obsession with crushing communism and the nearby Soviet Union; this unfortunate preoccupation with anticommunism resulted in the failure of the 1918 Siberian Intervention and the disastrous 1939 Nomonhan (Khalkhin Gol) Incident.[10] Meanwhile, the growing power of the GMD greatly alarmed local Japanese commanders. The expansion of Chinese state power within its own borders could certainly take on the appearance of a kind of domestic colonialism,[11] but on the level of discourse, the GMD did not feel the need to justify its conquests, speaking positively of unity and liberation.[12] The Nationalists' primary goal was to "revitalize" *(fuxing)* the Chinese nation against its enemies—which, from the 1927 Jinan Incident onward,[13] was a long list of foes dominated by imperial Japan. Indeed, considering the GMD's constant attempts to exterminate communism in China, its desire to liberate Asia from "Western" imperialism, and Chiang Kai-shek's initial admiration of Japan, the devastating 1937–1945 war is truly perplexing.

As a consequence, Japan's war against the Chinese Nationalists has been one of the dominating themes of modern Chinese history.[14] Despite the stalwart resistance offered by the GMD and, secondarily, by the Chinese Communist Party (CCP), the Chinese people suffered terribly during the period of Japanese aggression.[15] Of all nations in the Second World War, only the Soviet Union can compare with Chinese losses: China suffered an estimated 3.2 million military deaths and many millions more among civilians and GMD officials. Despite some scholars' low estimation of the GMD as a political and military organization, under the Party's leadership, the Chinese launched a tenacious defense almost entirely on their own.[16] Some 186,000 Japanese troops died during the fighting in China up to 1941—a figure that does not include Japanese sick, wounded, or the "Puppet Armies" conscripted in Taiwan, Korea, and Manchukuo.[17] Thus, well before Pearl

Harbor and the United States' entry into the war, actions in China had cost Japan hundreds of thousands of military personnel, and economic mobilization in East Asia was already arcing quickly toward its peak. In fact, a year before Germany invaded Poland, the 1938 National Mobilization Law in Japan had already launched civilian rationing measures. Thus, two of the most developed economies outside of the "West" were already engaged in a modern, total war before a single Panzer rolled into Polish territory.

A TRANSNATIONAL HISTORY OF THE WAR:
DIARY WRITING AND SUBJECTIVITY

At the end of *The Great War and Modern Memory*, Paul Fussell humorously recalled that the "generic identity" of his book "seriously puzzled some readers."[18] I hope that this book may not similarly confuse my readers, but it does engage with various fields including social history, literature, and philosophy. I have done so because, in seeking answers to difficult questions such as what "truth" means in a soldier's account of a battle, I have found that all of the most useful solutions to these problems cannot be found in a single discipline or methodology. Consequently, this will not be a straightforward military history such as Stephen Ambrose's *Band of Brothers*, so I ask for some patience from the reader who is unfamiliar with, for example, language philosophy but is interested in war diaries; similarly, I hope that those who are interested primarily in diary writing will not dismiss the importance of the complexities behind the political, military, and social history of the war itself. The issues involved in studying war diary writing are complex and confusing, so it is important to approach them cautiously. As Stephen Kotkin pointed out following the opening of Soviet archives, new sources, like diaries, do not always lead to new ways of historical thinking.[19]

The political and military story behind the conflagration in the Asia-Pacific Theater is important, but this book is not, primarily, such a history; there are already many such studies. Furthermore, in seeking explanations for why individuals participate in mass movements, dangerous political parties, or oppressive social organizations, scholars typically turn to points of common origin for modern identity (such as nationalism).[20] Consequently, theoretical explorations, as well as historical scholarship, tend to focus on the history of institutions and public discourse. In order to assess the effectiveness of state and media forces in guiding thought and behavior, we must also look at the various selves that individuals create in their personal narratives. Because I wish to examine the language that encouraged many men to make such dramatic sacrifices, both in the "West" and the "East," this will be mainly a study of diary writing and the self. This is because, in order to understand how modern governments managed to mobilize ordinary people so effectively, we must thoroughly investigate the mechanisms of "subjectivity."

Put simply, subjectivity is the sum total of what an individual thinks to be true about himself and the world around him and, consequently, what he thinks is possible. If "agency" refers to any action, thought, or speech of which an individual is actually capable, then subjectivity is that which he *believes* he is capable of. Subjectivity is of interest particularly to students of history because it helps us investigate issues of possibility and responsibility surrounding historical events. Why, for example, did so many Chinese men die fighting fiercely for the Nationalist Army in 1937 Shanghai, when we know the Nationalist Party to have been extremely corrupt and widely despised?[21] Why did so many Japanese servicemen kill their prisoners of war? Were U.S. servicemen motivated by racial hatred when they conducted themselves with such brutality in the Pacific?[22] Subjectivity is a powerful analytic tool not only for understanding issues germane to this project or the history of the Second World War but for discussing the process of understanding and decision making altogether.

The concept of the "Chinese traitor" *(hanjian)* in GMD discourse is a good case for how the use of subjectivity can help us better understand historical events. Historians have already demonstrated why, for many Chinese, collaboration with occupying Japanese forces was a reasonable decision.[23] When encountering mention of a "Chinese traitor" in a GMD war diary, it is often impossible to investigate whether the person in question was actually guilty of treason. GMD officers such as Liu Chongzhe suggested that loyalty was simply a matter of indoctrination and obedience to the state:

> [Our training] results are good. The people can help [the resistance] by getting right in front of the enemy. The people loathe the traitorous bandits, and their minds are already quite clear [*renshi yi qing*]. They already have an established knowledge of ideology [*zhuyi*] and faith in the government.[24]

Despite the ambiguity of what it meant to be a "traitor," the term itself was of great consequence for Liu and his men. By identifying certain categories of Chinese people as "traitors," the diarist set boundaries for both his and others' behavior. Discussions of "traitors" could thus be used for mobilizing oneself to act patriotically or even more brutally when facing these enemies. GMD officer Luo Zhuoying wrote that "every officer should search their vicinity for these traitors, selling their country and committing crimes, and execute them by firing squad," and there is some evidence to suggest that locals would capture, beat, and then turn over suspected "traitors" to assistance organizations, such as the Chinese Scouts.[25] Subjectivity, as a definition of self and one's world, is therefore extremely important: it helps us to understand what kinds of "knowledge" put limits on and opened possibilities for individual actions, including those we consider unethical. This does not mean, however, that we are discovering some "authentic" self. In her study of medieval and early modern Chinese travelogues, Xiaofei Tian argued that the "naked, undifferentiating, innocent eye meeting the world without trying to make sense of it [. . . is] something we can never know or prove."[26] Nevertheless, we cannot fully divorce a diary from the author who wrote it and under what sort of conditions it was composed.

How we decide to use these texts is therefore important to the construction of our continuing collective memory of the Second World War, and up until recently, that tale has been told in very limited ways. On U.S. action in the Pacific, some scholars have used diaries and other personal accounts to piece together compelling stories in the military history genre.[27] In Japan, military historians at Tokyo's National Institute for Defense Studies have used officers' diaries to compose their official history, but Yoshimi Yoshiaki was the first to use them as social historical sources.[28] Sadly, there has been no comparable social historical study of Chinese war diaries from this period. In contrast to detailed records of military operations or narratives that aim to describe the unity of national experience, some historians of the Second World War have adopted an atomized approach to writing about soldiering, influenced by trends in social history, such as the "people's history" *(minshūshi)* in Japan and the "new military history" that arose in the 1970s and 1980s.[29] John Keegan's *The Face of Battle* (1976) was groundbreaking in its use of personal accounts to reduce the history of warfare to the gritty level of the individual soldier.[30] This approach was adopted by many future historians, including those outside of the traditional focus on

war in Western Europe: Catherine Merridale researched the quotidian experiences of Soviet infantrymen,[31] and Peter Schrijvers examined how wartime American identities and themes were inspired by external influences
such as fiction, religion, and film.[32] Still, Keegan's methodology, historically, had a political purpose behind its construction. Writing at the end of
the conflict in Vietnam, he also inspired horror for war itself by presenting
it from a soldier's perspective.

Such an approach would have been quite at home in Japan, where another writer influenced by Vietnam, Honda Katsuichi, opened a political
Pandora's box in the 1970s by revisiting Japan's atrocities in China. Meanwhile, Japanese "Peace Museums" *(heiwa shiryōkan)* have used the horror of
American firebombing campaigns to support the Japanese government's
official renunciation of war; indeed, despite claims that the Japanese have
not faced the wartime past, the country hosts more peace and war museums than any other in the world. Although scholars in the People's Republic of China (PRC) still lag behind, researchers in Japan have recently taken
an interest in narrating the war directly through servicemen's diaries. For
example, Fujii Tadatoshi's recent monograph *The Soldiers' War* (Heitachi no
sensō) was very similar to Yoshimi Yoshiaki's article-length study from fifteen
years prior. Fujii salvaged textual evidence often overlooked by historians in
order to make claims about how servicemen experienced the war, showing
that Japanese records of battlefield experience match or even exceed texts
elsewhere. Most significantly, Fujii linked the study of personal writing to
servicemen's identities in order to discuss the connection between Japanese
society's wartime militarism and the cultural history of soldiering in the
modern era.[33] Fujii, Merridale, Yoshimi, and Schrijvers, like Honda and
Keegan, aimed to retrieve factual information from reliable sources in order
to achieve the task of composing a narrative of the war that included as many
regions as possible, as well as penning a story that would bring the individual
soldier back into history—this was a truly admirable task. None of these authors, however, critically engaged with sources such as war diaries, or the
myriad methodological pitfalls that surround using them in historical research. I want to show just how dangerous these documents can be and how
they help us to explain the brutality of the Second World War. By doing so,
I hope to illuminate how self-discipline, or the individual's construction of
his own subjectivity, helps us understand the mass support for total war.

THE PERILS OF SELF-DISCIPLINE: CONDUCTING A PROPER EXAMINATION OF WARTIME DIARIES

A diary's reliability is often perceived to be a function of how private it is; what this means is that any diary subject to the gaze of others is likely to be edited by the author out of fear or simply to appeal to an "intended audience." Even scholars who take up diary writing as a subject of inquiry for the most part insist on the privacy and authenticity of these accounts.[34] First, privacy itself is arguably more a product of legal definitions of property in Western history than it is a coherent philosophical concept. Second, language is not something that we privately create ex nihilo. As Ludwig Wittgenstein famously argued, the use of language forces even the most private of confessions to adopt public conventions; we do not own our language but only borrow it, no matter how private we believe it to be.[35] Even the act of translating a truly private language would change it into something public, as all languages are transformed through acts of translation. Third, "intended audience" itself is a problematic concept because it implies that the intentions of the author are accessible (we are historians, not mind readers). With diaries, where content is frequently in flux from one day's entry to the next, even intended audience as defined by genre (for example, epistolary form: "My wife, I write this diary for you") cannot be maintained for the reading of the entire document—diarists are always changing how the diary is composed, responding to shifting conditions.

Avoiding any effort to measure the reliability of these war diaries along the public/private divide, I argue for an alternate method for reading them, namely, that battlefield diaries are both tools for and evidence of what I call "self-discipline." Self-discipline is understood colloquially to mean methods employed by individuals to become more efficient and effective as a person, which is included in how the term will be used in this book. I am also referring to the concept of "discipline" as it is used by historians influenced by the philosophy of Michel Foucault, who argued strongly for the importance of modern institutions such as schools, barracks, and hospitals on the development of our subjectivity. I add the prefix "self" to emphasize that this is a practice in which the subject is acting on himself, underlining the importance of the individual's contribution to this process. Without paying close attention to the actions of individuals in creating their sense and experience of selfhood, we will have considerable difficulty discussing the ethical responsibility for their behavior, which is a dangerous road to go down when it comes to the study of war.

This book focuses on writing war, particularly in diaries, in order to illuminate how the struggle between the individual and large organizations, such as the state, occurred. On the one hand, during the course of a self-disciplinary project, like keeping a diary, individuals used public discourse, such as war reports and patriotic literature, to narrate their experiences; this effectively invited the state, military, and mass media to define who they are. On the other hand, diarists also willfully subverted or simply misinterpreted such discourse, particularly when extreme experiences, like combat, put pressure on them to find new ways to write about their lives. They then continued to formulate their views of self and the world (subjectivity) on the basis of these subversions and "errors." Put simply, the merchants of language (government, religions, newspapers, schools, military barracks, etc.) sold soldiers a product, but they could not determine how these men decided to use it—they ultimately had to leave that to the individual. When a soldier developed a coherent voice in a diary, he was in the process of piecing together an entire identity and worldview. This has profound implications for social discipline in times of total war: as strange as it may sound for the wartime period, ultimately the state did not simply command, it had to suggest,[36] and even then its success was dependent on the willingness of individuals to accept (and their ability to understand) its message. Furthermore, when writing about the war, a soldier had to adopt a voice and, in doing so, put on a performance of the self—either as implied author, narrator, or protagonist.[37] His authorial voice operated more according to the conventions of language and genre than to his internal wishes (or "intent"). In other words, the self that we create in a diary is not us, because it is in part defined by cultural, linguistic, and historical conventions.

Still, war diaries and their authors are different from the writers of fiction, poetry, and, for that matter, science textbooks and stereo instruction manuals. First, the structure of the war diary pressures the author into a particular method of record: "fact" and battlefield experience are usually important to military men. Also, the context in which war diaries are produced makes them difficult to separate from their authors as objects of analysis. For example, pocket diaries (Jp. *techō*, Ch. *shouzhang*) are very small, which allowed their authors to transport them under any conditions while providing precious little space for expansive prose. The large, tablet-sized diary notepads used for field diaries (Jp. *jinchū nikki, nisshi,* Ch. *zhenzhong riji*) have enough space for copying action reports, telegraphed orders, troop position, and events of the day, but they were more difficult to carry and were usually kept only by officers or medical personnel. Some diaries were published during the war for circulation among one unit, an army corps, or an entire bureaucratic state apparatus, or they were simply mimeographed for a few officers' perusal and were potentially subject to editing. Servicemen typically kept diaries close to their bodies, in breast pockets or hidden in trousers, tucked into socks or stowed in helmets. In every case, the records in a diary consist of those events and information that the author deemed important, personally experienced, and gathered on a day-to-day basis. Servicemen did not use a consistent voice in their diaries because their manners of expression, personal beliefs, and conditions of writing were constantly changing. Most important, however much we must remove the truth value of the text from our readings, diarists usually accepted them as true reflections of themselves in a way that most writers of fiction, news, and stereo manuals rarely do. Even though we cannot equate the diary with the author, pulling him totally away from his diary, as well as the experience of the war itself, is unwise.

At the same time, it is essential to separate the connection of a diary to its author from the rhetoric of truth that surrounds diaries themselves, with particular caution for how contemporary society links "truth" to the concept of "privacy." East Asian literary culture enjoyed a plethora of confessions, diaries, and other self-narratives that tested the boundary between "fact" and "fiction." Mishima Yukio, a Japanese author who was all too familiar with the techniques of public performance of self, declared in *Confessions of a Mask* that "only a mask can confess." In fact, a tradition of faux sincerity and deceptive confessional rhetoric was alive and well in both modern Chinese and Japanese literature. Edward Fowler pointed out that Japanese authors, who struggled with "camouflaging" the "fictionality" of their texts, were not successful in this endeavor: "the very act of expressing themselves in writing, they realized, was in effect to don a mask, to supplant a person with a persona."[38] Use of the diary in fiction was not merely an entertainment device: Ding Ling's *Miss Sophie's Diary* (1927) embraced the format to address gender issues in the construction of a modern female subjectivity. Furthermore, Lydia Liu underlined Lu Xun's "profound distrust of the author-reader continuum," especially with regards to formative works such as *Diary of a Madman,* giving rise to confusion over author and narrator, audience and object.[39] Lu Xun, like Mishima and Ding, knew all too well how inconsistently the reading audience grasped irony, metaphor, and satire, and to add insult to injury, the authors themselves were sometimes unclear where authorial subjectivity ended and a fictional narrator began. For most ordinary diarists, however, parodies and investigations of self-narrative, while rich with canonical literary allusion, were not the ideal to which they aspired for their own stories. In an interview I conducted in February 2003, Okamoto Masa, a former "special attack pilot" (*Tokkōtai,* or "kamikaze"), read his wartime diary to me, repeating aloud the ultranationalistic rhetoric he had once embraced. When I asked him how reading the diary made him feel today, he replied, "Without this diary, I would have probably believed like everybody else that I was dragged unwillingly into the war, that I never accepted this propaganda. This diary is essential to my self-criticism [*hansei*]."[40] Okamoto's embrace of a diary's "truth" is a testament to how critical the diary was to sincere projects aimed at disciplining the self, even if it does not represent "the whole truth" of his war experience.

It is clear that these authors were extraordinarily dedicated to keeping diaries. U.S. marine Thomas Serier complained in his diary that the bunks on his troopship "are only 18 inches apart, and lying down writing is quite a job."[41] After fleeing a particularly vicious American artillery bombardment in a Philippine jungle, Japanese army officer Jōji Tsutomu wrote, "Finding a place of solace, I tried to report on our movements based on my diary [*nisshi*], but I could not keep the powerful emotions from burning in my heart."[42] Most important, however, was the soldier's acknowledgment of diary writing as integral to his sense of self. On New Year's Day 1944, Chinese Nationalist supply officer Wang Wenrong listed a series of resolutions to improve himself as a soldier and a person, including a focus on keeping healthy during periods of shortage; more important for this study, however, was his fourth resolution: to "keep a diary every day." Living at the edge of the Japanese Empire came with many perils, and unfortunately, a month later Wang had already reneged on his promise to write. Nevertheless, he renewed his dedication to the diary, which he recorded faithfully until the end of the war: "Not keeping any diary is like taking time away from oneself. I must carry on with the spirit I have today and continue to write."[43] Men such as Serier, Jōji, and Wang composed their personal accounts under various circumstances, including while residing in dangerous combat zones, underdeveloped hinterlands, and tropical jungles. Writing a diary in these conditions, an author could be attacked by the enemy, interrogated by hostile superior officers, or even have his hands bitten by insatiable hordes of bloodsucking mosquitoes.[44]

Consequently, soldiers considered their personal records precious: Japanese servicemen, for example, tied their diaries to the inside of their thighs in order to avoid confiscation during routine inspections.[45] Writing a diary was like stealing a moment away from one's ordinary duties. Ishikawa Tatsuzō, in his wartime novel *Living Soldiers* (Ikite iru heitai), described a young lieutenant quietly jotting an entry into his pocket diary while on a train.[46] Because a diary was so important to the writer, however, it was also considered potentially dangerous by his superiors. In Japan and the United States (the case in Nationalist China is unclear), commanding officers frequently prohibited their men from keeping them, but those who wrote diaries either ignored these orders or their officers neglected to enforce them.[47] Also, when an officer prohibited a diary, it was an act of hypocrisy. All modern militaries had traditions of official field diary writing, so in most instances unit commanders were required to write some sort of log; still, the expectations could vary regarding who precisely was meant to keep them, how they were to be composed, at what level they were to be written, and to what extent they were subject to peer or superior review, which could be determined according to the branch of the armed forces (army or navy), whether the unit was engaged in combat, and whether the unit was operating independently or part of a larger unit (such as a division). Because so many older soldiers kept (and published) diaries, in many cases men in combat, both high and low, were merely imitating behavior they had been exposed to before.

Because that history is so complex, Chapter 1 of this book examines the modern history of military diary writing and war reportage in an attempt to understand some of the major precedents for the texts soldiers would eventually compose. Military thinkers realized that total war demanded that troops be self-disciplined rather than simply follow orders. This had as much to do with heightened interest in the "everyman" in modern culture at the turn of the twentieth century and the rise of mass politics as it did with the visions of prescient bureaucrats or ambitious military planners. Chapter 2 addresses the transformation of self-expression as it was put to the test on the battlefield of northern and central China from 1937. Before arriving on the battlefield, Japanese and Chinese soldiers used their diaries in acts of "self-mobilization," involving, for example, vilifying the enemy and generating anger. The chapter then juxtaposes changes in language with the combat conditions within which they were composed, which will show the impact of experience on language. When the authors accepted this record as a "truthful" representation of their experience, these moments of battlefield chaos could become the foundations of new selves. Chapter 3 analyzes the relationship between diary writing and disciplinary projects launched by centers of authority. Barak Kushner argued that the relationship between the battlefield and the home front was negotiated by the state and its mass media collaborators like the spokes connecting the inside and outside of a wheel.[48] In order to analyze this dynamic, first the chapters shows the collapse of personal narratives and political authority through diaries from the Nanjing Massacre; then, by revisiting diarists from the previous chapter, Chapter 3 will demonstrate how servicemen used their diaries to process information disseminated by authorities through print media and define who they were.

Chapters 4 and 5 largely switch theaters from Asia to the Pacific, defining self-discipline as a transnational phenomenon and exploring how the public/private divide does not help us understand diary writing, discipline, or subjectivity. Particularly during the process of self-mobilization, the courage and fearsome rage expressed in diaries by American and Japanese servicemen were as likely to appear in print as they were in a so-called private account. Responses of soldiers to the collapse of Western dominance in the Pacific mirrored Chinese accounts of the failures of the GMD. It would seem that America's history of press freedom and privacy rights had little bearing on the selves that soldiers would eventually create. Chapter 5 looks at the American counteroffensive and, secondarily, the struggle of the Chinese Nationalists to survive during the 1940s; by comparing diaries of the collapsing Japanese armed forces, the difficult Chinese resistance, and the increasingly powerful American invasion, the chapter demonstrates how the persistence of "individualism" in U.S. mobilization is a myth. Also, the transnational nature of linking one's personal involvement to the "historical" importance of the war will be demonstrated by looking at Chinese, Japanese, and American diaries. Finally, Chapter 6 addresses the consequences of self-discipline for veterans in the postwar era and whether postwar societies in Japan, the Republic of China (ROC, Taiwan), and the PRC were willing to admit veterans' version of the "truth" into the narratives that constitute our historical memory of the war. Because East Asia, unlike America, had no "Great War," the tools for constructing collective mourning were unfamiliar and need to be examined on their own.[49] Chapter 6 examines how and when veterans have tried to "set the record straight" by participating in public discussion of the war and how professing the "truth" was merely the result of their wartime self-discipline.

Charles Dickens wrote in *Great Expectations* that "All swindlers on the earth are nothing to the self-swindlers." Even though we must be skeptical of concepts such as truth and privacy when reading diaries, the fact that these beliefs were (and are) so prevalent, and that many diarists believed in the existence of a (truthful) private sphere, is too important a factor to ignore. Michel Foucault insisted that "truth," when backed by power, is not the same truth as championed by philosophers but is rather a "weapon," and for those who do not wield this power, "universal truth and general right are illusions and traps."[50] When a soldier believed his diary to be a true reflection of his experience, how he narrated his own story inevitably affected his ideas about himself and the world around him—even if those ideas were inaccurate or came from public sources such as film reels or war fiction. The study of diary writing is thus an investigation into the phenomenon of self-discipline—that is, how individuals participate in the act of defining (subjectifying) themselves and the world around them. On the one hand, by using language, which is by nature public and dominated by centers of authority, servicemen invited the state, mass media, and military inside their minds even more thoroughly through the act of writing diaries and embracing them as true accounts of their lives. On the other hand, they were responsible for writing the diary. By selecting the content of the diary, servicemen exercised agency in the construction of their sense of self. This is a view of subjectivity that cannot be seen through a study of schools, hospitals, mass media, or prisons, and so it is even more important to understanding why individuals willingly sacrificed so much for state and nation. The diary was both a site for discipline and the evidence of the disciplinary process; it was a battlefield where the inarticulate desires of the individual and the well-spoken demands of authority conducted a daily struggle.

CHAPTER ONE

Talk about Heroes

Military Diaries in the Modern World

IF THE STORY of a modern soldier is encapsulated in his diary, then that story begins well before his birth. In East Asia, the modern history of diary writing is heavily marked by the intrusion of the state into what we now consider to be a "private sphere." By the time of the Second World War, guided diary writing, as a training tool in schools, government bureaucracies, and barracks, was widespread. On 3 May 1944, Tamura Hideto, preparing to become a Japanese soldier, exceeded even his training officer's expectations:

> Military discipline is the expression of a pure spirit of obedience. For example, [our superior] Private Masamoto's work detail constitutes a direct order [for us], and while some carry it out faithfully, others stick to selfishness and are not obedient. It is something they should be truly shameful of. If you don't execute your orders, how could you ever become a superior officer or soldier? It's impossible.

To this his commanding officer wrote a more realistic goal in Tamura's diary: "Do the best that you can within the limits of your strength."[1] Tamura routinely pushed himself in order to become the best soldier that he could, and he used this diary ("A Record of Self-Cultivation," or *shūyōroku*) to record various exhortations: "try harder," "suppress pain," or "be the best!" A war diary, then, is a critical piece of evidence for how individuals learned to direct their energies (many of which served the state) and why certain government goals were more successful than others. How did such a system come about? Although this book examines diary writing during the Second World War in Asia and the Pacific, some attention must be paid to the history behind how war diaries were written in Japan, China, and the United States—although the last has received some attention in Anglophone scholarly literature. Consequently, this chapter will focus on explaining how military diary writing evolved in modern East Asia first and compare these traditions with America to assess how transnational they might be.

MILITARY DIARY WRITING IN EAST ASIA

Military reform was part and parcel of the transformation that East Asian nationalists viewed as essential to preserving sovereignty. This performance of modernity included education, technology, and military prowess; as the Qing Dynasty's repeated military defeats demonstrated, "modernization" without thorough social and political change was unsustainable. Thus, inspired by the need for "unequal treaty" revision, gunboat diplomacy, and self-defense,[2] a form of "isomorphism" developed in East Asia,[3] where new forms of writing and social discipline took root. It is within this set of social, political, and technological transformations that state-led reform emphasized the discipline of national subjects, and the military, which defended sovereignty directly, was perhaps the most important modern institution of them all.

First, in order to properly analyze the evolution of modern diary writing in East Asia, one must pay attention to the history of war reportage and technologies of record keeping. In the case of military records, in Japan (in the 1860s) and China (in the 1910s), military authorities introduced precise textual methods for observing and disciplining the behavior of officers and their men. Meanwhile, in the early twentieth century, lyrical tales of battlefield heroism gradually extended their scope to narrate the actions of both commanding officers and the common soldier. By the 1930s, war reportage in China and Japan had borrowed many narrative techniques from both authors of leftist fiction and (private, for profit) mass media reporting to portray the experience of the "everyman," and this language was in turn embraced by diarists on the battlefield. Although wartime diarists would eventually come to develop their own language for describing war, these institutions and traditions were among the most powerful influences over their writing. Thus, to properly understand how and why servicemen kept diaries during the war in Asia, it is first necessary to examine how official "field diaries" and war reportage merged to form the foundation of self-expression among soldiers in the twentieth century. By providing soldiers a flexible genre of self-narrative, war reportage and the field diary were the foundation for how men used language to comprehend self and war.

In both China and Japan, the field diary (Jp. *jinchū nikki* or *nisshi*, Ch. *zhenzhong riji*) was an invention of a Foucauldian nature: through the threat of potential review, it effectively extended the gaze of central authority into the everyday decision-making processes of officers, regardless of whether that authority was actually looking or not. In other words, no one was looking over a soldier's shoulder while he wrote his diary, but he knew that his superiors had the authority to read it; this was far more efficient and effective than micromanaging one's men—or, as Foucault put it, the "perfection of power should tend to render its actual exercise unnecessary."[4] Eventually, as military planners hoped, the authors of these war diaries would come to accept military discipline as their own, internal, view of self and the world and act in a manner useful to state and military authorities. Furthermore, field diaries were deeply embedded in nineteenth-century discourses that described "truth" as knowable through the disciplined record of fact; this system of "knowing" came into East Asia through various channels, usually in cooperation with foreign powers, but it quickly became as integral to East Asian modern culture as it was in the West, and thus soldiers encountered it through domestic military training. By systematically recording, among other things, weather, direction of wind, troop strength, position, training and education activities, various reports, and, perhaps most interestingly, the ambiguous category of "notes" of the day's activities, the field diary attempted to grant its author control over his material universe through observation and textual practice. Writing in his diary every day, whether a Chinese warlord army's division commander in 1913 Nanjing or a Japanese Imperial Army lieutenant in 1944 Borneo, the author captured the salient facts of his unit's combat experience and furthermore established himself as a member of a community specializing in war. Though not a personal diary, the field diary became an equally powerful expression of the officer's identity as a professional soldier. Nevertheless, even with such a seemingly overdetermined structure, authors of war diaries still desired a language that would bring their stories alive.

Reportage, a slightly later phenomenon in East Asia, aimed to convey information not just as undigested data but as a story that exposed hidden "truths" and moved its audience to collective action. War reportage began in late nineteenth-century East Asia as a capitalist invention intended to increase the circulation of newspapers, but it was not particularly concerned with the virtues and tribulations of the common soldier until the arrival of mass politics at the turn of the twentieth century.[5] Twentieth-century war reportage in China and Japan thus represented a politically significant expansion of its fin de siècle predecessor's subjects. Strictly speaking, the most sophisticated reportage of the nineteenth century (historically tied to the rise of Marxism) had concerned itself primarily with exposing the plight of the working class. By constructing a unified subject (the proletariat or the farmer) and by gradually "exposing" the systemic nature of their oppression through lyrical description, reportage began as a form of agitation propaganda. Ordinary "reporting," claimed leftist thinkers, represented an empty litany of "facts," which taught one nothing of the "truth" of human experience; furthermore, while the upper classes concerned themselves with factual accounts of events, leftist intellectuals (and, presumably, the lower classes) were in search of a larger historical truth. Similarly, by exposing crimes against the nation and expressing the fundamental heroism of the armed forces, war reportage attempted to mobilize the public to support national defense. War reportage took as its aim capturing the true experience of war from the worm's-eye view and inspiring its reader (the worm) to participate in the ongoing struggle (mobilization). To a large degree, then, war reportage embraced the same writing techniques that were developed significantly by Marxist pioneers and simply replaced "workers" with "our troops."

In a slow and uneven process, war reportage and the field diary, as writing forms with roughly similar goals and similar objects, began to influence one another at the beginning of the twentieth century. This was probably inevitable, for the following reasons: (1) when defining themselves as fighting men, infantrymen and junior officers looked first to their superiors, all of whom were either accustomed to or familiar with the practice of keeping a field diary; and (2) whereas traditionally the field diary format provided a space for discussing experience in a more lyrical form ("notes"), war reportage offered the most inspiring language for these stories. In both China and Japan, even high-ranking officers were delighted by the moving tales of heroism penned by embedded journalists during, for example, the Northern Expedition or the Russo-Japanese War. Although they recognized that they might be inferior writers, servicemen high and low came to realize that it was they, the experts, who monopolized both the facts, recorded faithfully in their field diaries, and the "truth," because war was, in their eyes, first and foremost experienced by soldiers. When looking for a way to write that reflected experience and evoked memory, infantrymen who endured the war on the front line began to imitate earlier war diaries—even if those model texts were written by their "superiors."

Consequently, over the course of the first half of the twentieth century in East Asia, personal diaries were drawn into the same constricted model of official accounts (in fact, servicemen came to call their personal accounts "field diaries"), and official diaries were infected by literary aesthetics from other genres, including reportage. The diary became a sacrosanct space blessed doubly with claims of channeling experience into language. The war diary genre thereby attracted servicemen of all ranks and backgrounds who desired to record, and thereby exercise control over, the "truth" of their experience.

NEW TEXTUAL PRACTICES IN MODERN EAST ASIAN MILITARIES

Japan

Despite a long history of military epics *(senki)*, bureaucratic diaries *(nisshi)*, and samurai notebooks *(tebikae)*, field diaries were a new technology to the Japanese army. There is no evidence to suggest that the earliest imperial forces, comprised as they were by samurai from the revolting domains in the 1860s, employed them, despite the presence of Western military advisors.[6] Sometime during the late 1870s, however, after the last samurai rebellion had been put down in Kyushu, and the early 1880s, when the new government felt relatively secure in its own borders, the new Japanese national army began exhaustively reforming its training practices along Western military lines. This included the introduction of new textual technologies for increasing efficiency and accountability.

It stands to reason that the navy would have been the first to use official field diaries. First, naval officers were responsible for the most sophisticated and costly components of Japan's military arsenal; thus the admiralty would need to convince the central government and their fellow officers that this equipment was being used responsibly. Second, even in the West, superior naval forces that the Japanese were attempting to emulate were among the first to use military field diaries. In Japan's land army, "work diaries" *(sagyō nisshi)* appeared before other kinds of daily records, such as field diaries. Japanese officers used work diaries to record basic information, including troop strength, equipment, weather, training and education activities, and the events of the day. Every day the commanding officer in charge of units in training (likely a brigade or regiment commander) recorded in detail his troops' performance and the condition of their materiel. These work diaries were reviewed by the author's immediate superior officer (likely a division commander) to ensure that training was going according to schedule and, if not, to devise plans to improve it. By the time of the First Sino-Japanese War (1894–1895), field diary writing had been widely practiced for at least a decade and was firmly entrenched in the quotidian disciplinary practices of the officer class. These documents, though it is clear they were used widely, are difficult to find today.[7]

Following the 1894 Chinese intervention in the Tonghak Rebellion in and around Seoul, the Japanese government declared war on the Qing Empire over the fate of the Korean peninsula. The war against forces marshaled by the Qing marked the first time Japan had sent its newly minted modern army abroad, and as a consequence, many new practices were finally cemented.[8] Field diaries in the Japanese navy and land army for the First Sino-Japanese War (1894–1895) were typically simple documents employed primarily to record the success or failure of the military's tactics; although some more personal accounts exist, these tend to be more characteristic of the later Russo-Japanese War (1904–1905).[9] Important military documents were widely accessible due to a new technology: the military had adopted the mimeograph *(tōshaban)* and almost single-handedly launched the copying device in Japan.[10] Military authorities ordered specific sections of field diaries copied in order to keep a narrativized history of Japan's first modern war abroad for other officers. When the Qing capitulated and surrendered their hegemony in Korea and Liaodong to the Japanese Empire, official diaries became the basis for popular publications narrating the course of what most Japanese considered a "highly successful" war.

Mimeographed official field diaries were intended for an extremely limited readership composed of officers and specialist bureaucrats; thus, ordinary Japanese (including some who would go on to fight in Japan's later wars) learned about soldiering through Japan's growing mass print media. Besides newspapers, periodical publications that focused on the Sino-Japanese War featured nearly all forms of writing on wartime experience.[11] For example, the *True Chronicle of the Sino-Japanese War* (Nisshin sensō jikki) was published widely after 1895. This periodical included sections on battlefield poetry, tales of heroism *(bidan)*, abbreviated or short biographies *(ryaku* or *shōden)* of famous generals and personalities, and a diary *(nisshi)* that was dedicated to chronologically delineating the major events of the war. The publication aimed to satisfy the interests of readers ranging from amateur military historians to young boys with a taste for adventure. Printed on cheap paper, with each issue short and linguistically simplistic, *True Chronicle* was easily within the economic and literary reach of ordinary Japanese.

Of all the categories, the "tales of heroism" and the "diary" are of paramount interest to understanding how periodical publications helped provide the form and content for war diary writing. *Bidan* in this publication were paragraph-length vignettes attempting to capture the essence of the soldier and the nature of combat. In portraying the battlefield, the narrative emphasizes difficulty, loss, heroism (usually from the officer corps), victory, and remembrance or reward. The example below shows how these themes were developed within a lyrical and impassioned style:

First on the Hyŏnmu Gate

At the battle of Pyongyang, the Motoyama Brigade scaled and seized a high artillery epaulement, advancing from Ŭiju Road and opening fire with their cannon on the rear gate—the Hyŏnmu. The artillery bombardment was fierce, but the walls steadfast and impenetrable and, facing enemy artillery on three sides, the battle became most trying. Many of our men fell; it truly seemed as though our entire army was prepared to withdraw. Platoon Commander Lieutenant Mimura Ikunosuke shook with great fury. Fighting at close quarters on his own, he stood ready to breach the battlements.[12]

The tale goes on to narrate how Mimura opened the gates on his own and let in a flood of Japanese troops. These troops, running through enemy fire ("like rain"), seized the fortress. One of the survivors "having gained such honor, immediately was raised to the rank of superior private." Such stories not only inspire vivid personal memories of the battlefield and invite inexperienced readers to imagine it but also aim to reinforce the military values among its readership by suggesting that no victory goes without reward and no sacrifice would be forgotten.

Most *bidan,* however, focused on defining (in positive terms) different types of fighting men. The characters they introduced quickly became archetypes in literature on the military: the fearless lower-echelon officer, the self-sacrificing general, or the infantryman who does not bemoan his own demise. Some are eulogies for servicemen who will be "sorely missed":

> Answering the distant call to war and losing his life in a flurry of iron, the young lad could have anticipated his own demise, but, looking from an outsider's perspective, it is [still] enough to make one cry in despair. . . . During the attack on Pyongyang he fought heroically, and then, being seriously wounded, later perished in a field hospital—a sergeant, a beautiful young boy [*bishōnen*].[13]

These manly tales were replete with "beautiful young men" being utterly smashed under the merciless battle machine of the enemy or instructive parables narrating how the frugality of all the officers and men kept the entire unit from starving through a long march. By combining or juxtaposing tales of individual heroism with the harsh reality of the wartime environment, *bidan* allowed the protagonist to draw authenticity from combat experience and make the hero-protagonist the most important subject of the battlefield. Such vignettes were not tied to a specific temporal sequence, however, nor were they necessarily composed by the persons involved. They were highly dramatized descriptions of combat based on terse battle reports released to the press by the Japanese military—much like art from the period claiming to depict real battles from the war. Even at this early stage, representations of war, such as theater productions, relied on official military reports and press releases in order to underline their knowledge of the "actual conditions" (*jikkyō*) of the war.[14]

The "main narrative" and the "diary" provided essential elements of disciplined diary writing, but *True Chronicle* kept them separate. The beginning

of each edition of *True Chronicle* contained a main narrative *(honki)*, and
the end also had a one-page diary *(nisshi)*. The "diary" was a summary of
the "main narrative" at the beginning of the issue; in other words, the "main
narrative" represented a more lyrical, storybook version of the war based on
the skeletal details of the "diary." The diary contained only the "factual"
events of the war—those that were replicated from telegraph wires, battle
reports, or news headlines. For example, 23 September 1894 read: "Word
on the street is Ye Zhichao was seriously injured, dies on the road fleeing
from Pyongyang. The Qing Army at Pyongyang is heading north," and 15
October followed with "Li Hongzhang rumored to have killed himself"
and notices of various Japanese cabinet appointments.[15] The main narrative
expanded these entries and presented them in a novelistic form:

> The enemy numbered about one platoon, saddled on horses smaller in stat-
> ure than our own, and, suddenly, fired continuously upon us. Our reconnais-
> sance troops were also on horseback, firing back at them with rifle at a dis-
> tance of merely 200 meters and initiating a fierce battle. However, we were
> outnumbered, and on top of this they were quickly reinforced with about
> two hundred more horsemen, so we realized that it was pointless to wage a
> decisive battle here. Fighting and running at the same time, when we were
> about to withdraw from the front line, a platoon of enemy troops laying in
> wait suddenly leapt up and cut us off. . . . We said, *Now's the time to show them
> the true face of the Emperor's soldiers!* and met them again unflinchingly, fight-
> ing more and more ferociously until the Qing soldiers were dealt a hard blow.[16]

These stories became a staple for the popular readership in Japan, but they
did not immediately inspire servicemen to imitate them. Outside of the
well-educated elite of Meiji Japan (such as Mori Ōgai), the vast majority of
Japanese servicemen did not keep any form of diary during the Sino-Japanese
War. Even officers' field diaries are themselves rare documents today.[17] Despite its impressive use of Western military technology on the battlefield—
even primitive telephones—the Japanese armed forces were still in the process of transforming themselves into an effective modern military.

Consequently, in Japan, war reportage and diary writing did not exercise
extensive influence on each other significantly until the Russo-Japanese
War in 1905. The resounding defeat of the Russian forces (albeit at great
cost), elevated levels of literacy, and an expanded popular press spurred on

several publications of war reportage, "war diaries," and other war accounts. Nevertheless, there are two points that one should keep in mind when considering diary writing and war from this period: first, land army and naval accounts differed only slightly; second, "official" field diaries and personal diaries composed simultaneous to the events they describe were not radically different in form and content. The armed forces of late Meiji, then, were deeply divided between high-born, highly literate officers and infantry, 77 percent of whom, optimistically speaking, were functionally literate. In this sense, however, they were arguably little better or worse than most armies in the West at this time.[18]

During the Russo-Japanese War, the practice of field diary writing continued in the same manner as ten years prior: a typical Japanese field diary was kept on large sheets (roughly the same size as $8\frac{1}{2} \times 11$" vertically ruled paper, printed especially for the military) and was written with a brush or fountain pen.[19] This field diary would be submitted to one's commanding officer, usually at his request, some time after the conclusion of the officer's action. For example, Ijichi Hikojirō, commander of the Battleship Mikasa, prepared a diary detailing his activities during the Russo-Japanese War in 1905. He sent the diary to the minister of the navy, Yamamoto Gonnohyōe (Gombei), for review on 22 June of the same year, with the document arriving on 24 June. The diary's entry for 27 May 1905—during the now famous Battle of the Tsushima Straits—included the day of the week (Saturday), weather conditions (clear), wind direction (southwest), wind speed (three to five knots), and detailed information on temperature. After recording these observations for each day, Ijichi included what he believed relevant to the history of the battle:

> 1.44pm: With a cry of "On guard!" we unfurl our battle flag.
>
> 1.50pm: Gradually increase speed to 15 knots.
>
> 1.53pm: Message from flagship, "The success or failure of the Empire rests on this battle, all personnel must strive for excellence." . . .
>
> 2.07pm: Direction, east by northeast. We are facing the enemy head on, but assuming a position to cut off their front. At this point, the closest enemy ship, the "Oslavia," turns toward us first and opens fire.
>
> 2.10pm: At a distance of about 2,400 [meters], our left [battleship] attempts to fire, and from here our naval battle began. From then until the sun went down, from beginning to end, our battle formation moved to put consistent pressure on the enemy, delivering a considerable blow.[20]

Despite such meticulous entries, Ijichi's diary did not serve the function of a battle report: "The detailed facts concerning this battle were recorded in the battle report [*sentō shōhō*], and thus are summarized here." What, then, was the purpose of Ijichi's exhausting efforts to capture on paper the key events of the battle? Although he does not make any statement on this matter, field diaries in general were a kind of storybook account of war that officers—especially those in training—might read in order to fashion themselves after exemplars like Ijichi. Not all field diaries were reviewed, however; fewer were copied and archived, and even fewer still were preserved over the years. The first function of a field diary was for officers' self-discipline.

Although diary writing certainly predated the Russo-Japanese War, as Naoko Shimazu demonstrated, it was this conflict that helped generate the narratives, experiences, institutional practices, and social organizations that would help the state overcome local allegiances and create a new kind of self for soldiers to embrace.[21] Again, the public and the vast majority of potential recruits for Japan's future wars did not learn about soldiering directly from these field diaries, though these documents influenced the structure of more influential popular accounts in the mass media. Following the conclusion of the Russo-Japanese War in 1905, when Japanese pundits were quick to portray their country as the first Asian power to defeat a modern Western nation, a flurry of popular press publications capitalized on the public's desire to know more about the war. Works appealing to the public were produced in tandem with those aimed primarily at a military audience. Media output was thus connected to military propaganda efforts or produced directly by military officials. The establishment of the Imperial Reservists Association (*Teikoku zaikyō gunjinkai*) following the Russo-Japanese War by Yamagata Aritomo's protégé, Tanaka Gi'ichi, marked a major achievement for military forces in their struggle to mobilize the masses for war. Their publication, *Senyū* (War Comrades), reached countless soldiers, veterans, and boys.

The defining work of war literature from the period, however, was a personal account written by a veteran himself. Sakurai Tadatoshi's *Human Bullets* (Nikudan, 1906) was published after the conclusion of the war to great commercial success. An early edition of *Human Bullets* from 1909 contained poetry by Sakurai declaring allegiance to the Meiji emperor and an insert reproduction of the author's calligraphy, spelling out "heroism" (*sōretsu*). With a gold and silver embossed cover and several stunning color sketches of battle scenes (yet still affordable to the middle-class home), it was designed so that an upstanding Meiji gentleman would be proud to have it on his bookshelf. Repeating themes from, for example, Sino-Japanese War "tales of heroism" (concerning legitimate suffering, the nobility of the officer class, and the superiority of Japanese troop élan), in many ways *Human Bullets* was not a departure from previous war stories:

> A foreign reporter, said, "The battle cry of the Japanese pierced the heart of the Russians, and filled them with terror." . . . Several sudden assaults, throwing one human bullet after another against the enemy's defenses, ended with the blood of heroes spattered, their bones shattered. But these sacrifices were not made during a cowardly flight. . . . The officers hid their tears, laying down the lives of their men. . . . I must admit that the first attack ended in failure, but those human bullets who had been used to this end became integral initial stepping stones for smashing the enemy's battlements, bringing us closer to the time of its collapse.[22]

Sakurai's account was not a diary by any definition, but in narrating the events of specific battles, Sakurai forced his depiction into a strict chronological timeline. More important, he was a respected veteran who used the vivid language of previous war reportage accounts and literature in order to describe the emotions of servicemen in the field and the difficulties of war. Consequently, Sakurai's textual photograph of the battlefield was much more lyrical and moving than, for example, Ijichi's. Given the immense popularity of the novel, it is very likely that Japanese servicemen thereafter used similar language to describe their own experiences—if not merely to be able to express themselves in a manner understandable to a civilian audience.

Sakurai's heavily edited novel, however, would not have been easily replicated by a serviceman who was writing a diary every day on the battlefield. Thus, arguably more influential on servicemen's narratives than the 1906 *Human Bullets* or previous newspaper reports on the war was Tamon Jirō's field diary, published in 1912 as *My Participation in the Russo-Japanese Conflict* (Yo no sanka shitaru Nichiro sen'eki), which, along with *Human Bullets,* was highly popular. Although *Human Bullets* was widely known across Japan, the intended audience for Tamon's work was actual servicemen. Tamon claimed that he made the diary public in order to answer frequent questions from inexperienced recruits, such as "What happens during war?

What actions do lower-echelon officers take during battle? What do you think of [*kannen*] during a fight?" He believed that it would be good for "young cadets with no experience of war" and that it would provide material for "readers' future self-cultivation" *(dokusha shōrai shūyō)*.[23] Although Tamon insisted the diary was merely his own personal view—or perhaps *especially* because it was the personal view of a commanding officer so experienced—the diary could be taken as a teaching tool for how to command, how to be a soldier, and how to write a diary.

Because Tamon's diary would become a model for later writers, it is worth examining more carefully. Structurally, it imitated semiofficial field diaries by recording the day, the weather, and troop movements, thus giving it the veneer of truth and professional authority. More important, it established content categories that servicemen would have easily recognized and embraced. The diary began with Tamon receiving his mobilization orders *(dōin karei)*, his induction into the unit, farewells with friends and family, rumors among the troops, a rendezvous with his superior officer, and the boat ride to the battlefield. These were, of course, just a few of the events that servicemen before and after Tamon might experience, but they were episodes specifically selected by Tamon as significant to his personal account. This sequence of events would become a standard format for many war diaries. Finally, Tamon's diary borrowed broadly from reportage and literary sources both to compose compelling battle scenes and to record his personal feelings:

> When the regiment gathered in the village, there were small arms fire reports from an elevated area to our right, followed by artillery bombardment. We were shocked, diving under the cover of nearby residences. . . . A regiment commander came to us. He said something to me, then, unexpectedly, shouted, "I'm hit!" Looking on in surprise, I saw he was wounded on the shoulder. I was almost standing shoulder to shoulder with him, and a bullet flew through the space between the houses and hit him. . . . While the battle for the day has not even started, to witness this right before my very eyes made me very unhappy [*fukai*].[24]

Tamon was an officer of the most elite pedigree—trained in a military preparatory school and admitted immediately into the land army's War College (Rikugun shikan gakkō). He would have had access to the military diaries of famous foreign generals as well as Japanese personal and official accounts of the Sino-Japanese War. His comments in the introduction suggest that he was deeply committed to instilling practices of "self-cultivation" in the young cadets, and the complexity of his diary suggests that he was fully familiar with several modes of writing, from both East Asia and modern Western civilization. It is safe to assume that servicemen read and sought to imitate this highly successful officer's diary, as they would his professional life. By blending the language of war reportage with the discipline of diary writing for the purpose of "self-cultivation," the identity that emerges from Tamon's diary was emblematic of the ideal Meiji soldier: a master of Western technology who preserves the martial spirit of the Japanese people. Unpublished officers' diaries from the Russo-Japanese War, however, still exhibited traits closer to the semiofficial field diaries of the past. This suggests that Tamon's diary, while in part composed during the conflict, was modified for a broader readership of recruits for future wars (to make it more readable and compelling) and would go on to become important later.

Personal diaries from the Russo-Japanese War exhibit tendencies similar to Ijichi's official account. Yanagawa Hachihei, an officer in the Konoe Infantry Reserves, recorded in the simplest possible terms his daily activities on the battlefield. Yanagawa wrote in pencil and brush into a small notebook that he kept on his person at all times. Initially Yanagawa wrote with little punctuation as he delineated his departure from Tokyo on 4 June 1904 and his arrival in Liaodong: "as part of organizing the regiment, I departed by train with General Ishida Masao at 9am from Tokyo Shinbashi We reached the docks, ate lunch, had dinner in Shizuoka At 1:40am on the 6th I reached Hiroshima This cost 26.20[.]" Gradually, Yanagawa departed from this style of narration and forced his diary into a strict regimen in which he recorded date, precise time, weather, troop movements (with accompanying time), military activities, and, if relevant, personal observations. It is possible that he did this in imitation of officers whom he witnessed keeping field diaries. Yanagawa's unbroken text was thus effectively disciplined into separating date and weather from the body of the entry, and each day's entry typically began with troop movement and time. Yanagawa took time to record items of interest to him—such as Koreans leaving Qing cities by horse cart or the interaction between the Qing people *(Shinkokujin)* and the Russians. These entries, however, are difficult to separate from those of military interest—for example, the absence of food or the condition of roads—suggesting that Yanagawa restricted his story to information relevant to the functioning of the army. Although his diary was for the most part truncated, occasionally—usually following a battle—he would devote time to putting his battlefield experience into words:

> 31 July, Clear
> Departed at 2:30am, arrived at 5am in the vicinity of Qiaotou[.] At that time, the sound of rifles and artillery was intense[.] At 7am we engaged in an intense [*hanahadashi*] battle[.] The enemy had twenty-four artillery, five divisions of infantry and cavalry[.] Our 12th Division 47th Regiment, missing one battalion, mixed with the Konoe Infantry Reserve Brigade and attacked[.] We were bravely resolved for Japanese victory[.]

Yanagawa's diary was short and terse, rarely making any attempt—outside of complaints of cold and lack of food—to capture an internal state or physical experience in language. However, his descriptions of morale and casualties, in addition to the unpleasantness of military life, pushed the boundaries of the form of the military field diary, which his work imitated.[25]

Some chronicles contained little or no personal content whatsoever. Omoto Saburō, an officer of unknown rank and affiliation in the Japanese land army during the Russo-Japanese War, wrote on thin, vertically ruled paper with doves printed on the margins, using brush and black ink. It is likely that the existing diary is in fact a postwar copy of the field diary he kept for himself in China.

> 10 November: Land at Sundi village[.] We'll stay in this village until the 14th[.] At 1am we leave the area heading northwest marching for about 14 *ri*[.] That day at 10pm we reach a nameless mountain[.] That night we camp outside[.] At 3:30am on the 16th we cross the mountain heading south for about [?] 13 *ri*[.] We reach Bao Village at 12pm[.] We stay in this village[.] On the 17th at 11am we leave the area heading south for 1 *ri*, arriving at a mountain top[.] We spot the enemy[.] That day at 1700 hours we return to Bao and stay the night[.] Until the 21st in [?] we climb to the peak of the mountain, the enemy [?] At night we stay at the local [?] residences[.] We leave at 5am on the 21st[.][26]

Omoto's pockmarked text demonstrates the persistence of formalistic record keeping among Japanese servicemen, even when they were writing their personal accounts. For some, this kind of pared-down chronicle may have been a closer expression of truth—similar to a newspaper headline or a battle report—than literary conceit. Conversely, many more may have used them as a basis for writing lengthier, more lyrical "diaries" after their repatriation. If nothing else, it demonstrates the willpower of these officers to micromanage their daily behavior by using textual tools.

Another source of military diary writing was memorial albums published by particular units in the Japanese army. It is unclear when this textual tradition began, but editions from the interwar era are abundant. The 1925 memorial album of the Fifty-Fourth Regiment (Okayama) of the former Fourteenth Division featured commanders' calligraphy, the unit anthem *(taika),* and photos of the practice fields, unit officers (group and individual portraits), and regimental flag with rifles. Besides bemoaning the postwar demobilization of the unit (as part of the 1920s "military reduction" period), it described the departure and service of the unit during various military expeditions:

> On 21 March 1915, the Seventeenth Division was switched to the Thirteenth, and we were sent to stay in Manchuria. From 16 to 18 March, we boarded the *Kotohira-maru* amidst a chorus of cheers from the enthusiastic citizens of Okayama Prefecture and, after splitting up onto two ships, we set sail. When you think about it, the Manchurian soil had absorbed the blood of the courageous army of the Russo-Japanese War, so it was a land that bore the heroic names of those in the regiment who had gone before us [*senpai no eimei*].[27]

Although early memorial albums were likely marketed toward officers, it is possible that they were bought and read by ordinary infantrymen as well. They described the assignments of their respective units in a disciplined, chronological fashion. Combining calligraphy, poetry, official data, and photographs in an attempt to define experience of war through an entire unit, the memorial album was a media pastiche that was later imitated by servicemen of all ranks in their personal accounts.

Ichinose Toshiya demonstrated how, following the Russo-Japanese War, the Japanese armed forces increasingly used guided diary writing as a form of training for men in lower and lower ranks.[28] These self-disciplinary textual practices were therefore no longer limited to officers of elite origins, and we can see that diaries by enlisted infantrymen grew in number during

the period from 1905 to the 1930s. Adachi Ei'ichi, who signed up for the
Twenty-Ninth Regiment of the Konoe Division (Kōfu), kept a diary from
the moment he entered the barracks on 1 December 1912. He used the diary as a personal record of his daily life in the army but also as a study
notebook for memorizing the unit history *(butaishi)* and the 1882 Imperial
Rescript on Soldiers and Sailors.

> 10 December, Tuesday
>   Weather is clear, rose at 6am, ate breakfast at 7am. This morning we had
> a ceremony for the reception of our rifles. The Regiment Commander gave a
> speech, saying, the rifle is [a symbol of] our honor as soldiers. After lunch at 12
> I rested. Then we had evening classes; first section of reading skills. 5pm
> dinner, after dinner I went to the canteen [*shuho*]. 8pm lights out, went to
> bed and slept.[29]

Though this was a "private" account (not subject to peer or superior review
and not explicitly prepared for publication), it relies heavily on military precedents for minute management of daily activity through textual practice.
In the back of one of his large, black, bound notebooks, Adachi even drew
a bar graph recording the times he awoke and went to sleep. All evidence
indicates that practices formerly restricted to the officer class, as a result of
raised literacy levels and the diffusion of military education and training,
were voluntarily taken up by the rank and file by the 1930s in Japan.

Perhaps it was not a coincidence, but the period 1905 to 1930 was also
the time when ordinary Japanese began to demand a greater voice over government affairs. The age of the "everyman" was emerging in Japan, wherein
the call for popular enfranchisement and militaristic expansion were not
mutually exclusive phenomena. Andrew Gordon aptly described early
twentieth-century pro-democracy, pro-imperial populism as an "unwit-
ting" construction of Japan's oligarchical leadership, which sought to gar-
ner popular support for foreign wars; or, as Gordon put it, the Russo-Japanese
War "fostered the belief that the wishes of the people, whose commitment
and sacrifice made the empire possible, should be respected in the political
process."[30] Both civilian political parties and the military aimed to gain
supremacy over each other by organizing Japanese society in support of
their causes.[31] It was the era of the 1909 Press Law, which severely restricted
publishers in what they could write,[32] but in which "ordinary people" felt

compelled to read and write narratives portraying themselves as playing an important role in history; this was when, in 1925, all Japanese men were given the right to vote, but the Diet passed the Peace Preservation Law aimed to "guide" acceptable political activity. Just as the oligarchs had unleashed the beast of populism, so too had the military given the ordinary soldier the tools with which to discipline himself, often with unpredictable results.

China

Traditions of writing about the self in China predate those of Japan (and certainly the United States). Various forms evolved over the centuries, including travelogues *(youji)*, self-accounts *(zixu)*, autobiographies *(zizhuan)*, and "notebooks" *(biji)* from ancient times to the early modern era.[33] Court officials in the Qing Dynasty (1644–1911) who oversaw military affairs, such as Lu Chuanyin, kept diaries, but these were in the traditional style;[34] nevertheless, like bureaucratic diaries in early modern Japan, they reveal an abiding interest in record keeping among East Asian elites, even if this was limited to noting weather, appointments with other officials, and the time one began work *(ruzhi)*. Chinese authors of travel diaries in the nineteenth century made use of multiple classical genres, including poetry, to express personal life experiences in text. In many cases, they complained of the inadequacy of classical prose to describe the world, but Xiaofei Tian insisted that what "critics construe as the failure of classical poetic language or of parallel prose is . . . no more than a continuation of generic conventions."[35] Complaining about the inadequacy of the genre to capture experience was, in fact, part of the genre itself. In any case, many of the travel accounts and previous war narratives, dating back to the earliest periods of Chinese history, were published and widely available to later diarists, so the conventions were hardly unfamiliar. In strictly military accounts, Chinese officers would have been receptive to new techniques and technologies in diary writing because self-accounts were often tied, in Confucian tradition, to "self-cultivation" *(xiuyang)*. This meant something different to premodern diarists, however, and usually involved perfecting one's knowledge of the Chinese classics. Furthermore, presaging the embrace of other writings styles within the field diary, such as war reportage, premodern Chinese were already experimenting with other genres in their self-accounts. Pei-yi Wu, describing early modern Chinese autobiographers, wrote how in "telling their life stories some of them did display a willful embellishment and a sheer inventiveness that seem[ed] to disdain credibility," revealing literary influences in supposedly "factual" records.[36] In sum, Chinese records of self, whatever they might be called, were diverse and subject to broad experimentation, but they were significantly different from the military diaries that emerged in the modern era; nevertheless, the cultural predisposition to keep organized records of experience, critically evaluate oneself, and experiment with genre may help explain why Chinese officers would later embrace the modern field diary.

What is critical about the modern era is not merely the emergence of vernacular written Chinese or new forms of writing about the self but the state's interest in guiding these practices and their spread throughout non-elite classes. Premodern Chinese elites also took an interest in shaping the morals of the public through manuals, but traditional views regarding state-society relations persisted, in which the elites viewed the public as "dangerous mobs, capable of spontaneous and unrestrained violence."[37] Thus the intense interest that the state apparatus had in managing the thoughts and opinions of ordinary people, as Foucault described in the European context, did not significantly emerge until the modern era for East Asians. Indeed, the suffusion of technologies such as disciplined diary writing may have been as late as the "Nanjing Decade" of GMD rule, which William Kirby described as China's first "developmental state"[38]—although, as this book will show, the project of disciplining modern soldiers was carried out in an unsystematic manner throughout the early Republic. Of course, the lack of central state leadership did not stop private publishers from printing diaries and distributing descriptions of war, which would have inevitably influenced later accounts. Lithographic and letterpress accounts of the First Sino-Japanese War (1894–1895) were hungrily consumed by Chinese readers in large urban areas such as Shanghai, and these would have included "diaries" and other chronological coverage of major events; this also corresponded with an early emphasis on "objectivity and factuality" in reporting.[39] As Christopher Reed and Barbara Mittler have pointed out, however, these terms meant something very different to Chinese writers even as late as the end of the nineteenth century.

In fact, when exactly modern forms of self-accounting, like field diaries, entered into Chinese literary culture is unclear. Ongoing research concerning the Chinese Maritime Customs Bureau, which was administered by foreigners for the Qing government, has exposed some of the mechanisms by which modern techniques of record keeping were adopted in China.[40] As for the military, direct evidence does exist that officers were keeping field diaries since the time of Yuan Shikai's government (1912–1916). All evidence suggests that field diary writing in China began much as it did in Japan—as a textual technology aimed at perfecting officers' discipline and modernizing the armed forces. In fact, it is likely that these techniques were adopted during the late Qing period by many of the future "warlords" who received their training in Japan, where military diary writing had been systematized since at least the 1880s.[41] These military figures, such as Yan Xishan, were convinced not only of the need to train a populace into supporting military mobilization but also of the usefulness of modern techniques for doing so, which included widely divergent practices such as logistics, technology, and accounting.[42]

It is unwise to assume that the 1911 Republican revolution itself was altogether decisive in changing writing practices in China, but changes did quickly follow thereafter. Future "warlords" such as Cai E, and their allies in the Nationalist Party, including Huang Xing, immediately following the revolution embraced conscription and announced that to "train a good soldier is to train a good citizen."[43] By the 1920s, Chinese mass media publishers, such as the Shanghai Commercial Press, were printing "model diaries" *(mofan riji)* for children who, once they had reached adulthood, would have been old enough to serve in the Second World War. These texts often contained political content as well; indeed, the early Republican Era (1911–1928) was characterized not only by the expansion of the reading public but also by close links between print media and political movements, culminating in the May Fourth Movement.[44] Leading up to the 1911 revolution, military officers, scholars, and reformers worked together, sharing information, technology, and ideology; fatally for the Qing, revolutionary activity was also located right within its own "New Army" barracks.[45] For a brief, fleeting period at the start of the Republican era, the national consciousness and modern military techniques that emerged at the end of the Qing Dynasty were shared in many parts of China, despite the strong history of localism;[46] the "systemic" nature of Chinese military training was mainly because military leaders did not yet wield personal power as regional warlords but also because of their shared experience of training abroad in places like France, Britain, and, especially, Japan.[47] Furthermore, the professionalization of the officer class at the end of the Qing, combined with rising standards of literacy for recruits and the introduction of foreign pedagogical techniques in schools, meant that the new generations of officers in China were ready for "modern" techniques of record keeping and writing about war.[48]

It was within this context that the oldest known "field diary" *(zhenzhong riji)* was composed, belonging to the commanders of the Third Division and Artillery Regiment of the Second Army (1913).[49] Each day was split into five main categories for entries—date, weather, activities, orders, and intelligence reports. It used a form of official modern Chinese, which was a major departure from how a top military document would have been composed in years previous. Printed on mass-produced paper, it was almost a direct imitation of Western and Japanese models. The authors did not devote considerable space to describing battles or heroism, but they did take time to reflect on the changing needs of soldiering in the modern world. Despite the bad reputation warlords have traditionally received as barriers to China's modernization, the diarists were keenly aware of the need to transform the military. One author wrote, "Educators take the development of the total person [*yangcheng renge*] as their aim" and therefore must pay attention to a soldier's moral character *(daode)* so that he does not revert to his thieving and barbarous ways *(daoben hengchi)*. Thus, spiritual training "must be superior to that which we have conducted in China in the past." He also presented a litany of chivalrous and filial virtues for his men to emulate, in keeping with the increasingly Confucianist tone of the Yuan government's final years—these virtues included "helping those in distress" and, when dealing with the people, "believe the truth, respect the elderly, and be generous."[50] As the author attempted to employ artillery to force his rival to submit, the descriptions of battles were simplified in the extreme. As Edward McCord noted, despite the attempt of the officer class to instill these values into their men, ordinary Chinese soldiers, many of whom were drafted during the desperate years of the revolution, were perceived to be lawless bandits: "Middle and lower officers were unable to command their soldiers; senior officers could not command their subordinates. All sense of obedience to duty was gone."[51] Nevertheless, Chinese military leaders had ambitions to create a force of literate, well-disciplined troops, and they were familiar with the techniques and value of military diary writing.

Civilian governments were eventually made subject to regional military power, giving rise to "warlordism," but this did not erase the progress made toward professionalization of the officer class during the late Qing and early Republic.[52] Regional warlords embraced disciplined diary writing, and foreign observers were often surprised at the levels of literacy among their field officers. An examination of these texts reveals much continuity between warlord and GMD forces in strategy and tactics, as well as what would prove later to be liabilities for the Chinese during the Second World War. During a 1926 regional skirmish between Sichuanese forces based in Chengdu and a rival army to the north, the brigade commander used his field diary to describe the battles: "We sent in Zhang Wei's unit to attack the city of Shi head on, and had a different battalion stand guard. . . . At this time, the northern forces had already entered into battle at Wushan. It was a huge battle that went on without end. They seemed to be using this as an opportunity to invade Sichuan!" He recorded their pursuit of these invading forces from the north, which included the use of plainclothes units and collecting intelligence from local Buddhist temples. The chaos and ruthlessness of warlord combat is clear: porters and other laborers were too afraid to enter Chengdu, resulting in a lack of coal and transportation paralysis; homes were burned down for "security" reasons; and in one instance, a cavalryman was caught selling his ammunition and shot.[53] It was misbehavior such as this that alienated warlord governments from local gentry, disrupting revenue streams and inhibiting mobilization efforts—which meant that China was in no shape to resist a well-organized enemy such as the Japanese Empire.[54] In the 1920s, then, it was becoming painfully obvious to warlords in China that "untrained troops could not face up to battle and inexperienced or ignorant officers were incapable of command," inspiring wide-ranging military reforms across the country, including reviewed diary writing.[55]

Nevertheless, prior to the Nationalist victory in 1928, there seemed to be a lack of consensus within the forces regarding how war diaries should be written. Although most Chinese officers serving in Sichuan's warlord armies, for example, were trained at China's premier military academy, Baoding, some came from regional military schools that may have had different diary writing practices. Disorganization seemed to be a common trait among warlord armies. Indeed, although later GMD forces would have special presses to print their diary paper and other stationery, warlords picked up their materials from various schools and booksellers. Several of these accounts complain of orders not being transmitted properly, of not knowing the location of their subordinates, and of theft. That being said, there were clearly some precedents for these texts. In the Sichuanese diary above, the brigade commander ended each entry with "presented by" *(zhuancheng)* and "inspected by" *(zhaoyue)*, followed by their personal seals. Another diary from this period, by Li Hongkun (commander of the Shandong Army's First Route), included the same categories of date, weather, position, and unit activities that would become standard fare in GMD documents.[56]

The Chinese Nationalists *(Guomindang,* GMD) embraced the disciplined diary writing practices of the warlords right away in part, ironically, to create soldiers who would be more loyal than those of the warlords themselves. Field diaries were kept by GMD field officers as they drove north to unify China during the Northern Expedition. Some were simple notebooks, others were more personal accounts, but most were disciplined accounts of unit activities. In addition to describing all that occurred under their command, some officers took to including others' reports in their account. Following the Japanese and Western fashion, the sections of "notebooks" *(biji)* or field diaries that described important battles would be requested by the central command at a later date, copied by a professional scribe *(wenguan)* seconded to the military, and made available for limited review. Such documents meticulously delineated facts such as troop movements, weather, and supply in a narrative unbroken by formatting or punctuation.[57] In doing so, the GMD tried to systematize militarism and escape the chaos of the early Republican era.

The GMD took diary writing seriously because it was, as much as the cannon and medicine, a characteristic of a modern military force. During the Northern Expedition, these diaries might be submitted directly to Chiang Kai-shek for review and were also often a space to paint an unflinching portrait of the ferocious nature of war: "Against the remaining defeated troops around Yuanjian, we must apply terrible pressure upon them and wipe them all out."[58] The importance of keeping an accurate record of these events, simultaneous to their occurrence (i.e., unlike memoirs), was repeatedly and strenuously emphasized. A 1926 diary from the General Staff office strongly advised that diaries "should contain record made while the events take place, or its value is lessened."[59] Despite the centralizing ambitions of the GMD General Staff, however, many officers continued to conduct diary writing in their own individual idiom. General Staff officer Wu Guanzhou used his notebooks *(biji)* to record a "war diary" *(suijun riji)* after the conclusion of the Northern Expedition in 1928. This was not merely a personal account, however, as it still adhered to the form and content of official field diaries: recording orders, reports, and "events witnessed" *(suo jian ji shi)*. It was also a space for Wu to inscribe his political views: "The purpose of this revolution is to directly alleviate the suffering of the people at the hands of bandits and warlords." He mentioned the importance of providing these materials for "the consideration of military historians" and made sure to "prepare the various impressions from each period." Wu also often used the diary to record "errors" in tactic and how those mistakes could be avoided in the future; he evidently submitted this text to the central government voluntarily.[60] The gradual emergence of political and personal views into the war diary was also a reflection of the influence of the Soviet commissar (political officer) system within the early days of the Huangpu Military Academy.[61] Jochen Hellbeck showed that guided diary writing, as a kind of political education for soldiers, took place in Russia at the very beginning of the revolution.[62] Because the GMD also saw itself as a revolutionary force, this practice was readily adopted by many in the "Revolutionary Army" *(Gemingjun)*. In sum, for the Chinese Nationalists, the diary served as a record of personal achievement, military history, and, eventually, political discipline.

By the early 1930s, even volunteer corps *(yiyongjun)* in northeastern China—before, during, and after its seizure by the Kantōgun and transformation into the puppet state of Manchukuo—kept field diaries of their actions against Japanese troops stationed there. The one surviving document (a Japanese translation) shows that the original diary must have been used primarily for recording reports *(tongbao)* and orders. Day, time, and location were followed on the next line by numbered contents. Some orders, however, were followed by descriptions of battles that attempted to employ more lyrical descriptions.

> Report October 8th, 7:30pm, Fulaer headquarters
> 1. Today at 3:30am about four to five hundred enemy troops opened fire furiously on our house at Changsheng. Our 2nd Battalion 5th and 6th Companies were under pressure from the enemy until 7:30, when they withdrew to Xiaohei. We were sure that over half of the enemy troops were Japanese. One Type 6 heavy artillery piece, two mortars, and many, many light and heavy machine guns. Day after day they dispatched a single plane to bomb our position, but today they increased to four. Their technique for bombing seems to consist of six or eight blasts each time, but they are terribly inaccurate.[63]

Captured by the Japanese, these documents were of intense interest not only for their strategic value but also (judging from the material selected for translation) for what they taught the Japanese about their enemies. In that sense, soldiers accepted their war diary not only as a true reflection of themselves, they also sought the diaries of enemies in order to see what kind of men they faced.

Many of the earliest field diaries written in China have been lost or destroyed, but evidence suggests that it was a practice that gained rapid approval among Chinese officers—particularly once the Nationalists seized control of China and Chiang Kai-shek consolidated his power within the GMD in 1927. Although late Qing reporting experimented with mixing "fact" and literary prose, these concepts were different from foreign press models, because literary techniques in China had traditionally been used interchangeably in both "fact" and "fiction" writing.[64] Plus, soldiers did not at this time systematically practice factual record keeping, because they had not yet developed an approach to do so—the establishment of the "New Armies" leading up to the Republican revolution in 1911 was decisive in introducing new kinds of textual practices in Chinese armies. These were embraced by the GMD, and in the 1930s, Chiang Kai-shek would expand diary writing among his officers and officials. As a consequence, the genre of military diary writing would develop in unprecedented ways.

A NEW LANGUAGE FOR EXPERIENCE

Yoshimi Yoshiaki described the 1930s as a time when the state had to "conquer" the divisions inherent in the widespread anger over military expenditure, populist imperialism, "panics" over foreign conflicts, and failures in the rural economy.[65] Meanwhile, the Nationalist government had to solidify its control over China by harnessing the power of growing populism and anti-Japanese sentiment without allowing those forces to destroy the regime's power and control. Ironically, in a time rife with contradiction and popular activism, soldiers frequently narrated their battlefield experiences from a unified subject position: in other words, the "I" in a war narrative frequently became "we." The archetypal "soldier" (*heitai* in Japanese, *shibing* in Chinese) in this new literature was the fighting equivalent of the "everyman"—a person to whom most anyone could relate. Although this monolithic identity promised to help overcome the problem of building popular support for war without concomitant demands for popular sovereignty, its origins are still somewhat mysterious. Early East Asian war reportage devoted considerable space to depicting gallantry and sacrifice, but these accounts typically were concerned with the experience of officers; this was to change in the 1930s. While the GMD was trying to establish a coherent community among its officers, it was also attempting to mobilize the people to support the army or sign up. Meanwhile, democracy and imperialism were converging in Japan. Many forces struggled among each other to give the "common man" a voice in both China and Japan, and one of the most influential in both countries was proletarian fiction. War literature, and thus diary writing, would be indelibly marked by the conflicts inherent in the arrival of mass politics in East Asia.

The construction of the "common man" in part derived from a seemingly unlikely source. Writing a narrative where many individual human beings are collapsed into one identity is often a tool of agitation propaganda. "Agitprop" literature is a form of writing that inspires masses of people to act in a similar fashion. Consequently, we may infer that accounts of the common soldier in East Asia have a discursive etymology stemming in part from proletarian literature. In leftist reportage and literary practice, the primary subject was almost always "the proletariat." Since "the proletariat" could not be a single person (individualism was considered characteristic of bourgeois literature, symbolized by I-novels, travel diaries, and memoirs), it was typically represented in language as a pluralized subject—the sailors, the men, the troops, the workers, and so forth. This unified identity was the locus of experience as well as the origin of action. In 1920s Japan, authors such as Hayama Yoshiki tried to breathe life into this kind of gargantuan subjectivity:

> Because of the extreme hard labor, the sailors were put to sleep without resistance . . . the structure of the whole ship and the basic, common sensation that enveloped them all alike, was a lot like the penetrating feeling of the usual senselessness and boredom and the four prisoners being eaten away by tedium, staring blankly up at the window. . . . When [the leaders of the revolution] passed by their entrance, the sailors cheered. It echoed all the way to the salon.[66]

By the 1930s, Japanese authors portraying the experiences of servicemen had learned to assimilate the language of proletarian fiction in order to move a mass audience. They replaced the lone, noble officer with mud-caked, suffering commoners. One motivation for this sleight of hand was almost certainly commercial—more customers could identify with faceless archetypes that closely resembled themselves than the scions of Meiji era "Sat-Chō" officer pedigree.[67] In this style of narration, one soldier blurred into another until they became indistinguishable. No one employed this style more skillfully than the war reportage author Hino Ashihei:

> My car was soon taken in by the soldiers. It was clear that they had been marching in the blazing heat, as they were dripping with sweat and their uniforms were soaked. . . . In the afternoon, the previously noisy soldiers quieted down, and [marched] without raising a voice, so I thought I might sleep. Then, suddenly, someone started singing we shall win [*katte kuru zo*] in a low, manly voice. And then, as if they were waiting, soon others began to harmonize, their voices grew louder, and finally they began to hit their thighs, tap their leaflet pouches, stamp their feet, and the chorus had there begun.[68]

Texts strongly supportive of the war effort, such as Hino's, and those with more nuance, such as Ishikawa Tatsuzō's, used the trope of the mass subject (soldiers) as a putative window into the world of the infantryman. Multiple individuals were thus collapsed into one experiencing subject; the reader's feelings were also engaged, and one was invited to become part of the crowd. It was a subjectivity so encompassing that even the author himself often claimed to be part of the movement.[69] That the mass subject could appear in works with such different political perspectives only serves to demonstrate the ease with which this discourse migrated between texts, irrespective of authorial intentions; it is a testament to the seductive power that this mass self held over textual representations of soldiers' lives.

In China, too, leftist reportage was well established in the early twentieth century, with a history longer than the Nationalist Party itself. Thus, the narrative techniques of proletariat literature were mobilized by GMD propagandists (who were often leftists or connected to the CCP to begin with) as early as the Northern Expedition in 1926. Progressive writers in Republican China—inheritors of the legacy of Lu Xun—abandoned realism for what Mao Dun and others referred to as "a literature of blood and tears."[70] This bloody rhetoric was dyed a deeper red by the influence of Marxist ideology. Directly after the Northern Expedition, authors of reportage proudly proclaimed that "on the surface reportage focuses on 'reporting the facts,' [*shishi*] but, this is not like taking a photograph, mechanically taking reality [*xianshi*] and making it manifest in text [*zi*]. It must have a target, a sure direction. This target is socialism."[71] However, many of these very same socialists would go on to deploy such graphic description and moving cries for action to support the GMD.[72] They moved from the political left to the right by changing as few as a handful of words.

This may seem improbable to those who are more familiar with the post-1949 CCP memory of the war; nevertheless, the transition from inciting the suffering workers to mobilizing the suffering Chinese people was as short a leap as it was for Mao Zedong to go from serving the Nationalists as a propagandist to overthrowing them within twenty years.[73] To begin with, the GMD offered its own version of bloody revolution well before the outbreak of war with Japan. Even a short glance at GMD training manuals will provide many examples of the kind of language that appeared in reportage, field diaries, and personal accounts:

> What is meant by the "Blood of the Fallen Heroes" [*xianlie*] is that we should be affected by the flow of their blood—that we should follow the flowing of their blood. Blood is the essential component of life, and it can flow—which means it can be sacrificed. What is meant by the "Flower of Ideology" [*zhuyi*] is that we should use our warm blood to nourish the growth ideology; ideology is fed by the flow of fresh blood from the Huangpu [Military Academy].[74]

This graphic prose would not remain in the halls of the military academies—it would reappear in novels, newspaper articles, and even pamphlets for the Chinese Boy Scouts.[75] The language that GMD mobilization introduced to the daily lives of Chinese people was truly revolutionary and not simply because many of their propagandists were also members of the CCP; writers not aligned with the Communists utilized the language of reportage and GMD political and military discourse as well. Xie Bingying combined battlefield vignettes, descriptions of warlord oppression, and revolutionary soldier camaraderie in a diary format. She served as a field medic for the GMD army during its drive from Wuhan to the north from 1927 to 1928.

In her diary (serialized through the popular newspaper *Dagongbao,* later published as a book), she strove to capture the essence of the emerging Nationalist heroes:

> On the grassy side of the railroad there were three tough wounded soldiers. One of these comrades was wounded in the left thigh and stomach, his body dripping with blood; except for the outside of his collar, everything was soaked through with fresh, red blood. No matter who heard this man's groans, his painful cries—no matter if his heart was made of stone—he would be heartbroken and driven to tears. It would also inspire his courage, and, stepping in pools of blood of the fallen, he would continue the unfinished task, strive to grapple with our foes! At this time I really wanted to go the front line! I want to go to the battlefield of blood and sacrifice!

Retelling the story of how the warlord soldiers committed offenses against local women and children, Xie tried to articulate her fury—"those repugnant bandits" *(wan'e tufei),* "grinding my teeth in anger over the warlord's barbarism," and "gentry bastards, running dogs [of the warlords]" *(wangbadan de tuhao lieshen de gouming).*[76] During the Northern Expedition, authors of war literature, whether privately allied with the CCP or the GMD, drew both on the techniques of leftist reportage and the political ideology of the Chinese Nationalist military; their diverging dreams for the future of China did not prevent them from sharing the same style of writing war.

Meanwhile, growing literacy in China and Japan resulted in an expansion of diary writing practices, and the state was becoming more interested in harnessing the potential power behind these developments. By 1930, the historical changes in these two countries seemed to be drawing them inexorably together. Diary writing, particularly among the elite and the well educated, was so important and so ingrained that partisan forces in Manchuria kept diaries and even Japanese spies kept them. Oda Makoto penned a top-secret document in 1928 that was indistinguishable from a field diary save for the title—"A Report [*hōkoku*] on Studies of the Shanghai Front." Leaving Nagasaki on 3 May 1928, he arrived the next day to investigate the military of the newly dominant Nationalist Party. On 6 May, he took a stroll around the Naval Headquarters. He was immediately alarmed by the presence of anti-Japanese study groups nearby, which threatened the "total massacre of Japanese people in Shanghai." By 16 May he had returned to

Yokosuka with some fairly firm opinions on what he had witnessed and recorded in China. Looking back on the armed forces in Shanghai, he sneered,

> Currently the Chinese army consists of private soldiers belonging to various
> powerful figures; it is contrary to national defense and preservation of public
> order. . . . Being that each figure is in haste to successfully expand their
> power, in their eyes there is no country, and the people do not exist; they
> just use private armies to fight amongst each other. Yesterday's enemy is to-
> day's ally, today's bosom friend is tomorrow's traitor.[77]

Oda deplored the notion that any armed force in China could make a spirited resistance to a dedicated foreign invader, but he also aimed to strike
fear into the hearts of his commanders by recording the extent of well-
organized civilian anti-Japanese activities, the numerous volunteer brigades
springing up in Shanghai, and the threat they posed to Japanese citizens
living outside the leased territory. Through his diary record, he positioned
himself as an expert observer of the deplorable Chinese condition: GMD
incompetence, civilian unrest, and the intense anti-Japanese hatred that
threatened imperial subjects in Shanghai. Like many officers, Oda wanted
authority on a particular issue (whether Japan should seize Shanghai) and, as
an aspiring authority figure, felt compelled to keep a disciplined record of
"facts" in the form of a diary. Being a good soldier, then, became inextricably
linked to the practice of keeping a disciplined record of one's activities and
experiences.

A PREVIEW OF COMING ATTRACTIONS:
RAPID CHANGE DURING THE 1930S

A meteoric rise in military diary writing took place during the 1930s. One
factor was undoubtedly the rapid expansion of military forces in both Nationalist China and Japan. Also, the Japanese seizure of Manchuria (1931–
1932) and the invasion of Shanghai (1932) were major events for both Japanese and Chinese servicemen and probably did more to establish the
discourse on soldiering than any military action that preceded it, not only
because of the narratives of the event itself, but also in the way that it inspired both nations to rapidly prepare their forces for a conflict that seemed
inevitable. The invasion in particular forced the GMD to pour more and

more of its attention and resources into building an effective army consisting of "modern soldiers."

First, the brief conflict between Japan and Nationalist China in 1931–1932 ended inconclusively. The GMD, under Chiang Kai-shek, ceded vast tracts of land to the Kantōgun (Japan's Northeastern Army, stationed in colonial Korea and in China's northeast). Later, in the politically disastrous Treaty of Tanggu (1933), Chiang was forced to abandon any armed resistance against the establishment of Japanese-controlled Manchukuo to the north. Nevertheless, Chinese citizens, servicemen, and ideologues, particularly in the south, never surrendered hope that the "Three Eastern Provinces" *(dongbei sansheng)* would be returned or retaken by a legitimate Chinese government. Additionally, Japanese forces were fought to a standstill by GMD troops in Shanghai, whereas, in the north, they had faced regional forces under former warlords, many of whom were commanded not to resist the invasion.[78] Military personalities from the brutal defense of Shanghai, such as Zhang Zizhong, were later apotheosized for their unwillingness to submit to the Japanese invaders. The Japanese, however, believed they were punishing the GMD for offenses its soldiers and cadres had committed against the empire in Shanghai, so they looked on with great bitterness when the GMD celebrated their successes against the IJA. In fact, the results of the Japanese invasion seemed, if nothing else, to embolden forces in the GMD to take an even harder stance against Japanese interests on the mainland. Considering the great sacrifices made by their beloved comrades, Japanese servicemen took this as a grave insult and vowed to "finish the job" in Shanghai.

The armies that met in Shanghai were already on a path toward modernization in both materiel and tactic. Though it is often not recognized today, Chinese forces in that area were increasingly literate, well trained, and well respected in central China for most of the 1930s, even if they were generally inferior to the Japanese army.[79] They were armed with up-to-date weaponry and were held in high esteem in the south—a major transformation from the warlord era, when common wisdom held that "no good man becomes a soldier." At the same time, the Japanese army was beginning to pull out of a long period of "military reduction," during which, famously, they reduced the number of active divisions but used surplus funds to update their arsenal. In China increased levels of literacy and new recruitment policies that focused on educated urban, middle-class sons (along with the establishment of the Huangpu Military Academy) meant that, at the very least, officers going to war in 1931–1932 had been exposed to diary writings and were capable of reproducing them. Armies in the north, the glorious tradition of Baoding notwithstanding, were of a markedly lower quality. Most important, Chiang Kai-shek's exposure to ubiquitous war diary writing practices while studying in Japan ensured that this model would have been part of his concept of a "modern military."[80]

Japan's expanding empire combined the boredom of serving in the hinterland with new technologies of rapid communication, giving servicemen ample time and opportunity to experiment with self-narrative.[81] Tanimura Kanzō was an infantryman from Kyoto who was assigned to a Kantōgun heavy artillery regiment in Port Arthur. On 6 October 1932, his unit departed from Port Arthur and went to Manchuria. In a regular ruled notebook (for civilian use), Tanimura kept photographs, newspaper clippings, and his own drawings mixed with his poetry, vignettes, and diary entries from northern China. His unit moved their large artillery pieces by truck instead of horse, impressing on Tanimura and, especially the fresh recruits, "the majesty [ikō] of the rapid Northeastern Army." The morning before they spied the Chinese forces, they ate "frozen rice mixed with wild vegetables." After serving in several battles, Tanimura found himself closer and closer to the front line. In 1933, he was involved in the clash of Chinese and Japanese forces at Rehe. Writing in hurried, staccato prose, he scribbled a narrative that tried to both record information relevant to the military expedition and capture the feeling of the moment:

> 28th: The flag of the Rising Sun is flying high. . . . The Imperial Army, with never a moment's rest, advanced towards Beijing[.] The enemy inflicted damage on the streets and railroads in this area in order to defend themselves from our pursuit[.] There are remnants of battle The corpses of enemy soldiers are scattered about[.] We advance on Miyun without much of a battle. . . .
>
> 11th: First day of Battle for Xinkailing: The battle began at 3am, with the whole army taking a deep breath and beginning to fight right away, a battle right after we passed Nandamen Moving with the air forces, the Imperial Army advanced on the entire front line of the enemy's position. . . . The fierce battles since the Manchurian Incident, the battles of the Shanghai Incident, and the lightening-quick speed of the army's movement, the bombardment of forty-nine artillery pieces large and small have defeated the enemy soldiers. . . .

The Division Commander expressed gratitude for the heavy artillery: "Good work boys, thanks to you we won the battle!"

However, Tanimura did not restrict his descriptions to battles or heroism; he also wrote poetry about a woman to whom his thoughts strayed and even sketched her from memory into his notepad. The poem was entitled "Thoughts at Night":

"Are you sleeping?
Are you awake?
A moon over a quiet town in fall
Listless after saying 'adieu'
The sigh from thoughts
Which never cease
Seek your far-off affections
My weak heart is conflicted."[82]

Nevertheless, such "weak" deviations from his voice as a soldier in the Imperial Army were few and far between. The first page of his war diary featured an object of arguably equally powerful affection, written in large, bold letters: "COMRADES" (senyū). Tanimura's diary demonstrates that Japanese servicemen were interacting with mass media to an unprecedented degree and doing so in accounts of their personal experience.

In the years following the Manchurian and Shanghai Incidents, instead of focusing on the Japanese menace, Chiang Kai-shek once again turned his attention to wiping out "bandits" (tufei), including the CCP. Consequently, many servicemen whose diaries survive from that time were engaged in so-called bandit suppression campaigns that diluted GMD forces across the interior. Meanwhile, the Japanese military was waiting for its opportunity to weaken or eradicate GMD influence on northern China. Most GMD officers used their diaries to condemn or justify their participation in a civil conflict while the Japanese were active on their doorstep. Some, like Hao Mengling, went on campaigns as far south as Guizhou to fight a medley of Communists and smugglers—an act he referred to as a waste of national strength. A common defense for internal military campaigns was the suppression of drugs and other sundry crimes: in Guangxi Province, Nationalist soldiers claimed that smugglers were forcing locals to buy drugs (presumably opium), thus necessitating the intervention of the Revolution-ary Army.[83] Whether for or against using the armed forces against Chinese citizens, official or personal, GMD diaries had become spaces for express-ing one's views on Chiang's policies and the author's consequent behavior.

Assigned briefly as a teacher to a middle school in Hubei, one unnamed Nationalist veteran of the Northern Expedition was suddenly asked to serve in a unit fighting "bandits" in Jiangxi. He "deliberated about this for some time," composing various opinions in his diary, and eventually justified participation by writing,

> Working to nurture revolutionary youths, this is a crucial task. We are now in a national crisis and bandits are running amok. If I don't go immediately to suppress them, they'll be certain to spread all over, endangering nations everywhere. I am a military school graduate, and trained to be a soldier. I sacrifice everything and throw myself onto the battlefield. Consequently, I decided to join the ranks; this was my motivation for participating in the bandit suppression campaign.[84]

Like Xie Bingying, this anonymous diarist was driven by his compassion for the people (whom he thought oppressed by internal enemies) to use his status and training as a Nationalist soldier for making revolution. He spent much of his time among the people he strove to mobilize into "volunteer brigades" *(yiyongdui)* and Peace Preservation Corps (PPC, *baoandui*). When two of his volunteers were beaten to death by local bandits, he and the townspeople held a public funeral. He covered their faces with white cloth and wrote, "It was a mournful silence demanding respect, extremely sad and painful; all of the officers and men—everyone—was moved to tears."[85] He used the diary, of course, to demonstrate his dedication to the Nationalist cause, which was a public performance of political bona fides, but the text was also useful for thinking about how life should be lived. For Nationalist officers such as this man, the diary was becoming an important tool not just for strict record but also for self-fashioning. Of course, it is possible that there was no such person and the diary itself was a construct of Nationalist ideologues; nevertheless, this was the sort of personal record that the regime was encouraging its men to compose, and in the 1930s, they were doing so with remarkable alacrity. As this nameless military diarist trained civilians to form armed organizations, he reflected on the need to imitate great leaders like Chiang Kai-shek, who had militarized his daily life. In China, he speculated, only the good people are disorganized—by establishing local militias and teaching them how to be soldiers, he hoped to change that. Disciplined diary writing, for soldiers, now combined good soldiering with meditations on life in general.

Fortunately for the nation, not all forces in China were directed toward killing other Chinese. "Don't be a slave in a fallen country" *(bu yao dang wangguo-nu)* was a ubiquitous battle cry emanating from GMD cadres, spurring the people to support the war in whatever way they could. Particularly in Shanghai, where many soldiers had fought the Japanese directly and harbored little but spite for their enemy, men were in training throughout the 1930s to defend the city from what they believed to be an inevitable and cataclysmic battle. Northern Expedition veteran and appointed mayor of Shanghai Wu Tiecheng left a handwritten notebook on training men during this period; this notebook demonstrates that the intensification of efforts in the GMD to improve its various fighting forces was matched by the suffusion of disciplinary documentation. "Training soldiers at this time of national crisis is not easy," he began, delineating the strategies and texts used to educate Shanghai students on tactics and maneuvers. Writing about the education regimen for everyday life (a duty overseen by the head of the *ban*), Wu noted that the "*ban* is the foundation of the combat unit [*budui*], so activities there are referred to as 'basic training' [*jiben xunlian*].[86] Its purpose make our hearts one [*zhongxin yizhi*] and bind our spirits together, to move with perfect cooperation, and inculcate a 'live together, die together' ethos." Indeed, by combining the communal existence of the barracks with political education, the GMD hoped to fuse Soviet and Japanese models to produce a superior soldier. Actual fighting ability, however, was recognized by Wu as equal in importance to the creation of a community of soldiers through political education:

> Military education at the company [*lian*] level is the most important. The head of the company should take all responsibility for its education, spirit, and order. The company commander must become a man of worth for all of his officers and men, and should do his utmost to nurture their military virtues [*meide*], encourage patriotism, and carry out the spread of Sun Yat-sen's philosophy and spiritual unification [*jingshen tuanjie*]. The company commander should at the appropriate times educate the men, fight steadfastly, throw one's

self onto the field of battle, and sacrifice without fear for his country and his people. All of this can only be achieved through peacetime training—[only when we have achieved this] we can be called modern soldiers.[87]

Thus, despite the Japanese military's attempt in 1932 to cripple the GMD in Shanghai by bombing Chiang's industrial heartland, the Nationalists still managed to rally their forces for the conflict. "Heroes of the people" *(minzu yingxiong)*, or those servicemen who had participated in the fighting in Shanghai, were given medals and widely lauded in the popular press.[88] The GMD also employed textual methods for mobilization: diaries and interviews with GMD servicemen who fought the Japanese in 1932 were picked up and published in Shanghai soon after the withdrawal of the bloodied Japanese forces. While some of the accounts of "young soldiers" *(qingnian shibing)* kept the vignette style of oral histories or reportage, others combined the narrative form of diary writing with the narrative strategies of war reportage. Wildly popular and decorated with modernist art on the cover, they became foundational texts for later diary writers.[89] To many, publishing accounts that memorialized the GMD's successful resistance to Japanese invasion in the south was essential to remobilization and national salvation. In these texts, servicemen seemingly called out to the nation from the heavens with the voices of holy martyrs. Indeed, the Commercial Press of Shanghai, after discovering its machine shop untouched by Japanese bombing, prophetically proclaimed, "[The Japanese] damaged the machines but overlooked something that could raise the dead to life."[90] GMD authorities embraced this spiritual language as enthusiastically as they did the language of "blood and tears."

Personal diary writing became so omnipresent in the armed forces at this time that the Japanese General Staff began directing them at every level possible. For example, recruits in the Japanese air force kept diaries that were subject to review by their internal affairs education officer *(naimuhan kyōkan,* usually a lower-echelon officer, for example, a *gunsō* or *sōchō).* Where the GMD had limited its powers of observation to field diaries kept by specific officers in a unit, the Japanese army now began to take tentative steps toward extending its gaze to all men. Naturally, it began with the smallest number of elite recruits. Flight recruit "Morita Tatsuo" in the special training program of the Japanese air forces *(yokaren kōhosei)* began in 1936 to keep his compulsory diary—evidently in earnest; after completing his physical examination, he wrote, "I'm filled with happiness, as I take the first step towards being a soldier. I'll strive to do my best, and become a fortress for the fame of the Empire!" Very quickly, however, Morita found that army life was full of its spiritual and emotional doldrums. Even on his second day in the barracks, he found himself bored, watching the torrential downpour outside his window: "Besides eating our meals, we didn't do anything special today, just sat around bored. Nevertheless, my lack of any overwhelming desire to study is really a shame. From now on, I swear, I won't waste my free time, I'll use it appropriately!" Although Morita's laziness and (probably feckless) self-encouragement initially escaped his internal affairs officer's watchful eye, pretty soon he was busted: "What are you doing every day?" Sergeant Takamatsu exclaimed in red pencil scribbled large and messy on the margins of Morita's diary (followed by his personal seal), "No matter how difficult it may seem, you must take your diary [*hanseiroku*] seriously! It is your 'mirror of truth' [*makoto no kagami*]. It will be your last will and testament [*igonsho*]!"[91] Morita thereafter made sporadic attempts to become a better soldier. Through guided diary writing—even more invasive than the field diaries of the past—the military hoped to make such discipline seem like second nature to these young men. Ideally they would open their mouths and speak with the same voice as their exemplars.

EAST ASIAN EXCEPTIONALISM? MILITARY DIARY WRITING IN THE UNITED STATES

The United States Armed Forces had a longer tradition of formal war diary writing than any force in East Asia, even if the American history of diary writing itself was far more recent; in fact, it appears that mass-produced blank diaries had appeared as early as the Civil War, although they were not specifically for soldiers—that industry would not fully develop until the mass mobilization of literate troops during the twentieth century.[92] U.S. military traditions are deeply linked to the country's historical ties to the British Empire. Early modern English war diaries were more similar to epic tales such as Julius Caesar's *Partitioning of Gaul,* but in the eighteenth century the British navy promoted the systematized composition of ship logs among its naval officers. Thus, Anglo-American culture enjoyed a long history of civilian diary writing; there has never been a point in American history when servicemen did not keep war diaries. Even during the American Revolution, naval officers kept diary accounts of their military exploits.[93] The Anglophone history of diary writing itself predates the colonization of North America; war tales and diaries written among the noble classes of the British Isles flourished in the early modern era just before settlers began moving across the Atlantic. Thus, it is necessary to ask what aspects of diary writing are "military" and "modern" when discussing American war diaries.

By the time of the Second World War, personal diaries by commanding officers often mimicked the form and content of official diaries, so there was considerable precedent through the years for how to write a war diary. How did it all begin? First, texts from the American Revolution, in accordance with the literary conventions of the day, contained fairly ornate language, but most authors did not pay as much detail to the disciplined record of "facts" that would later come to characterize modern war diaries.[94] Despite the emergence of "military science," war diaries were, in terms of genre, still more closely tied to personal "confessionals" and reminiscences. Furthermore, despite the comparatively high levels of literacy in the early Republic, American war diary writing was still largely an elite phenomenon. Finally, it was not systematically required, nor was there any apparent form to which war diarists were expected to adhere.

In contrast to eighteenth-century accounts, the nineteenth-century preoccupation with empirical discourse and scientific record had a more powerful influence over military doctrine, leading to narratives that focused heavily on objective measurement and observation. In particular, naval officers' diaries could contain far more detail on "factual" information such as weather, position, troop strength, and other notes salient to military record. William Henry Powell, crew member of the *San Jacinto* (the same ship that delivered Townsend Harris to Japan), mixed some inflammatory rhetoric with attempts at precise observations about Chinese military capabilities during a naval skirmish near Hong Kong in 1856:

> Our work of distruction being completed we returned on board our ship and thus was the insult to our flag revenged[.] [T]he chinese own to a loss of 500 men[.] [T]here were in these forts mounted and well supplyed with ammunition and well manned 168 guns some 68 pounders some 32 & 42

pounders. [T]hese were taken by two sloops of war and not more than 500 men the four forts having fallen into our hands in the short space [left blank by Powell] hours from the time that we first struck the shore.[95]

Powell also gave precise measurements of Chinese guns, including length, greatest circumference, least circumference, diameter of bore, probable weight, and metal composition. Such precision was uncharacteristic of eighteenth-century American records and signaled the arrival of "military science" within individual records of war experience.

By the mid-nineteenth century, record-keeping practices more common to the U.S. Navy had spread to the army as well. By this time, blank diaries and fountain pens were mass-produced for civilian consumption but not specifically for soldiers.[96] Civil War diaries were not only penned by more soldiers, but they also increasingly featured factual information such as weather, troop strength, position, and tactics. A diary by Michael Houck shows us that even soldiers incapable of using proper grammar and spelling had been influenced by "factual" military discourse. In a fairly graphic passage, Houck's narrative, while including some personal observation, still follows the "facts" he considered salient to a military record:

> Revilee at four had now breakfast this Morning. My pardner lost all we had. some severe skirmishing this morning. Report of Gen Longstreets command bein captured and that the Rebs are getting pretty badly whiped on the Potomac. we are progressing finly here. but are losing heavily. at twelve we started for the field and at three we opened on the Rebel Fort. we don some very heavy firing at six our Touniver straps broak. and that disabeled our Gun we worked all night but only got the straps off. this is the bloodiest fight of the War. it was horabel to see the sights of the dead and wounded.[97]

Although Civil War soldiers were not as well trained, literate, or disciplined as Americans would be in the Second World War, they produced an impressive number of personal accounts.[98] Also, like their Meiji Japanese and early Republican Chinese counterparts, they tended to mix and experiment with various genres, but their texts were mostly grounded in records of "factual" information that was an expression of their professionalism as soldiers.[99] Like many wartime diarists, even personal accounts of the Civil War featured acknowledgment of potential readership outside of the "private" sphere.[100] Record keeping during the Civil War was not nearly as organized as it would be in the twentieth century, but it did inspire the creation of the Command and General Staff School in the United States in 1881, which, for the first time, introduced officers to the systematic use (and production) of war diaries.[101] More important, perhaps, was the memory of the Civil War in American military writing, symbolized by Ambrose Bierce's influential *Tales of Soldiers and Civilians* (1891). At the turn of the century, nearly simultaneous to the explosion of materials in Japan concerning the Russo-Japanese War, American readers consumed dozens of accounts describing a conflict from nearly half a century prior, establishing a linguistic foundation for future diarists.[102]

Nevertheless, war diaries were still a fairly elite pastime until the beginning of the twentieth century; soldiers' accounts arguably took off most rapidly during the First World War. This suffusion of formal and personal record keeping was largely driven by technology—namely, cheaper paper and the invention of durable writing instruments at the turn of the century—but it was also inspired by John J. Pershing, commander of the American Expeditionary Force in the First World War, who asked for an official war diary composed by officers.[103] Such a task would require meticulous documentation at multiple levels. Consequently, formal military diary writing expanded more broadly and deeper down into the ranks in the United States. Paul Cheney's 1918 prison log shows the increasing bureaucratization of the armed forces, even in such menial tasks as prison watch. Recording the names of men, charges, time of arrival, and the company and regiment of the prisoners, "Remarks" could be added at the end of the record in which Cheney described any relevant events that occurred in the prison. Like the war records in Japan and China, this formal diary was countersigned by another officer, attesting: "I have personally examined this report and find it to be correct."[104] American officers during the First World War continued the tradition of reporting "facts" in their diary accounts, such as the weather, troop movements, times of departure and arrival, and other salient details of command experience. George A. Morrice's diary shows an attention to detail necessary for combat experience narratives, as well as how the boundaries between official and "private" accounts could be quite close for officers:

Got our first real taste of war. A fleet of submarines has been following us. We are in the Bay of Biscay and sighted land about 2:15 pm. About 2:30 a

submarine rose on our starboard side and fired a torpedo at this ship. Barely
missed us. Italian ships fired on it and naval officers claimed it was sunk by
first shot. It is so entered in log.[105]

The training of officers did not include specific lessons on how to compose
personal accounts, but these seem to have been, as they were in East Asia,
heavily influenced by the language for official reports, which was a consequence of direct instruction. The publication of unit histories (invariably by
experienced, highly ranked servicemen) would have also taught aspiring
officers how to write about war in the idiom of military science.[106] In sum,
the strong trend of diary writing among the officer class was an outgrowth
of the increasing professionalization and bureaucratization of Western armed
forces altogether.

What had changed, however, was the explosion of "everyman" accounts,
such as diaries by army infantrymen and ordinary sailors. As Paul Fussell
noted in the British case, Americans were living in an age of popular education and "self-improvement," for which the diary was ideally suited.[107] Self-
narratives by ordinary soldiers were aided in part by the publication of cheap
blank diaries; these texts were sold under titles such as "Army and Navy
Diary" and included some French terms, spaces for friends' addresses, "autographs of comrades," and tables to help servicemen with foreign currency
conversion.[108] Also, publications of these accounts in the Anglophone world,
such as C. B. Purdom's *Everyman at War* (1930), instructed future generations of soldiers on how war was written.[109] Some of these texts created a
mass subject—the ordinary soldier—by refusing to state individual author-
ship over the text: for example, *What the "Boys" Did over There* (1920) is
described as written by "Themselves." Because these accounts were written
by "grunts," the diaries would be more vivid than their predecessors, and
they were more likely to describe actual frontline experiences, as U.S. marine Henry Kindig's account demonstrates:

> "Over the top" at 8:00 a.m. no barrage. Fouke wounded was only two feet
> away from me when hit. Dressed his wound and got stretcher bearer to take
> him off field. I was one of the six men left in rear wave when we reached
> objective. Dug in with McCarroll. Nearly dead for water and food so Parks
> and I volunteered to go for water. Found water in ravine where hundreds of
> dead were laying. Finally reached front again with water after forming a

good target for German snipers and machine gunners. Hit twice on the blouse and once on my cartridge belt with bullets. How I ever escaped this day is a mystery to me. The field was a living hell.[110]

As in East Asia, newspapers promoted support for troops among civilians by publishing accounts of combat—even after the end of the war; such accounts rarely included descriptions of serious privations or bodily harm amongst the Allied troops. For example, in 1920 the *Charlotte Observer* serialized Willard Newton's record, including battles, but in an overall triumphalist tone:

> At last we are at the beginning of a real battle between prussianism and democracy and we are to fight on the side of democracy that the world may forever be free from the peril of prussianism; that never again will we have to leave our peaceful pursuits and cross an ocean to fight against such barbarians.[111]

It is telling, indeed, that the U.S. Armed Forces turned to Ernest Jones, both a pilot and a magazine publisher, to document the exploits of the emerging air forces; Jones's approach exemplified the developing relationship between mass media, populism, and military science that defined the modern war diary in the United States, China, and Japan, instructing unit commanders to find "picturesque accounts of notable air battles and the human story of their participants" and to

> present facts of dramatic, comic, or tragic interest, tales of obstacles overcome, of discouraging conditions, of problems of personnel, equipment and supplies, transportation or maintenance, or tests and experiments that may have historical value.[112]

The expansion of diary writing among the lowest ranks of the armed forces, which in turn encouraged the widespread publication of such documents in the public sphere, was a turning point in the experience of war for the West. By the Second World War, the publication of previous war narratives encouraged ordinary soldiers to write and circulate often literary descriptions of what it was like to be in a modern war. Paul Fussell famously referred to the conflict as a "very literary war," in that soldiers were becoming increasingly reliant on mass print culture to find the right words for their narratives.

After the conclusion of the First World War, however, military historians still struggled to collate documents for a proper record of the conflict, which was increasingly expected to include the accounts outside of the upper echelons of the officer class. The scramble to compile comprehensive records during the Great War in Europe inspired U.S. military leaders to place a greater emphasis on formalized diary writing leading up to the Japanese attack on Pearl Harbor. Consequently, immediately prior to the war, U.S. Navy officers in the Pacific were already submitting diaries to their superiors on a monthly basis, even if there was not much to tell. Like their allies and enemies in East Asia, "official" war diaries were often a group effort or, when composed by individuals, subject to peer or superior review in order to ensure their accuracy. The similarity between Chinese, Japanese, and American war diary writing arose from a common understanding of what "modern" warfare meant, belying most assumptions about irreconcilable "cultural" differences.

First, the reports, orders, and narratives that served as the raw materials of an "official diary" were signed by the servicemen who submitted them. For example, the U.S. forces in charge of Guam in the 1940s were commanded by Major-General Henry L. Larsen, who composed the "narrative" of their activities at the beginning of every monthly submission of the war diary; subsequent reports, however, including details of engagements with the Japanese, would be signed by his subordinates in charge of those activities. Very few entries into a diary were "anonymous," so the author was held to account for any claims he might make. In some cases, the diary might be dominated by the commanding officer and include fewer subordinate reports—a lack of uniformity among U.S. Armed Forces' record keeping that was shared with their Chinese allies. This was particularly true among units that were not in especially "hot" zones. For example, Commander Frank Jack Fletcher of the North Pacific Force signed (and presumably composed) most of the diary for this unit, whose main area of operation in 1944–1945 was between Alaska and the remote Kurile Islands (north of Hokkaido, near Russia); in addition to a few bombing raids on the lightly defended area of the Kuriles, his force was to "deny the North Pacific Ocean Area to the Japanese," and so his diary was very brief and did not require extensive reports by subordinates.[113] Still, for the most part, U.S. diary accounts were a communal practice that was designed to ensure mutual observation and adherence to the "true" account of the war. Thus, U.S. war diaries employed factual information to reinforce their claims to representing the "truth" of battle experience just like their counterparts in East Asia.

Second, the war diary in the United States was a didactic tool that, like in East Asia, served to extend the disciplinary gaze of the state. Conveniently for readers today, Guam Island commander Larsen explained the practice at the beginning of one of his "narratives":

> This diary is designed to make reports to higher echelons of command concerning the activities and accomplishments of the Island Command of Guam [and subordinate units]. . . . To make the diary a more direct and complete report, the various important functions under the Island Command have been requested to submit accounts of activities within their organizations. Material contained herein can be of value in planning future operations. For that reason, many suggestions and recommendations are included.[114]

Personal diaries of commanding officers in the field could take on the character of official battle reports as well, particularly in their focus on specific description of battlefield action and lists of men who were killed in action, missing in action, or serving meritoriously.[115] This was a common practice in both the armed forces of East Asia: in October 1937, the commander of the GMD Sixteenth Army Corps, nine division commanders, and two artillery regiment commanders convened near Shanghai to discuss the purpose of their war diaries. The commander instructed his officers on the proper form of the diary and suggested that the documents would one day be studied by "experts" in order to compose an internal "military history" *(zhanshi)* that would narrate their achievements and areas for "improvement and reform" *(gaishan yu xiuzheng)*.[116] The Chinese commanders also frequently named subordinates whom they thought should be promoted. The language used by Chinese and American servicemen here is the same, so overemphasis on putatively different cultural practices is misleading when considering the diary traditions that soldiers embraced.

In all cases, the reason for wanting servicemen to keep war diaries was twofold: to learn from past mistakes and successes but also to potentially hold soldiers accountable for their actions. The diary helped to internalize this process of scrutiny, making it a form of self-scrutiny—or, as I call it, self-discipline. In China and Japan, premodern Confucianist terms were deployed, just as the word "diary" itself, in English, has emerged from an ancient textual tradition, but the mark of modern discipline is impossible to erase and clearly transnational. By the Second World War, whether in the "East" or the "West," modern soldiers were taught to discipline themselves, and this would have profound consequences both during and after the war.

Disciplined diary writing practices in the military, on the one hand, and literary trends that were profoundly shaped by popular politics and mass media technology, on the other, shared a relationship of mutual influence at the turn of the twentieth century; this appears to have been a transnational phenomenon among societies prepared for waging modern war. In the Western world, military diary writing became the sine qua non of effective armed forces. Although diary writing in East Asian armies began as an imported textual technology of control, it quickly became an accepted standard. Furthermore, both Western and Eastern war diaries were influenced by the gripping reality expressed in reportage, and authors now could use literary conventions to record more for posterity than just the weather or time of departure.

"Discipline makes individuals," insisted Michel Foucault, and it turned people into "instruments" of the exercise of power; as servicemen were told what it meant to be a "soldier," then, their supposed individuality was determined by the institutions that aimed to train and guide their thoughts and actions.[117] Field diaries were immensely useful tools in this regard. Officers gained powers of observation over the natural environment, tactics, and logistics, and they were influenced by the "panopticon" effect of mutual observation through potential review. These documents were also, however, a form of self-discipline. By learning to restrict their entries to contain only certain kinds of information—and simply through the act of religiously keeping a diary every day—servicemen learned to think of the truth of their war experience as a kind of disciplined activity that could be captured in writing. As a consequence, the power exercised by a disciplinary institution like the military was limited by its ability to consistently describe war in a way that soldiers would accept; this would prove to be an impossible task, particularly in the chaos of the battlefield of a total war. Nevertheless, war diary writing was something that soldiers took seriously; that their personal accounts so often mirror the official only further demonstrates the fact that they linked this kind of formalized discipline to their supposedly private selves.

Meanwhile, the mass media began circulating personal and official descriptions of combat with incredible efficiency, and this coincided with the rise of mass politics in East Asia. Soldiers indulged in reportage literature, such as Sakurai Tadatoshi's 1906 *Human Bullets* and Xie Bingying's *War Diary*. They borrowed the lyrical language of professional authors to make their personal accounts of warfare more compelling. As literacy improved, men in every rank imitated the various styles of recording experience in their own daily lives at the front. By the 1930s, the soldiers constituting the armies of the United States, GMD-controlled China, and the Empire of Japan were thoroughly immersed in cultures with "war diary" traditions that were as old, if not older, than they were. Once they found themselves on the front line of a total war, however, the previously honeyed voices of their literary heroes, military exemplars, and national martyrs would quickly turn sour for them.

CHAPTER TWO

Self-Mobilization and the Discipline of the Battlefield

The Battle for Shanghai and Northern China

FROM 7 JULY to 15 August 1937, the Republic of China, dominated by Chiang Kai-shek's Chinese Nationalist Party, and the Empire of Japan, under the direction of Konoe Fumimaro's cabinet, abandoned decades of limited engagements over Chinese sovereignty for a massive conflict that resulted in the deaths of millions. Chiang's "total war of resistance" *(quanmian zhanzheng)* called on Chinese people from all walks of life to make every sacrifice in the effort against Japanese aggression, and ultimately the empire was unable to overcome Chinese resistance; Konoe's "holy war" *(seisen)* against the GMD included a refusal to negotiate with the Chinese government and thereby entangled Japan in a war from which there was no egress. This eight-year conflict transformed East Asia and, by depleting the empire's critical resources, forced Japanese planners to prepare for a war against the "West." To understand the Second World War, then, it is necessary to see how millions of people in East Asia became committed to this conflict.

The story below is composed of linguistic battle scars, as seen through the diaries of Chinese Nationalist and Japanese servicemen during the first few months of "total war" in East Asia. Although experience consists primarily of silence—that is, things ultimately beyond expression such as sensation and thought—soldiers tried to capture "what war was like" in diaries. Records of combat experience would later become the foundations for personal conclusions about self and the world, so the context in which these diaries were composed is still important to understanding why and how they were written; therefore, these diaries are, to the fullest extent possible, juxtaposed with the events of the war and our current understanding of its battle conditions. In this way, we may better understand what it was that these individuals attempted to control and overcome and also where their practice of diary writing took them.

This chapter will explore diary writing acts such as "self-mobilization," soldiers' creation of personal chronicles, and authors' experimentation with different genres. While some soldiers had been avid diarists for many years before the war began, others started writing only when they were drafted—a presentiment perhaps of the momentous events about to shape their lives. To servicemen in China and Japan, diaries were both records of the past and tools for future growth as they negotiated the demands of powerful organizations and the temptation of their individual desires. Although the language they used was, for the most part, dominated by the ideology of stridently autocratic governments during wartime mobilization, diarists adapted this language to reflect their ever-changing experience of the war. In order to more fully understand how such experiences change writing, and how that writing then transforms self, we must first examine soldiers' accounts of the war very closely.

CONSTRUCTING THE SELF DURING THE MOBILIZATION FOR TOTAL WAR

After the First World War, it dawned on military commanders all over the world that success in war was largely dependent on the commitment of all servicemen (and not only officers) to their mission;[1] this was why modern armies not only paid more attention to "spiritual" or "psychological" training but also experimented with directed diary writing. Examining disciplinary regimes such as the state provides only part of the story; soldiers also used diaries to discipline themselves according to their own sense of proper conduct. Convincing themselves of the need to commit to the war effort, often through the act of diary writing, soldiers in China and Japan were engaging in "self-mobilization."

Chinese soldiers in the opening days of the War of Resistance used their diaries, first, to inspire dedication to their cause and, second, to soothe stinging emotional losses and humiliating technological inferiority, usually by apotheosizing their war dead and praising their comrades' élan. Japanese servicemen, most of whom were drafted in Japan and sent to China after the hostilities began, similarly attempted to establish a coherent voice in their diaries before experiencing the battlefield, often by asserting their "resolve" *(kakugo)*. Although the self-mobilizational acts practiced by enemy forces were similar, the Japanese would be engaging in them at home while many Chinese Nationalists were doing so facing units in the Japanese army directly. In the end, however, they by and large arrived at the same destination: the battlefield. This was a space marked more by chaos and disorganization, not heroism and coherent narrative, and so the narratives of self-mobilization they so painstakingly constructed would necessarily be rewritten.

The Marco Polo Bridge Incident of 7 July 1937 involved a "missing" Japanese soldier, which resulted in an IJA infringement of Chinese territory. The "incident" was purposefully enflamed by reckless Japanese field commanders in order to execute their plan to fully separate northern China, especially Beiping (now known as Beijing), from GMD influence. It is typically noted for being the start of the war in East Asia, but at this time the civilian governments of both the Republic of China and the Japanese Empire were still trying to contain the conflict.

Consequently, GMD officers in northern China used their diaries to document a rather slipshod mobilization; the forces in the north were caught completely unprepared for war. Things began routinely enough: when division commander Deng Huanguang began mobilizing his unit, each man received three days' worth of food, 150 bullets, one sleeping mat, an overcoat, and a brown uniform.[2] Initially, Chinese intelligence was poor: after the conflict erupted, wild rumors flew into Ye Tiaoquan's regiment that white Russian mercenaries had been deployed by the Japanese army. Discipline, too, was abysmal: Ye frequently castigated his troops for their behavior, informing them that "for logistical reasons, we must protect the roads and cannot humiliate train station employees."[3] Deng similarly chided his officers and men for overstepping their authority during "this time of national emergency [*guonan*]," reminding them that the relationship with rail officials is still very important. All our soldiers need to protect the order of the roads and investigate forced rail departures or the hitting/humiliating of rail staff, etc. This kind of violation of traffic regulations and order not only threatens rail safety, it also influences military logistics.[4]

By the end of August, Huang Yong'an was even forced to send party personnel to conduct "secret investigations" of his own regiment's abuses of local merchants.[5] GMD officers diligently documented other signs of a poor mobilization. Deng noted that "experts" *(jishu renyuan)* came from the central government merely to document "the various atrocities of the invading enemy that drive both man and heaven into fury" *(ling ren tian gong fen)*, placing propaganda before preparedness. Even while the Japanese were at their front door, Liu Binghuan's men were attending classes and practicing marching.[6] Fifth columns and spies became a preoccupation among GMD troops. Like many other Chinese officers obsessed with the existence of "traitors" *(hanjian),* Huang endeavored to teach his men how to defend their military secrets against Japanese espionage while Ye noted that spies and traitors were "detonating food stores, ammunition dumps, key bridges" and donning the garb of military laborers.[7] Meanwhile, Chinese officers used their diaries to whip themselves into a fury, recording one offense after another: traitors were inciting villagers to rebel, spying out their positions with Japanese and Koreans, aiding missionaries in selling blueprints *(sixing huizhi)* of secret areas, and building "puppet facilities such as newspaper companies, publishing houses, pharmacies, photo shops and coffee houses, etc."[8] Still, these fears were arguably overemphasized. Despite the genuine concern over enemy subversion in northern China, Deng should have paid more attention to other issues: for example, his antiaircraft gunners were mistakenly firing on Chinese planes. Unfortunately, in the early days of the Japanese invasion, GMD officers spent little time overseeing basic combat training and were more preoccupied with administrative matters.[9]

While the situation deteriorated in northern China, servicemen in the south began the process of transforming their anti-Japanese sentiment into effective military action. Reflecting on the Japanese invasion of 1932, company commander Cai Yizhong composed a tract in the idiom of war reportage. He tried to stir up emotion in his work as other writers had done in the past: "These past five years, our people [*minzu*] have suffered indignities and deception that have added to our fury; at the same time, however, they have also become a source of boundless inspiration." Examining the sites of the invasion—"those broken fences, those ruined walls"—he observed an irrepressible tide of enthusiasm in himself and others:

> Time has passed too slowly for our brothers—those who have all buried indignation deep in their hearts. This is because, when night falls, the Japanese inevitably come to our encampment to provoke us. At that moment, the pain and anger accumulating in our hearts through the decades has finally been given a chance to be released, to be exhausted.[10]

Although many GMD army officers seemed to be searching for a chance to loose their pent-up desire for revenge, their proclamations did not immediately inspire coordinated war mobilization. The captain of the Third Flight Group in Jurong (near Nanjing) complained that his men were "unwilling trainees," noting that "when the days seem calm and peaceful, our staff still takes time to go home and relax."[11] It is also possible that they were merely in the dark: once Song Zheyuan had alerted the party of the conditions of his flailing army near Beiping, even the atmosphere in otherwise laissez-faire units began to change.[12] In late July, while arming their airfield with antiaircraft guns and artillery, the Third Flight Group's men were suddenly energized, and their commander consequently translated this excitement into his diary:

> News came that the situation up north is becoming extremely grave. . . . The Japanese slaves [*wonu*] have tried every scheme and trick in the book, but they have only incited anger, so now they are going to try their last hand—military force! Because of this, our unit is on a heightened state of alert; my fellow countrymen are also unusually excited—all waiting for the opening of the War of Resistance so they can kill the enemy.

He later noted enthusiastically that "in the last ten days, when applying themselves to their duties, all of our officers and men are courageous and possess a will to work hard" and that this was a great "comfort" to him when thinking of the resistance.[13] Observing the movement of Japanese civilians out of major coastal areas put Chinese officers on alert for a repeat performance of 1932.

While civilian officials in Japan and the GMD leadership wished to avoid a serious conflict, the Japanese military had other plans, going so far as to ban the press publication of a short-term cease-fire in northern China for fear that the Japanese public would call for peace.[14] Soon enough, the situation in Shanghai was brought to a head. On 9 August 1937, at 6:30 p.m., a naval lieutenant named Ōyama Isao and an accompanying soldier, Saitō Yuzō, drove their jeep directly into a Nationalist Chinese guard post in front of an airfield near Shanghai, provoking a gunfight with Chinese Peace Preservation Corps (PPC, a militia) that resulted in the Japanese servicemen's deaths.[15] News of the incident spread instantly among Chinese officers.[16] According to one Chinese officer's diary, the Japanese military representatives who arrived shortly afterward to inspect the men's bodies were infuriated by their "defilement."[17] The commander of the Japanese Naval Headquarters in Shanghai, Vice-Admiral Hasegawa Kiyoshi, ordered marines (rikusentai) deployed from Sasebo and requested land army forces mobilized while Ōyama's and Saitō's bodies were still being inspected. His subsequent demands amounted to a total elimination of the Nationalist presence in Shanghai.[18] Chinese officers were not receptive: "So, on the one hand the Japanese are using agreements to solve this problem through negotiation, and on the other they are increasing their troop strength in order to threaten us."[19] The commander of the Third Flight Group also scoffed at the Japanese proposal for Shanghai after the Ōyama Incident: "This case just further exposes the motives and schemes of the hated Japanese. Without inquiring whether the act was right or wrong, and never appealing to reason, they just dispatch thirty troopships from western [Japan] and demand the removal of our PPC units in order to invade."[20] The GMD central government, which had already taken a position of total resistance, was similarly unconvinced by the Japanese offers of peaceful negotiation.

Armed with such resolve, the GMD response in the south painted a picture completely at odds with the bungling that occurred in the north. The government ordered a halt to all civilian rail traffic and rapidly began moving GMD land forces into Shanghai—willfully violating a 1932 cease-fire treaty that had banned China's national armies from entering its greatest city. Citizens of Shanghai were elated to see GMD servicemen—many wearing medals painted blood red and engraved with the words "Hero of the Chinese People" (minzu de yingxiong)—marching into their hometown, which had been divided up by foreign powers.[21] Ordinary citizens, horrified, angered, and exhilarated by the Japanese attack, rushed to support the GMD by joining organizations such as the Girl Scouts and the

Chinese Red Cross, even though many were also filled with fear of a war on their doorsteps.[22] Anticipating the possibility of war, Zhong Song, like many Chinese officers, used his diary to make declarations of resolve: "The situation [in Shanghai] has changed dramatically; military conflict is already unavoidable."[23] On 13 August, the GMD attacked, and by 15 August, the Japanese and Chinese governments had forsaken their policy to contain the conflict. Chiang Kai-shek finally ordered the national mobilization of China to prepare for total war.

Chinese soldiers' diaries exploded with fear, excitement, anger, and graphic detail as they used these documents to motivate themselves for combat—the phenomenon I have dubbed "self-mobilization." Even during those extreme times, these soldiers energetically and proactively sought an appropriate language to describe the war. Gao Zhihang, informed by the GMD that the Japanese "plan on taking Shanghai in order to threaten our capital," rushed to the skies from Nanjing to conduct the first air strikes; his and others' acts of heroism were dutifully recorded.[24] Diarists also tried to capture the sights and sounds of modern war in language: as the Chinese and Japanese armies clashed at Shanghai's Bazi Bridge, Zhong, declaring that "negotiations are ineffective," described the sound of enemy artillery blasting in the distance and the poisonous fumes from flames that would engulf the city.[25] Close-quarters fighting broke out on the cobblestone streets and in the cramped housing districts; witnessing this firsthand, Xu wrote, "there were furious rifle reports from the Bazi Bridge and many enemy bullets were ricocheting around the houses in the surrounding area."[26] Servicemen scribbled with surprising detail in their diaries, attempting to capture as closely as possible combat experience in whatever style they felt was "realistic."

The textual fever of self-mobilization spread quickly to Nanjing. Hearing the news in the capital, Ma Chaojun, head of air defenses and mayor of the city, whipped himself into a state of near frenzy, describing GMD officials as "beside ourselves with excitement" (xingfen). He castigated the "hated Japanese," claiming that the GMD would "wipe you all out." People discussed and argued about the war on the streets, and soldiers were "as numerous as blades of grass."[27] In nearby Jurong, a diarist in the Third Flight Group declared a new state of consciousness among the pilots and staff there, echoing the words of Chiang Kai-shek: "Sino-Japanese relations have already reached the final juncture [zuihou guantou]; now our forces can only launch a spirited War of Resistance."[28] The citizens of Shanghai looked on anxiously. Antiquated Japanese Type 89 fighters and rickety Chinese Curtis Hawk IIIs clashed furiously over Shanghai. Two Chinese aircraft burst into flame and crashed into the city.[29] The sudden attack, the cowardly foe, and the exhilarating pursuit were all transcribed into field diaries as Chinese pilots started their engines with fuel pumps still hanging from their planes.[30] Chiang's officers, who felt themselves imbued with the invincible "Huangpu Spirit," had unleashed themselves. Cai, who had reflected on the swelling tide of battle élan among the GMD, described the taking of Bazi Bridge:

I don't know how I managed to suppress my joy [*kuaihuo*] at that moment—oh, I was so happy I could jump!—and then our brothers in the rear came forward cautiously. Even though the enemy had shot at us and surprised us with an artillery assault in the night, because our brothers were possessed by a terrible anger, in the end we took Bazi Bridge.[31]

Chinese officers, seeking to prove their worth, began enshrining their martyrs and defining themselves as potential heroes in their diaries. Despite Gao Zhihang's unit having to flee Hangzhou (in Zhejiang Province, close to Shanghai), the bravery of the Fourth Flight Group continued to inspire others to emulate them.[32] The same day Gao was wounded in battle, four Japanese bombers from the First Flight Group (Kisarazu) flew to Nanjing. A Chinese pilot lauded their "valiant" counterattack, writing, "The enemy aircraft, after hitting our tough attack [*tengji*], crumbled and could not regain their formation, scurrying away."[33] Men under the command of Zhong Song, who had held tight through artillery bombardments all night, "leaped and danced in glee" when they saw seventy Chinese planes bomb the Japanese. Zhong, like so many Nationalist officers, saw this as an opportunity for GMD officers to distinguish themselves on the field:

The Battalion Commander saw a chance for great honor here [*jian dayi suo zai*], waiting for the order to go into battle. The Japanese unit's situation was dire and, after [our unit's] surprise attack [*qixi*], they immediately collapsed into retreat [*pimo*]. . . . The battle was extremely intense, but luckily the spirits of our officers and men were soaring.[34]

Defeating China's chief imperialist foe would legitimize the Nationalist government like nothing else could, and so GMD officers told themselves that now they could fulfill their roles in this historic event. They took every opportunity to make their heroism a matter of record. Spotting Japanese Type 96 heavy bombers heading toward Nanjing, antiaircraft gunners "fired ferociously into the enemy devils" as Chinese pilots scrambled to their aircraft.[35] Ma wrote that these servicemen had sent the enemy "scurrying off" after shooting down two of their aircraft, and he noted, "The heavy task of defending Nanjing is a great honor, because the safety of the Committee, top government officials, and the lives of hundreds of thousands Nanjing citizens rests on my shoulders."[36] The consequences of this sort of self-discipline could be immediate, however: truly embracing this heroic identity would make surviving the war extremely difficult.

The Chinese Nationalists knew more than anyone that they were facing a formidable foe. A common misconception states that a reviewed diary, because of its lack of privacy, would only "say what the reviewer wanted to hear." In fact, these diaries did not simply reproduce propaganda: in them, GMD officers acknowledged Japanese technological superiority and their own failures. While praising the troops' dedication to their cause, one Chinese officer did not hide the brutal reality of the GMD's inadequacies in his diary:

> Today our artillerymen unleashed a very accurate, terrific bombardment on their targets, but because [the Japanese] were so tightly defended, the attack did not live up to our expectations. . . . Our artillery pieces were fired so intensely that their barrels were damaged; one or two exploded, and one cannot fire at all. . . . Our air forces operations were very heroic and precise, but the enemy's antiaircraft cannons have electronic devices which increase their destructive power and range, making their bullets fall like rain.

The technological inferiority of the GMD was further exposed when the battleship *Izumo,* armed with a steel net around its hull, drove straight through a Chinese minefield on the Yangtze River, destroying the defenses in an impressive display. A Chinese officer watched this and wrote, "When the mines exploded, the sound shook the heavens and all the glass in the surrounding houses shattered." A Chinese naval vessel behind the blockade then fired on by the Japanese fleet burst into flames and sank into the river before all those looking on from the shore, prompting the diarist to write, "The ship's officers and men, giving their lives thus, is a difficult thing to bear."[37] Acknowledging the dangerous possibility of widespread panic, the central government began to offer comfort services *(weilao)*. A pilot in the Third Flight Group described a surprise visit from Chiang Kai-shek's wife, Song Meiling, who tried to assuage soldiers' fears that their families would be neglected in the rear *(houfang)*; then, a General Staff officer told the men that they should "struggle to slay the enemy, fulfilling your destiny [*tianzhi*] as a soldier, upholding our air force's spirit of striking fear into the hearts of the enemy and protecting our homeland!"[38] GMD diaries in Shanghai such as Zhong's, however, were still partly individual records of the destructive power of modern warfare:

> Japanese troops are arriving nonstop. From 9am there was intense Japanese artillery fire—as if it would level the mountains and wipe out the sea [*pai shan dao hai*]. The Yuedong Middle School and the Patriotic Girls' School [PGS] were reduced to piles of burning rubble. Airplanes and tanks are moving about furiously. [Our units] in the school buildings took furious enemy artillery and rifle fire and, due to the buildings' total collapse, losses were very heavy. At 12pm, after the enemy employed its artillery's devastating bombardment, they sent out tanks as forerunners for about one company of infantry, advancing to the PGS. . . . Because of this intense fighting, we lost hundreds.[39]

Meanwhile, suffering a surprise air attack, Ma and his officials scrambled to take cover in their office: "The sound [of the explosions] shook the office, and we all crouched very low. Remaining in the office, there were many among us who had looks of terror on their faces."[40] Because of failures in communication, antitank units lost men and equipment,[41] and Zhong wrote that Japanese "reinforcements arrive constantly; they use land, sea and air superiority to drop many bombs, firing and creating destruction everywhere" as the Japanese attacked with new vigor.

GMD officers, despite their initial losses, continued to use their diaries as a space where GMD servicemen could become national heroes—in effect, mobilizing themselves for war (and death). While acknowledging GMD technological inferiority, Zhong transformed loss and failure into victory through his record of the war. He wrote on 21 August 1937, "Even though the battles are unbearable [*ji xing canku*], our officers and men's spirits seem very courageous," but he hastened to point out that Shanghai was ideal for the combined land-sea-air assault launched by the Japanese. He concluded, "In this war to liberate the people [*minzu*], our army is inferior in every respect, but we have also achieved the spirit of the people's warrior [*minzu zhanshi*]."[42] Even as far away as the military academy in Lushan, a Chinese Nationalist officer noted that many of his countrymen had already abandoned "selfishness" *(siyi)* and that some of his comrades in Shanghai had, through their own volition *(zhudong),* died gloriously in battle. Listening to his trainees' responses, he wrote down his observations on the "mentality" *(xinli)* of the recruit, copying down dialogues that came directly from his interaction with them: "Why aren't we fighting the Japanese right now? . . . Are we supposed to resist the Japanese *now* or aren't we?—of course, *now* we must resist."[43] Despite the material shortages and initial setbacks, GMD servicemen convinced themselves that the spirit of the Nationalist Army must prevail *(bisheng).*[44] In effect, the GMD had wagered its legitimacy on defeating the Japanese invasion. An army of millions dug themselves in physically and mentally, waiting for Japanese resolve to crumble. Chinese servicemen had mobilized themselves for a decisive battle, particularly in Shanghai, but Japanese troops would be engaged in similar acts of self-discipline.

On 16 August 1937, the first mobilization orders in Japan came at a time when the conflict in China had hit a total standstill, and Japanese commanders began to wring their hands in anxiety—could they conceivably lose to the Chinese? The Japanese civilian government, more concerned about the growth of Soviet power in northeast Asia and maintaining good relations with its largest trading partner, the United States, was deeply divided over attempts by Japanese field commanders to expand the war in China.[45] All kinds of men were rapidly drafted all over Japan to be sent to the China front, ostensibly to defend Japanese citizens in China. Before their departure, Japanese diarists were subjected to discourses and rituals that attempted to control the meaning of the war and soldiering.

On a textual level, there were several immediate influences on the way that diarists described their departure experience. Many diarists who were mobilized to fight in 1937 began their diaries by recording their draft notices *(akagami)* and mobilization orders *(dōin karei)*—a part of the soldier's "departure script" as penned in previously published war accounts. Like childbirth, marriage, or death, the receipt of a draft notice was a major event, immediately changing the tenor of the local community. Umeda

Fusao, a villager from Shimane Prefecture, was drafted into the Fifth Division (Hiroshima) on 28 July 1937:

> 4:10pm: received my draft notice. I thought I was prepared for it [*kakugo shita*], but now that the red slip is actually in my hands, I'm moved, excited, feeling all kinds of extravagant emotions. First I showed it to my wife, then my parents. Everyone looked thoughtful, and then everyone sighed and held me for a moment. Dad went to tell my uncle at our branch house, let them know, then went around informing all the villagers. Before long the villagers gathered to prepare a farewell party. . . . Watching them [prepare] like this, the reality of it all hit me. I wonder how heavy my responsibilities will become.[46]

Local organizations typically would deliver a thick envelope to the draftee and his family entitled "Letter of Farewell." The Women's Defense Organization, Imperial Reservists Association, and the Youth Group might draft a joint letter and deliver it in person with the personal seals of all of the organization heads. A typical letter addressed to a "Hero of the Sacred War" *(seisen yūshi)* was suffused with laudatory proclamations of his bravery and assurances that those at home "will fulfill all [their] assignments," inveighed against the "barbarity" of the GMD, and stated boldly that the Nationalists had become China's "curse."[47] Servicemen also drafted a will and testament that largely reiterated orthodox ideology. In one example, the author encouraged his mother to embrace his dedication to the "greater obligation" *(daikō no michi)* and stated that he wished to give his "seven [reincarnated] lives to the country" *(shichishō hōkoku)*. Characteristically binding wartime national goals with household and individual interest, the author also expressed his desire to "brighten the door of my household with honor" and exploit this "opportunity—no bigger than the eye of a needle."[48] In some cases, the recipient bought postcards expressing thanks *(reijō)* and sent them to everyone who supported his departure, promising to "smash my bones and destroy my body for the sake of the nation."[49] Given this profundity of text, it is not surprising that servicemen's diaries should initially so resemble official discourse.

Spoken language and ritual interactions also affected the way Japanese servicemen narrated their departure. Induction into the unit introduced new language into servicemen's lexicon: Nagatani Masao recorded a speech by his company commander, who encouraged the men in the unit to faithfully carry out their duties as soldiers for the sake of the unit's honor. Nagatani then described his departure from Tadozu in language that imitated such propaganda: "I have taken up my path as a soldier [*seito ni noboru*]. It gives us joy. We are sent off by shouts of 'Banzai!' by our enthusiastic country-men [*kokumin*]." Many Japanese soldiers were first sent off by local organi-zations or enthusiastic mobs, but these nationalistic gatherings were often followed by more personal farewells. Nagatani continued:

> Dad came to the 12pm visiting hours. This is the end. If I stick to it and fall in battle with dignity, I think he will rejoice with me. . . . In reality, I couldn't conceive the fact that I was going to war. We're in the situation, however, when a few among us, perhaps a few dozen, perhaps the whole company, might come back as bleached bones. . . . I promised that I would become a splendid man. I swear that, without fail, I will do this. I don't know where we're going, but when the faces of those who came to see us off at Marugame come to mind, the people of the city who were thus moved on our behalf, unable to withstand the sincerity and emotion of the people of the prefecture, we were resolved.[50]

As a reservist in the same unit, Yamamoto Kenji was required to undergo training but would not depart with the initial invasion force. Nevertheless, he was similarly "sent off with a great chorus of farewells by the villagers" as he made his way to Fukui to join the barracks.[51] While others fought at the front, he read Japanese *waka* and *Shufu no tomo,* wrote letters and nearly fifty *reijō* to those who helped with his departure. Reservists could be im-mersed in this exhilarating environment for weeks.

Seasoned servicemen, however, often wondered how serious they should take the events in China and initially kept only simple records. Hamabe Gen-bei, a serviceman from Shizuoka who had served during the Manchurian In-cident, was inducted into his unit as soon as his notice arrived. Hamabe kept his entries brief—a mere list of notes to jog his memory later. He recorded where he stayed, when he had visitors, his unit affiliations, and time of his departure. He was, however, soon surprised at the scale of the mobilization in Hiroshima.[52] Similarly, Sakaguchi Jirō, a veteran of the China front from Na-gano Prefecture and an otherwise prodigious diarist, kept his notes brief. Soon he too was impressed by the mobilization in Mito ("befitting these extreme times"), even though he was also thoroughly familiar with the procedure:

20 August: Independent Machine gun Unit, attached to the 14th Division: At last the time for induction into my unit has come. Our car reached the gate, which was very impressive. At 7 I was inducted, and, according to orders, the Matsumoto unit's area was pretty much all folks from Nagano. . . . There are a lot of old war buddies here—mostly fifth-, sixth- and, seventh-year soldiers. There was an order to separate the reservists from the combat soldiers. I was determined to be a combat soldier.[53]

Sakaguchi spent the remainder of August training, waiting for his chance to prove himself on the field. After he had passed his exams, he was shipped to Osaka with servicemen drafted from all over the country. Receiving his travel compensation, he sent a postcard home notifying his family of his imminent departure and wrote: "At 8pm the regiment worshipped at Jōban Shrine. We were sent off by the congratulatory voices of the city folk, getting on the train at 10:10, hearing 'Banzai, Banzai' nonstop all the way down the Tōkaidō."[54] Once he arrived in Osaka, the local chapter of the Women's Defense Organization met the unit to comfort them *(imon)* before departure. While fighting raged on in China, he wrote about sightseeing in Osaka with his buddies.

Not all draftees described themselves as aspiring heroes or professional soldiers. In Kyoto Prefecture, Azuma Shirō, the eldest son of a well-to-do rural family and a "literary youth" *(bungaku shōnen),*[55] was more lyrical in his story about being drafted. He had left his hometown, the family business, and his sick father to report for duty in Fukuchiyama. Although Azuma had a farewell celebration in his town, he chose not to write about it in his diary. Azuma's descriptions of family in his diary greatly resemble the development of characters in fiction, while emphasizing the importance of ritual in establishing resolve. For example, he met his stepmother, birth mother, and brother at a hotel in Fukuchiyama for a final farewell:

Mom said, "This is a tour of duty that you couldn't buy for a million dollars. Be happy about it. If, through some misfortune, you are captured by the Chinese troops, use this to cut your stomach open and die. I have three boys already, so if I just lose you, it won't bother me." Then she gave me a dagger with the character for "Chrysanthemum" on it. These words, how happy they made me! I wondered at how impressive [*erai*] a woman my mother was. Before now, I had no idea. Then, I swore in my heart, *I will go to death happily.* My stepmom cried when we parted. She expected my safe return, she prayed for it.

Azuma attributed his stepmother's ignorance *(ninshiki no kando ga tarinai)* to the fact that she was raised in the countryside, whereas his birth mother's "rich understanding of the times" *(jikyoku ninshiki ni tomu)* was attributable to her urban upbringing. After making arrangements with his birth mother, he left "with a clear heart and absolutely no regrets."[56]

While Azuma tried to find the literary route to becoming a soldier, Kimura Genzaemon, a teacher from rural Akita, approached the experience in a language both cool and cerebral. Four days after receiving his notice, Kimura's rural hamlet held a farewell celebration *(kigansai, buraku kigakai),* and he was soon inducted into a medical unit. Kimura endured tests and examinations of every stripe daily. By the time this process came to its conclusion, Kimura produced his notebook and pen and wrote the following entry in anticipation of his departure from Hirosaki:

> 6am lecture from the squad commander. Dreams of the battlefield and running about the barracks. Every night my dreams are not about my home, not about my wife and children, but actually an image of myself on the battlefield. The most beautiful thing in the world is "truth," an "image of one who seeks truth," a "process toward truth." If there is anything beautiful about war, it is the "truth" that only war can possess.[57]

Kimura reflected on what the war meant to him and why he was participating in it as a soldier. Then Kimura's diary transformed briefly into an extended farewell letter to his wife and children whom he had to leave behind. If he could only embody a life of "truth," he wrote, even if he was "covered in blood and tortured by all the pains of this earth," he could face his children after the war.[58]

Even before battle, almost immediately Japanese servicemen were confronted with the less romantic aspects of military life and had to find a way to integrate this experience into their personal war stories. For those who were going to the battlefield, they sailed across the Sea of Japan in a voyage lasting a few days; they were escorted by Japanese destroyers that appeared and disappeared in the night like mysterious ghost vessels. Their troopships were a suffocating, cramped space, where men were forced to sleep within one foot of another man in every direction. Although Japan is an island country, many men had never sailed far from shore and some had never been on an ocean vessel before in their lives. Furthermore, the food on the ship was terrible—

sometimes even rotten—and the stench of many unwashed bodies was for some unbearable. Nagatani described his trip to China in unflattering terms:

> I got up in the morning, but, no matter what, I feel terrible. I lay in bed for a while, but I just can't get over feeling ill. I tried going to the bathroom. When you're actually on the sea there's nothing doing about it. Land army soldiers are no good on the water. I didn't eat lunch or dinner, just went out on deck and sprawled out—which made me feel a little better. . . . I don't know where we're going, but, wherever it is, we have to go. Wishing it to come quicker is no use. I almost think it would be better to die quickly and get it over with.[59]

The days on board were excruciatingly hot, especially below deck, and the nights above deck were freezing cold. Sakaguchi complained, "The inside of the boat is so, so hot. We're rolling around in our beds naked." As his boat crept north toward Tanggu, he wrote, "This afternoon the wind kicked up the waves, making many of the men seasick. All of a sudden it got very cold, making us shiver as we slept."[60] Although some soldiers wrote more lighthearted accounts of the camaraderie aboard the troopship—telling stories of home and singing military ballads (gunka)—most diarists complained bitterly of the ship as a smelly, sickening, stifling hole. Azuma described life on board as "unbefitting even the lowest of Koreans," as a "human sardine can" bestrewn with human filth, flies, and dirty mats, where soldiers "roll around naked reading torn bits of magazines in a daze." Despite Azuma's repulsion at the conditions of the ship and the state of the men—comparing them to "writhing maggots"—he still managed to muster his strength in order to imagine them in a better light. He looked ahead, fantasizing about their transformation on the beach, writing, "Once they put on a military uniform, they'll show their true selves [honsei]."[61]

Not all Japanese servicemen's experience of mobilization followed the same script. Many were already serving abroad in the Japanese Empire or Manchukuo when hostilities erupted in July and August. Kawakami Yoshimitsu, a newly promoted corporal, had departed from the Korean peninsula, where his headquarters were located, with considerably less fanfare than those who had left from Japan.[62] Taniguchi Kazuo, a medical officer, shared a first-class room with three other officers that he described to his family as "wonderful." While the battle raged in Shanghai, on 28 August he drank beer until he felt "quite good," gazed comfortably out on the port of Tadozu, and wrote letters home as their ship raced ahead.[63] In his initial correspondence from Pusan, he described the relative luxury in which he lived and "the feeling among us all that we are bored to death and want to get to the front, but have no choice." Japanese officers were not subject to the same grueling conditions as the grunts. Nevertheless, even in such privileged accounts, many conventions consistently emerge that also appear in the diaries and letters from the poorest farmers of Japan: closing each letter with "your unfilial son," Taniguchi attempted to continue directing the affairs of his household from the battlefield, instructing his children to wear their overcoats in the cool fall evenings, study hard, and listen to their grandmother.[64] For Japanese men high and low, being sent to the battlefield was a serious disruption of their primary task as patriarchs: running their households. Prior to landing in China, many Japanese servicemen viewed the war as an inconvenience rather than a great adventure.

When Japanese troops hit the beaches near Shanghai, they would discover that their acts of self-mobilization had not adequately prepared them. On 22 August, the first wave of the Japanese land army arrived in central China. At first glance, the army's arrival seems to have been seamless, and the majority of Japanese servicemen were champing at the bit. Up north, a few days after his landing at Tanggu, Sakaguchi wrote, "Today we rested near the unit walls, taking care of the base, tents, horses, and laundry—all our battle preparations. You can really hear the artillery blasts; the time has come to fulfill one's duty on the battlefield, to be one of the Imperial Army."[65] At times it is impossible to discern whether the diarists are trying to convey excitement or fear. Hamabe merely recorded that he could see enemy units moving on the shore just north of Shanghai and that they could not manage a smooth landing because of Chinese troops hiding in the rocky bank. Before too long, Japanese troops all had set foot on Chinese soil, most for the first time in their lives. Nagatani simply wrote: "Our landing has finally come. This is it."

NORTHERN CHINA: THE BOUNDLESS BATTLEFIELD

In the final months of 1937, Japanese and Chinese servicemen became entangled with each other in the vast expanse of northern China. Diarists struggled to find a way to narrate this seemingly endless war because the experience became more psychologically and physically challenging than anticipated. For example, once they had actually seen the battlefield, many Japanese troops decided to buy life insurance: for 73.8 yen Japan Life (Nippon Seimei) sold a policy that would pay two thousand yen in the eventuality of death.[66] Thus, it seems that some Japanese conscripts were willing to bet on the possibility that they would die. Meanwhile, Chinese officers haphazardly switched from recording "atrocities" and the activities of "traitors" to recording the unexpected catastrophe of total war, and the identities that Japanese servicemen developed during the war deviated far from their prior self-mobilization narratives. Bullets bearing injury or death became the basis of a kind of communication between the men who fought each other in late 1937; as they inflicted suffering on each other, they forced transformations in how their enemy narrated self and the outside world. Thus, there is no "Japanese" or "Chinese" story that can meaningfully stand alone. Because this was an inherently dialogic experience, I have chosen to interweave their stories.

The scale of the Japanese invasion overwhelmed many diarists—no one alive had seen war conducted on this scale in East Asia. Sakaguchi, arriving early in Tanggu, spent the day breaking his back loading supplies onto trucks in the rain and mud. Running into one friend from Nagano after another, he wrote, "First of all, everywhere you look there are Japanese soldiers, a flood of soldiers. It's shocking." The next day, his unit arrived in Tianjin, where the local chapter of the Japanese Women's Defense Association served them tea, donated tobacco, and cakes. Private Ueda Masaki drew maps of northern China and recorded his experiences in neat, brief, and miniscule script. For Dairen, on November 8, 1937, he wrote:

I went shopping for sashimi, boiled tofu, dried bread, and fish. The apples are cheap and delicious. Schoolgirls are waving their handkerchiefs at us, which is very moving. . . . If you take a bath, you have to get in with [all of the other Japanese troops], so some unfortunate soldiers held back. I bought binoculars in a town called "Shīyōtoru" . . . went to sight-see Dairen's bright lights and other attractions . . . and drank tea in a café for the first time. Where the hell is the war?[67]

Indeed, most Japanese servicemen's experience in soldiering began as a dreamlike fantasy. On the train from Tanggu to Beiping, Taniguchi wrote in a letter that the cars were full of "soldiers sleeping haphazardly, talking in

their sleep—dreaming perhaps of their hometowns."[68] As these troops prepared to leave secure urban bases, however, servicemen were treated to a rude
awakening. Azuma's commanding officer delivered the following address:

> From here on out you're on the battlefield. On the battlefield, there are ene-
> mies. Plainclothes units are operating even in positions we have taken. After
> tomorrow, anyone who falls out of line will die like a dog in the fields. This
> is because out there we have no field hospital, no triage unit; it is a place with
> only GMD soldiers, plainclothes units, and hostile locals. You better re-
> member that falling out of line means dying like a dog. You're not allowed to
> die like that by falling out before reaching our destination. You should save
> all your strength for the front line, so make sure you economize your energy
> and perseverance until we get to the front. I don't care if you take a dive and
> die right when you get there.

Moving on foot and by boat south from Tianjin, through the countryside
along the Ziya River, Azuma saw villages emptied of their inhabitants,
Japanese supply troops shot in the back by Chinese plainclothes units, and
frightened Chinese villagers huddled around foreign missionaries in their
churches.[69] The shattered remains of GMD defense structures were littered
with rotting horses and Chinese soldiers' bodies, creating an "unbearable
stench." Kimura watched birds feeding on Chinese corpses and wrote that
"their cries and caws are appalling." Wounded troops trickled in from the
battlefront to makeshift triage centers, as Japanese units wiped out entire
villages.[70] It was a trying time for would-be heroes. Kawakami Yoshimitsu
had been committed to such an image of himself before the war began.
Chinese resistance, however, unnerved him. He noted the evidence of Chinese mobilization in the north, such as a poster that read "Wipe out the
Japanese Demons!" Enemy fire from camouflaged concrete bunkers plagued
his unit. As he burned the remains of men in his unit, he and his comrades
killed five Chinese "scouts" and executed twenty-one villagers. In the process of chronicling these difficult experiences, Japanese servicemen like
Kawakami were transforming the language they used to describe the war.
As Kawakami's unit advanced, he noted that the faces of all of his men were
"black and filthy."[71] Similarly, while grunts devoured their rations, Taniguchi wrote in his diary disparagingly, "When eating, men greatly resemble
animals. It is repulsive [*asamashii*]."[72]

Despite the powerful interlocutors of war reportage, official propaganda, and heroic self-narratives, a serviceman's individual experience of the war and how he viewed himself could greatly affect his diary. Still in Japan, Ishida Gi'ichi, an artilleryman in a privileged "secret unit" of the Japanese army, had no individual basis for viewing the war as anything other than a grand adventure: he noted that everyone was "joyous" to reach the continent, "feeling as though we're going on a trip."[73] While based in Fengtian, a conscript in Captain Akiyama Toyochi's flight group hurt himself falling out of a tavern window drunk. Akiyama, playing the responsible commanding officer, was exasperated. He also ranted in his diary that another soldier "caught cold today and is in the hospital. I wonder if he's not up to fighting and will go AWOL? The atmosphere here is all like this. I thought: my pain as a commander has begun at last."[74] Others found the war more pleasant; Taniguchi traveled with embedded reporters from the *Osaka Daily* and described the piles of ammunition and food at the base in Liangxiang as "magnificent." From the rear, he wrote that the Japanese aircraft's exploding bombs and booming artillery "echoed in my heart" and "froze the enemy's spine." When an intense firefight erupted nearby, Taniguchi was delighted:

> The sound of rifles and cannon grow, and the circling of aircraft is intense. There are carefree [*nonki*] times on the battlefield as well! Rather than feeling as though they're in the middle of a war, the men feel more like they're at play [*asobi*]. People at home shouldn't worry. . . . Nearby some men sleeping outside groan in their dreams while others sit and scratch their noses.[75]

In contrast, grunts like Kawakami were on a brutal, seemingly endless march in pursuit of an enemy they rarely saw, abandoned by Japanese army supply lines. Kawakami's story became increasingly inglorious: picking ripe, wild jujubes to feed himself, he wrote that he had become "inhuman" *(ningen rashiku naku natta)*; stealing chicken from local farms and digging for potatoes, he tried to scrape together dinner for himself (and also for officers like Taniguchi); at the end of a typical day, he had blisters on his feet and was exhausted, writing, "the pain is indescribable."[76]

The difference between how Taniguchi and Kawakami portrayed the war was tied up in their sense of who they were as individuals—the lens through which they viewed their lives. Officers such as Taniguchi struggled to keep themselves separate from the grunts, calling conscripted men like Kawakami "mud dolls."[77] Kimura, the former schoolteacher, scrutinized the men who fell into line beside him harshly, finding even low-ranking officers woefully uneducated—a state that "devastated the power of the Imperial Army" *(kōgun no iryoku messha)*. Kimura then offered, in his view, an even more serious accusation: "One wonders how much they are really superior to the Chinese soldier." As his own carefully constructed self-identity threw him into sharper contrast with those around him, the objects of his scorn expanded:

> The only person who welcomes the call to war is one without education, such as children, ladies [*fujin*], and the (uneducated) elderly. The intellectuals, as a whole, are bystanders. Does the Japanese Spirit [*Nippon seishin*] find culture so intolerable? There were certain ladies who prayed for our troops. Something about it struck chords of anger in my heart.[78]

Soldiers like Kimura had no time to reflect and give the war meaning, however, as their commanders pushed them mercilessly forward.

GMD and Japanese forces clashed fiercely over the key Hebei provincial cities of Shijiazhuang, Zhengding, and Baoding, where servicemen were pushed to extremes on both sides and their narratives came apart. At this time, Azuma noted that he was ordered to execute Chinese civilians for the first time and that he witnessed Japanese officers using their swords to kill old men.[79] Similarly, Sakaguchi described corpses of Chinese soldiers who had been captured and beheaded; he slipped in the muck and was constantly soaked by rain; his unit pulled their equipment to the front as their horses collapsed; he was frequently forced to "requisition" goods from the locals. "Today we start the battle for Baoding," he wrote, "these GMD regulars have the *Army Handbook, Handbook for the Revolutionary Soldier,* and so on—a real pain in the ass [*shaku ni sawatte shikata ga nai*]."[80] The battle for Baoding began at dawn:

> We took off before dawn, got out of the car, went to battle, took direct, concentrated fire from the city walls, and lost nearly the whole Third Battalion. It was 9am. Our Fourth Platoon lost three men, seven wounded. The squad lost one, three wounded. At 11am, we shouted *Banzai,* and the Hi-no-maru flag was raised high. We were one hundred meters from the enemy. When we shouted *Banzai,* I was moved beyond control.[81]

Baoding was one of the most important sites of Chinese military tradition; many of the GMD officers fighting the Japanese at this time were graduates of its academy. Liu Binghuan's unit was sent to defend the city, but he noted several impediments to their mission: the Japanese had blown up the bridge inside, separating them from the city; roads were too pockmarked to be used and trains were abandoned because they were too damaged; Japanese planes had relentlessly bombed Baoding and Shijiazhuang, setting the cities on fire. Finally spotting the enemy, Gao Jingbo led his company to engage them, describing a "devastating fire" *(sanmie sheji)* that they unleashed for hours. With no friendly unit to cover them, however, he noted that "the situation turned into uncoordinated fighting," and soon Japanese aerial bombardment forced them to flee in disorder.[82] Neither Gao nor Liu made any attempt to disguise these disasters in their accounts. Meanwhile, Sakaguchi swelled with pride at the fall of Baoding but quickly added that "there aren't words to describe the pain and exhaustion."[83]

After the sting of conflict, the process of comprehension began. Taniguchi, who had turned his nose up at the state of Japanese infantrymen, suddenly found himself thrust inside their world:

> There were piles of corpses collapsed on the road, women and children, their faces pale from loss of blood—there is no end to my pity for the misery of a fallen people. . . . The roads have turned to muck. In the afternoon, at Longmenkou, another unit picked up three captives, whom they will deal with tonight. Starting tonight, we'll be camping out in the field for three days, so there are no supplies. We just gnaw on hard tack. We have to requisition foodstuffs for breakfast. It feels truly desolate [*kokoro-bosoi*] being out here.[84]

In nearby Liangxiang, Kawakami embraced his heroic victory, dreaming of walking through his home village and proclaiming proudly, "I was in five battles!"[85] The very same day, the cities of Beiping and Tianjin were plastered with signs—presumably written by Chinese residents—reading "Congratulations on the Fall of Baoding." Akiyama Toyochi saw these signs and was dumbfounded: "I struggle to comprehend the minds [*shinri*] of the Chinese people."[86] The GMD diarists, conversely, did not accept these losses so easily. Falling back from Baoding to Shijiazhuang, they chronicled their collapse as an ongoing tragedy. Gao Jingbo's unit met with an unmitigated disaster as they attempted to ford a dangerous river. Burdened with heavy equipment, the Japanese enemy was close behind:

> Because the river was deep and flooded, and the waters were gushing by, we could not move the artillery across. Our forces broke up and fought to cross the river—we did not know the enemy's position. . . . We first had to try sending the large vehicles across, but the water was very deep, to the point that all of the clothes, machine gun ammo, official documents, maps, equipment, provisions, etc., on four vehicles and four or five horse-drawn carts were washed away. We could not cross, and thus stayed out in the open on the north shore. (Five civilian employees went missing).[87]

After the officers collected themselves on the south side of the river, they found that the Japanese were approaching them from the north just four days behind. Japanese aerial bombing killed more horses than men, but this was equally crippling for artillerymen. By 1 October, Liu Binghuan's brigade was in full retreat toward Zhengding, and all of the outskirts of Baoding had been secured by Japanese forces.

After key military areas such as the city of Baoding fell in the north, the Japanese army pushed into a formidable hinterland, full of wild rivers and rugged hills, with both sides resorting to dirty tactics. Umeda Fusao departed Ujina to join the Fifth Division while Deng Huanguang's Sixty-Fourth moved slowly to the same front. Just one week before Deng complained of the activities of Japanese plainclothes units and Chinese "traitors," Umeda wrote of the "numerous barbarous acts of the [Chinese] plainclothes units." While the Japanese army sent "Manchukuoan Education Brigades" to "disturb" Chinese units and marched with Mongolian conscripts, Deng's Division sent guerilla forces to attack Japanese supply routes—which Umeda was assigned to defend.[88] Worrying about his family in Japan and narrowly evading ambushes, Umeda described the conflict in the mountains: "We sleep out in the open in spite of the rain, facing the enemy head on as dawn breaks. Both friend and foe fire away for our lives. We're in a trench, and don't dare to move a muscle." Meanwhile, on the opposite side of the same battlefield, Deng proudly announced that "the Huang Battalion's bitter assault felled [kuibi] many [Japanese] and there are over one hundred Japanese dead from land mines." Then intense Japanese artillery bombardment from Umeda's side of the river scattered the Chinese forces. The next day, Umeda, "stumbling on [Chinese] corpses," struggled to stay awake as his unit advanced over muddy roads. The Chinese, meanwhile, were waiting for them with snipers, mortars, and land mines. A corporal in Umeda's unit was shot down by the Chinese, shouting, "Tennō heika banzai!" Umeda wrote, "It was so sad; there was no medic here for him, so he was carried away by his comrades." The next dawn, however, Deng wrote that Chinese positions "at the front were attacked. Our officers and men perished while holding the line [*bingsi zhiju*]." GMD forces withdrew without collecting their dead, and Japanese wounded lay scattered in ditches and on the fields. As his unit inched forward once again, Umeda described the scene:

> While looking for other Japanese casualties in the trenches, I came across wounded Chinese soldiers [*fushō shita tekisan*]. Shocked, I led them to the unit commander. It was sad to see them undergo different kinds of interrogation [*torishirabe*]. *So this is war,* I thought, but an hour later they finished the inquisition and the Chinese were led to the rear by Lieutenant Yamane. They were probably killed. Even though they're our enemies, they're human beings with a soul like all other living things in this world. To use them as helpless tests for one's sword is truly cruel. There's no place as cruel and unjust as the battlefield.[89]

Meanwhile, in the first week of October, the preliminary fighting for Shijiazhuang-Zhengding began, and many soldiers' accounts were filled with pockmarked descriptions of loss and gore, as if language itself was scarred by warfare. At Shijiazhuang, Huang Yong'an stood in front of his thirty-nine officers, ninety-one men, and civilian staff and ordered them to "strictly uphold unit order and defend our nation with your bodies [*yi shen wei guo*]."[90] The Japanese, however, were to unleash a terrible assault on the GMD forces, which Liu described: "the Japanese bombarded us horribly with heavy artillery and, at 9:30am, attacked us from the northeast. Company Commander Lian Ruilan died right there at his observation post." Japanese artillery attacks cut off Liu from the various companies under his command, and in a state of panic, he pulled his forces out of position near Zhengding and fled.[91] Kimura, firing on "suspicious looking people" in the fields, arrived at Baoding on 3 October; he marveled at what he saw around him: "Stayed in the barracks of the Baoding Military Academy, the bodies of Chinese in many piles along the way, everywhere signs of extreme battle, seemingly endless rows of soldiers'

barracks."[92] Kawakami and his men chased Chinese forces across the Hutuo
River and then took cover when the GMD fired back from the other side:

> The night march was the most excruciating. It was completely black. The
> engineers were digging in the sand next to the Hutuo River in front of the
> Chinese with their bare hands. Enemy bullets came flying at us with that
> "zip, zip" sound. The water was deep—so cold it froze your guts. We crossed
> the river at 8am, and finished a half-hour later. At dawn I thought we had
> quite a few casualties here at the battle, but there weren't so many after all.
> Nevertheless, it was tough. I thought I was done for.[93]

Liu, who had heard nothing from Zhengding, was ordered to abandon Shijiazhuang and, "while strictly upholding military discipline," to flee south to
Zhangde.[94] As Huang's unit ran away, they were warned from Nanjing that
units in the north were reporting that the Japanese had been using poison gas
in northern China, which only added to the consternation of Chinese forces.[95]
Soon thereafter, Kimura set foot in Zhengding and described the scene:

> We pull out to the edge of the city gates and spend the evening there. Chi-
> nese dead are piled up on the city walls—I cover my eyes. The city is full of
> corpses, and I am overwhelmed by its ghastliness [*sakimi ni semaru*]. . . .
> They say Shijiazhuang will fall. How far are we trying to go? We can't find
> the unit; we don't know where we'll sleep. The waning moon is alone over the
> city of Zhengding, brilliant. . . . Even when I gaze at the Chinese dead—
> forcing myself to look at them until I feel I can no longer stand it—no
> "awakening" [*satori*] comes of it. I still cannot untangle the problem of
> where in one's heart practical bravery comes from.[96]

Sakaguchi's unit then marched in next to Kimura's, crowding into the
town of Zhengding at the same time. Having crossed four icy cold rivers
and likely looking at the expansive Hutuo in front of him, he remarked in
despair: "I have no idea how far this will go."

Even though language cannot fully express internal thoughts and feelings,
in an effort to capture some "truth" of what they were witnessing, servicemen
filled entries in their diaries with descriptions of sensation. Sakaguchi collapsed into his lodgings in the middle of the night after the long marches.
When the effects of the drugs he took to stay alert began to fade, a pain so
intense came over him that he wrote, "I could almost cry."[97] Discovering a

sudden (if ephemeral) egress from the brutal demands of war in the dead city of Zhengding, Kimura revisited his concern for "truth" but now, after experiencing the battlefield directly, tied it explicitly to physical self-management. He was now concerned with "bodily health." Still mired in Zhengding the next day, he swore to work hard on the battlefield for his family but wrote that his body failed him. That night he had a nightmare of his daughter being sick in Japan and awoke to pray for her health.[98] While his body was wracked with illness, Kawakami received the first letters from home since his departure. Although he wrote that "there's nothing more joyous" than receiving correspondence, it only made his illness and nostalgia more difficult to bear.[99] Sakaguchi went to visit his war buddies in the Japanese field hospital, which housed over a thousand casualties: "They laid mats out on a brick floor, and the men were on top of them; it was truly a pitiful sight. Next they came to see us off to the station. Their hair and beards were all grown out. When I look at them, they are really a pity."[100] After seeking refuge in a soothing bath, Kimura lay down to sleep, but Chinese partisans burst into his unit's camp with submachine guns and shattered his calm. Overwrought, he wrung his hands for want of a cigarette, but there was no more tobacco on the battlefield.[101] Jotting down these events and sensations with no apparent narrative to string them together in meaning, Kimura seemed lost in China.[102]

Meanwhile, Chinese diarists were adding new fervor to their description of the war tragedy, adding sight and sound to the record. Three days after the GMD abandoned Shijiazhuang, Japanese battalions such as Sakaguchi's caught up with Liu. Liu could hear them launching "a huge artillery bombardment; large numbers of defeated Chinese troops were in the swampy roads." He added, "Our situation is desperate."[103] One of Liu's subordinate's, Yang Tiejun, reported, "At about 10am, while on the march, I saw enemy planes blasting us incessantly, and the sounds of artillery shells thundered in our ears without end." The roads turned into rivers of mud, immobilizing their artillery pieces. Then they were attacked by Japanese plainclothes units, and Yang's march turned into an utter catastrophe:

> Horses and men were slipping in the muck. I heard the roar of enemy artillery very near to us. . . . I saw the blinding flash of the artillery explosions. Other units on the road fought each other to race ahead, completely panicked. They abandoned much of their equipment on the muddy road; everything deteriorated to the point where they were fleeing for their lives.[104]

While struggling to cross the Zhangde River, Yang and Liu were finally able to arrive with what artillery and infantry they had left. The very next day, Yang wrote, he could hear furious bursts of machine gun fire on the river banks as the GMD tried to keep the Japanese from overrunning them. Constantly on the move, Liu eventually crossed the Yellow River, leaving the area entirely to the Japanese, but Yang, his subordinate, lagged behind. As Yang and his men struggled to escape the Japanese assault, enemy artillery pounded them, and Yang noted that the sound of machine guns became "more and more fierce," at which time all battalions fled in desperation.[105] Hebei, the province of Beiping, had been totally surrendered.

Next scattered Nationalist troops organized in isolation to carry on their resistance as guerilla forces, and Japanese servicemen wrote in increasingly divergent ways about this new element of the war. Kimura and his men were attacked by hundreds of Chinese soldiers disguised as civilians, sometimes from rooftops, which was terrifying and disorienting. Soon after Kimura was writing about "war and morality" and about trying to be reassigned to guard duty in Qingdao.[106] Kawakami's unit also fought hard against the scattered GMD forces in the closing days of October, trudging through trenches and over the dead. He wrote that he beat wounded Chinese troops with a stone and sliced open a captive with a Chinese sword *(Qinglongdao)*. Kawakami explained, first and foremost to himself, that such behavior was acceptable, right, and even pleasurable. Pursuing retreating Chinese troops into the mountains of Shanxi, he seemed to grow more and more impatient, and by the end of the month he had become extremely brutal:

> In Shanxi, everyone is in the Communist Army, so there isn't a single local to be seen. If we find them, we kill them all. We eat whatever is on the Chinese dead. These are miserable circumstances. The position on a hill outside of Bojing village was tough. Shooting the fleeing enemy soldiers from here is fun [*omoshiroi*]. Also, playing around [*itazura shitara*] with the wounded and making them kill themselves was fun.[107]

Publicly, the fall of Hebei at the end of October was lauded in Japan as a great victory. Servicemen in the rear such as Ishida Gi'ichi celebrated the victorious aftermath—Chinese residents of Zhengding posted signs for the occupying army congratulating this "victory" as they had for Akiyama for the fall of Baoding. For the most part, however, Japanese servicemen, mired in the continuing chaos of a mammoth battlefield, did not describe the fighting in northern China in this way. It is unlikely that, at this stage of the war, they even knew how these events were perceived at home. Furthermore, their views depended heavily on their individual experience: unlike Kimura, Ishida did not want to get out of the war and, unlike Kawakami, did not take pleasure in "playing around" with Chinese wounded.[108] Regardless of these differences, most Japanese servicemen painted a portrait of themselves within their individual understanding of war with the "truth" of the experience underpinning the decisions that they made.

Meanwhile, the Chinese Nationalists indulged in their desire to kill the enemy as the Japanese embraced their fury over the Chinese resistance, congealing into a vicious cycle of self-mobilization, chronicle, and increased brutality. In craggy, mountainous Shanxi, a report came into Deng's unit stating that the most effective Chinese units attacked from a distance, employing heavy machine guns, keeping underground and out of sight: "This kind of battle technique is very suitable to our army's needs in this War of Resistance. . . . Not only can you kill or wound the enemy but also can strengthen your fighting capabilities [zhandouli]."[109] Hiding in ravines, the Chinese forces over the next week brutally repulsed one assault after another by using this method. Umeda described this battle from the Japanese side: "There are enemy troops on all four sides of us. There's nothing we can do. I went back a bit and into a crevice, where I met seven others." At this point Umeda and his comrades were attacked with grenades, and Umeda was hit in the face. "At last it was dark, and five of us went forward a bit. . . . Entering a Japanese position, we embraced each other, crying with joy."[110] If a camera were to pan across the valley to catch Deng's expression, however, he probably would have been smiling while he recorded the suffering of Umeda and his men:

> Today two Japanese main forces attacked Pingxingguan, martyring many of our defenders. Reinforcements had to come and attack in order to cut the enemy into two sections and their losses were great. At 4pm the enemy for the most part went back to their original position at Hunyuan, moving further west. They were in total disorder.[111]

News of the miserable scene at Pingxingguan traveled fast through the Japanese military,[112] but witnessing the real thing with one's own eyes left a stronger impression. However difficult it may have been to capture this experience with words, Umeda felt compelled to attempt such a description as he saw the final, terrible clash of Chinese Nationalist and Japanese forces in Shanxi:

> This time the battle was particularly harsh. Japanese losses were also horrible. I had seen them [just] yesterday, but there were dozens of mobile units that got done in—many cars charred on the roadside with their burned drivers still at the steering wheel. It was so horrifying I couldn't bear to look at it. The Twenty-First Company's supply lines were hit, with men, vehicles, and horses scattered about one *ri* from the road, dead. That gut-wrenching image is beyond description. Everything on the caravan was stolen by the enemy, with rice and sugar scattered about—their wanton theft [*ōryō*] is despicable. I wonder if the people at home, overjoyed with the thought of ever-victorious Japanese soldiers, understand the unending pain that comes with this victory.[113]

Dividing the defenders and combining infantry assaults with aerial and artillery bombardment, the Japanese were finally able to threaten the field headquarters of the Chinese army in Shanxi. In full retreat, Deng used his diary in an attempt to understand his nation's failure. He complained that Nationalist troops frequently mistook Japanese maneuvering for retreats, bemoaned the infamous GMD communications failures, and noted that the Japanese "leadership and supply" could change their tactics "quickly and energetically."[114] Despite their hatred of the Japanese, Chinese Nationalist diarists felt compelled to recognize their enemy's military superiority, sounding sometimes dangerously defeatist. Meanwhile, Japanese servicemen's accounts often crossed the line from mimicking gritty war fiction to a language that would have struck the military police as "antiwar sentiment." Nevertheless, diarists on both sides rarely shirked from pushing the limits of their ability for self-expression in an attempt to capture the "truth." In part, this was demanded by the war diary genre itself: in order for the text to have any value to diarists as a record, they had to be willing to accept it as accurate—even if it did not represent the "whole truth."

As the war dragged on into months, many Chinese diarists began to establish a recognizable pattern in their diary writing—recording killing the enemy, brave sacrifice, and Japanese technological advantage—but others struggled with their position as GMD officers. Wang Jingguo, though commending the Japanese "gutsy and rapid drive south," claimed that "the heroism of our officers and men" was responsible for the killing of three thousand Japanese troops near Yuanping; two brigade commanders, three staff officers, and three thousand men were "valiantly sacrificed" *(zhuanglie xisheng);* three regiments were "utterly sacrificed" and "there was not a single day when we weren't locked in a death struggle with the enemy." He used his diary to record the historical significance of the battle:

> The 196th Brigade at Yuanping launched a tragic, bloody battle, locked with the enemy for ten days or more. During this battle, our regiment commander Jiang Yuzhuo fought and died valiantly [*zhuanglie chengren*]. Because of the stalwart, ferocious battle of Yuanping, we were able to allow Xinkou to prepare more easily, where we commenced the now famous Battle of Xinkou, surely the most shining page in the military history of the Second War Zone.[115]

The apotheosis of the war dead served as an ad hoc epilogue to an otherwise scattered, episodic inscription of war experience. Later some of these diaries would be used by military historians and strategists to write more consistent narratives, but in the meantime, they were only tattered notes representing the chaos of experience.

Other Nationalist officers, however, did not disguise their failures with such triumphalism and instead tried to decide (in their diaries) how to lead men against a superior enemy. The diaries of army commander Hao Mengling and his division commander Liu Jiaqi demonstrate the dynamic cycle involving self-mobilization, experience, and chronicle. In August 1937, they begged the GMD to send them off against the Japanese in Hebei.[116] Within two months, they had crossed many provinces to arrive in Shanxi's biggest city and Nationalist military outpost: Taiyuan. Hao's diary reveals not only how GMD officers promoted self-mobilization among one another but also how the diary was the site in which this discourse was put to record:

> Woke early, chatted with Regiment Commander Chen and Brigade Commander Kong. The gist was that this war is for the survival of our people [*minzu*], so we can only sacrifice. If we retreat again, say to the banks of the Yellow River, there'll be no more soldiers left and, if so, how could the officers survive? We mean: "If I die, the country lives; if I live, the country dies." Also, we're going to deal with the traitors and the cowards [*lianzuofa*].

There may have been more to the officers' resolve than mere guts—after all, those who turned and fled too easily before the Japanese were dealt with harshly: "Perhaps because Li Fuying will face the firing squad, all of the high ranking commanders in Shanxi are very committed."[117] Nevertheless, the possibility that failure would result in death was a very real one, indeed, and GMD officers such as Liu took it seriously:

> The officers and men in this division are not making any effort in building our outer defenses, and more than a few cannot follow the regulations. I am deeply concerned about this. I'm good at cultivating a spirit of meticulousness during a period of peace, but once we get our orders, it is not such an easy thing to do. From here on out, regarding our fighting spirit, if we are not resolved to die in battle, it is going to be extremely difficult to achieve victory. The officers and men in the division are spineless [weimi jingshen], our system of punishment and reward is unclear, so I'm truly concerned about our battle against the Japanese.[118]

Indeed, Hao's and Liu's trip to the front was not without its difficulties: they abandoned malfunctioning trucks and were harassed by Japanese aircraft constantly; soldiers coming back from the front "looked as frightened as mice"; provisions at Yuanping had been seized by the Japanese, meaning that the enemy was "eating our rice—just like in Baoding and Yizhou." Approaching the advancing Japanese force, Liu was suddenly attacked by doubts that he could effectively lead his men:

> My heart is not full, with little progress from before—something is lacking. I need strength to correct past mistakes, to be careful of my words and composure, showing absolutely no weakness [hanyang] or wavering [yincao] so that no one will look down on me. When I'm in front of the Japanese, I need to make plans with a clear mind [xuxin] in order to overcome this tough adversary. This is my intent, and I dare not predict what the future will bring, but right now I am lacking in authority. I have a will that I cannot enforce—what should I do?[119]

These officers had to find their resolve, particularly as they faced death. Hao selected 10 October, the anniversary of the founding of the Chinese Republic, as an opportunity to reflect on the hardships of past GMD leaders and wrote: "If we allow this much of northern China to fall into the hands of the Japanese, we've not done enough, we haven't shown our spirit."[120] A battalion under Liu's command spotted a Japanese armored unit and, rushing toward the tanks, threw hand grenades and Molotov cocktails at close range. Excited by a victory on such an auspicious occasion, Liu wrote, "On such a clear day we engaged in combat and achieved victory—the future will undoubtedly bring satisfaction!"[121] Liu and Hao had written the possibility of victory into their personal stories, which seemed to make victory all the more possible. Even as the odds stacked against them, they scribbled positive foreshadowing into their records, perhaps hoping that this act alone might contribute to victory.

Ultimately, however, Chinese officers, bound by their commitment to truthful record, could only find ways to narrate their own tragic failures. When Yuanping fell on 11 October, Hao witnessed the flight of defeated Chinese soldiers and wrote, "I fear we cannot hold the town,"[122] while Liu wrote bitterly, "Tonight the Japanese sleep soundly as their puppet armies from Manchuria and Mongolia are on night patrol."[123] Hao heard that Chinese forces were retreating from Niangziguan: "At this rate, the graves of our ancestors will fall to the enemies—it breaks my heart."[124] While gathering his troops for a counterattack, Hao was shot dead by his enemies. Traumatized by his commander's fall, Liu tried to muster his "authority" and rally the troops to counterattack when a mortar canister exploded near his head. In the midst of being pulled off the front to be treated by field medics, Liu was shot numerous times by a nearby Japanese machine gun and killed.

While the GMD narrated their failures, Japanese servicemen were left to explain their "success." Japanese servicemen—even medical officers such as Taniguchi—were quick to admit that they had frequently fled in terror before the Chinese. In November, Taniguchi's unit was moving through Shanxi when a surprise attack from Chinese troops armed with machine guns and artillery forced them to flee in disorder. Taniguchi saw a lieutenant take a bullet in the gut, groan, and die "tragically" in front of him; other officers were stabbed to death and fatally shot. Scrambling through the hills, they "spent an uneasy night listening to gunshots."[125] In addition to trying to describe their own fear of death, Japanese servicemen were burying their friends on the field of "victory." Umeda, arriving in Liu's and Hao's area a week after their deaths, found that many of his comrades had been killed. One friend, shot in the head, was buried in a trench after Umeda collected the man's personal belongings. Unable to give the soldier even the dignity of a hero's burial, Umeda and his friends were forced to erect a grave marker in their "hearts only" *(kokoro bakari no bakuhyō)*. Umeda thought that his friend "was really a hard-working and good man" and worried about "how shocking this will be for the people back home." Nevertheless, even amid such fear, terror, and physical privation, servicemen like Umeda remained committed to chronicling what they experienced as a testament to the truth of their experience. While collecting his friend's personal belongings on the battlefield, Umeda discovered the man's personal notebook. "I took care of him [*sewa wo shita*], and the battle was so fierce that I had no idea if I would survive either," Umeda wrote in the back of the dead soldier's diary, which was addressed to the bereaved family. Umeda was then hospitalized from an illness that he had contracted on the battlefield and returned home two years later, presumably with both his friend's diary and his own. He died shortly thereafter, having delivered both testimonies.[126]

It might seem that the hollowness of victory and the desolation of defeat might break an individual's ability to engage in self-discipline. Indeed, most servicemen's heroic narratives of self-mobilization devolved into barely coherent, episodic chronicles of battlefield experience. Such a state might resemble madness—what field doctors used to call "shell shock." Japanese and Chinese servicemen, however, would later demonstrate an impressive ability to heal their own wounds through the medium of language.

SHANGHAI: "DRIVING BOTH MAN AND HEAVEN INTO FURY"

Japanese servicemen who had experienced the Battle of Shanghai referred to the city, with little affection, as "the meat grinder," and GMD officers wrote of their "great personal humiliation" and unbearable sacrifices defending it. Shanghai generated close to 85 percent of the income for forces directly under Chiang Kai-shek's command, so he was committed to keeping it out of Japanese hands. Once Japanese land army troops landed in the northern suburbs of Shanghai, it became one of the bloodiest fights in the entire war. The war smashed servicemen's self-narratives as it did their bodies, and these would have to be rebuilt. Because disciplinary mechanisms such as the state, mass media, and even the military did not reliably provide guidance on how to describe this experience, servicemen relied on themselves.

At the beginning of the battle for Shanghai, Chinese officers frantically scribbled down and phoned in Japanese attacks, recording in their diaries brutality, ferocity, and consternation. A Chinese officer stationed at the command headquarters near Shanghai copied his primary order under the category "Resolution" *(juexin):* "the army has decided to encircle the landing enemy forces and wipe them out."[127] GMD intelligence, however, was poor—they could not predict from where the invasion would come, so they scattered across the entire shore. A company commander composed an account that tried to capture the atmosphere of nervous frustration:

> The planes of those Japanese bastards are a little annoying. Every day they circle our battlements, buzz buzz buzzing, but we're getting used to seeing and hearing them now. To us they're like ducks and birds in the sky. Some of my brothers get a little upset and go shoot at them with their rifles, but this is actually a pretty ignorant thing to do. It not only doesn't hurt them, it just gives them a target to bomb. After I warned them severely several times, they do this sort of thing less often, but, really, it can't be stopped. It is unavoidable because it is an expression of my comrades' hatred for the enemy. Even though I know my orders through and through, I can't put a stop to their feelings, which burn like fire.[128]

The Chinese air force was struggling to regain air superiority over Shanghai and Nanjing, but in late August the Japanese had deployed sophisticated antiaircraft guns to Shanghai and a new kind of monoplane aircraft, the A5M2a, or Navy Type 96 Carrier Fighter. Consequently, Chinese air force commanders complained that their foes often flew away faster than they could pursue, and the aircraft under war hero Gao Zhihang's flight group met with intense antiaircraft fire, their pilots returning severely injured.[129]

Without air superiority, naval power, or reliable intelligence, the initial landing of Japanese forces in Shanghai (starting 22 August 1937) filled Chinese commanders with extreme fear. Luo Zhuoying recorded chancing upon four to five thousand Japanese soldiers on the beach, where they "fell into a bitter battle [*kuzhan*]" until "the Japanese abandoned their dead and fled north."[130] Chinese officers in fact sometimes led their men to the front line in total darkness for fear of Japanese air assaults. Peng Xi proudly reported that their artillery assaults were pushing the Japanese back when, suddenly, a Japanese force of "unknown size" came south toward their position. The Chinese scrambled to meet them when at about seven, two hundred Japanese troops started attacking our Sixty-Second Regiment. The more we fought, the more they came, and they were very savage [*xiong*]. We ordered the Sixty-First Regiment back to Xinzhen. At around eight our Sixty-Second Regiment's left was encircled by the enemy and it turned into a battle of clashing blades [*yan cheng baidao zhan*]. . . . In the end, blocking the enemy's advance has not been easy—Zhang Lie was wounded and we've had a mess of casualties among the officers and men. The battle is becoming a standoff.[131]

Back north, just outside Luodian, Li Weipan coordinated battles on the field to force the Japanese from the village of Lujia. Li was wounded during the battle, as was his regiment commander Wei Rumou, and they lost company commanders and infantrymen totaling almost half their number. Li wrote:

The left wing threw themselves into the battle with no care for death or injury, heroically counterattacking the enemy at close quarters, making the situation even more intense. At about eleven, the enemy had even approached Luojia Road. Because Cai was desperately outnumbered, many positions began to show signs of faltering. The situation at Luodian is unknown. Our 398th went forward to reinforce them at Luodian when the situation turned dire. The Japanese losses were also horribly heavy; they do not dare come too close to us.[132]

While many fought and died, others lost their courage and fled in panic; in Jiading, which was hit by a Japanese air attack, the district chief and the police chief both fled the area for the interior, abandoning the Chinese army completely. Panic was widespread, and the evidence of these feelings is dappled with bravado in GMD diaries.

The clash of these two forces unleashed many powerful emotions. On his first day in China, Japanese veteran Hamabe wrote, "Enemy bullets are falling like rain. I was shocked by our hurried landing. The feeling that 'this is a war' wells up inside me—much more so than the [1931] Manchurian Incident."[133] Where the Japanese landed, hidden GMD regulars or PPC units fired on them. Close to where Nagatani's and Hamabe's units were landing, Zhong was writing, "The Japanese are making a fierce attempt to land. . . . Five times already, one after another, we've killed many enemies, over one thousand, trying to land, reinforcing themselves endlessly. Luckily, our heroic officers and men hold their positions."[134] Those Japanese that survived the landing witnessed the remains of over two weeks of modern warfare, and many tried to capture it on paper. Nagatani, who had been so passionate about his dedication to becoming a hero, wrote:

> I feel like I'm still on the boat—rocking and swaying. Everywhere you look, the place is brutally torn apart from air raids. I'm finally able to truly under-stand the cost [*kachi*] of war. This is how you know how horrible, how sav-age a thing it is [*makurumono*]. Right where we were resting, under the shade of a tree, were soldiers who had just come back from an intense battle; I was filled with a sense of fortune and gratitude for having landed safely on this land, taken by the blood and tears of the marines and forward land units. I offered a small prayer to the spirits of the war dead and faced toward the Emperor in the far, far East. While feeling how grateful I am for my country Japan, I was able to sense how horrible [*zankoku*] this thing called war really is.

In contested Wusong, Nagatani was never safe: during the day his unit fell under a furious Chinese artillery assault, and at night the Chinese would try surprise attacks. Nagatani, attempting to command his squad, could not find the proper words to describe what was happening to him: "When I'm repeating my special orders, no matter what, I can't keep my voice steady, which is really a shame. I know I'm doing it, but my voice still shakes. Getting your assignments under enemy fire is, also, an intense [*kakubetsu*] feeling."[135] Some Chinese servicemen were awestruck by the renewed force of Japan's modern army, and their military inferiority became painfully ap-parent. Zhong's unit was forced to hide under canvas bags when their makeshift trenches filled with water. Wang was amazed by the power of a Japanese aerial bombardment even as he fled for his life: "This was the first time in my life I had seen such a grand spectacle. This time we had no inju-ries; only that poor grove of trees with which we had grown so familiar, in one moment, was burned to the ground."[136] Luo copied reports of buildings all over the Shanghai area being reduced to smoldering rubble from Japa-nese land, sea, and air bombardment.

Chinese losses and failures inspired increasingly emotional prose—even in official documents—and GMD officers used their diaries as a means of defining a target for this anger. In fact, anger, loss, and failure frequently shared the same page: Luo copied a report on the loss of Luodian, writing

that the Chinese army "was unable to eliminate the stubborn Japanese bastards [*yuankou*] completely from the riverbank, for which we feel deeply
humiliated [*xushen cankui*]." Similarly, copying from a report by Regiment
Commander Ye, he described the brutal form of street warfare that the GMD
was adopting—that advancing units should spray alleyways with machine
gunfire before entering, adding the injunction to "hold your position to the
death and never retreat."[137] One Chinese soldier's anger grew exponentially
until his targets included more than enemy units; he let loose his hatred for
"cowards" and "traitors":

> This place is crawling with traitors. Every day when we move we're threatened
> by Japanese air forces and spied out by observation planes, and at night signal
> flares. The traitors also follow our units on all sides and fire flares at will, so the
> enemy knows all our military movements clearly. In addition to this, the en-
> emy uses its battleships as base areas, attacking us at will and sending Chinese
> traitors to open fire on our positions with small arms during the night.[138]

Even in the government capital in Nanjing, as yet unthreatened by land
invasion, the commander of the Third Flight Group received a surprise visit
from two officers. Although he had previously expounded on his unit's "desire to kill the enemy," these men questioned his unit about the area around
the airstrip, "worried that traitors would seize the opportunity to disturb
them" and advised him to augment the guard.[139] Meanwhile, Luo copied
an intelligence report concerning "The Madness of Chinese Traitors" into
his diary, which constructed a most sinister image of China's internal foe: a
man who spied out positions for the Japanese, writing in a little notebook;
his chest and thighs were covered with scars from knife wounds (evidence
of torture); he wore black and red Japanese jackboots; he poisoned wells,
killing soldiers and good citizens *(liangmin)* indiscriminately.

The supposed madness of the Chinese traitor, however, was equally matched
by the unbalanced fervor with which Nationalist servicemen, officials, and civilians subsequently proceeded to seek them out. Luo wrote that "every officer
should search their vicinity for these traitors, selling their country and committing crimes [*hanjian maiguo lunzui*], and execute them by firing squad."[140]
Even in areas where civilian organizations were especially watchful, GMD officers, though soldiers and not judges, could be asked to summarily adjudicate
such accusations. Citizens beat suspects viciously and even turned them over

to the Chinese Scouts for execution.[141] Wang, leading his men through a small village, had such an experience as a mere company commander:

> The villagers of the hamlet Shimian caught a traitor and brought him to us, saying that he put poison in the well in order to kill the villagers and the units here fighting the Japanese. After a public hearing that I held, the traitor would not recognize his crimes. *Hanjian*—this is a serious problem. I've been the target of many enemy plots, and they've all been the result of these traitors. If there were no traitors in our midst, I have no doubt that the enemy could never have made it one step beyond our mines. The more I think of this, the more infuriated I become. Why don't our comrades in the rear [*houfang*] eliminate a problem as serious as this?[142]

The GMD, of course, had its share of spies as well, and Chiang Kai-shek had openly advocated their use from the very beginning.[143] As early as 28 August, orders were circulated among the officers instructing them to send "plainclothes units [*bianyidui*] out to collect information, infiltrate the enemy's rear, and disturb their troops—all in order to make the [Japanese army's] situation clearer and exhaust the enemy." As in the north, the GMD was willing to use any means to defeat what they saw as an illegal invasion of their land but were simultaneously infuriated by Japanese attempts to employ the same tactics.

Although it may seem that the act of recording "violent acts" *(baoxing)* would lead inexorably toward violence in reprisal, such records in fact could lead to different conclusions.[144] In September 1937, Japanese units in Shanghai were encountering Chinese noncombatants for the first time during the war, and the impeccable morality of the war hero was torn asunder for many. While listening to friendly units advance with rifles against GMD artillery forces, Nagatani's unit found an old Chinese couple behind their lines. "We did them in right away," he wrote and seemed to think no more of it. Over the next few days, however, Nagatani's unit captured over 500 Chinese soldiers during night attacks. The more the prisoners flooded in, the more Nagatani was forced to "dispose" of them, and the more his language changed:

> We got four more of them in the night. When we left for our night attacks, we shot three and sent one to the rear. At midnight, we were on alert. In the afternoon we attack, at night on alert. I'm getting a taste of how hard this

thing called war really is. [One day later] Today at 7am, we made breakfast. Caught three more—killed them all. They straggle behind here and there, which is dangerous, so we have no choice. . . . At one the Third, Fourth and Seventh took three hundred. . . . At five we tied up two hundred, shot them with a machine gun, and burned them with dry leaves. Then, some of them, who had only feigned death, started to run, so we stabbed them one by one. It felt horrible [*hizan*], like a living hell. People shot one after another, all kinds of people.[145]

Some servicemen recorded these acts but did not seem to think poorly of themselves for committing them. For example, going into the fields and towns, Hamabe merely noted they "procured" *(teire)* horses from the locals in order to pull their equipment.[146] The idea that the Japanese army was capable of "barbarity" *(manxing),* of course, was nothing new to the GMD officers. One GMD officer proclaimed: "Ten Japanese transport ships are on the move, each ship holding 500 or so men, heading west to unload their troops, who are creating havoc, burning, killing, and looting."[147] For the Nationalists, Japanese brutality fed an equally fierce desire to kill and drive the Japanese out of China altogether. While Japanese servicemen such as Hamabe might record his acts merely as a matter of record—thereby making such acts commonplace—Chinese officers such as the one cited above were trying to capture all of the offenses that he heard and witnessed— thereby capturing such acts as further evidence of Japan's aggression on the mainland. For Nagatani, this chronicle of quotidian violence was building toward a personal transformation. Whether they sought change or stability of self, these were, for the diarists, not just meaningless lists of data.

By September, Chinese and Japanese servicemen close to the Shanghai front began to settle into a miserable wartime existence, and they recorded their deprivations. Hamabe complained: "the one thing you can't get a hold of on the battlefield are sweets. We have no sugar, so everyone is sucking on sorghum. Some went out to collect sorghum in the fields, but they got nailed by enemy fire and came back empty-handed."[148] Hamabe had spent a whole day fighting in Yangxing with nothing to eat. Medical attention was also by and large nonexistent; Japanese medical officers *(eiseihei)* were renowned for their incompetence. Nagatani, seeing his platoon leader off to the field HQ to rest because of a pain in his stomach, lamented, "He had done so well for us up until now, but I would have never thought he'd end up like this. It is such a shame; especially so when someone is sick and you can't even care for them."[149] Chinese servicemen fared little better. Although they were supplied through various support organizations, constant Japanese bombing made the delivery of those supplies inconsistent and unreliable. Chinese servicemen slept in abandoned houses or out in the fields, like animals. One Nationalist soldier, perhaps seeing similarities between his fleas and the Japanese, wrote:

> Later I still felt there was something itching me back there, but this time I just couldn't take it. I ran as quick as I could to a grassy hill and sat down facing the sun. I took off my old uniform and searched it thoroughly, finding quite a few fleas. Picking them off one by one with my fingernails, the crunching sound and fresh blood flying was strangely satisfying. I struck swiftly and surely in order to get my revenge on this irritation. Fleas—under any normal circumstances perhaps a person would find this terribly ignoble, but we in the army don't see it that way. In times of war, a soldier can't prevent fleas like a worker does, and doesn't have the time to root them all out. People may think that this is a rather unheroic thing, but we can only allow them to do as they please.[150]

Japanese commanders, losing face each day Shanghai did not fall, forced their men to the front, turning Shanghai into a savage killing field. Meanwhile, Chinese officers such as Zhong took pleasure in shooting at the Japanese troops:

> The sounds of the assault and killing could be heard up into the heavens. At this time the enemy soldiers lost their artillery support and thus were facing us as equals in battle. The Japanese did not consistently reinforce their position, and in the end, our officers and men's courage and ferocity beat them back at 9pm. When the mist cleared, the enemy soldiers pulled out. They saw that there was nothing that they could do [to defeat us], so they took their revenge by blasting us with their artillery.[151]

While one side advanced to write of satisfying violence, the other might retreat into bare-boned records of victimization. The same day as Zhong's attack, Nagatani led his squad through intense enemy fire to sweep out hamlets in the area. His entry for the day was uninspired: a list of deaths and wounds kept in great detail.[152] With so much death around them, many were at a loss for words; Hamabe and Nagatani resorted to simply recording the deaths of their comrades.

As the battle dragged on, servicemen continued to experiment with language in order to find an appropriate voice, as if they were attempting to establish a new genre for war experience. As the GMD momentum in Shanghai was blunted, Chinese officers in the south found a pattern for recording their experiences just as those in the north had: noting Japanese technological superiority, GMD sacrifice, and stalwart defense of their territory. Material disadvantage was particularly distressing for the GMD—as Zhong wrote, "the Japanese are constantly landing before our very eyes with modern weapons. From morning to night the enemy uses its planes to spy and bomb. The enemy artillery fire is unceasing and maddening."[153] Luo's diary records further bombardment and destruction of Chinese defenses in Shanghai, while others listed the officers who had perished in various units, the figures mounting higher and higher each day. The Chinese were taken aback by the ferocity of the new Japanese forces, but GMD officers kept experimenting with different phrases: they observed that "the officers and the men held their positions to the death" and that "despite intense artillery bombardment, our men did not budge an inch"; they qualified these observations by adding "but our losses were enormous" and "we have lost nearly half a battalion." While one Chinese unit replaced those exhausted from holding the front line, the diarists worked hard to find the right words for what they were witnessing.

In conditions such as these, the reemergence of the language of self-mobilization might seem, from our perspective, tragic and even absurd. At the same time Chinese officers such as Luo were suffering under Japanese bombardment, Nagatani's unit began marching on a GMD stronghold. Soon he complained of a pain in his chest. "It is nothing," he told himself, "I'm going to put my best foot forward." After arriving in Yuepu, two more of his men were sent back to headquarters for treatment. Reflecting on the men he had seen die since arriving in Shanghai, Nagatani's language begins showing signs of instability:

> I thought everyone would go home ok, but now there's just nothing I can do. Why this bad fortune? I killed my boys [*buka*]; there's nothing I can say about it. I have to avenge them. If I don't get back out there on the front line and do my job, I just can't take it. . . . For better or for worse, I made it alive. I might live a little longer. I asked my parents to think of me as an honorable man if

something bad happened to me. . . . I have to stay alive to avenge my comrades.[154]

Nagatani, who had been straining to describe his horror after he killed Chinese civilians and seemed tempted to curse the war itself, finally managed to remobilize himself by using the trope of "avenging" his comrades' deaths. Two days later, while his unit drove north from Yuepu, Nagatani was shot in the head and died outside of Luodian. Knowing that the military police would confiscate and burn it, Nagatani's comrade picked up the diary from his friend's body and protected it for the remainder of his tour of duty. The Japanese army sent Nagatani's body back to the rear immediately to be burned in the fields.

As reservists flowed unceasingly onto the front line from Japan and casualties increased, increased exposure to warfare correlated to changes in language: as Shanghai got "hotter," servicemen's diaries became more gruesome and bizarre. On 12 September, in Shikoku, Yamamoto Kenji recorded hearing the names of those who had been assigned to active duty. In response to hearing his own name, he wrote, "There is no end to my happiness" and notified his father by telegram. He traveled toward Tadozu, sent off by the enthusiastic cheers of flag-waving civilians. Given the timing of Yamamoto's arrival, it is likely that he was setting foot on China the same day that Nagatani's remains were being shipped back to Shikoku. But Yamamoto's heroic resolve crumbled even more quickly than had Nagatani's:

The remnants of fierce battles are everywhere. In wide, flat fields, you can see the white walls of destroyed homes, surrounded by trees. There are abandoned horses. On the bank of an irrigation canal, there was a dead child, and a bit further down, two adults' bodies with no heads had been carried to the bank by the stream. It is so horrible, I can't look.

Transport troops are moving ammunition and provisions on emaciated horses.

Yamamoto's unit moved as quickly as possible down sopping wet dirt roads, from Shidongkou to Chuansha, staying in dirty, abandoned hovels. He complained of "the horrible stench from Chinese soldiers' corpses, collapsed on canal banks." Engineering officers had him digging trenches nearby, and he was kept awake by "gunshots which continued incessantly through the night."[155] Yamamoto and the others gripped their rifles tightly until morning. Meanwhile, Hamabe watched the men under his command killed one by one, only to secure short stretches of land along the coast near Shanghai. The reserve of this normally terse diarist split open and text poured out onto the diary page:

> It is one month to the day since I was inducted into the unit. We haven't heard from the Twelfth Company since the night of 16 [September], which is really worrisome. Platoon Commander Nagajima seriously injured his hand and came back after not having eaten for a whole day. . . . No matter how you look at it, central China is full of canals and is a major hassle. It looks like there have been a lot of deaths among the reservists who came the other day. In my own platoon, too, about twenty-five men have died. . . . In the evening, when the usual three or four night attacks come, there is such a din of pistol firing that you can't even talk to the man beside you, and bombs fall right before your eyes—I just don't feel well. Then, at night, the enemy planes attack us.[156]

Suzuki Hideo, a lower-echelon medical officer in the 101st Division, wrote about the gruesome tales servicemen brought back—men blown in half, whole battalions decimated, and no progress on the front—until such narratives "became a kind of empty slogan [serifu]."[157] Yamamoto described men in his unit being shot by hidden assailants while going to irrigation canals for drinking water.[158] By the 27 August, Hamabe hoped for the fall of a certain town, whose name he did not dare to write, to put an end to the fighting. Whereas some officers such as Lieutenant General Kimura Matsujirō could write that "there are a lot of dead soldiers" with no apparent narrative affectation or remorse,[159] Yamamoto tried desperately to capture the horrors in stuttering prose. First, he drew on the language of war reportage for his battle scenes: "The bombardment is a success, we've suffered no casualties!" The next morning, however, they advanced, "stepping on the corpses of dead Chinese soldiers," into a "nameless hamlet," and his style of writing shifted:

> It started to rain. We're covered with mud. Tanks advance. The korian stalks snap and crack, echoing in the field. Someone says: "I'm hit!" Someone else says: "XX is hit, he's wounded!" Advance, advance. My comrades are taken away, covered with blood, but nothing can be done. We only advance, advance. The tanks pull up 50 meters from the enemy and open fire. We jump

into an irrigation canal, right into an enemy position. Oh, we've finally taken Xiaotaizi. At night, we're counterattacked twice, but we beat them all back. Nonstop firing.

As his difficult experiences increased, Yamamoto's language becomes increasingly broken and odd. He and his comrades went to bury the Chinese war dead—"which are horrible to look at." He described them lying in piles in the trenches, their stomachs bloated and bodies stained with blood. Graphic entries creep in: "I touched one of their heads, and the brains came out."[160] Yamamoto and Hamabe had been pushed beyond their usual manner of self-expression, leaving them apparently disoriented and confused. Although we cannot know exactly what these two were "actually" feeling or thinking, it is clear that their experience, both physical and psychological, when combined with the act of record, profoundly destabilized their war narrative.

Casualties in Shanghai were so heavy that more units from all over Japan and China were mobilized, feeding more "meat" to the "grinder." Servicemen on both sides struggled to make sense of what was turning into a major military disaster. Private "Honma Masakatsu" wrote in his diary that, two days after landing in Shanghai, he had killed eight Chinese women and children. Itō Kihachi, a private in the Thirteenth Division from Fukushima Prefecture, brought out fifteen Chinese noncombatants and shot them, simply describing it as "horrible."[161] Meanwhile, the GMD scrambled to replenish its forces at the front line, attempting to keep pace with the carnage. With bloodied units coming back and fresh units rushing ahead, all under Japanese air raids, Battalion Commander Yu Yanling captured the chaotic scene in his diary:

It seems like common sense that, after our previous long march, we'll have a few days to rest and regroup, but these days we're constantly getting orders from above telling us to board a train forthwith, rush under starlight to XX and await orders. What they say is true: "Military commands are like an avalanche." Thousands of men are running like clouds swirling in rushing wind, advancing straight to their destinations.[162]

Chinese servicemen, however, quickly found themselves operating under extreme circumstances; they narrated events in short, staccato language but made sure to get down as much as possible. After rallying themselves for an attack, a Nationalist officer had to quickly explain in his diary that "because enemy [artillery] fire was so intense, our base was utterly destroyed and casualties were very high, so our position fell apart."[163] Like his Japanese enemies, Luo resorted to writing short snapshots of the battlefield but added touches of vivid description: "the battle conditions are intense, and the enemy casualties are high; dead bodies are littered across the fields. We are locked in with the enemy throughout the night."[164] Zhong Song and his men, after incorporating fresh recruits at Kunshan, staggered when Japanese unit fired explosive 75mm shells directly into the sandbags and rubble comprising their defensive line, "smashing us with their fire." Zhong ordered another company up from the rear to reinforce their position. Japanese aircraft and artillery bombed Zhong's men, and then an infantry unit launched a sudden assault:

> The Sixth company commander Li Haishou fought bravely, with no regard for his life, and fighting the Japanese bayonet to bayonet [*duanbing jiezhan*] for an hour. Our communications were cut and enemy planes buzzed us, making our rear and front unable to communicate with one another. We fought with the enemy for three hours straight and, in the end, among the horrible casualties, Li was killed. Following the enemy's land and air bombardments, falling like rain, all of the men heroically sacrificed themselves; not a single man made it back.[165]

The Japanese found the grinding brutality of the war equally disorienting and alarming. The sight of wounded men coming back from the front line assailed Yamamoto daily, who recorded that they were "covered in blood, moaning on their stretchers—a terrible sight." Elderly Chinese civilians, abandoned, hurt from shrapnel, or otherwise unable to flee, meandered behind Japanese lines. What words could possibly capture the experience of witnessing this? Yamamoto, perhaps feeling the inadequacy of the ideology that so thoroughly suffused his early entries, drew instead on the fiction and poetry he enjoyed so much. The words began to flow much more easily:

> In a flooded rice paddy, I sit down to put pen to paper. The sunset is reminiscent of the famed paintings of Tai Xi. Here and there amongst the expansive cotton fields, there are clumps of sorghum growing tough and strong. The sun in the western sky burns like fire. The lake is quiet as clouds illuminated

by dusk blow gently across the darkening sky. I am delighted by the white flowers on the banks and the gentleness of the reeds under the water. Under the trees of the bank, the cries of the butcher-birds have sometime gone silent. From time to time I hear gunshots from our side and theirs. The dull thudding sound of artillery explosions reverberates, but the view at sundown is silent.[166]

That servicemen such as Yamamoto tried to write at all is impressive by itself; after similar experiences, many simply did not have the energy. Hamabe was certainly not poetic—overwhelmed and wounded, he became markedly less verbose. He spent two weeks trying "to rest while listening to enemy bullets [flying by]."[167] The same day Hamabe's and Yamamoto's units were reinforced—13 October —Commander Yu's replacements arrived as well. Moving into a village that had "been reduced to rubble," Yu built his defenses. When they received orders to prepare for an attack, he wrote that his men were excited, eager to "show their stuff" *(chuqi)*—they had worked themselves into a frenzy. "The enemy is truly cowardly," Yu wrote, "once you see them, they just take off, but our men pursued them vigorously from behind. The little demons that couldn't run too fast were finished off by our men." Despite a clear GMD policy against killing captives, Yu took no prisoners. When a Japanese bombardment forced them into retreat, however, Yu was pursued by unlikely adversaries:

I heard the men say that when they were facing the enemy behind an embankment, they heard enemy troops calling out randomly, "Oh countrymen! Don't be so cruel! We are Chinese too! Most of us here are from Dongbei, forced to come with the Japanese. What choice did we have? The Japanese demons are pushing us forward, so we can only go ahead. But we're just shooting at the sky; the light machine guns are being used by the Japanese only. We want you to know this, countrymen! Do your best! It is terrible to lose your land!"

Yu was disgusted and reflected later on how "foolish" the people from Manchukuo were; he could not believe that these men were forced to serve, that they "could not kill a Japanese man with a Japanese gun." Was Yu using this text as a space to rationalize killing these men? Similarly, were Japanese and Chinese records of killing and trauma pushing them in a particular direction? It is possible, of course, that Yu composed this diary strictly for the purposes of propaganda, but the language echoed through all of the unpublished diaries from the period. In the end, despite the chaos of the battlefield, diary writing continued to serve as a space to mobilize oneself, record "facts," and draw conclusions. This self-discipline, however, served the needs of the state less and less; it was a disciplinary apparatus gone awry.

As the month of October drew to a close, the fate of Shanghai was still unclear. Both sides were bloody and broken, and their self-narratives either exploded with excessive self-confidence or were as scarred and crippled as their bodies. Yu was directing his men under the cover of night to rebuild their defenses for the following day. "Running to and fro under the cover of the pure white moonlight," Yu tried desperately to control the 500 men under his command. Then, unexpectedly, he was hit by an enemy bullet. He exclaimed, "What an idiot!" and continued ostentatiously:

> I heard tomorrow morning the enemy will execute a massive attack on our position. I also heard they will be using tanks. I had always planned on facing the enemy one on one, to see what he's really made of. But later events have gone contrary to my hopes and have made it impossible for me to continue this work. Even though my wound is light, a major blood vessel in my leg was broken, so I cannot move. I must leave my unit, go to the rear, and nurse my wound; I will prepare to meet my enemy again and take his life.[168]

Some had been pushed beyond their limits, however. In the Fourth Field Hospital, Itō languished merely in boredom, suppressing his desire to "return to my unit," eating canned fruit, and receiving comfort packages from the imperial family. Simultaneously, in the Third Field Hospital, Hamabe weakened day by day. All around him, Hamabe saw servicemen from the front die in their beds—sometimes two or three men a day. Hamabe wrote, "It makes my heart sick with loneliness." Men died in their beds calling out the names of their wives and children. Soon Itō too wrote of the painful loneliness of the hospital, far away from one's comrades and surrounded by dying men. After looking out over the "miserable Chinese homes" destroyed by artillery fire, Itō dreamed of happy, healthy children at play.[169] The next day, Hamabe's wound oozed and caused him another sleepless night, but the hospital was woefully understaffed. Near the end of his life, he simply wrote, in disgust: "I've had enough [korigori da]."[170] Attempting to attack the Japanese again at Bazi Bridge, Zhong's unit was pounded by Japanese artillery fire; they tried to take the bridge four times, but their losses were unbearable, and he suffered his second major defeat. Zhong was broken. He wrote: "Heaven feels the sacrifices of these heroes—it makes the gods cry."[171]

Piecing together broken selves and war narratives was impossible for some and certainly difficult for most, presaging the coming struggle to reorganize China itself. The Japanese army scrambled over the ground the GMD ceded as they fled, encountering streams of defenseless refugees,[172] seeking out GMD army stragglers and spies for execution. Army medic Suzuki Hideo haphazardly pieced the Japanese wounded back together—cauterizing missing legs, performing arm amputations, and bandaging those wounded from friendly artillery fire. His makeshift physical repairs reflected his often feckless attempts to give narrative coherence to the events around him:

> Lieutenant Watanabe killed a man (an old man). We take our rest in a temple. PFC Fujisaki and some others capture three GMD regulars. Tie them to a tree. Young faces. Two are from the Youth Leaders Brigade [*seinen kyōdōtai*], and one looks like their leader. We show them a pamphlet, dropped from our aircraft yesterday, saying, "Throw down your weapons and give up. The Japanese Army will not harm prisoners." The youngest has a deep, conflicted expression on his face. I do not understand the plea he wanted to make. Another is laughing. In a place about 100 meters away, they are killed by sword. The self-satisfied face of junior officer K. Children, women, and old folk watch from the road. The [Chinese] soldiers cry out in despair.[173]

Later, in November, Hamabe was still stuck in a field army hospital. Despite promises that he would be sent home or to a nicer hospital, the Japanese army seemed too preoccupied to do this—he had been there for nearly a month. Hamabe's writing had become garbled, probably through his fear: "Clear. Last night, because it had been handled so poorly, my wound began to bleed. They administered treatment twice. I'm worried. My throat is dry."[174] He died that day, without having any time to think through his experiences, and a comrade furtively mailed his diary back to Shizuoka through the uncensored hospital mail system. Meanwhile, Yamamoto heard news that his friend Kunizaki had died in battle. He tried to make sense of these events with what words he could muster: "Kunizaki, how the hell did you die? Death! Was it real? I thought we would go on living together. Death! Was it real? . . . Thinking about him, I couldn't get any sleep. That night the sky cleared, and the stars were shining."[175]

Here Yamamoto appears to have exhausted his ability to use language to give meaning to his experience. Kimura, who was committed to "truth" and dedicated to his personal records, also struggled to arrive at a conclusion regarding war and the human condition. Similarly, GMD officers such as Zhong Song did not seem to grasp the reasons for and consequences of their failure to defend their homeland. Neither side managed to comprehend the meaning of the hundreds of thousands of servicemen and civilians sacrificed in just three months of war. Diary writing on the battlefield was not actually a space where great "truths" convenient to overcoming trauma were discovered—though not for lack of trying. Rather, diaries were the raw materials for subsequent narratives with that ambition. As Isaac Babel discovered by recording his own military service, however, in defining the horrors, victories, and hatreds of the battlefield in these documents, diary authors set limits on the kinds of people they could become and how the war could later be described.

In the Battle of Shanghai, from 9 August to the beginning of November, the Nationalist Army lost its most effective fighting force: three-fifths of these men were wiped out, and about 10 percent of the field leaders (mid- to lower-echelon officers, largely trained at Huangpu), who frequently led their men directly onto the field, were killed.[176] Consequently, on 6 November, Ma met with officials in Nanjing, where Chen Bonan told them in no uncertain terms, "Regarding the battle for Shanghai, everything we had— not only the personnel lost under artillery fire but also their weapons—was simply buried under the earth. In light of the heroic sacrifices at the front line, as with the expenditure of materiel, they cannot be replenished."[177] The Japanese suffered thousands of casualties in Shanghai alone up to October 1937.[178] Because of these losses, the mobilization for total war in modern East Asia could not rely exclusively on the disciplinary machinations of the state; its success came to depend even more heavily on self-mobilization. Thus, in spite of the efforts on behalf of the state, mass media, and military, all of which held great sway over many prior to arrival on the battlefield, servicemen ultimately tried to write according to what they saw and felt, drawing from diverse linguistic sources. This is why they used voices that were often wounded, despondent, and seething with volatile language. Their diaries changed as their sense of self did, like organisms that struggle to survive in radically new environments. Or, to put it another way, these diaries are the remains of the increasingly divergent paths upon which they set out—like boot prints in mud or scars left by stray rifle fire.

CHAPTER THREE

Assembling the "New Order"

Reconstitution of Self through Diary Writing

THE SERIOUS WOUNDS inflicted by the war needed to be sutured; this was as true for language as it was for the human body. State and mass media actors orchestrated the healing of wounds at the level of public discourse but also attempted to enter the personal realm of individuals who were trying to heal themselves. The final throes of the first stage of the Second World War in East Asia—the decisive defeat of GMD forces in Shanghai in November 1937, the rapid fall of Nanjing (the Nationalist capital) in December, the establishment of a new capital under Wang Jingwei in March 1940, and a gradual shift in Japanese military strategy from rapid pursuit *(tsuigeki)* to military sweeps *(sōtō)* and limited punitive expeditions *(tōbatsu)*—coincided in both China and Japan with, on the one hand, the mass publication of selected personal narratives and, on the other, individual servicemen rewriting their diaries on the battlefield. The momentary victories for Chinese forces at Taierzhuang and Wuhan in 1938 became foci for the memory of the War of Resistance—a narrative of previous events that many struggled to define while the war was still going on. Beginning in late 1937, there was a radical transformation of space and discourse: the elimination of the

GMD's political presence in eastern China and the construction of a new polity under Japanese "guidance." During this confusing period, servicemen would use their diaries to make sense of it all (and themselves) in a rapidly changing context.

This chapter thus examines how servicemen were "smashed" and then "remade," and the role the diary played in this process. First, it will examine the period beginning with the fall of Nanjing (December 1937) and ending with the fall of Wuhan (October 1938) through the diaries of Chinese and Japanese servicemen in order to show how the chaos of the battlefield influenced diary writing and, consequently, servicemen's sense of self. When this chaos threatened military order, the state, mass media, and armed forces cooperated to "rediscipline" their men through the creation of a historical memory of the conflict. The final two sections will analyze how servicemen, who had grown accustomed to disciplining themselves, reacted to these efforts and adjusted to the stalemate in China from 1939 to 1945. In the end, despite the state and mass media's ability to shape public discourse, in each instance it was the self-discipline of individuals that determined the success or failure of efforts to define the war experience.

TERROR, PUNISHMENT, AND COLLAPSE: SHATTERING THE SELF, 1937–1938

The Chinese Nationalist government's capital was in the city of Nanjing, a short distance by rail (or the Yangtze River) west of Shanghai, where both the GMD and the Japanese armed forces were locked in a terrible struggle. In early October, two new Japanese forces changed the nature of the war in the south: fresh divisions landed in Wusong, and the army succeeded in carrying out an ambitious landing at Hangzhou, thereby outflanking the Chinese forces. With the Chinese army in full retreat, Nanjing was left nearly defenseless. From this point onward, the Japanese army would begin a reign of terror over the GMD heartland, aiming to root out the social, political, and economic mechanisms that had produced such loyal soldiers for the party.

Both sides immediately intensified their battle rhetoric in diaries. Corporal Hamazaki Tomizō, after arriving in China at the end of 1937, wrote a menacing proclamation in his diary: "Look upon the land and the sea,

Chiang Kai-shek, you did not know the resolve of the Imperial Army and defied us! Now we're closing in around your neck."[1] Staring down these forces directly, Tao Zhiyue told his men that, in the war, "even though there have been terrible losses, it is inevitable that we will get our revenge and clear our humiliation in order to comfort the souls of our fallen brethren [*yi wei xianlie*]."[2] Between November and December 1937, the Japanese army switched from their earlier goal of pushing the Nationalists out of Shanghai to obliterating them entirely. The terror in Nanjing was in fact merely a small part of a larger political extermination campaign that would reach Xuzhou, Wuhan, and many other critical cities. Nevertheless, the ruthless assault on the heart of Chinese resistance would have devastating consequences for both the Chinese and Japanese forces, including the revision of heroic narratives, contending with catastrophic failure, and coming to grips with the extraordinary emotions unleashed by the Japanese campaign. Terror and fury gripped diarists on both sides as centers of authority—commanding officers, national capitals, and confidence in total victory—were either absent or destroyed.

In fact, by late October and early November, the men dug in on both sides at Shanghai had already begun showing signs of collapse. Japanese infantryman Yamamoto Kenji, though diagnosed with malaria on 5 November, assisted others in the wind and rain by collecting and burning dead soldiers—"one indistinguishable from another"—in "nameless" Chinese hamlets.[3] Life near the regimental headquarters was a little better than being on the front lines. He bought canned fruit and other luxuries and was able to send and receive mail through the military postage system *(gunji yūbin),* but such censored correspondence rarely offered even the slightest inkling of their poor conditions. Motojima Saburō wrote a typical letter to his aunt and uncle:

> I hope you are both doing well and in good health. I am receiving your letters from time to time, and I am sorry that, due to my hectic duties and fearing my messy handwriting, I haven't been writing as much. Please forgive me. Because of your prayers, I am getting better and better, so please do not be concerned. September is nearly upon us, and I bet right about now the rich, golden waves of Aizu are wonderful to behold. My heart is filled with appreciation when I think of you all working in the hot sun back at the home front. . . . These days I have been soaking up the Fall moonlight of central China, and the rice harvest here has begun. The sound of crickets in

the grass reminds me of home. It has been raining every day, and I have been lonely most of the time.[4]

As a result of harsh living conditions, many at the front began falling ill, although Ma Chaojun (head of Nanjing's air defenses) suspected that this sudden outbreak of illness was mostly disingenuous, pointing to a serious decline in morale.[5] The collapse of GMD forces at Shanghai struck fear into the hearts of those in nearby Nanjing. Seeing bright flashes of light, antiaircraft personnel panicked and argued amongst themselves—were these secret Japanese planes with silent engines or chemical weapons detonating nearby? Ma wrote that it was once again an example of "over-sensitive nerves and a lack of common sense amidst an atmosphere of heightened tensions."[6] As each army entered the chaotic war zone, guerrillas, turncoats, and assassins seemed to lurk everywhere. Hamazaki was unnerved by stories of "disgusting things" (imawashiki mono) from his comrades and was jolted awake by enemy attacks in the middle of the night.[7] Japanese planes bombed Wuxi, Suzhou, and Nanjing incessantly. Ma, watching the Japanese launch a surprise attack on a Chinese airfield, was convinced that "despicable traitors" in the GMD ranks had given away the positions of their planes with the use of radio transmitters. He wrote in exasperation, "Oh god, our planes had all gathered there, and then this. We had no wireless telegraph to inform them, no way to know where they are; our complete technological inferiority is excruciating!"[8] As news of the collapse in Shanghai reached Nanjing, higher officials such as Ma began withdrawing into the interior, and Ma himself fled Nanjing by the end of November. Once GMD officers abandoned their men, order in the ranks dissolved; the troops mixed with Chinese civilians behind the Japanese front line, resulting in a truly dangerous situation.

As the Japanese approached Nanjing, servicemen on both sides increasingly wrote entries in their diaries emphasizing feelings of anger, horror, and despair, but they also used the text to express their desires. For example, as a result of Chinese guerrilla tactics and fierce resistance, some Japanese servicemen were eager to "get even." Their revenge would be terrible; researchers have already demonstrated the magnitude of the murders that took place in Nanjing, even if an exact figure is elusive.[9] Private Ueda Masaki, arriving in Nanjing on 15 December 1937, tried to capture the scale of these mass killings:

Word is out that 15,000 unarmed [Chinese] soldiers without uniforms were caught and surrounded with machine guns, and another regiment was found in concrete bunkers; they're both being guarded. So, we went into the canals [looking for fleeing GMD soldiers]. It's fun to go searching for them and pull whatever is there out. . . . We marched to Zhongshan Mountain to look at the remnants of the battle. There were about five hundred corpses at the gate, shot and left there in piles. [The scale] was beyond any man's ability to measure [*ningen mo hakasanai mono nari*]. Bodies with their hips torn apart, skulls with the face ripped off . . . they had been prepared to resist us for over a month. . . . Went on patrol in Nanjing and its suburbs. . . . Five or six hundred fleeing Chinese soldiers were killed by the Watanabe unit.[10]

Given the widespread and detailed accounts by observers of different stations, forces, and national background, it is clear that a large, often well-organized campaign of murder occurred in Nanjing. Many felt compelled to record the massacres in order to make some sense of what was happening around them, even if their conclusions seem disturbed today. Some were horrified, but others recorded a sense of achievement. Private Itō Kihachi once stood on a hill in Kunshan and proudly looked over "a pile of Chinese soldiers' corpses as high as a mountain."[11] In the midst of the massacre occurring across the Jiangnan region, Kurozu Tadanobu decided to cling to the fantasy that China would embrace them:

The houses of the Chinese are flying our Imperial flag with signs that say "Welcome Japan!" The refugees from Zhenjiang have more or less returned. . . . We spent the night here. So far, Zhenjiang has been the most culturally sophisticated town in China, with tall buildings and electricity. It is fabulous. . . . There was a Chinese man who had lived in Japan for a while; he spoke Japanese, made us tea, and welcomed us here.[12]

From Kurozu's vision of a pacified, subservient China to Itō's satisfaction over China in ruins, soldiers were using their diaries to articulate where they hoped the war would go.

Servicemen who were troubled by the events tried to find the proper words to describe it, but this seemed to have been difficult for them. Private Ōdera Takashi arrived in Wusong on 3 December and, like Itō, encountered a harsh battlefield reality. While still on board, there was an "uproar" (*ōsawagi*) among the troops when Chinese corpses, bloated from the water *(dozaemon)*, began floating down the river past their ship. Ōdera disembarked and went immediately to take in the "remnants" of battle and artillery bombardments *(tatakai no ato, hōgeki no ato)*. He tried to keep a cool record of what he was experiencing but soon deviated into more graphic descriptions:

> The Chinese defenses were, at the closest range, barely one hundred meters from our own. They had bombarded the school with artillery mercilessly until they felt satisfied. Horses lay dead, their innards carved out and eaten by dogs, stinking and unbearable to look at. Many of the pockmarked walls look like they were hit by naval bombardment, and the ones that had collapsed into a shapeless mass were from aerial bombing. There was ample sign of small arms fire. At the Wusong artillery platform . . . human corpses had not yet been disposed of, with their flesh rotting—only bones and clothes remained. We saw the raw remains of battle until noon, and there were some things that were emotionally unbearable.[13]

Many servicemen were shaken by what they saw, and the language that they used to describe their experiences began to depart from the heroic stories that they penned at the beginning of the war. Yamamoto wrote sympathetically of the "pitiful children and old folks" who were caught up in the Japanese advance; they fled burdened with personal effects and wearing dirty clothes. Near Suzhou, Yamamoto's unit passed by three or four dead Chinese women, "an ugly sight" *(minikuki sama nari)*, and he wondered in horror, "Did Japanese soldiers do this?" After pondering the possibility of Japanese-committed atrocities, Yamamoto described how he and his friends used ladders to break into Western-style homes, where they pilfered gold watches, sugar, and other "rare" goods while running the record player. As he visited each dot on the map to Nanjing, Yamamoto also tried to capture something in words—the flowers, the people, the horror of war—sometimes abandoning the paucity of prose for poetry: "I trod on the corpses of Chinese soldiers without care / for my heart had become wild and disturbed" *(araki kokoro)*.[14] The extreme nature of what men like Yamamoto experienced, coupled with deeply ingrained, historical practices of "factual" record keeping, put pressure on them to capture these moments. It seemed difficult for them to decide, however, what kind of language could best describe these extraordinary feelings and experiences, so they began to experiment with various genres and styles until they hit upon something that felt "true."

It appears that many Japanese servicemen convinced themselves in their diaries that the fall of Nanjing would bring an end to the awful war, so some men wanted to utterly destroy the GMD at any cost. After the collapse of the Shanghai front, personal suffering on the battlefield and anger over stubborn Chinese resistance became a justification for striking down the Nationalist capital. For example, Yamamoto used his diary to convince himself of Chinese treachery: Japanese infantrymen washing vegetables on river beds were hit by Chinese snipers, GMD troops straggling behind *(haizanhei)* charged Yamamoto's unit while it was at rest, and he complained bitterly of stumbling through towns leveled by enemy artillery fire. Writing "To Nanjing, to Nanjing," Inoue Yasuji and his unit moved west along dirt roads from Wuxi. Chinese soldiers feigned death by collapsing when he opened fire—which he described in uncharacteristically wild handwriting as "real goddamn annoying" *(kore ga honma no kusoYAKE)*. Having adopted a scorched-earth policy, the field artillery of the GMD incinerated hamlets and fields; the sight of fields and farm houses on fire all around Inoue were "deeply unsettling" *(kimi warushi)*.[15] Japanese army engineers ran through the fields, roads, and streams, dripping with sweat, trying to repair roads and bridges and clear debris. GMD reprisals could generate intense fear: Ōdera went to get orders and found that a Chinese soldier had caused a major fire in their base camp, writing, "I'm afraid to go out alone."[16] Fear and anger were closely linked: months of terror and fighting a determined enemy could generate powerful hatred. Talking with a soldier from Yamamoto's unit, Ōuchi Toshimichi listened to horror stories of the battlefield and reflected, "The Chinese army has become really despicable [*nikurashiku*] to me; I want us to wipe them out [*senmetsu*] as quickly as possible."[17] Thus, while the history of diary writing was steeped in writing fact, these entries were not simple chronicles—they were also intended to convince the authors that these thoughts and feelings were justifiable. In this case, self-discipline could lead to acts of extreme violence, even what we now call war crimes, and they help postwar audiences to understand why the Nanjing campaign was so brutal. Japanese troops literally talked themselves into becoming ruthless adversaries.

Once Nanjing was surrounded in early December, soldiers mobilized themselves for (what they assumed would be) the final confrontation and faced off in Nanjing. A critical part of their self-discipline was to transform, through the act of writing, powerful emotions to rational justification and then rational justification to direct action—making the diary a crucible for subjectivity itself. Jiang Gonggu, an army medic who had served under the GMD during the Northern Expedition, answered the call to service in August 1937. While many other top-ranking officials pulled out of Nanjing, he decided to stay on to look after the wounded. Amidst desperation and mounting fear, the head of the Second Army Medical Unit delivered a speech that raised their spirits:

> At this time of great peril and distress, Commander Li was able to gather sufficient men to assume responsibility for field medical service inside of a week—thus one can see that each and every man here is a patriot and a comrade. We have all served as soldiers or officials in the past, so naturally we are rich with battlefield experience. But this time everything is different than before, it is a critical juncture in the survival of our people and our nation [*guojia minzu de cunwang guantou*], so you must go forth with a spirit of great courage and compassion [*daren dayong de jingshen*] and fulfill your duties.[18]

On the offensive side, Japanese troops turned their fear into acts of terror against their perceived enemies, including noncombatants. Japanese servicemen hunted down GMD supporters just outside of Nanjing: Inoue's unit searched five Chinese soldiers and "found one of them"—a Nationalist Party member—sealing the captive's fate. Turning up around one hundred more GMD men in a "hunt" *(mori)*, they lined the captives up against a canal and shot them, making "a sea of blood in order to terrify the locals."[19] Meanwhile, GMD officers tried to harness their strong feelings to fulfill their duties in the face of overwhelming Japanese military superiority. On 8 December, Jiang and his commanding officer, Li, were encouraged by an officer from the general staff to flee: the enemy bombed the capital incessantly; the sounds of far-off machine guns and artillery shell explosions disturbed their meetings; at night, Zhongshan Road, the main thoroughfare of the capital, was pitch-black to prevent air attacks. Nevertheless, Jiang was moved by something Li said to another official: "I, a man with great responsibility, can't take off whenever it pleases me. If I go with you to [Wuhan]. I would call that running away [*tao*]. Those who flee may keep their lives, but what face do they have to show others?"[20] Jiang tried to inspire himself to carry out his duty, although this put him in great danger. Indeed, self-disciplinary acts that transformed emotion to action, in the context of total war, could come with terrible consequences.

Diarists sometimes could only admit that their feelings crippled them, whether inspired by fear or simple trauma. The attack on Nanjing had begun by 9 December, and the GMD forces charged with defending it gradually abandoned inspired patriotism for panic, especially as the scene in Nanjing deteriorated around the defenders. As Japanese units poured into Nanjing proper, Jiang heard "shrill cries calling for help" as the "incomparably evil dogs, the *hanjian*," shot at passersby. Wounded Chinese soldiers came flooding up from the south, and Jiang struggled to move them to Xiaguan, where one could cross the Yangtze River and leave the city. When he learned that the GMD army had collapsed outside of Nanjing, Jiang went with his commanding officer to Xiaguan to assess the situation:

> We did not anticipate the fact that [units in the GMD army] had already taken it upon themselves to cross the river and retreat. We couldn't see even a sliver of light—everything was simply covered with an inchoate mass of human shadows, moving along on foot in shock and terror like the living dead. It was a horrible sight. There were a number of large ships at the river bank loading automobiles. There was an intensification of fire from the other side of the river. This, of course, meant that [other Chinese units] would not allow us to cross, but that was terribly hypocritical of them. . . . After midnight artillery fire intensified, all aimed at the city center. I had not slept all last night because of [the artillery], and was so utterly exhausted that I did not feel the danger of the situation.[21]

Being on the "winning side" did not dissipate fears of being killed or failing in one's duties; Japanese officers were using written expression to contain their panic as well. Hamazaki lost his sword right before the attack on Nanjing, then turned to his diary to sort out his fear and wounded pride:

> I have no face to show my superiors or the men; there's no excuse for losing a weapon necessary for battle, and nothing can be done about it, but *seppuku* is even more unfilial [*fuchū*] at this time. How can I fight without a weapon. . . . After losing my sword, I should die on the front line. No matter what method you use, a fatal wound cannot be cleansed.

Hamazaki did "cleanse" himself of the wound of humiliation, however, by encouraging self-improvement in his diary: "I won't be taken by this [mistake] and let it darken my heart; I'll use my error as a basis for preparing for the next battle." As the battle to surround Nanjing intensified, however, like Jiang, Hamazaki felt more and more pressure building on him as a commanding officer, responsible for the lives of his men. He tried to console himself with the bitter reality of the battlefield, writing, "Today for the first time I lost two men under my command. Whether by luck, fate, or my bad leadership, we neither tended to them nor looked back, just advanced; this is the true face of war. If you rest for one second and reflect, you're emotionally overwhelmed" *(kanshin muryō)*.[22]

On 13 December 1937, the Japanese began the massacre in Nanjing proper, and servicemen on both sides, overwhelmed, used their diaries to make simple and sometimes unemotional records. Deciding to flee, Jiang and Li were fired on by Japanese troops immediately, whereupon they mixed with civilians and soldiers running in panic:[23] "We had no particular destination in mind, just ducking as we fled with the mob." After dozens of civilians had been shot near the hospital, Li ordered everyone to stay inside the refugee quarters. Dark figures fired on Nationalist officials, civilians, and servicemen who tried to cross the river and flee west to Wuhan.[24] Having captured the city and driven off its defenders, the Japanese military tried to wipe out any remaining resisters; it was an unbearable sight for some, but for others, it was something that needed to be recorded. Private Uwada Hiroshi described what seemed to be senseless, disorganized massacre:

> I ran into a cornered Chink [*chanko*] unit of about two thousand that had raised a white flag and surrendered. Old men mixed with young in a million different outfits, they had thrown all their weapons away and were all over the road, a real sight. They had been killed in all different kinds of ways and just left there in the street.[25]

Many Japanese lamented the massacre. Lieutenant Maeda Yoshimasa witnessed a multiple murder of noncombatants that erupted over a simple argument between an infantryman and a GMD captive. He subsequently wrote, "One must admit, it was an error over which the Imperial Army has lost face."[26] Others rejoiced in the killing and took no apparent shame in describing it in their diaries. Kindō Eijirō fired on refugees with light machine guns, writing it "was fun [*omoshiroi*]. Looking down on defeated [Chinese] soldiers while riding on horseback with Nanjing in front of my eyes didn't feel too bad, either."[27] Sensitive servicemen, however, might sympathetically describe their enemies, even as they killed them. Azuma was impressed by a dying GMD officer. He wrote Azuma a message in a small notebook and accepted death with a smile.[28] Ultimately, the massacre surpassed reason, and there was no explanation for why it happened; as a result, the diarists could not fully control the story. Saitō Jirō wrote a diary that was suitably ambiguous: he alternatively expressed fear, anger, and horror while imbuing his vision with a ghoulish ambience:

> I walked through bodies piled high, their numbers uncountable, and a foul wind blew, stinking of murderous intent. We kill XXX prisoners by the river banks. Until yesterday, the moon was shining brightly, but now it is cloudy, almost diaphanous, and a rain like mist is descending. A cold wind blew as if to slice my ears. One of my comrades who had gone to execute the prisoners was shot through the stomach, and his cries of mortal pain [*danmatsuma*] cut through me.[29]

Saitō's expression "murderous intent" *(satsuki ga tatsu)* connoted both a desire to kill and a feeling of gruesome abhorrence, but such Janus-faced reactions are not necessarily disingenuous. By acknowledging his role in the massacre, Saitō indulged in self-recrimination of the most severe kind: the Buddhist term *danmatsuma* is an agony experienced by the damned, and he carefully juxtaposes it with his own anguish. Like so many other diarists, Saitō was drawing on the language of Buddhism to paint a portrait of an underworld into which he had fallen.

Conventional wisdom holds that soldiers "don't talk about the war" and deliberately avoid discussing its horrors, but that is true less often than one might think. Even simple, reserved chronicles could serve as a mnemonic device; a diarist might later use more poetic language to force order and meaning onto these experiences. For example, Kindō coolly noted his "victories" over the Chinese but sometimes took time to reflect on the more unsettling aspects of war. In a single entry, he noted that the unit had decided to kill one-third of 20,000 GMD captives for "arson," simply stating: "we took care of them all. We bayoneted those who were still alive." Afterward, he reflected on the cool beauty of the pale blue moonlight, writing, "there is no greater horror than the cries of these stricken by the agony of mortal blows. One would not hear such sounds were this not the battlefield, and it is a scene that cannot be forgotten for the rest of one's life."[30] Indeed, in order that they would always be able to remember, Japanese infantrymen employed recording-keeping skills to capture the massacre of the Chinese Nationalists and their supporters.[31] They moved more and more to poetic language when they felt willing and able to understand its broader implications. For some, such epiphanies occurred on the battlefield, but for others it would take decades. Meanwhile, Chinese authors such as Jiang provided textual snapshots of the barbarity of the Japanese and the terror that they unleashed. For Chinese Nationalist servicemen like Jiang, writing and maintaining an accurate record of these atrocities was one of his most important tasks, even if he did not understand why at the time. Despite being broken by the horrors of this total war, soldiers would one day return to these records and think about what sort of men they were.

DESTROYING POLITICAL AUTHORITY:
TAIERZHUANG, XUZHOU, AND WUHAN, 1938

By mid-January, after the massacre in Nanjing had abated, the Japanese government announced to the world its intention to destroy the Chinese Nationalist Party entirely.[32] After Nanjing, the battles for Taierzhuang and Xuzhou (Spring 1938) and Wuhan (Fall 1938) signaled the end of Nationalist power and the beginning of Japanese dominance in East Asia; accordingly, Chinese and Japanese servicemen were deeply affected by the emotional highs and lows of these (seemingly) final conflicts. Japanese staff officers such as Kawahisa Tamomochi now openly declared that the purpose of these climactic battles was to "obliterate" the GMD army.[33] As the Japanese army moved in for, again, what the General Staff assumed would be the final blow, Japanese troops began to assume the role of an occupying force. For the Chinese, it was essential that they survive the onslaught. The 1938 execution of Han Fuju, who had fled his post in Shandong, galvanized Chinese officers to unite under Chiang Kai-shek, as the 1937 execution of Li Fuying had demanded such obedience from units in Shanxi.[34] Many GMD officers evidently embraced the new unity—at least in their field diaries—and they organized an impressive defense. It was, however, the excessive losses of their best men and many of their most sincere officers, and then the total collapse of regional armies, that finally gutted the GMD military of its élan.

In order to recover from the stinging losses of 1937, the GMD reemphasized political work among troops so that diarists never lost sight of the significance of the war, and self-mobilization could continue. Thus, the emphasis on self-discipline continued and even grew during 1938, building on the GMD's history of militarism. Liu Binghuang's artillery unit moved into Taierzhuang and participated in the GMD's brief victory there. A new company commander, He Xiuhan, recorded the content of Battalion Commander He Yuting's speeches, such as "A soldier's God-given task is to obey, and to possess that special ability [*texing*] to withstand pain and suffering."[35] Records of Japanese atrocities that the GMD had been collecting since the beginning of the war served as emotional whips to excite anger. When they had retaken one of their positions outside of Taierzhuang from the Japanese, Zhang Kuitan claimed that the "people of Taierzhuang have been oppressed by the Japanese. . . . There are corpses of men and women here, many were murdered. The people of the surrounding hamlets have fled; they are all empty."[36] Diarists rallied behind positive emotions as well. Despite many setbacks due to incompetence—especially among newly promoted officers— even the smallest victories could inspire the diarists to recall their highest hopes from the beginning of the war: after receiving good news from Taierzhuang, Gao Jingbo wrote, "We also heard that every city and town offered their own congratulations, lighting lanterns and setting off fireworks; the final victory begins here!"[37] With each victory, then, came a lesson in dedication, and diarists inscribed these lessons into their accounts. Intertwining political education and records of battle experience continued to be an important factor in GMD self-discipline, even after the loss of their capital city.

The effects of losing so many dedicated men, however, were beginning to show in the GMD armed forces. Desiring to link Japanese occupied territory in northern China (for example, Beiping, Tianjin, and Manchukuo) with their conquest of Nationalist strongholds in the south (for example, Shanghai, Hangzhou, and Nanjing), the IJA had to secure the critical railway junctures in the city of Xuzhou (and hold nearby Taierzhuang). Observing signs that the GMD was falling apart in early 1938, they felt that "there has never been a better time, and the opportunity will never come again."[38] Internal discipline was indeed collapsing among GMD units. As early as February 1938, Chinese officers such as Ye Tiaoquan—

who had previously lectured his men on the treatment of rail employees—described complaints about the serious lack of order:

> An investigation regarding the retreat of our forces revealed that officers of every rank frequently abandon their troops, creating disorder in the ranks and weakening our ability to resist. When retreating, officers must be sure to control their men. If there are any who leave the ranks on their own accord, they must be punished by death.[39]

In part, the GMD failures at Taierzhuang can be attributed to the increased use of chemical weapons in the Japanese artillery. Liu Binghuan described it vividly: "The enemy in the Fanxia district is using massive amounts of poison gas. In the least serious cases, our officers and men are crying uncontrollably, but in the most serious, they are all collapsing."[40] To add insult to injury, the officer class was failing in its basic duties: men were being promoted too quickly through the ranks, causing a deleterious decline in competence. For example, according to one lieutenant's diary, he spent the better part of the day on 7 March 1938 simply keeping track of the constant shuffling of the ranks in his unit.[41]

Another (perhaps more important) cause was that the Japanese were giving the Chinese plenty of reasons to be despondent: one GMD officer in Henan recorded that the Japanese were parading their motorized artillery and heavy machine guns in occupied towns.[42] Thus, in addition to being less competent, Chinese officers were also demoralized. Gao Jingbo noted that the regiment commander had to circulate among the officers and sit them down for "individual discussions" (gebie tanhua) regarding their understanding of the War of Resistance.[43] Demoralization led to what might be considered fanciful denial. As Liu's unit pulled out of the vicinity of Taierzhuang and began to flee west, company commander reports became sparse and formulaic, followed by Liu's outrageous statements of victory in the field. By November, he wrote that his men had asked him to retire from the field due to illness, so that he could better attend to "the heavy responsibility of defending the river." It could very well have been that Liu, like Li Zongren, was overcome with guilt over the loss of so many of his men; still, when their men collapsed at the front, the GMD officers all too often abandoned them and fled—they covered their tracks and tried to assuage their guilt in their field diaries with outlandish claims regarding enemy casualties. The cost of the GMD's failure to defend Xuzhou was enormous, for now Japanese forces could move freely from the north to the south and held most of the GMD's wealthiest cities. Four days after Liu's retreat, north of his former position, the Japanese were sweeping the area looking for the families of GMD servicemen and executing them.[44]

Despite Chiang Kai-shek's destruction of control dikes on 20 June 1938, which led to massive flooding and civilian casualties, the Japanese invasion could not be stopped. Nevertheless, die-hard Nationalist supporters and Chinese patriots tried to rally themselves one last time in Hubei Province. In the south, during the defense of the major city of Wuhan (and nearby Jiujiang), GMD commanders circulated constant calls to "preserve élan and military order by rousing the spirits" of the men, copying these cries into their diaries. They agreed that Wuhan, Jiujiang, and the surrounding area were the last line of defense for the entire nation's existence. They noted that "the officers and men work day and night, pouring rivers of sweat, so that they won't have to pour rivers of blood when the time comes to fight."[45] Chinese officers such as Third Division Commander Zhao Xitian tried to resurrect the spirit of the defense of Shanghai, proclaiming: "Ever since the beginning of total war in July 1937, this division has asked for permission to slay the enemy [qingying shadi]." Self-mobilization, however, quickly gave way to chaotic records of the devastating battle for Wuhan, the last GMD stronghold in eastern China.

The Wuhan campaign was even more costly than Shanghai for both sides, in large part due to the massive Chinese mobilization. Zhao was a newly minted commanding officer (CO), having climbed the ladder once his superior officer moved on to become an army commander, and was filled with enthusiasm characteristic of many who had come to defend the center of the War of Resistance. He tried to impart this enthusiasm when recording his diary, as he surely did when leading his men into action:

> The city of Jiujiang was already burning from enemy fire from the banks, including this division's entire position. In the midst of this heavy encirclement, even though we were surrounded and suffering horrendous casualties, fortunately our officers and men were glorious and honorable, throwing their lives into the Resistance; we didn't move an inch, fighting this terrible battle all the way until 10pm.[46]

Finding such units extremely difficult to dislodge, the Japanese suffered heavy casualties, even though the Chinese troops there were not as well trained as those in Shanghai (only less vulnerable to sea and air bombardment). Many of the higher-ranking Chinese officers were exasperated when their junior officers and men turned and fled before battle techniques that they did not understand.[47] The Japanese proceeded to use chemical weapons extensively against stubborn Chinese forces, creating almost instantaneous panic and disorder. The battlefield in Wuhan was exceedingly brutal, and the Chinese officers there, as they had in Shanghai, rarely made any attempt to disguise it. Zhao described a climactic battle in Wuhan thus:

> At 3:20pm to 7:30pm the enemy employed field artillery and mortars in order to attack [one unit's] position six or seven hundred times, using poison gas repeatedly. Our Seventh and Ninth Company losses were very heavy; the Seventh Company commander and one squad from the same company were all poisoned [by the gas]. The enemy infantry numbering five or six hundred men used this artillery fire as cover, and then attacked our Sixteenth Regiment's Third Battalion position fiercely. Our soldiers on guard kept their heads down and fought back hard until dusk; they are still fighting.[48]

During battles, diarists like Zhao recorded these events in a staccato voice: the commander sent his men forward; they advanced "bravely" into artillery and machine gunfire; patrols attempted to cut through Japanese supply lines; they did not return; all attacks failed; Japanese planes strafed and bombed them in retreat. While events were unfolding, no comprehensive analysis was forthcoming. The momentous, often chaotic battle over Wuhan could be recorded only in short bursts, like gunshots in the dark, because its outcome was uncertain.

Finally, under heavy bombardment, GMD officers led their remaining men out of the last stronghold of the Nationalist Party, in some cases leaving behind their equipment, dead comrades, and even their diaries.[49] When they arrived "victorious," Japanese diarists were appalled at the state of the area after the GMD decided to abandon it:

> The deaths of the soldiers, various people, and horses are horrible, and even some captives have been killed. While we are marching occasionally a surrendering soldier is shot. While heading to X town, because of the stench of

dead horses and men, some men collapse. . . . In the town of X, because of the bombing, there are maybe two houses that haven't been destroyed. On our way here, as well, we saw the aftermath of the bombing everywhere.[50]

As officers such as Zhao fled, they must have looked about them in despair, bearing witness to the Nationalist Party's miserable failure. On the road out of Wuhan, inclement weather forced his unit's escape to a grinding halt, and Zhao wrote in his field diary, "Because of all the army traffic on the road, the scene is pretty miserable [*fengji kuijia*], and many of the local people are [also] in flight."[51] Caught in such a quagmire, it dawned on many Chinese officers that their fighting capacity was effectively finished. As early as January 1939, top military officials acknowledged the policy of disengagement:

> The army must strive to maintain its current status, mobilizing the strength of occupied areas to check and sap enemy troops, exhausting them. This must be done to buy time, to protect the growth of the national army's new forces . . . so that, later, they can switch to attacking the enemy.[52]

The loss of some of China's greatest cities, including Shanghai, Nanjing, and Wuhan, was simply unacceptable for the Nationalist regime; it would never recover, and these blows would later abet the growth of Communist power. For the Japanese, the cost of taking them had sapped the national economy (on rationing since 1938), cost them hundreds of thousands of lives, and put them on a direct course of conflict with the United States and its allies in the South Pacific over critical military resources.

Meanwhile, servicemen who experienced these events used their diaries to try to comprehend events as they unfolded. Indeed, if subjectivity is the basis on which individuals decide what kinds of actions are appropriate and possible, then these diaries were a kind of drafting board for it. Across the fields and city streets of China, from Shanghai to Zhenjiang, Suzhou to Nanjing, Xuzhou to Wuhan, there were scattered many broken bodies and shattered ideals. Although servicemen had been forced to stitch themselves together for the most part without guidance from a central authority, the near complete chaos of the battlefield was not to last. The invaders had smashed the GMD's strongest bases of support and left a vacuum of political power, like an empty page waiting to be inscribed. In September 1937, when a sailor from Osaka captured the diary of a student in Shanghai, the young Chinese man's lackadaisical narrative of his carefree days in the great metropolis—taking exams, going to foreign movies, and smoking about the house—gave way to the sternly disciplined Japanese military voice of the soldier as he made the diary his own.[53] The Japanese military intended to fill the space created by the Nationalist collapse with its promise of Asian brotherhood, but this turned out largely to mean the subjugation of the Chinese to Japanese interests. For each capital or base destroyed, however, the GMD simply built a new one, mobilizing man and text to continue their resistance and preserve their legitimacy, and the two forces began a subtler war for "hearts and minds."

RECONSTITUTION AND MEMORY: DIALOGUE BETWEEN STATE AND SELF

In 1940, the Japanese at home were enjoying the "2,600th Anniversary" of the Japanese Empire, a celebration of "imperial Japan at its zenith";[54] by contrast, the war in China had become a quagmire, and the Japanese armed forces struggled to "pacify" the areas that they putatively controlled.[55] In September 1942, in Hebei Province, a Japanese army officer, speaking to Chinese initiates in the "New Citizens' Youth Group," admonished his subjects to abandon their "selfish" and "dependent" ways and "temper" their hearts in order to earn their independence from Japanese rule. One of his pupils submitted a composition for the officer's approval. The student used the mobilizational rhetoric of the GMD, except he now spoke as a supporter of the Japanese army, spitting out phrases such as "because those communist bandits had not one bit of strength in them, they fell easily and were wiped out."[56] The Chinese language essay was saved by the Japanese, presumably for its excellence, and survives in a Tokyo military archive. At nearly the same time, Japanese captives of the GMD began writing diaries, with the encouragement of their captors, to embrace peace through self-criticism.[57] The confusing, divided nature of authority from 1939 to 1945 was mirrored in the hybrid voices of the diaries themselves—combining elements of discipline, experience, doubt, and anger—as individuals situated themselves, through self-narrative, inside unfamiliar and unstable political terrain.[58]

Before looking at their process of adaptation to a new political order, however, it is necessary to examine what authorities were trying to have them say. Japanese and Chinese servicemen were broken by the massacres that took place in China in 1937 and 1938; these were cuts inflicted not only on human bodies but also on political space, individual subjectivities, and discourse. Governments, mass media, and individual servicemen all tried to heal these wounds and build a new order on editorial cutting boards and committee meeting tables. Wang Jingwei's cooperative Nanjing government signaled an emerging political space previously unknown to China, even as it drew life from the language of the departed GMD. Indeed, in imitation of Chiang Kai-shek's "New Life Movement," the collaborationist Wang Jingwei government organized a "Committee to Promote the Movement for New Citizens" *(xinguomin yundong);* among other things, it closely followed GMD practices when training a new corps of cadres in leadership, China's revolutionary history, and pan-Asianism through guided diary writing.[59] Meanwhile, the GMD itself continued to fight physical and ideological wars from their new capital in Chongqing, offering alternative political and discursive authority. Although we are accustomed to thinking of historical memory as a postwar event, attempts at control of memorialization occurred during the war on the battlefield (military), at home (state), and were aided by private enterprise (mass media). We have already examined the movement of experience to language; now we can turn our attention to how authorities attempted to organize language into memory.

State and military officials on both sides quickly established a system to manipulate the understanding of the war, and the most important objective was to keep the chaos of the battlefield from affecting home-front mobilization. On the Chinese side, the GMD needed to maintain a large enough force to resist Japan. Although the central government took steps to ensure that military dependents were freed from tax burdens and supported financially, local governments also coordinated efforts with the high courts to handle criminal behavior among servicemen (damaging to public support) and family members who attacked draft officers.[60] In China, home and battlefield were frequently too close for comfort, but the GMD nevertheless tried to control correspondence between servicemen and their families through prefectural governments.[61] The Japanese had similar concerns, although they had an easier time keeping the home front and the reality of war as far apart as possible. On 22 February 1938, the Home Ministry advised the Ministry of War to have military police conduct examinations *(ken'etsu)* of men going home at seaports and on troopships. They were searching for evidence of any "malicious criminal activity" *(akushitsu hankō)*, but they were doing so to "ensure military order" *(gunki wo shinsa shi)*. This directive presumably included those who might harbor "antiwar sentiment" *(hansen shisō)* but also those who, perhaps in imitation of behavior not unusual for the battlefield, might commit brutal crimes in Japan that would reflect poorly on the armed forces.[62] In February 1939, following the fall of Wuhan and repatriation of some men from the front, a Japanese military official circulated a notice condemning soldiers' raw narratives of the battlefield, as well as other offenses that affected discipline or threatened to show a "lack of public support for the China policy."[63] Back at home, the Japanese press cooperated with authorities under the 1925 Peace Preservation Law to eschew publishing battlefield narratives that might erode public support, even while trying to make the people feel "closer" to fighting men through the clever use of propaganda.[64] Local chapters of the Imperial Reservists, military police, the special higher police, and neighborhood associations monitored servicemen's behavior and tried to keep them from disturbing those at home.

The armed forces and the state cooperated to guide wartime remembrance rituals as well. On the battlefield, the Japanese military made a conscious effort to orchestrate memorial services.[65] First, officers organized these services *(ireisai)* for the war dead *(senbotsusha)* in occupied areas. Religious practices included Buddhist and Shintoist rituals, led by the battalion commander and occasionally by unit priests.[66] Chinese servicemen carried out similar acts of remembrance, sometimes leaving evidence behind: GMD officers erected a grave near Xuzhou commemorating the death of Sixty-Second Division Battalion Commander Kui Kaiqin, and unit memorial services to commemorate the first anniversary of the war were ubiquitous in 1938.[67] GMD officer Wang Wenrong described his visit to the graves of "unknown soldiers" near Xi'an:

> We visited the public graveyard for the Fifty-Seventh Division, which was surrounded by earthen walls on four sides—it was crudely constructed. In front of [one of the] walls was a small memorial monument, and in front of that there were many small flowers growing. It was very rough, and it makes you feel wounded inside. These warriors of the people [*minzu zhanshi*], I hope you are resting in peace. I hope that the local government will look after this memorial and allows the old folks to tend to it, so that these dead soldiers can be at peace [*jiangshi anshin*].[68]

Some celebrations, such as "Double Ten Day" and memorials for Sun Yat-sen, were highly ritualized mobilization festivals that refocused self-discipline toward state goals. Division Commander Ai exhorted his troops:

> If one's heart is insufficient, nothing can be achieved, so I hope that everyone—officer, soldier, and the people—can maintain a spirit of enduring hardship and fury, no matter what may come. You must remember that we here are righteous [*zhengyi*]; therein you will find absolute resolve and your mind will not retreat a single step. . . . On this day of memorial you must think back on the past, and meticulously self-reflect [*zixiang fanxing*] in order to reform so that you do not commit errors in the future. Go reflect on yourself, castigate yourself, encourage yourself [*qu fanxing ziji, huiguo ziji, mianli ziji*].[69]

The GMD also commissioned films to memorialize their war dead, which was their attempt to use servicemen's sacrifices as an emotional appeal for support and unity in the rear *(houfang)*. In one example, uniformed men and women stood over the body of a fallen officer singing a hortatory military ballad, while a GMD star, the symbol of the party and the national flag, faded in superimposed over the body and the vocalists, binding them together in an ethereal light.[70] Military commanders' ambitions for memorial hegemony, however, were not successful. In a manner similar to their imitation of official diary writing, servicemen spontaneously conducted their own services when priests and officials were not present, leaving simple grave markers behind them for other units to see. This did not dissuade the authorities from their ambitions, however: most famously, Matsui Iwane oversaw the formal memorial for the entire army in Nanjing after it fell in December 1937. As if they were merely another knot in a net of remembrance ritual, Yamamoto's unit held their first official memorial service for their war dead in occupied Chaozhou, directly after the New Year and only three weeks after the fall of Nanjing.[71] As soon as the rituals of remembrance and conquest were complete and Nanjing was controlled by the Japanese Empire, letters from home poured in for the men, "consolation packages" arrived, and the Japanese military established a "comfort station" in the former GMD capital.[72] Far away in Chaozhou, Guangdong Province, Yamamoto, even while pitying local prostitutes, indulged in similar "pleasures" with his friends, and authorities continued to soothe soldiers into thinking that they had "conquered" China.

The state and the mass media worked closely together in China and Japan to shape the language of wartime experience by controlling correspondence between the battlefield and the home front.[73] Although manuscript correspondence in China during the war is nearly impossible to come by today, wartime publications certainly selected "appropriate" examples for the general public.[74] A Chinese reporter wrote that he read a letter sent to the front by a seven-year-old boy who proclaimed, "When I get big, I'm definitely coming out there with you guys to kill those despicable Japs!" and laughed alongside the men.[75] Besides these comfort letters *(weilaoxin)* written for the general audience at the front, newspapers published correspondence addressed to individuals as well. One little girl wrote of her experience consoling wounded men in the field hospital: "I saw many wounded soldiers and, uncle, I was very upset. My cousin told me that they were wounded protecting us and I hated those Japanese demons."[76] Chinese servicemen also wrote back, convincing their loved ones, like the Japanese, that their sacrifice for the nation did not violate their obligations to the household. In "An Undelivered Letter Home," a GMD serviceman proclaimed he would respect his mother's wishes to "honor the clan and ancestors" *(guang zong yuan zu)*, "add to the glory of the family" *(gu li zeng guang)*, and "fight for the honor of our people" *(wei zu zheng guang)* by striking a blow against Japanese imperialism. How could he reconcile giving his life to the nation when he had responsibilities as a filial son? He replied: "To be loyal to the nation is to be filial to one's parents."[77]

Japanese wartime correspondence that passed censors used remarkably similar language—just like their farewell letters examined earlier—binding the interests of individuals and households to national goals. Japanese and Chinese servicemen who wrote letters similarly swore "bloody revenge" on their enemies. In Japanese censored correspondence *(gunji yūbin,* usually postcards), one serviceman promised to "smash my bones and destroy my body for the sake of the nation,"[78] just as a GMD soldier, witnessing the Japanese "splintering our national territory," would "be willing to split my body and smash my bones for mother just as I would plunge into boiling water and leap into fire for the nation."[79] Despite sharing their views on battlefield sacrifice, Xie Bingying, as a woman, could only "console" servicemen and not fight herself; Chinese wartime discourse established a gender boundary that was difficult to transgress. Likewise, Japanese media corporations produced postcards depicting men on the front and women working at home in the fields and factories.[80] Nevertheless, war correspondence was able to frame identities at home and on the battlefield in favor of wartime mobilization not simply due to government intimidation but because these efforts parasitically attached themselves to the only tie between loved ones in East Asia.

As Gregory Kasza described, the Japanese state directed the mass media through various tools, including a series of forced mergers to eliminate independent local news and a paper rationing system that privileged pro-government publications.[81] In fact, most segments of the Japanese mass media during the Second World War were already well prepared to give the common soldier a heroic narrative. Private Ueda Masaki observed reporters from the *Asahi Mainichi* driving about in their automobile, taking photos, and firing furiously across the wireless telegraph at the same time the Japanese artillery blasted Nanjing.[82] Although embedded journalism had expanded greatly during the Manchurian Incident (1931), reportage authors covered the war between the Japanese and the GMD to an unprecedented degree.[83] The triumphant return of Japanese "tales of heroism" *(bidan)* from previous eras of reportage was perhaps inevitable but surprising nonetheless in its magnitude. *Kingu* published *bidan* written by (or cowritten by) Japanese servicemen that scripted every aspect of a soldier's life: descriptions of farewells to family and friends, induction into the unit, intense fighting in Jiangnan, heroic deaths, and the sad return of servicemen's remains. These accounts even provided dialogues from which servicemen could draw lessons regarding appropriate language and comportment for daily life on the battlefield. One commanding officer consoled another who began sobbing over his men's sacrifices: "You did a good job, son, and it was tough. . . . No need to cry. It's war. Don't cry, now. Here, how about some whiskey?"[84] Even *kamishibai,* or "paper plays," tried to capture the lived experience and dreams of Japanese men serving in mainland China.[85] Designed primarily for selling candy to children, *kamishibai,* a series of illustrations narrated by the candy salesman, also served to make soldiering both accessible and palatable to a general audience. Such plays frequently equated soldiering with adventurism, such as the myth of Momotarō. A soldier's desire to see his mother was a popular theme in wartime media, aimed at binding men in the same unit more closely together. Nevertheless, bringing home and hearth to the battlefield made such texts highly unstable and open to interpretation: Japanese servicemen working for the GMD used the same theme as a basis for antiwar propaganda.[86] Although some might find these materials rather kitschy today, they were avidly consumed and provided a template for many soldiers' personal writings about war.

Chinese wrtiers were certainly not strangers to mobilizational texts or "the literature of blood and tears," but the war was a transformative moment for Chinese journalism. As professional writers struggled to unify themselves and capture the voice of the fighting man, the boundary between personal narrative and public remembrance became increasingly blurred.[87] One of the newspapers most deeply entangled with the project of giving meaning to servicemen's experiences was *Field News* (Zhenzhong ribao). *Field News,* published by the Fourth War Area's Political Division, gave up considerable space in order to serialize selections from Battalion Commander Yu Yanling's diary as early as the end of October 1937.[88] Like Yu's account, the October 1937 publication of Shi Hezhang's diary from the battle for Shanghai was a part of a general mobilization effort across the south during the final days of GMD-controlled Jiangnan. Shi passionately described the seesaw battles of the "Eastern Front" *(dongxian)* in vivid, often grotesque language: "That night, we held the enemy's former position inside the trenches amidst the smell of fresh blood, and with a large pile of corpses; we trampled over them, but their flesh was already smashed beyond recognition." As GMD officers had tried to achieve in their field diaries, however, Shi too reinscribed the values of the Nationalist army in order to mitigate the horror of this slaughter. From this repulsive mess of blood and gore arose, in startling contrast, heroes to be remembered. Riding in on a white horse, shrouded in fog like a mythical warrior, Shi's platoon commander, a young but battle-hardened man, gave his men a rousing speech:

> I remember he said in a stern voice: "We're soldiers—we don't fear death or seek riches; we protect our citizens [*renmin*], our people [*minzu*]. . . . We must shed our last drop of blood for the nation. A soldier's blood is as beautiful as a flower. . . . We must bear witness to our own beautiful flowers, so we should let flow our last drop of blood on the front line . . ." Truly, he was cut out to be our commander. After he finished speaking, he fell for a moment into thought, and then would not speak.

Shi's memorial text, however, was still dappled with inklings of uncertainty: what was the commander feeling when he found himself unable to speak? Later, when the Japanese counterattacked their position with bombardment from land, air, and sea, Shi could only cry out in dismay, "Ah! The cannons of the enemy won't stop for one moment, and when we all retreated, the rear was hit from the air and the sea!" He continued on with disconnected snapshots of the battlefield: "more than a few of our men were sacrificed under their artillery that night. There was no moonlight, only the glare of fire, spreading everywhere during the night! . . . Once this was a lively village, now only a pile of rubble; it was a dangerous layout, not easy to defend."[89] The movement from strictly controlled narrative to a tangled collection of disparate scenes is similar to the literary process later employed by reportage authors such as Shi Tuo in his *Shanghai Correspondence*.[90] With the smooth intermigration of language between reportage and diary writing, dangerously irreconcilable issues of life and art are immediately threatening: which is the simulacrum?

After the fall of Jiangnan, printing companies in Chinese-controlled cities such as Wuhan and Chongqing were contracted by both the GMD and major newspapers to produce large quantities of soldier narratives for various audiences. Well-known newspapers including the *Wuhan Daily* published articles such as "Visiting Soldiers on the Moonlit Battlefield" and, although written primarily for those behind the front lines, described soldiers' stoic endurance under artillery bombardment and their indefatigable spirit. Aside from delineating what these men needed from those behind the front line, the author of the article wrote, "When our artillery fired, they yelled, 'Look! That one got 'em. Ha!'" The author also wrote that GMD soldiers, who relied primarily on an inconsistent supply of newspapers and field reports *(zhenzhong shubao)*, crowded around him and begged for information, asking, "How is it over there? How is it on such-and-such front?" These articles tried to give voices and personalities to Chinese servicemen, even as they made them convenient tools for mobilization—men who "look at their life as a paradise, and none see it as painful—truly they are the great soldiers of the Revolutionary Army" *(weida de gemingjunren)*.[91] The GMD also had its own in-house publishing industry, run by and for servicemen, epitomized by the publication *MP Weekly*. Founded by Li Zhuoyuan on 30 April 1938 (before the fall of Wuhan), it was printed by the Eastern Military Police Command Headquarters' Political Training Division *(Dong xianbing qu silingbu zhengxunchu)* as a "tool for MP education" which included, among other things, the Confucian-inspired philosophy of "rectifying oneself so that others might be pacified" *(xiu ji yi an ren)*. Thus, they released articles such as "I'm a Soldier" by Ze Guohua, in which Ze promised, among other impressive proclamations, to "spill my blood to cleanse our national humiliation."[92] The intended audience for the paper was clear, as the editors compiled advice most useful to officers, such as how to inspect units for hygienic and medical *(weisheng)* violations.[93] The Chinese mass media, then, like its counterpart in Japan, searched for coherent narratives that were deemed useful for continual mobilization, aiming these stories at the public but also, importantly, at men on the battlefield.

After Jiangnan fell into Japanese hands, some newspapers, such as Ma Shuli's *Frontline Daily* (Qianxian ribao, Third War Zone), made more of an effort than the large dailies, like *Field News* had done before, to approximate soldiers' language, often by allowing servicemen to write pieces. Although *Frontline* was distributed widely among civilians, articles in the newspaper—particularly those written by servicemen—many times mirrored the language used in GMD field diaries, suggesting that the intended audience also included men at the front. In "Remembering the Bloody Battle for Jiangnan," Chen Shuxun pieced together for his audience a memory of a costly victory on the banks of the Yangtze achieved through the sacrifices of his battalion. The text is rife with military expressions easily found in GMD war diaries. He begins with a lyrical snapshot of the calm, peaceful Yangtze flowing by, followed by the menacing arrival of five Japanese ships. His battalion "swore to resist [them] to the death" *(shisi dikang)*, and half of their number were annihilated under a Japanese naval bombardment, "fully realizing the 'live together, die together' spirit" but ultimately forcing them to retreat. When they returned with reserves, they "felt the time to wipe out the enemy had come," whereupon they attacked the Japanese at 1:00 a.m. "fiercely like savage tigers who had shown their spirit" *(ru menghu chushen ban de)*, sending the Japanese "scurrying away." The Japanese shelled them from the sea again, Chen recalls, sending the Chinese back for supplies and reinforcements. In the final stage of this seesaw battle (typical of those in the early fighting in Shanghai), the GMD and Japanese units fought at close range, thereby eliminating the Japanese navy's ability to overwhelm the Chinese forces with aerial and sea bombardment. The Japanese infantrymen could not overcome the GMD in battle, and Chen described their disordered flight as "hurried as a dog that lost its master, as panicked as a fish that tumbles into a net."[94]

Newspapers were walking a fine line between the mobilizational rhetoric of reportage and the chaotic language of the battlefield. Chen's use of GMD military ideology and vivid battlefield description seems to have come directly out of a GMD field diary, except that now, months after the event described and in the relative safety of Wuhan, he tied these disparate events together into a narrative with coherent meaning: the article impresses upon the reader the indomitable élan of the Chinese soldier, even in the face of a technologically superior foe. Where precarious narratives did arise, they did so fleetingly: *MP Weekly* briefly carried Lin Dafu's hospital diary, which was littered with aggressive language. Lin, a military policeman, accosted his hospital neighbor, whom he called "A-kun," for dumping his medicine out (in order to stay off the front), saying: "Can't you take the pain?" Later, when Japanese planes bombed a building one hundred meters from his window, he exploded: "You vile, savage bastards! Your final days are coming soon! How long do you think we'll sit and watch your barbarous acts? Huh? *I* will avenge these dead and stricken comrades! I swear it, I must swear it!"[95] For the most part, however, newspapers stuck to "noble tales" *(jiahua),* various reminisces *(zhuiji, zhuiyi, jinian,* and so forth), articles, war reportage pieces, and straight news—in other words, narratives that made more sense.

In addition to the daily reporting, both sides published cumulative works of reportage fiction and diary writing that looked back on the momentous events of the recent past; in effect, consciously or not, editors took account of the stories published episodically throughout the early stages of the war and then attempted to organize them into a form of public memory. The Japanese homeland and centers of Chinese resistance, such as Wuhan and Chongqing, experienced an explosion of war narratives in novel and novella form. Authors such as Hino Ashihei became rich and famous by deriving authority from witnessing the battlefield even while maintaining narrative distance from the fighting man—ultimately establishing themselves as unassailable, unsullied experts. When *Mugi to Heitai* was published in 1938, two afterwords to the text, one by a certain "Lieutenant Takasaka" and another by one "Umemoto," attest to Hino's status as a soldier and aver that his bravery exceeded that of any reporter. Even as Hino tried to create unity among Japanese soldiers (and his readership), however, he always narrated his subjects from a distance—from the roof of his automobile or on a hill. In his uncensored 1938 manuscript, Hino went so far as to distance himself from the horrible crimes Japanese servicemen were committing abroad, stating simply: "I had not become a demon."[96] Hino and antiwar authors such as Ishikawa Tatsuzō required such authority to narrate the war as objective observers.

Chinese authors typically attempted a closer union with the "fighting man," making large statements such as "In ten days of life in the war zone, I have had a taste of this kind of life soldiers live, I understand them, I am able to see through to the despondent and courageous moods in their inner hearts. . . . Unless you have personally had a taste of mortar attacks and charges, the solemn sacrifices of our Nineteenth Army are impossible to understand!"[97] Leftist writers had been proclaiming their proximity to the working man since the May Fourth era, and they had already begun the "patriotic" process of replacing "proletariat" with "soldier" in their discourse. Still, GMD-aligned authors without ties to the CCP spoke similarly or were simply soldiers themselves. In fact, the Communists did little fighting in the early stages of the war, which may be why their authors were so eager to "become one with" the average grunt. Readers—soldier and civilian alike—hungered for tales from the fighting man himself. Consequently, especially during the final tumultuous months of the defense of Wuhan, the GMD and various publishing houses cooperating with the war effort published war diaries such as those of Yu Yanling, Hao Mengling (posthumous), and, most famously, Xie Bingying.

Xie Bingying was one of the most well-known war reportage writers in modern Chinese history, first making her name known during the Northern Expedition (1926–1928). Nevertheless, she was never paid for her *New War Diary* (Xin congjun riji). Published in July 1938, before the fall of Wuhan, it was based on notes she took in a pocket-sized notepad four inches long and two inches wide, written in characters "as small as peas."[98] Despite the similarity between this title and that of her Northern Expedition diary *(Congjun riji),* Xie wasted no time alerting her audience to the fact that this war was categorically different than those that preceded it: "How is it that, during the Northern Expedition, everywhere we went, tens of thousands dropped their ploughs and came to welcome us, but now that we're fighting the Japanese, when the people should be exhilarated, everywhere it seems cold and desolate? Where did they all go?" She wondered how the GMD could achieve victory without the help of the people—a thinly veiled appeal to her civilian audience. Significantly, Xie devoted considerable space to channeling the voices of her male comrades coming back from the front; these ad hoc interviews crystallized much of GMD military discourse for her readership and doubtlessly appealed to servicemen as well. Phrases uttered by wounded men might as well have come directly out of a GMD field diary: "The enemy soldiers are really afraid of dying, and they're weak at fighting. If they weren't hitting us with aerial and artillery bombardment, we would have killed every one of them long ago."[99]

Xie's position as a writer was an interesting one: during the Northern Expedition, she carried a firearm while on the march with Chiang Kai-shek's army. In this war, where women were not allowed into regular units, she always made it clear, through descriptions of her writing implements and feelings of impotency, that she was now a woman of letters and not a soldier. Nevertheless, Xie also actively tried to shape the direction of servicemen's discourse through her own writing. First, she attempted to capture the moment when returning officers would narrate their battle experiences for their comrades. Then she inserted her own voice in a clearly didactic tone. On 14 October 1938, a battered officer observed to her: "I think war is in reality unbearably cruel! Men are the highest form of life [ren wei wanwu zhi ling] and should therefore love peace. Why then must there be war?" She replied,

> We all know war is terrible, and those evil criminals who start wars—those profiteering, unjust, and savage animals who despise humanitarianism—the militarists and imperialists—they are the common enemies of the human race, and we must wipe them out, or there will always be war. When that day comes when we have struck down all the world's imperialists, then we will have realized a true peace.[100]

Books such as Xie's New War Diary were printed on cheap paper and sold for little, making them widely available to men of all ranks and the urban citizens who provided support. When Xie wrote disparagingly of "Chinese traitors" (hanjian) and Japanese propaganda leaflets (which encouraged GMD troops to surrender), she deployed her authority as a witness of the battlefield and a literary figure in order to engage in the bitter ideological warfare with the Japanese that followed the actual fighting. By circulating her Diary, Xie was posing as a model for proper thought, inviting readers to imitate her example.

Japanese and Chinese mobilization forces in government and mass media drew on personal diaries for authenticity, but servicemen were also inextricably connected to the language and literature that gave life to their traumatic experiences. In fact, some were directly connected: Yamanaka Sadao was a film director and deeply involved in theater, but he was also participating in the war directly as an infantry sergeant. His uncompleted and often incoherent field diary *(jinchū nisshi)* contained scenes he imagined for a future war film, intermingled seamlessly with descriptions of his daily life. He invented gags and silly dialogues starring personalities he knew from the war:

> —"What's *wode?*"—"*Wode* is me in Chinese."—"Oh, really?"—"Hey, Wode private first class!"—"*Wode* private first class? What are you saying?"—"It's you, isn't it? Wode."—"No, *wode* is 'me.'"—"Yeah, so, you're Wode Private First Class." "No, you idiot, *wode* is Chinese for 'me.' You don't know a damn thing."—"What the hell did you say? *You're* the stupid ass."

Yamanaka's ad hoc mixture of the theatrical and the quotidian became so ingrained through diary writing that even his military drills came to resemble "play acting" *(gokko)* in his fertile imagination (and capacity for biting sarcasm). For Yamanaka, fantasy and reality were not meaningfully distinguishable—that is, until he was killed at Xuzhou in 1938.[101] Nevertheless, Yamanaka seemed to have accepted not only that art and language provide us with the means through which we remember experience but also the converse: that language and art are impossible without experience. Why else would the experience of war inspire so much artistic production, suffused with assertions concerning the author's authority and the text's authenticity?

One explanation is political: in desperate times, authority can aid collective efforts through organized leadership. Thus, as Xi Qun proclaimed in 1938, "we have understood the solemnity of theater and its forcefulness [zhandouxing], so we have abandoned the idealism of 'art for pleasure' and destroyed the fantasy of 'art for art's sake.'"[102] Perhaps it is best, however, to move beyond simplistic realpolitik understandings of how individuals contributed to wartime discourse. If one is willing to accept that literary forces helped determine the content of battlefield narratives, then one should also allow that battlefield experience was in most cases the foundation of wartime literature; art and lived experience are inextricably linked. Kimura Genzaemon, who was normally a very dry writer, seemed to be filled with creative inspiration when he wrote, "In the endless plains we formed a long line like a snake, a military formation of one million solemnly advancing. One man in this million, I gaze on them tirelessly. Surely this is a new form of three-dimensional art for the twentieth century."[103] More often than not, the struggle between power and the individual reveals the triumph of the former; that being said, even during a time of national mobilization, influences on soldiers' diaries need not always have emanated from reportage or training manuals.

Azuma Shirō became one of the most famous war diarists when he published his records in postwar Japan, but the process behind the production of these texts was extremely complicated. First, when he was decommissioned in 1940, this self-described "literary youth" rewrote his field notes into a diary *(nikki)* and did so in a steady hand untroubled by any immediate threat.[104] Putting one diary on top of the other, he created a textual palimpsest in trying to narrate experience—he added meaning to recorded evidence through subsequent written interpretations, like a Confucian scholar's official commentary on one of the Chinese classics. Azuma's later edition expanded on what might have been inscrutable in his original pocket diary: when he attempted to free Chinese women captured by his murderous comrades, he used his field diary to try to communicate with them, "I wrote in my pocket notebook, 'You run 11pm.' . . . and at last they understood they were fated to be killed tomorrow, were afraid, and cried aloud." He styled his diary as a work of soldier fiction *(heitai bungaku)* in imitation of writers such as Hino Ashihei, but Azuma also added other literary influences. When recording the ill-fated women's recapture, he preserved the lecherous dialogue between his comrades ("I think I'll satisfy this broad") as it would appear in racy Shōwa-era fiction; when he saw one of the girls being taken into a nearby home, he compared her to the tragic noble ladies kidnapped by the demon Shutendōji. Despite Azuma's efforts, however, the reconstituted diary did not erase all evidence of the original text and its mobilizational rhetoric. During the battle for Nanjing, he wrote,

> The sergeant's sword shone before my eyes, cold and white. The trench terminated in a grass field. The grasses and weeds wrapped around and sometimes clung to our boots. When we had walked about one hundred meters, we heard the sound of rushing water. The small stream gave forth a pitiable sound as it flowed. . . . In my heart there was only one phrase: "I'll be first, before all the others." I followed behind the sergeant. Our enemies were at

the top of this hill. *I'll surpass the sergeant and go first,* I thought. The sergeant was moving ahead of me with utter stealth. My heart ordered that I should go ahead of him, but, no matter what, fear would not quicken my step. Going first could mean instant death. Going first was still a very difficult thing, but following others is easy.

Nor did his diary erase moments of weakness: Azuma felt impotent before a wounded comrade who begged to be shot and wrote, "Nanjing is near. Maybe we can go home alive?" Coming upon a GMD officer gasping for air in a trench among the dead, he found himself strangely "endeared" to this man, "a hero who will die for his fatherland. He committed no crime. He was following his orders." In the end, Azuma used his diary to fuse his literary self with the soldier, but this was a constant conflict. When trying to describe the murder of some seven thousand unarmed GMD captives, Azuma wrote:

> This herd of ignorant sheep, lacking both discipline and order, walked in and out of the darkness trading whispers. That this pack of beasts was the "enemy" who had until yesterday fired artillery upon us is unthinkable. . . . [The next morning] While we were on patrol, groups of two or three hundred captives were assigned to each battalion and killed. I heard the only officer among them, an army doctor, knew where their secret provisions were held, and asked us to use it to feed them. Why were all these men killed? I have no idea. But I cannot think of this as inhuman [*hijindōteki*] or horrible [*hisan*]. One can only consider it as an incalculable, unjust [*futō*] act. Seven thousand people erased in one moment is a seemingly unbelievable truth [*jijitsu*]. On the battlefield, life has no more value than a fistful of rice. Our lives are discarded in a great trash bin called war—thinking thus, I felt a terrible hatred for war.

By combining literary and authoritative voices, Azuma did not aim to merely create a work of war fiction—he aimed at writing *the* work of war fiction, at the same time producing a personal record that was also truthful. It was beautifully written, bringing in new possibilities for expression and identity; for Azuma, as it had been for the supporters of the war effort and the nationalistic officers of the 1930s, his diary was the true work of a real soldier—it was his mellifluous "mirror of truth."[105]

After the trauma and excitement of personal experience on the battlefield, men turned to reconstituting their knowledge about themselves and their world; the military, state, and mass media scrambled to assist. In fact, these forces combined their efforts to produce new kinds of field diaries for servicemen. They restructured the physical form of the diary, in an effort to align the content of the writing of the individual with the directions of the state. Until 1937, most of the blank books used as personal field diaries were produced for civilians. After 1937, blank diaries, as well as the "War Notebooks" *(jūgun techō)*, were designed especially for servicemen. These mass produced pocket-sized books contained addenda such as popular military ballads *(gunka)*, handy Chinese phrases ("Who's there? Stop! Who are you?"), and photographs of the "peerless Imperial Armed Forces" *(muteki kōgun)* on land, sea, and air.[106] Although they were not (yet) drenched with the symbols and language of emperor worship and state Shintoism, they provided a forum in which a man might be both a proud soldier and an individual force for Japanese imperialism. Thus the state extended its guiding hand further into the minds of its citizens. Some men, however, would continue to slip between their fingers.

NEW WORLD DISORDERS:
JAPANESE SERVICEMEN REASSEMBLED

In mid-December 1937, medical officer Taniguchi Kazuo noted that Chinese refugees were flooding back into cities in Shanxi with "smiling faces."[107] As the heavy fighting of 1937–1938 began to die down, Japanese newspapers, novels, and films flooded into China. The Japanese army produced cheery postcards for soldiers to send back home that depicted happy Chinese children, embraced by the empire's heroes, waving the flags of Japan's mainland puppet governments. Blank diaries published after 1940 commemorated important Japanese military victories.[108] Did this work? Was any soldier truly fooled into thinking that Japan was somehow victorious?

Powerful forces in government and media shaped the public record of the conflict in what was increasingly a war of propaganda. Both sides attempted to force life into their patchwork creatures of politics and popular discourse through, among other means, the lightning-like powers of the modern mass media. Caught between the competing political spaces created in Nanjing and Chongqing (and, for 1938, Wuhan)—namely, eastern China and western China—servicemen continued to use diary writing to situate themselves in new contexts. This section will thus analyze how the servicemen from Chapter 2 made sense of themselves after the most heated battles concluded and they found themselves occupiers of a foreign land. Furthermore, in order to evaluate how wartime discourse and battlefield experience affected servicemen's personal writing, it is necessary to examine the diaries of men who were subject to these forces.

As military staff officers and cooperative popular press editors made efforts to shape and profit from remembrance, individual servicemen found their own ways of doing so in their diaries and other documents. After the fall of Taiyuan, Shanxi Province, Taniguchi found that being a representative of the Japanese Empire in nearby Yuci afforded him copious free time. Taniguchi initially felt some remorse for the powers he had been given: when Chinese residents attempted to return to their home in Yuci, they were curtly rebuffed by Taniguchi, who wrote, "It is actually their home, and here I am acting as if I am the owner. It is really too bad." He also began to write an article, almost certainly based on his diary record, about the dramatic and narrow escape from certain death he had experienced in November: "Maybe when it is finished," he wrote, "I might be so bold as to submit it to the Empress." Taniguchi never strayed far from his role as an extension of empire and, even after everything he had seen on the battlefield, managed to reattach himself to the sources of that authority.[109]

As the pace of the war slowed, Sakaguchi Jirō wrote letters (censored) and read newspapers even as his unit was involved in intense battles with retreating GMD regulars. In his home prefecture's paper, the *Shinanō Mainichi Shinbun,* he saw a photo of a corporal wounded in his unit and an article that proclaimed that his division's battles "were of historic importance." Sakaguchi dutifully copied the "Song of His Imperial Majesty," which was sent to army dependents in Nagano along with a small cash award. At the same time, however, Sakaguchi, a veteran of the Manchurian Incident, knew better than to take official news channels too seriously: "They said that Shandong has become independent, and that there is no anti-Japanese resistance, but I also heard that we don't know if this is true." Sakaguchi continually wrote of how the sights and sounds of conquered China (his unit raised the flag of the new Chinese government over conquered towns in early December) reminded him of home and, on days with good weather, proclaimed that it would be a fine day to go home (trium-phantly). In a letter to his father, he wrote that his three months abroad had passed "like a dream" and speculated that he might return soon. Through-out his entries during the transition from heavy combat to occupation, he had difficulty resolving his desire to go home and his sense of duty.

It was, in fact, a personal tragedy back home that proved a crucial turn-ing point for Sakaguchi, and his delicately constructed self underwent a change. A week after Nanjing fell, he received news that his father had passed away. The heretofore stoic, disciplined infantryman poured out, "I thought, 'Is this a dream?' and was caught in this tragedy." In the very next line, he noted with characteristic brevity, "Our objective—to punish the Chinese—is finished." For Sakaguchi to write this, after priding himself as an obedient soldier for so long, is quite surprising. While recording the preparations for the New Year's celebrations and establishing a new coun-try, however, he composed descriptions of his "first" and "second" major engagements, attempting to put the events of the year behind him. On the first day of the new year in 1938, he wrote that he "would not be lax" in building the new government in northern China and that, "I will go bravely forth filled with new hope, and strive with a new energy." Sakaguchi's be-havior, however, became less heroic. His duties shifted away from engaging in major assaults toward minor anticommunist "expeditions," and for the first time he acknowledged "playing with Korean pussy" (Chōsenpii to asobu)—that is, visiting "comfort women."

These dubious pleasures, however, would not exorcise the specter of his father's death or bridge the distance from home. Waking up from bad dreams, he wondered whether he was becoming "neurasthenic" (shinkei sui-jaku) and encouraged himself in his diary to be more "light-hearted" (har-eyaka na kokoro), but while on a lonesome guard duty, he finally conceded to his diary: "With every thought of home and dad, I try to forget but I cannot. I think of the future, but it merely reminds me of the past." He could not have imagined that he would be spending the next New Year's in an even more depressed mood. Trapped on top of a remote mountain in January 1939, bereft of contact with the battalion or Japan (even after the fall of the last GMD stronghold in Wuhan), he could see no way home. A few days later, however, it struck Sakaguchi that he had transformed into a resilient and capable fighting man, and this seemed to give him some final comfort:

I want to stop living in holes in the ground and go home [even if] temporarily. Another victorious spring here at the Holy War, and, looking back, I think our work is pretty impressive. This just confirms the fact that we still have a job to carry out: punitive expeditions and working hard to build northern China—striving even harder than before. When I think about it, I've been sleeping on top chestnut shells all this time, and yet there's nothing wrong with me physically; when I consider the fact that I've conquered all of these hardships, although it has a limit, a man's body really goes quite far. Even when it is your [own body], you can't help but be surprised.[110]

Even officers such as Corporal Kawakami Yoshimitsu were thrilled to hear the news of Nanjing's fall and imagined Matsui's triumphant entry into the city "as a gay affair, a procession with lamps held high in the night. The day of our triumphant homecoming is close." Although he was stuck in desolate Shanxi, he calculated when the army might send him home and wrote, "I'm living full of energy on the battlefield now." Like many others, he ate, drank, and made merry every day, "since there are no battles anywhere," repeating the phrase "these are the fat days." However, even as Kawakami's days grew "fatter" and he amused himself with "Korean and Chinese pussy," he missed home more and more, stating, "The only thing that consoles me is the sun and moon in [a clear] sky." Even his New Year's resolutions, outside of "promising to splinter my bones and smash my body for the Emperor," centered around business ambitions he would pursue when he returned home to Japan, and in the days following he was assailed by memories of New Year's celebrations past and fantasies of what those at home were doing in the present to pass the holiday. Speaking with his comrades about the events of the previous year, he remembered a New Year's trip to scenic Matsujima and the fun he had at Tsurubashi: "When memories of dad from nine years ago came to me, I just couldn't take it. No matter how much I try to forget, I just can't do it. . . . Today I won't do anything but sleep."

By February, Kawakami felt sick at hearing the phrase "I want to go home" so often. Soon after the New Year, he was dispatched into the frigid, bitter Shanxi mountains on "punitive expeditions" against GMD and CCP forces scattered in the hills, but his unit claimed only one casualty against an enemy patrol for the whole campaign—a captive whom they killed—and

suffered one casualty among their own men—a private whose grenade exploded in his hand. As time dragged on, Kawakami led one "expedition"
after another as platoon commander and fell into an almost daily habit of
chasing down women when at rest. By the time he was killed by Chinese
troops in September 1938, Kawakami had become a hardened lower-
echelon officer *(kashikan):* he enjoyed booze, whoring, and meat for dinner;
he could trek through the harsh wilderness and "wipe out" pockets of
Chinese resistance; he could record his unit's losses without being moved.
According to his diary, Kawakami's world revolved around a few simple
things: food, women, physical pain, and correspondence from home.[111] In
effect, he had adopted an identity that he felt was well suited for a soldier in
occupied China and had done so on his own.

When Yamamoto heard the news about Nanjing, he simply wrote: "tears
poured down my face." Soon after, when he received compositions and pictures from Japanese schoolchildren, he felt that fate had intervened: he believed it miraculous that he of all people would receive correspondence from
children in his hometown. Perhaps due to some sense of finality after the
fall of the GMD capital, Yamamoto began writing letters back to them. At
first, he wrote fluently in the voice of wartime reportage (which, his diary
reveals, he had been reading once he left the front): "Dear Beloved Schoolchildren: It was August, under the blazing sun with the clamorous sounds
of locusts, when I departed from the school, sent forth by your brave cries
of *Banzai!*" After dispensing with epistolary formalities such as describing
the weather, he assured them of his continued good health and his dedication to fighting the enemy. Nevertheless, his months of exposure to a battlefield without newspapers or voices of authority had made its mark—
Yamamoto, in finding his own way to narrate the war, had forgotten what
constituted acceptable speech. His letter to the children changed in tone as
he delineated salient categories of his experience in China:

> I've leaped into canal beds, into the enemy camp, and stabbed Chinese sol-
> diers to death [*tsukikoroshita koto ga arimashita*]. I've shot Chinese soldiers
> when they came to attack us at night, too. Also, while drinking soup made
> from chestnut husks when thirsty, chewing raw garlic and daikon when
> hungry, I shot the Chinese at close range while they fled. If I went on about
> the fighting and such, well, there's a lot of fun stuff [*omoshiroi koto*] to tell,
> but in order to maintain military discipline [*gunki no hochi*], they won't let

me write about it. Maybe when I come home I'll tell you. But this body has been offered to his Imperial Majesty. This is a body [*shintai*] that will be on a battlefield, where it might not see the light of the next day. Will I ever see you all again?

Even acknowledging the threat of censorship, Yamamoto used inappropriately graphic language in his attempt to communicate with the children. In his next letter, he told them that while they were playing and sleeping soundly next to their mothers, many Chinese children (left behind or lost) lay crumpled dead next to burning buildings while others wandered aimlessly crying for their mothers. He asked them to mind their mothers and listen to their teachers and promised to work hard for the emperor. Yamamoto tried to use his new voice—one that encapsulated both heroism and brutality—to communicate what he had learned on the battlefield before "this body" might be destroyed. It is unclear whether these letters were ever delivered.

Yamamoto also used his diary to process the growing propaganda that aimed to redefine the purpose of the war. After reading the *Sunday Mainichi,* he wrote, "The China Incident is not merely an incident [*jihen*] between China and Japan, but a battle [*tatakai*] between fascism and communism. I wonder if all of China will become communist?"[112] When it became clear that the war would not be won any time soon, Yamamoto diligently copied into his diary events surrounding police action against an antifascist labor movement (the "Popular Front Incident") and the Japanese government's suppression of the political left.[113] Like Sakaguchi, he visited prostitutes, drank, and played cards, grabbing every chance he could to indulge himself now that he was away from the front.

Something had, however, changed: Yamamoto now cried at the movies, which he thought was "due to my being on the battlefield," and he simultaneously became even more engaged with fiction and film. By the end of January 1938, Yamamoto learned that one of his reflective poems on war, "Taking up the Gun" (*Jū wo toritsutsu*), had been recommended for publication. This gave him "no end of joy"—the same emotion that he felt when he was called up for active duty, expressed in the same language. His memories of the Shanghai battlefield, composed later in peaceful Guangdong, take up the remainder of his diary and, through poetic letters to "Mr. K," he created a persona that spoke both beautifully and in the voice of a good soldier. Tempted by literary fame like Hino Ashihei, Yamamoto censored his own poetry in the back of the diary notebook by marking "X" next to questionable lines such as "They say that the representatives of the Imperial Comfort Services buy women in Shanghai and then go home / Such a representative from my hometown departs without seeing the troops."[114] By the end of his diary, Yamamoto had sublimated his repulsion at the suffering of the Chinese in order to produce compelling (and acceptable) poetry for publication.

Kimura Genzaemon maintained his typically cool distance from the events surrounding him, indulging in (often esoteric) zetetic exercises regarding the relationship between individuals and between peoples and the goals of education. Like Yamanaka Sadao, the script writer-cum-infantry sergeant, Kimura had abandoned "art for art's sake" and continually longed for a form of writing that felt closer to "life" *(seikatsu)* and was imbued with "realism" *(riaruizmu),* which would also empower the text or at least "smash the misconception that words [*bun*] and writing [*bunshō*] are mere decoration around 'fact' [*jijitsu*]." Like Yamamoto, Kimura used his diary as a space to digest state-sanctioned discourse: "newspapers, correspondence, consolation letters, and letters to home, work evaluations, field diaries and every other kind of writing I see still has that beauteous Meiji-era literary style, setting not one foot beyond the highest delusions [of the era]." He cast his aspersions on letters to the front, even from children, detecting insincerity in such state-sponsored correspondence. Kimura snorted at the opposition to the status quo as well: when Japan's leading liberal intellectual, Kawai Eijirō, claimed that Japan would be "saddled with a heavy burden" in the management of northern China, Kimura, who felt himself already deep in the process of building the empire there, recorded his belief that, under Japan, these regions' future "would be much brighter." He later wrote of Kawai: "Did they really have such damn idiots at Tokyo Imperial University?"

Kimura's views of the war show that he had been growing ever distant from his "comrades." He was one of the very few diarists who made no mention at all of the fall of Nanjing, dismissing the discussion of the delay in the unit's triumphant return by writing: "Everyone looks depressed, but I don't feel a thing. . . . I shipped out with the proper determination [*tadashii ketsui*]. There's no way they'll send us home that easily. I'll do what needs to be done." Despite Kimura's distaste for modern China and the sense of superiority that he derived from being part of an occupying army, he never condoned senseless slaughter and recorded indignation when the self-appointed "heroes of the Holy War" solicited prostitutes. He carved a niche for himself in contrast to those surrounding him, seeking self-perfection and trying to use the war as a means to learn about fighting men, pedagogy, and the differences between peoples *(minzoku)*. When Kimura nonchalantly mused on the nature of war and gambling, he perhaps unwittingly revealed the self that he had created through his war diary:

> In all competition [*shōbugoto*], in order to feel a fleeting sense of superiority when victorious, one must gamble against the danger that, when defeated, one feels remorse and regret, as if one is doomed—and that is what war is like. . . . Therefore, only those who stink of vulgarity will engage in competition. In other words, competition is something only mankind does, as a game. . . . If this is some bellicose nature [*sōtōsei*] inherited from our primitive past [*yasei jidai*], then no one is quite as primitive as he who is obsessed with competition. But, within this competition, there is an opportunity that one should take to perfect oneself [*mizukara wo migaku beki kien*].

Even when he grew frustrated with his prolonged stay in China, he still wrote with the same dry and cynical tone: when infantrymen from the Twentieth Division returned "victorious" from Hankow in December 1938, he noted that "not a single one of them had looks of excitement on their faces" and that "after one and a half years of working as a human target, all burning emotions have dissipated." Near the end of that year, he reflected, "If a man can discard those little emotions, everything in this world is, really, quite clear, I think." When he finally made it to his home in November 1939, Kimura wrote that he felt moved for the first time in over two years.[115]

Sakaguchi and Yamamoto had similarly maintained detailed personal records after the war cooled down, using the diary as a space to reconsider what they had done. Some may doubt that servicemen such as Azuma wrote such extensive lyrical accounts during the era of *Wheat and Soldiers* with no intention to publish them, perhaps because the more ambitious among us cannot imagine a person who exerts himself without promise of fame or fortune. Nevertheless, they did. Cynics might point out that newspaper "diaries" and those published for internal military consumption merely mimic the chaotic language of the battlefield in a hackneyed and more manageable manner. Rather than seek to separate authentic from inauthentic language, it is more important to identify when it moves from newspaper to diary and then from personal narratives back into the press. There is no authentic language of the battlefield, but soldiers did write about war according to what they believed was truthful; sometimes that included messages from authorities trying to influence their behavior, but other times soldiers rejected those attempts. That so many of these men could, even with such impressive and thorough discursive fetters, stray so far from the political objectives of the state, mass media, and the military shows that those disciplinary mechanisms have a tenuous grasp over our identities and rely on our support for their effectiveness.

CHAPTER FOUR

The Unbearable Likeness of Being

The Transnational Phenomenon of Self-Discipline during the Pacific War

IN EARLY 1942, only two months after Pearl Harbor, an unorthodox American corporal named Evans Carlson stood before his marines—a new outfit dubbed the "Raiders"—and had them shout out a phrase he had unwittingly invented by himself: "Gung Ho!" This story was turned into a popular film, which soldiers watched on the battlefield, and the word has become a permanent fixture in the English language.[1] The term was drawn from the short form name of the CCP Industrial Cooperative *(Gonghe),* but Carlson, inspired by Chinese Communist dedication, told these elite marines that the term "called for self-discipline and implicit belief in the doctrine of helping the other fellow." Thus, in addition to the functions of camaraderie, Carlson had learned from guerilla commanders such as Zhu De the importance of a serviceman's ability to think for himself and to understand the purpose of the war he fought, both of which were essential tools of self-discipline. Describing Carlson's inaugural speech before the Raiders— poised to spearhead the U.S. counterattack in Asia and the Pacific—Carlson's biographer wrote: "There was a split-second of silence in the ranks. . . . But the words [Gung Ho] came and the grove of eucalyptus trees in the middle of San Diego County heard a thousand voices say a strange and foreign phrase that, in the necessary coincidence of human history, was as American as it is Chinese."[2] Some U.S. marines who had witnessed the devastation of the Second Sino-Japanese War while seconded to Chinese military units would bring their knowledge of and hatred for the Japanese with them to the United States.[3] Indoctrination and self-discipline were inextricably linked in achieving military success, and this was as familiar to U.S. servicemen as it was to those in East Asia.

The functions, desires, and consequences concomitant with wartime diary writing were not split apart by the putative divisions of race and nation or even the breadth of the Pacific Ocean. During the Pacific War, however, Japanese state and society moved into a stage of wartime mobilization unknown in the American historical experience since the Civil War. In Japan, state authorities often replaced peacetime educational curricula with military training. With the mobilization of students *(gakuto shutsujin)* in October 1943, the state began to draft young people in university and high school. Japanese university students found their educations truncated as they were mobilized for war; this meant that the military was drawing more widely for men, which changed the character of the armed forces by including those who were ambivalent about the conflict to begin with. Indeed, as early as 1941, Oki Seiichi, a sailor who would later die in the Solomons, wrote in his diary that imperial decrees to restrict education and send every young man to the front would ultimately be counterproductive:

> I think these orders were issued because of Japan's increasingly perilous situation. If not, then we are only harming university students and our culture in order to satisfy the reckless demands of the military. . . . [This] isn't just a matter of [lost] time. Three months isn't much, but when one considers the shock to the students, the impact it will have on their attitude towards study, the influence on the junior students, and the unease it will create amongst the soldiers, it has far too many bad effects.[4]

As a consequence of such widespread unease, authorities overhauled war diaries, further suffusing the "private" space of draftees with wartime discourse. It is unclear when exactly this process began, but blank "war diaries" *(jūgun techō)* mass-printed by organizations linked to the military were numerous in 1939 and ubiquitous by 1941. Thus, ideological indoctrination became increasingly important as the government drew from a more and more diverse group of men to serve in its armed forces. What we might not expect is that similar forces were also at work in the United States during mobilization. While more Japanese carried blank diaries printed with propaganda material inside, many Americans received similar documents for free.

Comparing American and Japanese servicemen's diaries shows that self-discipline through diary writing was a transnational phenomenon, particularly during the mobilization for the Second World War. The transnational nature of self-discipline in modern war can be seen through the compulsion to chronicle personal history (both good and bad), global willingness to self-sacrifice for state goals, the suffusion of mobilization techniques in personal writing, the illusion of privacy, soldiers' concept of "history," the role of American and Japanese soldiers as enforcers of colonialism, and even the use of religion in support of militarism. In such a bitterly divided world, how can we explain such similarity? This is particularly counterintuitive considering the different literary and cultural traditions of Japan and the United States, which extend to self-narrative. After all, Ruth Benedict emerged from her close study of wartime Japanese to claim, in *The Chrysanthemum and the Sword* (1946), that American and Japanese cultures handled psychological stress in completely different, culturally determined ways.

Soldiers on both sides of the conflict nonetheless turned to diary writing, even during the worst moments of their wartime experience. Psychoanalysts since Freud have used talk therapy to "heal" past trauma, but what if the use of narrative to extirpate the emotionally charged past was not an unveiling of hidden truth but the use of language as an attempt to control experience? If so, then diaries become critical and even dangerous documents, because the text wields considerable power over the author. By looking at the diary as a space for "cathartic" chronicle as conducted by the patient himself, regardless of whether it tells "the whole truth," we can move the discussion of self-discipline outside of the confines of East Asia and see it as a critical tool for shaping wartime experience globally.

THE COMPULSION TO CHRONICLE: THE COLLAPSE OF THE
WESTERN POWERS IN ASIA

Arai Yasujirō was a pilot who had been trained to fly a new kind of plane—the "Zero"—that was, at the time, the best fighter aircraft in the world. Part of an elite squadron, Arai was one of the first to find out that Japan was planning a war against America. "There were rumors of a war between Japan and the United States," he wrote in his diary, "but the first stage of launching the hostilities came from our sneak attack." He participated in the destruction of the U.S. fleet in Hawai'i. After his unit attacked Pearl Harbor, he felt his pride as a soldier grow: "I saw a heroic battle for the first time. As more and more [bombs] hit, pillars of water shot up into the air. To have been able to take part in this battle was, for a warrior [bujin], the greatest joy." Arai's words were not mere hyperbole; the attack on Pearl Harbor marked the world's first successful air assault on a naval force. He was amazed at the stunning success of the attack, writing: "looking at the results, you just thought, this moment is world military history [sekai senshi]."[5] Word spread almost immediately among U.S. forces, especially those overlooking the projection of American military power in Asia and the Pacific.[6] Two weeks later, while the Japanese armed forces stormed the Philippines, John C. Cash, in the U.S. Navy, described how American forces were "still holding out, but it looks pretty bad. . . . This is going to be a long and hard war."[7] Embracing the "historical" importance of personal experience, soldiers like Arai and Cash were compelled to record it and, in doing so, tied themselves to state goals; in this process of fusing individual to state and nation, the diary, as repository of "truthful" self-record, played a critical role.

Japanese soldiers had been keeping diaries since the nineteenth century because, for most of them, serving in the armed forces (especially abroad) was like being transported to another world, and they were desperate to get control of this strange experience. Still, many people keep diaries for the same reasons that scribes kept public chronicles: the records were inspired by a sense that events significant to the author must be recorded and must be done truthfully (according, of course, to what they accepted as truth); these men believed that they were part of history. It is difficult to argue with servicemen on this point: the Japanese conflict with Western hegemony in Asia was a momentous event that directly affected the lives of millions, and so it deserved to be recorded for posterity. In 1941, American military power in Asia was in most aspects inferior to that of the Japanese invaders, and this reality was shocking for U.S. soldiers stationed abroad. Subsequently, U.S. servicemen, like the Chinese Nationalists, felt compelled to document their failures in the first year of the war. A.C. Tisdelle reflected somberly on the decline of Western power in Asia and the Pacific:

> The war had begun five months earlier and I had gradually seen my American world collapse before the invading army of a foreign power. . . . The war was only in its 5th month but our defeat had not been accomplished in that short time, it had been invited long before.

Meanwhile, Japanese servicemen grew exhilarated by telling a story of being at the center of a momentous victory. Facing down the Western powers, Hara Kinosuke drew on the rhetoric of self-mobilization that had come to characterize Japanese war diaries since the turn of the century:

> I greet 1942, a year of great significance, with a body and mind as clear and clean as an azure sky. . . . In this year, more than any other, we must fulfill the Path of the Warrior [*bushi no michi*]. This year, we must unleash the potential of the Japanese Spirit [*Yamato damashii*]. This means we have to strengthen our bodies and minds, and wage war.[8]

As will soon become apparent, these were not cultural differences, but the separation between victor and vanquished.

American diarists felt the need to chronicle "truth" as keenly as did the Chinese Nationalists and the Japanese, even if, collectively, these records do not tell the same story. During extreme times, diarists could adopt a voice characterized by brutal honesty. For example, high-ranking officers and field commanders in the Philippines evidently were compelled to admit that they were pulling together a poor defense. Japanese air strikes wiped out American forces and established air supremacy almost immediately. Meanwhile, D. M. Moore complained of staff and command inadequacy, writing, "Col. MacDonald appointed chief of staff. He doesn't know anything. Parker gets rid of him. Difficulty with communications. Staff doesn't understand magnitude of the problems confronting them. Parker can't decide on how to rack up his staff."[9] Meanwhile, in Manila, shortly after the attack on Pearl Harbor, nervous antiaircraft gunners were firing on their own planes. American troops were not equipped to fight total war, as they were largely there to provide security over a colonial possession. American submarines came in to be serviced by Earl Sackett's ship, but then withdrew, "leaving us the 'Battling bastards of Bataan—no papa, no mama, no Uncle Sam.'"[10] The failure of the U.S. defense of the Philippines, of course, inspired much analysis both during the war and after. William Sharpe, for example, claimed that American pilots in the early stages of the Pacific War had only six or seven hours of flight time before being sent against vastly more experienced Japanese pilots.[11] Americans in defeat, then, were very similar to the Chinese, who also felt compelled to explain failure in their diaries.

In any case, the Japanese attack in the Philippines came quickly, catching American forces off guard. Sackett described how, in the course of a few hours, Japanese aircraft had rapidly destroyed new airfields and infrastructure nearby his ship. Like the Chinese, some Americans rushed to blame their allies and inferior technology when feeling the sting of defeat. Lieutenant Colonel Arthur L. Shreve was awakened by Japanese bombers the day after Pearl Harbor and wrote that the "result was too accurate for night bombing. We suspect 5th column."[12] Stranded on Corregidor with a pair of stone lions from Chiang Kai-shek (en route to President Roosevelt), A. C. Tisdelle composed angry entries about his frustration with technological inferiority in a manner strikingly similar to that of the Chinese Nationalists: "Anti-aircraft keeps them high but our powder train fuses just don't reach the little yellow bastards"; "If only we had a little modern equipment, a little aircorps, and a little more medicine and chow"; and "It's hell to have nothing to work with."[13] American officers used their diaries as a means of grasping facts salient to understanding the events unfolding before them. To consciously construct a fallacious account of the war defeated the purpose of the document, but individual bias can be easily found in any record—personal or "official."

Indeed, "facts" were always filtered through a diarist's subjective point of view. The importance of the individual's position when recording the "facts" becomes strikingly obvious when one switches sides: while Shreve and Moore wrote their disparaging accounts, Japanese pilot Hara Kinosuke was flying above them in his first attack sorties. Like many in the victorious army, he took delight in defeating the Americans: "I woke up and went right to the air strip. . . . Lately the attacks have been kind of dull, which I found a little disappointing, but today we had a real response [from the Americans]. Manila fell, and those bastards defending Corregidor are fighting like madmen. It is a lot of fun."[14] Contrasting views of "truth" were put into dialogue through propaganda campaigns: soon after Hara's attack, the Japanese army began broadcasting in English and dropping leaflets onto U.S. servicemen. While Americans attempted to mobilize themselves, then, their views were directly challenged by the Japanese, which Tisdelle observed mournfully:

> The damned Nips have got a new propaganda program that does not help our morale any. The men joke happily but underneath they are disquieted. [The Japanese play] American songs to American soldiers on Bataan and Corregidor at 2145 hours every night. Theme song 'Ships that never come in' followed by popular records.[15]

Still more painful were the conditions that the defending soldiers were enduring; as Louis Morton described their underground defenses, "Dust, dirt, great black flies, and vermin were everywhere, and over everything hung the odor of the hospital and men's bodies."[16] Despite these factors, the U.S. and Philippine forces managed to reorganize themselves in Bataan and Corregidor, exacting casualties against General Honma Masaharu's units and holding out (largely symbolically) against the invasion for a few months.

Nevertheless, the heroic image of American and Filipino soldiers uniting against a dastardly foe is a myth; indeed, more debilitating than Japanese propaganda campaigns were the divisions within the U.S. Armed Forces. Despite the frustration of the high-ranking officers, those commanding in the field felt American incompetence most keenly; in many cases they had to get right under Japanese artillery fire with their men to make them advance, just like the Nationalists did in China. Some felt that their courage was not recognized, which inspired Sergeant Bernard Hopkins to write, "I think my blood will boil when I hear of Generals and Colonels being cited." Their continuing complacency and impotence infuriated him, and he unleashed his anger in his diary:

> The war plans called for this area to be held—but the local big-wigs—plenty of them asleep on the matter and few of them knowing anything of the area. I've been there—felt that it would take the Jap 6 months to get in there.

Well, the Japs got into the area in less than a month. These same big-wigs didn't know there was a sugar cane railroad up into the area. . . . [The map] has been on file here (in HD Hq) for over two years now. I certainly hope someone gets wise soon, before the Japs start pelting us with 8" guns from over here.[17]

Americans also blamed other branches for these failures, which shows just how important the diarist's subjectivity was in determining what was "true." Paul D. Bunker, a colonel serving as an army field officer on the island of Corregidor, was part of the units defending Manila. His quarters were idyllic—complete with a full library—underlining the severe discrepancies between infantrymen and officers that were particularly egregious before the war. In addition to being a privileged soldier in a colonial setting, however, Bunker was also a disciplined, forthright diarist. As an officer, he keenly recognized the U.S. forces' failure to resist Japanese invasion effectively. He copied a report from another officer to the effect that the "Jap bunch there [Pucot Hill] are mature and splendidly trained men who talk American— even slang—and have outsmarted us at every turn."[18] On top of these privations, the U.S. Navy did not adequately supply the land forces trapped in southern Luzon, despite never seeming to be short of supplies themselves. Also, while the U.S. Army tried to defend the Philippines in trenches and barracks, U.S. naval forces were taking shelter by night in subterranean bunkers.[19] Finally, Bunker claimed, they refused to engage with the enemy:

I talked with HD Exec and asked why, since the Inshore Patrol say they are patrolling Manila Bay, they should not have investigated and broken up yesterday's formation of bancas off Naic. They have two gunboats still here plus several other armed craft that are all moored in "South Harbor" . . . while their officers and crews are hiding in the Navy Tunnel! The Exec said, "They won't do it." I replied, "Do you mean they refuse to obey orders?" And he astounded me by saying, "The Inshore Patrol is not under our orders." . . . This part of our Navy WILL NOT FIGHT!

After acknowledging similar reluctance in the "vaunted" British Navy in Singapore, Bunker exploded again: "Seems to be a lot of yellow in our Navy friends. *Try* to get one of those 105 naval officers out of the Navy Tunnel— just *try!*"[20] Officers also blamed their subordinates: wherever the fighting intensified, soldiers and service personnel stationed in the Philippines seemed to prove intransigent—Shreve reported officers using guns to get their men moving.[21] U.S. officers later used descriptions of this kind of foot-dragging and cowardice to demean the GMD forces of the 1940s, but U.S. servicemen's diaries show that they were hardly nobler in defeat, and they had been fighting the Japanese for only one month. Americans complained bitterly about subordinates, peers, allies, and superiors, pouring out frustration and anger onto diary pages; like the Chinese, whether accurate or not, U.S. soldiers used diaries to record the components of their evolving personal narrative of loss.

By April 1942, the American forces in Bataan were crushed, and by May 1942, the defenders of Corregidor similarly had to surrender to an overwhelmingly superior force; the Philippines were lost, and the Americans had held it only a little longer than the Chinese had held Shanghai in 1937. Like their counterparts in East Asia, American narratives began to lose cohesion as they tried to describe the chaos following the fall of the Philippines. First, as American dominance over the Philippines crumbled, so too did order in the army and control of the Filipino colonial subjects. Shreve, who had barely slept for four days, was trying to conduct buses near Bataan full of Philippine Army units that jammed the roads in retreat; he pushed them back and forth "with the aid of my pistol." Abruptly, he began to write valedictions to his wife and children in his diary, even though such entries were unlikely to ever reach them should he die. Before long, Shreve grew deathly ill, was moved with hospital staff under Japanese artillery fire, and witnessed the war in a morphine-induced haze.[22] Emotionally overwhelmed, Moore used short, ephemeral vignettes and displayed little apparent narrative control over the experience:

> Truck-civilian-busses soldiers jam road. White flags on vehicles. Dive bombers and staffing. Congestion all night—8–9 April. Consider going to Corregidor Ammunition dump—Nurses to Fort Mills difficulty in getting through—looting by soldiers. Our mission to Jap's. Wilson and I contact Col. Sato. Wilson get kicked in shins. My message to Elizabeth through Traywick—Hope it went through. American women in tent near war 6A—and drunken soldiers.[23]

U.S. servicemen's diaries and personal notes often resembled the total breakdown of language in similar documents by the Chinese and Japanese during the bloody war of 1937–1939. D. M. Moore's diary could very well be the English translation of a selection from Taniguchi—the medic who tried in vain to give coherence to his experiences during the Nanjing Massacre:

> Rumors good—It won't be long now. Difficult of concentrating. . . . Am convinced that we have too few officers who take the military profession seriously, and make an intelligent and concentrations study. . . . Dead bodies— burials—stiff arms bodies thrown in—#2 not read—tried to climb out— held down with 2 large rocks. / Bodies along the road—part of flesh torn and eaten by dogs—kick skull—north across rice paddy—foot-balls—men fell out of column—2 rifle shots—one less soldier—Phil. soldier falls out— across back w/ 2" × 4" hooks on w/ disgust. 2 strokes at base of skull—one less soldier—Man stops at pump to get water—bayonet through chest— gets back into line—see him drinking water later on.[24]

Americans, who had become accustomed to their roles as colonial rulers in the Philippines and comfortable in their superiority over Asian subjects, became acutely aware of their new vulnerability and subjugation, which affected their sense of self greatly. Even during the battle for Bataan, with American forces fleeing south and suffering constant bombardment, officers such as Wendell W. Fertig enjoyed "the most luxurious set up in Bataan as we have tentage with bamboo floors, a central shower and toilets, and excellent mess run by 'Lee,' the Chinaman from the Parasols Club."[25] Bunker was also served by a Chinese Filipino, who supplied him fresh, clean underwear every day. The rapid transition to being a failed colonial power was difficult for them to grasp. Americans described Filipino army regulars as unreliable, led by incompetent officers hired through "political appointment," and noted how they fled before the Japanese, abandoning their valuable artillery equipment. In one account, these troops ran "*laughing* and shouting and, holding up their 2 first fingers to form a V, call[ed] 'Victory,'" prompting Bunker to write, "These Filipinos were different than the ones who served with us in 1898."[26] After being captured by the Japanese, Bunker described how he and his comrades were paraded in front of the Filipinos, who looked on with curious smiles. While American servicemen languished in Japanese prison camps, dying at atrocious rates, some Filipinos were eventually released, and Americans viewed this with suspicion. In fact, more Filipinos died than did Allied soldiers, but American servicemen believed the Filipinos to be disloyal; it was a part of their attempt to narrate the experience of transforming from colonial overlords to vulnerable subjects.

When Japanese soldiers encountered the inhabitants of their new empire, they were often struck by how compliant these subjects seemed to be and how well white colonizers were able to live. Particularly in places like Dutch Indonesia, the world seemed ripe for Japanese intervention, and servicemen actively gobbled up government propaganda as a compelling language for their new role in the Pacific. Hara seemed delighted at how colonial peoples had learned to interact with occupying forces, and he quickly adopted the patronizing tone of a benevolent ruler. After landing at his new airbase in Kendari, Indonesia, he wrote:

> Before dinner I went out for a stroll about town with Miyamoto. I wanted to buy a monkey, but wasn't able to. We visited the homes of the local civilians and were treated to coffee. They have some trust in us. They receive us graciously and with pride. We are very fond of them [*kawaigatte iru*]. We have a hard time teaching them Japanese, but they are very serious, so they pick it up quickly. . . . The islanders are all filled with new hope, and can be seen everywhere working their hearts out. People are really simple and pure [*jun*]. They do have that trait, unique to the people of the South Seas, to mill about and do nothing, but the natives [*dojin*] here are better than those up until now.[27]

Undoubtedly, this response was a refreshing change from dealing with the Nationalists in central China, but the Japanese—suffering from a form of colonial narcissism like their predecessors from the Western world—were unable to understand the limited options available to colonized populations and mistook necessity for sincerity. Japanese invaders were also often confused by the complex situations into which the war had thrown them. Quarrels between colonial subjects erupted as the Japanese invaded, which was a subject of concern and fascination. Part of the 1942 Buitenzorg (Bogor, near Jakarta) invasion force, a Lieutenant Watanabe (only his family name was recorded) wrote that, in one Indonesian village, "the locals [*domin*] are fiercely resistant to the Chinese, so the Chinese all carry pistols." Still, Japanese servicemen like Watanabe were able to inscribe a heroic narrative on their advance in the Pacific:

Bandung at a Glance

Since we launched our surprise landing against the Dutch, we've crossed 100 *ri* in 13 days. A truly rapid advance, our entry into the final target of Bandung was tremendously impressive, and the majesty of our unbeatable Aoba Division was true to its appearance. The cooperative efforts of our units' action, especially the air forces, are worthy of praise. . . . The enemy knew that they should not resist us, and quickly announced their surrender.

Watanabe noted that they captured so many weapons, automobiles, and ammunition that they "are concerned with what to do with it all." Watanabe, like Hara, saw his role as a heroic destroyer of white oppression in Asia. He was amazed at, and repulsed by, the splendor of the houses of "white people" in Indonesia, where "the homes without personal cars were few indeed." He snarled, "It is a situation where extravagance has no limit, and it has been squeezed from the blood of the natives [*dojin no chi wo shibori aru jyōkyō*]."[28] Not long after, the dire news of a surprise American attack at Guadalcanal would reach Watanabe in Batavia (Jakarta), but he, like many others, continued to use a paternalistic tone strikingly similar to that of Western colonial powers. As Japanese soldiers wrote down their adventures in these "exotic" islands, they seduced themselves into believing that they were benevolent hegemons and invaluable leaders, as had the Americans before them. In moments such as these, when servicemen use their diaries to paint a convincing portrait of themselves and their world that could be dangerously inaccurate, self-discipline departs from any "truth" recognizable by an outside party and becomes a perilous form of self-deception.

The influence of the Japanese occupation on their colonial subjects (as well as postcolonial movements in Asia and the Pacific) cannot be limited to the establishment of state mechanisms or the construction of railroads and airstrips—it included the tools for constituting and reconstituting identity itself. In an attempt to capitalize on Pacific communities' unfamiliarity with the realities of Japanese imperialism, Japanese officers immediately sought out the "intellectual youth" *(interi seinen)* to recruit from among the "native troops" *(dominhei)* as translators and coordinators of the New Order—even though some diarists recognized that these young men might serve purely out of fear.[29] Self-discipline, however, was as unpredictable a tool as military armaments themselves; how badly the Japanese misunderstood their new subjects is clear if we examine the other side of this relationship.

Leocadio de Asis, captured in Bataan as part of the U.S. defense forces, was one of the Filipinos released from the Japanese prison camps for Allies; unsurprisingly, he quickly embraced his chance to escape. Japanese military officers, seeing that he was intelligent (and presumably not exceedingly loyal to the U.S. colonial regime), sent him to Japan. Immediately on his graduation from a Japanese preparatory institute in the Philippines, he began writing a diary. De Asis trod carefully in this text, examining all sides of the international situation and not fully committing himself either to the Japanese project in the Philippines, to the Americans, or to outright and immediate independence. For example, he began by describing a declaration by General Guillermo B. Francisco (head of the new "constabulary" force in the Philippines): "Never forget you are FILIPINOS!" Despite the initial euphoria of traveling abroad as a young man, de Asis never let go of his desire to return to the Philippines and was observant enough to discover that Japan was leading his country down a dangerous path. Filipinos in the Japanese imperial capital quickly bonded with one another and tied their personal identities to the Philippine nation even more tightly than they had under the Americans.[30] This experience proved to be a turning point for de Asis. In sports competitions *(undōkai)*, determined to show the "Filipino Spirit" (often to teams from around the Japanese Empire), de Asis frequently criticized Japanese arrogance and finally insisted on true independence for his country. While many servicemen in training used their diaries to motivate themselves for war, de Asis, as a result of his search for difference from the Japanese around him, departed from the language of wartime self-mobilization. While watching Japanese cadets training to be armed colonists for Manchukuo, he wrote:

> We left the academy immediately after lunch with deep admiration and at the same time a feeling of pity for those young boys who are leaving behind home and country, determined to dedicate their lives tilling the cold fields of Manchuria. Trained from their early years, I saw in those young boys veritable cogs in the huge wheel of the state, the course of whose very lives have been already traced by their country.[31]

De Asis was likely encouraged by his military (and colonial) superiors to keep a disciplined account of his daily life. What they did not intend, however, is that he would use this workspace to develop a self at odds with the aims of the colonial state.

The Japanese military followed decisive military defeat with public humiliations of former colonial rulers that were designed to break them down. American POWs, objects of this psychological and physical torture, dedicated themselves to keeping a disciplined chronicle of the experience.[32] Using their sophisticated armed forces to destroy the American, British, French, and Dutch military presence, the Japanese embarrassed civilizations that assumed their racial superiority based on technological dominance.[33] In Osaka, captives such as George F. Gallion were forced to wear their navy uniforms as they marched in front of Japanese civilians.[34] Japanese servicemen also humiliated their captives on an individual level. Shreve, after being robbed and nearly shot by Japanese infantrymen, described his harrowing captivity in a narrative style that further reflected the collapse of American military power:

> We were counted, then lectured by the Camp CO, a retired Capt. J. A. in substance; we are P.W. [POWs] and at his mercy; we are the eternal enemies of Japan. We have no rank, will wear no insignia, we will salute all Japanese regardless of rank. We will be shot if we commit various offenses such as attempted escape, arson, failure to obey and others. We and our things are searched again and again. . . . Thus, the days go by, [and] rice is our only food. . . . There is but one small pump to supply us, and the thousands of P.A. [Philippine Army] on the other side of the camp. No washing or bathing. We have no razors, so no shaving. . . . Then the terrible Death March up with no food, no water, [men] are dying by the scores. What little food we brought in is given for the sick. The older officers are pitiful. The end of their long service P. of W. Little hope of survival. Some of all ranks and ages just give up and die. God is good, I can eat the rice, I can work to keep the water running.[35]

Two years after U.S. forces had been captured in the Philippines and forced to endure terrible conditions, the decline of Japan's supply capabilities reduced the captives to those same conditions again. Forced on a ship to Japan with inadequate food, water, medicine, and toilets, William Miner arrived in Japan by swimming ashore after his boat was destroyed by Allied dive-bombers. He was placed on another "Hell Ship" and kept a bare record of the "most fantastic and horrible trip" of his life, scribbling on tiny notepads. The Japanese tried to humiliate men like Miner by making them lie in horse manure, and after arriving in Japan, he was "buggered in rectum by Japs Med. Corps."[36] Nevertheless, even when he was on the brink of starvation,

Miner kept a daily record of his life in Japanese custody, underlining the importance of the diary to soldiers' attempt to control their experiences.

It must have seemed that, at that moment, Oswald Spengler's prediction in *The Decline of the West* had come true: the age of materialism and individualism was destroyed by perfectly coordinated armies of invincible warriors obeying "strong men." Popular support for the war in Japan was strong: the Home Ministry reported gleefully that "the people are light-hearted and unconcerned [*meiryō kattatsu*], and we do not detect any reports of unease or wavering."[37] In the armed forces, Japanese men were aware that many of their comrades were dying, often needlessly, but this fact did not result in a collapse of support for the war. Tatsuguchi Nobu participated in the doomed invasion of the islands off the coast of Alaska beginning in June 1942—just a "cog" in a minor diversionary tactic to distract U.S. attention from the South Pacific. He was supportive of the effort, even though he was a medical officer and a Christian and despite the fact that everything was deteriorating around him. "Nervousness of our CO is severe and he has said his last word to his officers and non-commissioned officers (NCOs)—that he will die tomorrow—gave all his [belongings] away." While noting the panic that ensued among the men, Tatsuguchi criticized the CO who had abandoned himself, writing, "Hasty . . . The officers on the front are doing a fine job." The Japanese resilience was mystifying (and terrifying) to U.S. servicemen, and they sometimes indulged in fantastic visions of the invincible samurai warrior.[38] During the mobilization for war in the United States, this vision of the Japanese supersoldier would be critical to Americans' efforts toward abandoning individualism and embracing self-sacrifice.

Still, Japanese diarists were not, of course, unthinking "primitive" supermen, and they frequently expressed their frustrations in their diaries just as U.S. servicemen did. Tatsuguchi resorted to merely enumerating the horrible circumstances: frostbite, lack of food, bombardment from the sea, strafing from the air, and illness—Tatsuguchi himself "suffer[ed] from diarrhea and [felt] dizzy." Diarists often poured their most heated emotions into their diaries, sometimes writing what they would not dare say before their comrades. When Tatsuguchi heard that their final line was broken, his unit read the Imperial Rescript on Soldiers and Sailors, and he wrote laconically: "No hope of reinforcement. Will die for the cause of the Imperial Rescript." In the end, however, these nuances could be lost in group attacks on their enemies. After rations ran out and critical positions were lost, a general retreat was called off by the field commanders, who preferred to finish things in a climactic demonstration of the Japanese military spirit:

> The last assault is to be carried out. All patients in the hospital were made to commit suicide. Only 33 years of living and I am to die here. I have no regrets. *Tennō heika banzai!* I am grateful that I have kept the peace in my soul. . . . At 1600, took care of all the patients with grenades. [He composed valedictions for his loved ones.] It seems that the enemy is expecting an all out attack tomorrow. I have no regrets dying for the Emperor![39]

When the Japanese popular press valorized this unit's near extermination, for the first time in the war they would use a term that would later come to define the final stages of the conflict for the Japanese: *gyokusai,* or the "shattered jewels." It transformed their deaths into an object of reverence, allowing media, government, and military forces in Japan to mobilize men toward even greater sacrifice by ignoring the complex and conflicted reality behind *gyokusai.* Reading this propaganda or seeing Japanese units at their final stage of attack, Americans were thus encouraged to see the Japanese as unthinking fanatics. What is clear from Tatsuguchi's account, however, is that becoming a "shattered jewel" was a long process that involved considerable self-mobilization and sometimes ended with resignation.

Whether one is examining American responses to the fall of the Philippines or early Japanese "banzai charges," the fact that servicemen recorded such awful events suggests that the chronicle served a function. Psychoanalysts use catharsis as a means to help patients overcome crippling emotions by revealing and confronting the subconscious causes of those emotions through language (or "talk therapy"). In these cases, however, the guidance of the therapist in directing emotion to positive thought and action is crucial. As we have seen, battlefield discipline was self-inflicted, and directing emotion through language and writing would often lead men to less therapeutic destinations—particularly when subjects were under physical and psychological torture designed to break their will. William H. Owen described in his diary just what kind of decisions U.S. servicemen made in the prison camps after they had lost the first major battles in the Pacific: "Hospital orderly Havrill, confesses to stealing medical supplies. Vitamin tablets for sale. Marines attitude of superiority and attempts at mob rule. Lt. Polk again admonished by Major for attempting to stay in farm-work when marked duty. More drinking and he is to be severely punished. Two drunk and fighting at midnight."[40] Owen described these events with disgust, but others had decided that such selfish behavior was a helpful response to their deteriorating situation, and there were precious few disciplinary forces to correct them. Japanese troops, when they encountered these colonial forces, were thus encouraged to think of Americans as weak because of their "individualism." Subsequent months would show, however, that Americans could defeat their individualism through self-discipline in service of the state just as easily as the Japanese. Sergeant Bernard Hopkins, once captured in the Philippines, encouraged himself by observing, "We know just what Uncle Sammie can do, and will do, when he gets started."[41]

THE DEMANDS OF HISTORY:
SOCIAL ORGANIZATION, PRIVACY, AND MOBILIZATION

On 22 January 1942, Captain Ralph T. Noonan of the Massachusetts National Guard was sailing with a regiment of infantrymen near Cape Hatteras. He heard General Rose tell the officers and men that he was "proud" to fulfill this assignment and that the "best troops in the United States were selected for this task." Noonan did not know it yet, but on some level he was aware that he was going to the South Pacific to fight the Japanese. He pulled out a medium-sized daily planner and wrote, "The grapevine says that this is the largest and longest convoy in history. A strange feeling to be part of history."[42] Soldiers in both Japan and the United States felt strongly that the Second World War was an event of special historical importance. This concept of "history" acted on the individual diarists in unexpected ways, and individuals frequently expressed, either through embrace or resignation, that the course of history's events was totally beyond their control. Individuals often noted that the war came upon them uninvited and directed the course of their lives without their consent. Thus, the war did not just change the structure of army divisions or the nature of air power—it would utterly transform the individuals who served in it. Once pulled into the war, men engaged all their energies to win and survive it, even if it meant rewriting themselves in the process. In order to serve the nation at a time when choice seemed frivolous, Americans would sacrifice individualism, privacy, and even the notion of being "civilized."

What were servicemen talking about when they used the word "history"? First, "history" served to separate the war from previous conflicts, opening up life to previously inconceivable speech and actions. Even while describing the horror he felt on seeing rotting corpses in Guadalcanal, marine William Heggy also wrote with the pleasure of enacting revenge on the Japanese, "Radio reports claim that Friday's battle [21 August 1942] was history's greatest slaughter."[43] In this new context, massacres became commonplace for Heggy, changing his views of what the course of a normal life could be. Second, servicemen were encouraged to surrender the self in service of realizing their role in these historic events. For many Japanese soldiers in the war, sweeping away hundreds of years of Western colonial domination seemed the culmination of the nation's modern history. When the IJA ordered a desperate counteroffensive against U.S. forces in Guadalcanal on 1 October 1942, Second Division Commander Maruyama Masao warned that the Guadalcanal campaign was "under the eyes of the whole world" and would decide the fate of the entire empire.[44] Third, history encouraged individuals to see sacrifice as acceptable. Even those who surrendered wanted to be part of history's great machine: on the eve of his capture, Shreve wrote, "I believe also that history will prove that it was through our efforts and by our tenacity that Australia was saved for the allies."[45] Sublimating individual desire in order to be a part of history was just as important to the Americans as it was to East Asians. In wartime discourse, history was a part of mobilization: it required the individual to give up on self-preservation and not ask what alternatives existed for them and their communities. Why did Japanese and American infantrymen, many of whom were drafted from rural communities, simply not join hands and initiate a global populist revolution? "History" demanded this specific sacrifice, and it served this function regardless of national or cultural boundaries.

Thus, it is important to acknowledge the transnational nature of social management before we can examine U.S. government efforts to shape servicemen's narratives after 1941. Self-discipline was a crucial foundation for modern nation-states, and social organizations, many of which were inspired by the armed forces, were thus ubiquitous as societies became more regimented at the turn of the twentieth century. In Japan, for example, the Imperial Reservist Organization (Teikoku zaikyō gunjinkai), founded directly after the Russo-Japanese War, established chapters across Japan, especially in rural villages and towns. It encouraged military values through its publication, *Comrades (Senyū)*, and by directing preexistent social orga-nizations such as the youth groups *(seinendan)*.[46] In China, Chiang Kai-shek, while enrolled as a young officer in a Japanese military academy, was impressed with Japanese social and military discipline. Consequently, the GMD also directed (with widely varying success) social programs adjuvant to mobilization such as the Youth League of the Three Principles (of Sun Yat-sen: Sanmin zhuyi qingniantuan), the Huangpu Alumni Association (Huangpu tongxuehui), and the Chinese Boy Scouts. The crown of Chi-nese Nationalist social organization was the Society for Vigorous Practice (Lixingshe); it was founded by Huangpu Military Academy graduates, oversaw many of the organizations listed above, and, at its height, listed 500,000 members, ran university and high school military training pro-grams, and counted several ranking government figures in its midst.[47] Be-fore war broke out with Japan in 1937, Chinese society was organizing at a rate that seemed destined to threaten Japanese military power on the conti-nent. At a glance, it would have appeared that East Asia was hurtling to-ward totalitarianism, following in the footsteps of the Soviet Union.

The United States, although founded upon the principles of individual rights and private property, was a society even more organized than Nation-alist China and perhaps as much so as Japan. The American Legion, founded in Paris by U.S. veterans directly after the Great War, not only organized veterans as a powerful force in U.S. society and politics (through the U.S. Veterans Bureau from 1921) but also reached out to boys through initiatives such as the American Legion Baseball program. By the 1930s, the American Legion had over one million members. Similarly, the Boy Scouts of America, which had previously had a strong naturalist character, became militarized as a result of the Great War and helped spread these values through their nationwide chapters and publication, *Boys' Life*.[48] In 1917, the Boy Scouts of America (BSA) announced to the U.S. government that it had no less than 200,000 boys ready to guard railways, aqueducts, and bridges—by contrast, the Chinese Boy Scouts had just over 17,000 in 1930.[49] Like the Japanese military reservist-led youth clubs *(seinendan)* or Chiang Kai-shek's Blue Shirts, the Boy Scouts of America devised their own drill manual designed to provide military training for civilians. BSA leaders and their allies in the media countered accusations that they were a paramilitary organization by highlighting activities such as camping, hiking, and craft making. Although they did not have to defend themselves against similar charges, analogous

Japanese organizations also engaged in nonmilitary activities, such as improving rice irrigation networks, organizing local festivals, and serving as firemen.[50] Chiang Kai-shek also rarely bothered to engage with accusations of supporting a military dictatorship, because that is exactly what he wanted, but the Chinese scouts also tried to help the local community. All of these organizations aimed to valorize "traditional" life, foster national strength by toughening male bodies, combat domestic threats, promote military values (whether openly admitted or not), and teach self-discipline. The evidence above does not support arguments that any of these societies were more or less totalitarian, militaristic, or inclined toward "fascism" than the others; rather, it shows that these organizations in all societies were concerned with teaching citizens self-discipline and that the practices that they had used were strongly influenced by modern military tradition. These tools would also be necessary for total war.

In addition to growing U.S. social organization and cooperation with state objectives, reviewed diary writing became a part of the armed forces, even if these self-disciplinary practices were not as consistently applied as they were in East Asia. The gathering of diary accounts was split between American military and national archives, but the purpose of collecting these texts was articulated as a project that illuminated the history of the "experience" of war as well as strategic study, just as it had been in East Asia. After Pearl Harbor, the historical importance of record keeping was reaffirmed by the U.S. Navy through the establishment of the Office of Naval Records and Library, particularly because earlier incarnations of this office had performed so poorly in their collection of historical documents, including war diaries, after the First World War.[51] Still, official U.S. "war diaries," "logbooks," and "journals" were probably less abundant than their Japanese counterparts. Even in the U.S. Navy, which prided itself on its professionalism, some commanding officers considered it an aggravation to write diaries, even though there had been a precedent from the First World War. Dwight D. Eisenhower, who commanded U.S. forces in Europe and was acutely aware of the need for documentary evidence for future study, instructed his men to make record keeping a top priority. He kept a personal diary numbering several thousands of pages and advised his fellow officers to write as well. Like Chinese Nationalist officers, he saw diary writing and record keeping as part of a historical project to instruct later generations of military men. Still, the Japanese were, by the 1940s, much more dedicated record keepers than the

Americans. Judging by the existing archives, even the Chinese had a more systematized concept of diary writing than the United States, despite the fact that all officers did not strictly follow the rules all of the time. Nevertheless, it is important to note that military diary writing was consciously encouraged in the United States from the highest levels.

Critics might see such accounts, potentially subject to public scrutiny, as less reliable because of the lack of privacy. The use of "privacy" as a means of establishing a hierarchy of reliability for wartime diaries is fraught with methodological and philosophical problems. In fact, a belief in privacy can and did contribute to the increasing success of state, military, and mass-media forces' discipline of individuals in the modern era. Because the United States enjoyed a history of "privacy," grounded in legal rights over property vis-à-vis the state, examining the similarities between America and imperial Japan (where such rights were more easily violated by the state) will effectively demonstrate why historians should not attempt to define texts as "private" or "public." Before further analyzing American narratives of the Pacific War, it is essential to debunk any assumptions that American troops were categorically different than their counterparts in East Asia because they lived in a society that enjoyed greater freedom during the war. Examining the concept of "privacy" in diary writing is a good place to begin.

First, privacy itself is a historically determined concept; privacy in twentieth-century America was not the same as privacy in Victorian England. Throughout time, it has not been the same for all people; one hundred years ago, a woman's right to and experience of privacy was arguably different than a man's.[52] Second, texts composed in the tight homosocial confines of the armed forces can hardly be considered comparable to confessionals written in isolation on lonely mountain tops, and Americans at war enjoyed no more "privacy," however defined, than their East Asian counterparts. Both nations' armed forces, for example, exercised widespread censorship powers over the writings of their men. Sharpe, whose duties included censoring unit correspondence, noted that it could be "a little hard at first, reading other people's mail, and some of the letters are quite personal," but it did not stop him from making copies of "some very good poems" that he came across.[53] Diaries, in addition to letters, were also potentially under watch, even if they were not official field diaries. By 1945, blank diaries distributed to soldiers for personal use were printed with the following warning:

All members of the armed forces of the United States are cautioned not to
record herein any information which might be of value to any enemy of the
United States should this diary fall into the hands of enemy agents. Army
regulations require that regiments and similar organizations collect all diaries in the zone of operations and send them to the rear, where they will be
kept in a safe place.[54]

Surveillance was, therefore, ubiquitous, making the separation of "private"
documents from "public" ones a tricky venture, at best.

Having accepted the impossibility, or at least difficulty, of privacy in the
ranks, however, one should be careful not to embrace the opposite extreme,
namely, that the experience of war was entirely "public" all the time. Diaries from the South Pacific campaigns reveal that U.S. Marine Corps commanding officers, after using Japanese diaries as intelligence documents and
warning against such practices among Americans, were unable to prevent
soldiers from writing and, in some cases, simply gave their subordinates
freedom to write whatever they liked.[55] Stanley Rich, on his way to Guadalcanal in July 1942, wrote that the letter censors "haven't decided yet what
we can and can't say."[56] In fact, if VMF pilot Henry Miller's account is
accurate, sometimes military censors were "disciplined severely" for lax
enforcement.[57] Despite warnings about collection printed in blank diaries,
William Heggy did not trust the Marine Corps bureaucracy with his diary,
which was probably wise. He landed with the invading marines on Guadalcanal and was concerned about losing his diary of the momentous event, so
he went so far as to lock it in a bank vault while on furlough in Australia.[58]
Henry Miller noted in his diary that there was probably "a restriction
against anything like a diary," but he wrote one anyway, censoring his own
text to exclude dangerous information such as place names—something
Heggy did as well.[59] Letters, as the primary means of communication with
friends and family, were also very important to U.S. soldiers,[60] and so they
often tested the limits of acceptable language. Even servicemen who were
told not to write wrote anyway, assuming that censorship was purely for
tactical reasons; in other words, they exercised some self-discipline in keeping (what they judged to be) dangerous information out of enemy hands.
Nevertheless, U.S. military officials did sometimes confiscate and burn diaries when servicemen were preparing for repatriation, exactly as this system
was practiced in Japan. This happened to Stanley Rich's second, typewrit-

ten diary, which he had neglected to put in the "back of [his] shirt"—this was ironic because Rich often helped to censor his company's correspondence.[61] If the officers in charge of censorship flouted the rules, it would be silly to argue that ordinary soldiers followed them carefully.

The voices of authority were therefore incapable of sending a clear, consistent message on whether diary writing was acceptable; it only added to the confusion and chaos of writing war on the battlefield. First, the officer class was encouraged to write field diaries. Second, social conventions and print media were certainly working against any attempt by military authorities to squash frontline diary writing by ordinary soldiers; in fact, it seems hardly possible that armed forces anywhere were really determined to do any such thing. Diary writing was a Japanese modern military tradition since its inception in the late nineteenth century. Besides the massive market for civilian pocket diaries, the "Conquering Army Diaries" *(jūgun techō)* after 1937 were followed by Pacific war texts designed for soldiers (and the market for such pocket diaries expanded dramatically with increased conscription). The appearance of blank books entitled "Holy War Diaries" *(seisen techō)* signaled an increasing diversification of media interests profiting from servicemen's desire to pen self-narratives. By the end of the war, the Japanese Army was cooperating directly with women's groups and publishers to oversee the production of "Conquering Army Diaries" under the auspices of one of its own organizations: the "Land Army Courageous Soldiers Section" (Rikugun juppei-bu). If the Japanese armed forces strictly proscribed diary writing, why were they helping publishers mass-produce them for troops shipping off to war?[62]

Similar practices in the U.S. military show that Japan was not unique in this regard. Social support for "our troops" mobilized on a large scale is perhaps as old as war itself, but the mass production of blank "war diaries" was rather new. These blank diaries were published explicitly for servicemen shipping off to battle.[63] Some contained patriotic poems and songs, spaces to record comrades' names, and even "thoughts." The War Area Service Corps in China went so far as to produce a special version of a war diary for their servicemen, complete with Chinese holiday reminders and quotations from Confucius.[64] It is very likely that many of these diaries were given to U.S. troops by the Red Cross, along with, as one might guess, cigarettes, postcards (V-mail), and candy—just as their enemies in Japan would have received such items from patriotic social organizations. In some cases, in both the United States and Japan, "official" logbooks were also used as personal diaries, showing servicemen's remarkable tenacity for keeping personal records.[65] Similarly, Chinese Nationalist war diaries were often written on paper printed especially for the unit, with the division number printed on the margins of the blank diary. Chinese units continued to do this even as they retreated from China's industrial centers in the east, using handmade paper and portable field mimeograph machines. Although field commanders were certainly sensitive to the intelligence risk behind diary writing—and sometimes relayed orders to forbid it—diary writing among servicemen went on unabated.

Official "war diaries" in the U.S. armed forces were roughly comparable in form and content to their Japanese counterparts. For example, the Second Parachute Battalion's "War Diary" was evidently retyped and copied for distribution covering the dates from 27 October to 4 November 1943, just as "official" Japanese and Chinese diaries were copied by mimeograph from an original field notebook carried by a commanding officer (or one of his subordinate officers). Although the diary's content was mostly "just the facts" of a raid on Chousuei (in the Solomon Islands), the author used the first person ("I am in [Company Number]") and took time to describe events of import with more than just the robotic language of a record keeper: "The courage of these men swimming unarmed into territory which could possibly be in enemy hands, since there was no evidence of friendly forces and contact with the enemy had been imminent, is worthy of mention."[66] The diarist also used derogatory epithets such as "Nips" in the official document—a practice also embraced by the Chinese Nationalists, who frequently used terms such as *wonu* (Japanese slaves) in field diaries subject to superior review.

Nevertheless, U.S. troops continued to inscribe a sense of military professionalism into their records of war, and this tendency was not restricted to "official" accounts. U.S. Marine Corps Captain Robert P. Neuffer kept a personal diary of the invasion of Guam that was more or less the same as a "public" text. Neuffer recorded only those facts he deemed salient to capturing the essence of the war—from his perspective as a commanding officer. Thus, troop movements and battle tactics were meticulously recorded—some even by hours and minutes—and even when casualties arose, he made little effort to include his thoughts or feelings in lyrical detail. Also, much of the information was restricted to Neuffer's position: he did not always know what other units were doing, and he paid strict attention to whether the men under his command were receiving hot meals and coffee.[67] Neuffer's adoption of official form and content in his narrative is a reflection of his self-discipline as an officer. Similar habits were common among enlisted men, such as seventeen-year-old sailor Frances P. Cameron. His diary sticks to bare "facts" of ship movement, major activities, and the assignment of commanding officers. Even the end of the war did not merit any additional comment from him.[68] Jack Muecke, a sailor, included official congratulatory messages from General Douglas MacArthur and Rear Admiral Aaron S. Merrill in his personal account.[69]

It is important to point out the fundamentally transnational nature of twentieth-century military training; despite the seemingly vast differences in government organization, political ideology, and national culture, Japanese and American servicemen underwent very similar processes of discipline and experiences of war, even as late as 1944–1945. U.S. Marine Private George M. Dunn used his 1945 diary to record his induction into the battalion very matter-of-factly, noting sundry "chores" and the process of receiving his uniform, weapon, and immunizations. After his first day in the battalion, he added, "When I left the hospital this morning I had a funny feeling in my stomach as you feel the first day of high school or first day of work."[70] Similarly, infantryman Nakada Saburō's 1944–1945 pocket diary began with a simple chronicle of his induction, as well as notes on training lectures, names of commanding officers, and other information a soldier was expected to have at his command. Nakada described in his diary the harsh military training and near impossible standards for recruits but also how the quotidian existence of training and insect infestation made him think of the battles ahead:

> Due to the fleas and mosquitoes from last night, my head, neck, hands, and arms have itchy, painful sores on them. About 16, 17 bites every twenty minutes at night. When I think about how they'll come attack me tonight, I can feel the pain of the soldiers on the battlefield. . . . How can I beat back these insect night attacks? I was thinking while training for air raids: we stage retreats into escape trenches, but if there are air attacks, I worry about home. There is the feeling running amok right now—wanting to get to the battlefield and face the enemy.[71]

In the early stages of recruitment, then, most servicemen would have shared an experience very similar to those trained prior to the war or at its onset. Although the Japanese government would eventually, like the Chinese Nationalists, sacrifice adequate training for rapid deployment of more manpower, the process and experience of being mobilized seemed, according to the diaries, to have changed little during the war.

There were, however, some differences: when the U.S. government mobilized American society for war against Japan, Americans responded with venom that would have impressed even the Chinese Nationalists. As John Dower has shown, state-supported "racism" indeed exacerbated the willingness among men on both sides to commit acts of extreme brutality.[72] Still, Americans' personal and semiofficial accounts do not exclusively rely on this particular motivation for self-mobilization; in fact, other forms were more prevalent. For example, Americans bonded with one another according to other mutual affiliations. Often they were delighted to encounter men from their particular part of the United States (for example, New York City, a home state, and the South). Stanley Rich was pleased to discover that many of his fellow officers in the First Division Marine Corps were from his own Hobart College.[73] Young men were encouraged to fight by individuals with whom they shared a variety of relationships, and in their diaries, they selected the ones that provided them with a source of inspiration to commit themselves to the war.

As described earlier, the most important component of Japanese self-mobilization was the family, and this was true for the Americans as well. In Tennessee, pilot Clayton Knight begged the U.S. Army to move him out of Panama and to the Philippines, where U.S. forces were under attack and his nephew (also a serviceman) had disappeared. His anger was so intense that, when the army would not send him abroad, he publicly aired his gripe in the *Knoxville Journal.* Then he discussed his desire for revenge: "Wherever [my nephew] may be, I would like him to know that his uncle is only too anxious to meet those rats who have caused him all those hardships and who have brought perhaps death upon him. I hope that I may get the chance to even up the score." Even before the war, however, Knight was champing at the bit: he complained in a letter to his wife that, in the army, all he did was "eat and sleep" and that "a day's work would almost kill me now." Men like Clayton Knight came from farming communities and, like their Japanese counterparts, were accustomed to hard work. Also, like many born in rural communities, he was tightly connected to his blood relatives. Like men in East Asia, who had come to equate the war with the defense of the lives of their families, Knight's resolution was also deeply tied to his dedication to his loved ones, not only concern for the fate of his nephew, but even filial affection—a birthday card sent by his father became the foundation of Knight's resolve:

> In every fight you may battle hard
> And win what the world calls fame,
> But are you a pal with a true regard
> For the lad who will bear your name?
> . . .
> But best of all when the day is gone
> Is the chance to share your joy
> With the fellow who's proud of the fight you've won,
> The pride of your heart—your boy.[74]

It is possible, of course, that Americans, particularly those in rural or semirural areas such as those in the Midwest and the South, thought about the war in familial terms because their world was dominated by a multigenerational, extended family structure (similar to that of many Japanese). William Heggy, a marine recruit who departed in January 1942 for basic training, visited relatives and friends in a whirlwind of almost ritualized farewells that seem very similar to Japanese accounts. He recorded who he visited and when and in his diary noted, "All seemed to feel bad at my going away."[75] Servicemen also rushed to marry their sweethearts before shipping off. U.S. Marine Stanley H. Rich did so at the same time he was finishing college at Hobart. Rituals of marriage and graduation, then, were suffused by the presence of military mobilization, particularly as men began to participate in social events wearing their uniforms.[76] Even in great coastal cities, however, where smaller, nuclear families were becoming more common, people like Ralph Noonan explained that his sacrifice would keep his loved ones safe. He therefore used his diary repeatedly to strengthen his resolve by recording justifications that he could accept: "It is a queer thing to know that you are facing death with every minute. I suppose that is one reason for my being in this: so that my son will never have to face the same experience. It is not pleasant." When ocean waves at night transformed into phantasmal submarines in his eyes, he used this thought to control his experience of fear.[77] Stanley Rich tried to articulate the feeling of familial separation and anxiety as well, writing, "I suppose this and other thoughts are a part of what all people are subjected to in this queer war."[78]

Religion was also a large part of American social life in the twentieth century and thus could not be excluded from mobilization efforts during the war. We are much more comfortable in recognizing the role of state-sponsored Shintō in Japan and Buddhism in both Nationalist China and Japan, because historians have strongly associated these governments with oppressive political systems that harbor totalitarian ambitions (fascism, military authoritarianism, and so forth).[79] The role of religion in American mobilization, however, was also organized, ubiquitous, and guided by government and military authorities. For example, the history of military chaplaincy is as old as the United States armed forces, but the military began training its own chaplains during the mobilization of 1917.[80] The need for chaplains waxed and waned with the size of the U.S. military, but over one thousand were ready to serve by 1941. Some servicemen mocked religious comrades and chaplains, but U.S. soldiers, like Americans in general, were for the most part deeply religious people.[81] Alfred Tramposch, an army pilot, drew personal sketches of mass ceremonies conducted by military chaplains aboard ships crossing the Pacific.[82] Chaplains in the United States, just like their Japanese counterparts, performed mass funeral services on the battle-field, which the U.S. military organized in an attempt to guide survivors' memorial acts.[83] Judging from their diary entries, soldiers of all ranks and backgrounds made attending mass one of their daily routines and dutifully noted it along with their personal habits in letter writing and official duties, as well as drinking and gambling. In addition to providing spiritual counsel, chaplains also taught the men how to better read and write and educated them about history and geography. Building "character" through education and self-discipline was nothing new to religious authorities—Catholic organizations printed blank diaries that helped men remember important holidays and religious observances. This practice made its way to China by the twentieth century through Catholic schools, and these tools for religious self-discipline appeared in the pockets of Chinese youth in 1937 as the Japanese invaded. Many of these young men would die as soldiers in the Chinese Nationalist army. The strictures of self-discipline that came with religious life were advantageous for making the transition from civilian to soldier.

Self-discipline that results in behavior that is beneficial only or primarily to the state, however, cannot rely on the church; it requires the constant presence of a guiding authority, and government officials knew this. The Japanese state had already launched the project of consolidating and "guiding" the mass media, striving throughout the remainder of the war to eliminate any hint of the "critical, objective attitude of the past."[84] In the United States, President Roosevelt established the Office of Censorship in 1941, employing over 14,000 officials empowered to monitor all forms of communication. While the U.S. military censors allowed expressions of anger, love, and resolve to pass through their correspondence filters, they were relentlessly strict in excluding any reference to suffering or defeat. Letters arrived home pockmarked—scars of the process of government-guided memorialization. U.S. censors used precisely the same system as wartime Japan's—a censorship stamp marked "Passed By" was signed by the officer in charge, usually on the front of the envelope. In some cases, the letter's content was so thoroughly excised that relatives had to wait until the end of the war to discover what their son, brother, or father had wanted to tell them. "I hope my letters are reaching home without too much censored," began Private John Savard, "Well, it's so hard to write much, [so] I guess I will close [here]. By the way"—after which a section large enough for two more lines was cut out of the letter, followed by, "Well, that's all for now."[85] Some letters were probably self-censored. One serviceman, landing in Fort Kamehameha in Hawai'i two months after the Pearl Harbor attack, asserted rather incredulously that "the damage here has been grossly exaggerated."[86] Like the Japanese, Americans often emphasized in their correspondence how happy and committed they were: "I guess you wonder at times whether I regret my decision to leave. Well, I don't one minute."[87] Other writers tried to work around the censors. Paul Spengler, a doctor serving in Pearl Harbor, had to wait a year to mail "the dope" on the attack to his hunting buddies in Oregon: "You have read the official accounts. . . . I note relief in the mainland that it was not as bad as feared. If the truth were known, I don't think they would be so optimistic. . . . If you think these damn slant eyes didn't do a thorough job, guess again."[88] Prewar differences in legal systems notwithstanding, the practice of policing correspondence demonstrated that the U.S. government was not above exercising tight control over public discourse in the manner of wartime Japan.

The American mass media, for its part, accepted the Code of Wartime Practices in 1942, which demanded that war correspondents receive approval from military officials before publishing their work.[89] The U.S. mass media quickly produced America's version of the "common soldier" narrative written in diary form and, like their counterparts around the world, sent reporters to learn how soldiers speak and write in order to make their accounts sound more authentic.[90] Like Hino Ashihei and Xie Bingying did in their war accounts, Richard Tregaskis wrote *Guadalcanal Diary* as a reporter who made special claims to understanding the grunt at war. He claimed to have "come out here for action" and took great pains to describe the harsh life he shared with the marines, but while writing about "our losses" and the danger to "us," he also clearly defined his role as a correspondent. When fired upon by a Japanese sniper, Tregaskis described his precarious position: "I retreated behind a tent. And then anger caught up with me. Again the war had suddenly become a personal matter. I wanted to get a rifle and fire at the sniper. Correspondents, in theory at least, are non-combatants." This combination of objective distance and experiential proximity allowed him to comment on the marines with authority for the general public. Tregaskis also recounted the heroics of individual marines in a manner not unlike Japanese *bidan* and Chinese *jiahua;* he recorded their names and devoted a paragraph to their valiant acts. In the case of Private First Class Ray Herndon, of Walterboro, South Caroline, his last words could have come out of any military publication in East Asia: "You guys better move out. I'm done for anyhow. With that automatic, I can get three or four of the bastards before I kick off."

Tregaskis's marines, however, are even saltier than Hino's dusty (if hearty) lumpen proletariat. He tried to capture, as Azuma Shirō did, servicemen's prurient banter. When one marine ribbed another that he would only marry a girl he "could never make," his partner shot back: "F—— you, Mac. . . . The trouble with you is you never met a virgin." Like Hino, Tregaskis walked a very fine line when it came to describing the brutality of his own army; when a Japanese prisoner was brought into his camp, Tregaskis tried very hard to capture the truth of the experience without delegitimizing the marines' terrible anger:

As the Jap came toward us, there were angry shouts from the marines. "Kill
the bastard!" they yelled. "Kick him in the b——!"

This Jap did not have an inscrutable face. Now it was marked by signs of
terror obvious even to the Occidental eyes. The marine guard explained the
reason. "There were four of them," he said. "His three pals were cut in pieces."

Tregaskis was then ordered to escort the prisoner as a guard but remained
silent on whether he was guarding the Japanese soldier from being murdered
by the marines. Tregaskis was also less concerned than many of his contem-
poraries about avoiding discussion of American bodies—such as when he
described the gruesome sight of a marine hit by a Japanese 75mm shell. Yet
many of the themes addressed by Tregaskis, such as the historic importance
of their mission, were echoed in personal diaries. Tregaskis copied a colonel's
speech before the invasion of Guadalcanal, catching the officer during his
attempt to put his men into the proper state of mind: "It's the first time in
history we've ever had a huge expedition of this kind accompanied by trans-
ports. It's of world-wide importance. You'd be surprised if you knew how
many people all over the world are following this. You cannot fail them."[91]
The state, military, and mass-media management of discourse was particularly important in the beginning of the war: the beginning of 1942 marked
the ascendancy of the Japanese Empire, when it grew large enough to challenge the entire global order crafted by the Western powers.

One important difference between the U.S. mobilization for war and,
perhaps, the rest of the modern world was the extraordinary power of
American entertainment media. Paul Fussell remarked on this as important
to understanding why First World War narratives were "literary" but those
of the Second World War were not:

In 1914 there was virtually no cinema; there was no radio at all; and there
was certainly no television. Except for sex and drinking, amusement was
largely found in language formally arranged, either in books and periodicals
or at the theater and music hall, or in one's own or one's friends' anecdotes,
rumors, or clever structuring of words.[92]

Descriptions of films are ubiquitous in American diaries from 1941, underlining the impact they had on soldiers' views. Stanley Rich mentioned, like

many others, that, as early as June 1942, during the first U.S. invasion of Japanese-held territory, films were shown on his troopship every night.[93] His description of these events, however, does suggest that they were not quite the same thing as a trip to the movies today:

> First you have to show up early to get a decent seat (one brings a box or folding chair to sit on). Then, as it grows dark, flashlights play games on the screen or try to catch bugs in the beam and then you're in danger of getting burned as cigarette butts are flicked at the bugs. Finally, the show starts, maybe the sound is bad or the film breaks, but eventually the show goes on. Whenever a beautiful wench appears showing her shapely gams there is plenty of shriek-ing, groaning, and whistling, and whenever a particularly delightful bosom stares out at you from the screen there is a unanimous roar of approval. Should the movie have a hot dance number with plenty of bumps and grinds all hell breaks loose. . . . It's really pathetic to see the boys out here in a driving tropi-cal downpour patiently sitting and watching a rotten, old class B picture.[94]

Some servicemen recorded in their diaries every movie they saw—an almost daily ritual for years. This helped alleviate boredom and boost morale. Al-though Japanese and Chinese servicemen also had their own forms of enter-tainment, they were often less technologically sophisticated. The American media also left an imprint on servicemen's records that made them different than their East Asian counterparts: Americans encoded "buddy comedy" dialogues directly into their accounts of the war and the interactions they had with their fellow soldiers, which was something quite rare in East Asian diaries. Nevertheless, although Fussell was right that film was a new tech-nology that came to share equal footing with literature in servicemen's lives, to describe his experience in the war the ordinary soldier could not make a movie. For that, he still had to go back to the written word.

Mobilization for war with the United States placed even greater de-mands on Japanese servicemen; in this environment, diary writing became even more widespread. The Japanese military continued its practice of guided diary writing during the opening months of the Pacific War, with more offi-cers using training diaries as a matter of personal discipline. Most young officers used this space as they always had: a record of truth, a tool for self-mobilization, and a space to negotiate with popular discourse. Officer-in-training Marumoto Hideshi used his "Record of Self-Improvement" *(shūyōroku)* to push himself to ever higher standards of excellence, criticizing and encouraging himself by writing phrases such as "One must always throw oneself gallantly into self-conditioning [*renmatsu*], and [have] the strength of steel."[95] Pilots in training had dutifully kept diaries subject to review by their education officers—a process that would only accelerate in intensity with the formation of the "Special Attack Forces" *(tokkōtai,* colloquially known as *kamikaze).* As the war intensified, then, so did the state's involvement in observation of subjects through their diaries.

After Japan launched its war against the Western powers, it seemed that Japanese soldiers were encouraging themselves to accept a dangerous worldview through their diary writing. Special attack pilots in the Philippines were told by their superiors that "America's battle plan, seen rationally, seems like the result of an idiotic idea. We should attack them as if to expose [this idiocy]." This diarist wrote in detail that he could attack American transport vessels and noted how flying parallel to the sea at low altitude would be most devastating.[96] Tsuchida Shōji left his job at an airplane factory to enroll in a Youth Pilot Academy (Shōnen hikō gakkō) at age fifteen—the only alternative to the high school education that he could not afford. His "Record of Self-Reflection" *(hanseiroku)* reveals his enthusiasm for study, sense of being a part of history, and eagerness to receive guidance from older men who spoke with authority:

> I was told that, in order to become the best air force in the world, we need the best training. In my heart I made an unshakeable oath that through this year—no, this *life*—I [*jibun*] will show the spirit of the people of Shiga, and become someone who will leave his name for posterity.

To this his area commander *(kutaichō)* responded (with red ink in Tsuchida's diary): "Go for it [*ganbare*]!" Once his Special Attack Force unit had been organized, Tsuchida noted that in this stage of the war divisions between the homeland *(naichi)* and the battlefield *(senchi)* were meaningless, because it "will be a great, decisive battle [*kessen*] when the rise or fall of the nation [*kokukyobōji*] will be fought"—words that harkened back to the fervent Chinese Nationalist mobilization during 1937. "At this time," he continued, "problems with thought [*shisō*] are more important than those of materiel [*busshitsu*]," because young pilots like Tsuchida felt the weight of having to lead the entire nation to sacrifice by his own example.[97] Tsuchida's diary was an attempt to discipline himself in this manner—he assiduously copied superior officers' admonitions, praise, and lectures, incorporating all of these into his self-narrative. Perhaps because of such obvious dedication among the pilots, servicemen in other branches of the armed forces, as did Japanese civilians, idolized the Special Attack Forces, and a morbid cult soon developed around these young men. A Japanese officer in the Philippines, Obara Fukuzō, hearing of such a sixteen-year-old pilot, wrote, "In the sixteenth year of life to have attained such self-control, such enlightenment, is surely to have attained the sublime heights of the gods. This is Japan! This is Japan!"[98] Thus, the highly textualized self-discipline of the Special Attack Forces not only served the aims of training but also produced national exemplars who sometimes even exceeded the state's expectations. Still, some servicemen did not fool themselves and used their diaries to express skepticism. Sixteen-year-old flight recruit Nishimoto Masaharu, who toasted Special Attack pilots before their departure, knew better after over two years in flight school (yokaren) than to slavishly adore these heroes: "I wonder if the Special Attack pilots from last night made it safely to their target ships. . . . No way [masaka]."[99]

Nevertheless, many men felt compelled to follow in the Special Attack pilots' footsteps—even if they ended up at different destinations. Some might be surprised to learn that educated and intelligent men, drafted into the bottom of the military hierarchy, embraced guided diary writing, but they did. Nakamura Tokurō, who had completed high school and was pulled out of Tokyo Imperial University in 1942, wrote a diary (shūyōroku) that was subject to weekly inspections. Nakamura's diary was divided into sections for date, weather, records (kiji), and impressions (shokan). During his training, Nakamura had intense dialogues with his superior officers, who seemed to enjoy interacting with an "intellectual." "Your troop ship goes down," his internal affairs officer (naimuhanchō) barked, "Will you live? Will you die?" Confronted with imagining such a situation, Nakamura used his diary to ponder the possibility of death: "Every day death provides discipline [shūyō]," Nakamura wrote. "People who suddenly face death after not giving it a single thought are not likely to die with grace [rippa na shinikata]." Interactions with his superior spilled over into the diary because Nakamura needed to make these lessons a part of himself. Ultimately, Nakamura found a way to bind his "philosophical" nature to his military life, realizing that otherwise he was not likely to survive either the army or the battlefield:

Just ruminating on empty rationalizations [*rikutsu wo konemawashi*] is meaningless, he [Nakamura's superior] said. But that theory is too shallow. It is useless [*toru ni taranai*]. . . . At the moment of death, I will be fortunate if I can be satisfied and say, "No problem [*kore de yoshi*]!" We need an everyday lifestyle that makes this possible. I can't be one of those people who dies shouting, "Oh shit!" But most people are like this.[100]

Postwar accounts of military service, however, frequently emphasize the brutality of the ranks for those who did not correspond to military ideals—in particular intellectuals. Arbitrary and savage beatings were frequent.[101] Indeed, as Oki Seiichi wrote in his diary, "It's a mistake to assume there's no contradiction in sending 'intellectuals' into a mix of young officers and reckless, rough, and largely uneducated soldiers."[102] Ordinary servicemen, however, had just as many tales, and they were just as unforgettable: a private from Suita sketched a scene where a sergeant beat a green recruit in front of all of his comrades for a minor infraction.[103] Still, immediate postwar resentment notwithstanding, during the war, many were able to craft selves that allowed them to embrace a military that abused them daily and sent them far away to die in hopeless battles.

It may seem surprising that individuals would adapt so readily to an abusive system, but servicemen felt pressure to be part of the group in order to ensure their survival, and this "language community" had a set of values built into it. Indeed, most devastating to the concept that Americans' love of individualism and privacy set them apart from East Asians (or that such privacy would even be possible) is the fact that they created tight homosocial communities that worked strongly against independence of thought and action. Integral to the functioning of self-mobilization was servicemen's love for their war buddies; this was, however, only one part of the community values that servicemen embraced as they rewrote themselves in their diaries. Armed forces in Japan and the United States began by "breaking down" individuals through humiliation, then "building up" those same men to work as a team—official training techniques that were replicated in unofficial practices between soldiers.[104] This was reflected in their language. Japanese servicemen even substituted personal pronouns for "I" (*watakushi*, and so forth) for the indefinite "myself/oneself" (*jibun*), using these forms in their diaries to express individual membership within a larger group.[105] Japanese soldiers further expressed their tight group cohesion (*danketsu*) in their diaries by calling the nonmilitary world the "provinces" *(chihō)* and civilians "provincials" *(chihōjin)*.[106] In fact, Japanese servicemen and their American counterparts, through speech and an almost universally shared collection of printed text (newspapers, novels, and informational pamphlets), adopted an entire vocabulary essential for communication in the armed services.[107] Walter E. Lee, an officer in the U.S. Navy, recalled the terms used by the new group to which he belonged: "I learned a new language like 'What's the dope,' 'Chow,' and everyone in the Navy being called 'Mac.'"[108] Diaries and even spoken language in the Japanese armed forces were peppered with neologisms borrowed from Chinese, revealing the deep impact the occupation of China had on the armed forces. In postwar Japan, with many men returning only after enduring long years on the front, newspapers even printed glossaries of "Soldier-ese" *(heitaigo)*, including pidgin phrases derived from spoken Chinese but given with a distinct Japanese accent. For example, when demanding something be done quickly, instead of simply saying "hurry up" *(hayaku* or *sassa to)* in standard Japanese, servicemen said "kai-kai dē" *(kuai kuai de* in Chinese).[109] Soldiers designed a language community of their own on the battlefield, which was strengthened by bonds they developed for survival, and their strange cognates, neologisms, and technical jargon made them nearly unintelligible to the civilian world.

Men who went to war not only invented a new language; many developed new relationships with women, even while pining for their girlfriends, fiancées, and wives at home. This began even before the men had seen war. Walter Lee, a sailor in San Francisco, described how he frequented "girlie shows on Market Street," night clubs, and, "of course, Fisherman's Wharf. There were always pretty girls that joined us. There were no 'meaningful relationships' that I was aware [of]. Everyone just wanted to have a good time."[110] U.S. marine James O'Leary developed a long-standing relationship with a local woman named "Rosa," who was indignant when called "Mrs. O'Leary" by James's friends. Griffith, running about with women in New Zealand while recovering from malaria, remarked, "Mary [his fiancée] will probably give me hell if she ever reads this diary—if I'm there to hear her" but assuaged his guilt by adding, "little does she know what a strong deterrent factor she is in all my actions."[111] As O'Leary noted before the war, however, keeping women on the side was not a new practice among the U.S. Armed Forces—even when they were shipping off, prostitutes rode alongside of naval officers while older servicewomen such as nurses were forced to walk.[112] That the Japanese established a military-run system of enforced prostitution, the so-called comfort system, demonstrates the state's acknowledgment of this widespread phenomenon and its attempt to control it. War is certainly not the only social condition under which men join communities with inflexible rules and new relationships, but the ruthless logic of "kill or be killed" that pervaded their diaries put special pressure on them to discipline themselves in order to fit this community's standards of acceptance. Soldiering was not solely about brotherhood, however, as more senior soldiers often preyed on juniors coming into the ranks.[113]

Nevertheless, camaraderie presents insurmountable problems for those who want to read diaries as "private" documents or those written with an "intended audience" in mind. Servicemen allowed their friends' voices to commingle with their own—almost as if imitating the chaotic, multiparticipant commentaries in war reportage—suggesting a tendency (or desire) to fuse their identities together. George Gallion may have been keeping a record of his captivity for himself, his family, or even a broader "posterity," but sometimes his war buddy Don Henderson took the diary and wrote comic messages, after which George seemed to be writing for their mutual amusement. After using his diary to record the camp's inadequate rations, Henderson grabbed the book to tease the more serious Gallion, and a dialogue of dueling grunt banter (conducted in contrasting handwriting) ensued:

For lunch we had (corn, one GI spoonful, camote soup and a sukashi [Jp. *sukoshi,* "a little"] piece of cornbread with peanuts in it.

P.S. [in different handwriting] I feel as if I had not et [eaten]. Don J. Henderson.

If it stays this way, I will always feel the same.

Geo. should not complain—he went thru for thirds before I did. What a chow-hound he is!!!

Don is a bigger liar than I am.

That is only one man's opinion—ask some of the other boys that know him as well as I do.

I am positive that you will find they all agree with me.

That's a bunch of Manuck Tihee. Don J. Henderson.[114]

It is precisely at moments such as these that the instability of the diarist's "intended audience" is revealed. In some cases, the intended audience may seem quite clear: William Sharpe addressed his diary ("For My Honey"), but was he always thinking of his "honey" in every entry?[115] Patrick Noonan initially kept a disciplined military diary (evidently for no one in particular) but then began a new record for 1942 after he lost his previous account. He addressed this new diary to his son, Timmy Noonan, and proclaimed, "I'll keep this book of incidents of my wanderings, for you and 'Mummy,' Timmy. But it is not a diary, merely a series of observations, stories and facts that might be interesting to you."[116] Nonetheless, Noonan's subsequent account was frequently graphic and seems today to have been inappropriate for his young son. U.S. soldiers, like their counterparts in East Asia, kept diaries for various purposes, but trying to define the "intended audience" of these personal documents is like chasing after the wind. That servicemen allowed other men inside their self-narratives and neglected the conditions of intended audiences stated in the diary itself show not only how contested a diary's space was (after all, the language of the state and the mass media were in there as well) but also how this practice and official ideology (promoting camaraderie) continued to produce many unintended consequences.

Both Japanese and U.S. authorities in mass media, military, and government, however, accelerated their efforts to guide self-narratives. As mentioned earlier, around 1940 blank diaries printed for servicemen began to circulate in vast numbers in Japan. Private Ichikawa Jūzō bought or received one that featured photos of Mount Fuji and cherry blossoms as well as songs such as "The Patriotic March" *(aikoku kōshinkyoku)* and "The Bivouac Song" *(roei no uta)*. The back of the diary contained spaces for "Names of Officers" *(jōkan shimei),* "Names of War Buddies" *(senyū shimei),* and "records of correspondence" *(tsūshin memo)*.[117] Edward Hickman bought a similar blank diary in late 1943. Like its Japanese counterparts, the diary encouraged a sense of camaraderie among the men by allotting space for entering information about "My Buddies in the Service" along with chummy pictures of men marching together, playing music, and chatting in the barracks. The back of the diary featured a section for "autographs," which instructed the owner of the diary to "have each of your buddies write a verse, sentiment, or characteristic comment . . . and sign his name" and depicted servicemen laughing and sharing their diaries with one another. The body of the text featured space for Hickman's running narrative of his life in the South Pacific, but it was interpellated,

as often were his ideas about himself, with preprinted aphorisms and quotations about war and heroism. Ultimately, it is unclear where or when publishers
began printing these diaries for servicemen, but in both Japan and the United
States during the war, they were quite common and remarkably similar.

Still, the reality of military life made its mark on the otherwise heroic identity that state, military, and media actors had crafted for diary authors. The attempt to structure Hickman's narrative was not always successful—despite the
favorable progress of the war in late 1943, the considerable ideological output
from American propaganda, and the tradition of disciplined soldiering in
the U.S. Armed Forces. Even in the "Identification" section of his diary,
under the category "Birthmarks or Other Distinguishing Characteristics,"
Hickman enjoyed a clownish rebellion: "Ugly as ____, dumb as ____, mean
as ____, small as ____, red-headed, bow legged, high-tempered." Composing strict records of what he saw and did encouraged Hickman's irascible nature and therefore kept him from embracing an altogether heroic image of the
war against Japan. Above the encouraging phrase "What can alone ennoble
fight? A noble cause!" Hickman recorded "Jap nurses ran out of hospitals with
breasts showing and ripping their clothes off to keep Aussies from killing
them. Aussies shot them just the same."[118] Once on the battlefield, the American military response to potential anxieties was similar to that of the Japanese
in China, as shown in this speech given by a U.S. Marine Corps Major:

> Now what the hell, you joined this outfit to fight, and fight I've every confi-
> dence in you that you will. Forget about this dying business; you can't live
> forever. Think instead about the killing, concentrate on squeezing off those
> shorts, make every round land in one of those little yellow bastards. They
> kill easy. Sure we'll get bombed, sure we'll get shelled, sure its tough to take
> it, but I want every god-damned son-of-a-bitch in this outfit to stay in his
> position and keep thinking, "Let 'em come, brother, let 'em come," and
> when they do acquit himself like the man and Marine he is.[119]

Nevertheless, self-discipline did not necessarily mean simply imbibing
ideas about oneself and direction from authorities. Officers such as U.S.
Marine Corps (then First Lieutenant) Joseph Griffith suffered from as much
a lack of self-confidence in their command as Chinese Nationalists like Liu
Jiaqi did. Griffith observed, "others in general have actually cried when telling me their troubles. Half of them are older than myself—what can I tell

them?" Yet instead of drawing on the examples of the superior officers whom he despised, he employed humor to hold his unit together, constantly buttressing his own confidence through diary writing: "only by kidding and making a constant fool of myself can I keep them normal."[120] Nakamura, the would-be university student drafted right after high school, also realized that his ideals of military self-improvement did not always conform to those of his superiors; when he chided himself on his declining skills in German, his commanding officer wrote in large, clumsy script, "*What use* is German for a soldier who is dutifully waiting to die?" When the theft of his property led to daily "private punishments" *(shiteki seizai)*—that is, when men secretly beat and abused offenders on their own—Nakamura wrote that he wished the whole thing had never happened. He described the broken teeth, black eyes, and busted ears as a "hundred demon night parade" *(hyakki yakō)*. Most important, these incidents of perverse military discipline did not affect Nakamura's self-disciplinary practices; he merely redefined this concept for himself:

> It is easy to investigate others and dole out punishment. It is more difficult when, examining others' imperfections [*ara*] and calling attention to it, one critiques oneself [*hansei*] as well. . . . I think that there is nothing more grotesque than an impulsive act based on a kind of psychological or physical rage. To say that one's adrenaline was pumping is neither here nor there. I want to think slowly, and write with care. I want to discipline myself [*shūyō*]. I *must* discipline myself.[121]

Japanese troops were accepting the call from military authorities that they discipline themselves for war, but those same authorities could not ultimately control this process. In this sense, many Japanese soldiers' inconsistent responses to prevailing ideologies in Japan contrasts sharply with Americans' ability to overcome "individualism."

Indeed, U.S. authorities' ambition to convince soldiers to sublimate their individuality and embrace group cohesion ironically reflected their monstrous image of the Japanese enemy. American films produced during the war attempted to show U.S. soldiers in a unified way: directors attempted to show how differences between recruits such as regional and socioeconomic background were made insignificant by military training. Many Americans continue to believe, as they were told during the war, that the

Japanese military was full of brainwashed robots (or emotionally volatile warriors who would irrationally fight to the death). During the war, this belief was strengthened by the ferocity of the Japanese attack. An internal U.S. military memo, however, cast a shadow of doubt over the impressive image of the stalwart and sadistic samurai: it noted that most Japanese units were willing to surrender, provided the U.S. forces promised not to tell the Japanese government that they had been captured. This lesson—that the Japanese might respond to the right overtures—was learned at a terrible cost, after the U.S. suffered massive casualties in an attempt to exterminate what they thought to be an insane foe at Guadalcanal.[122] Even so, many American units persisted in their previous image of the Japanese and pursued an unwise military strategy while encouraging themselves to conform to the group and show no mercy to their foes.

Did these accounts prove that American diarists, because of the history of legal protections and cultural appreciation for privacy, resisted efforts to guide their thoughts and actions? Were men from countries such as the United States (or, for example, Australia) immune to the conditions that made the Japanese such merciless fighters? If we are to accept the examples here and in previous chapters of Nakamura and other diarists (even those where they were writing under the watchful eye of their superiors), then it would seem that cultural differences in "privacy," a problematic notion in and of itself, had little impact on the development of subjectivity in diary writing.

SELF-DISCIPLINE OUTSIDE OF EAST ASIA

In an interview about his book *The Captive Mind,* Czeslaw Milosz captured how tricky it is to separate the "real self" from a consciously created one. "Sometimes I even blame myself for 'wearing a mask' or several masks," he wrote, "But for all I know this may sometimes be a necessary condition of effective action."[123] Every self that we develop is a mask, and no identity is necessarily more authentic than any other. In order to meet the enemy, Japanese and American men had to become "soldiers," which involved training in the barracks and, more important, learning from battlefield experience. Gerald Linderman wrote that American soldiers were not very good at discipline, particularly when Americans lost their battles and ended up in POW camps.[124] Nevertheless, Chinese Nationalist soldiers fled from their trenches, and

Japanese soldiers were not simply stoic superwarriors in defeat. The ability of American troops to succeed during the invasion of the Pacific where Japanese, Chinese, and even the "well-ordered" British failed was, to a large degree, due to their willingness to be organized, to discipline themselves, and to self-sacrifice. In a sense, many of these perceptions of "disorder" are in the eye of the beholder: for the Japanese, British POWs appeared "undisciplined," and to the Americans, Japanese "banzai charges" seemed like disorganized madness.

It is important, however, not to overstate the similarities, particularly when it comes to war diary writing. It may first appear that servicemen in the United States and East Asia had adopted exactly identical means of self-discipline in the modern era. In fact, however, when one looks at the big picture, East Asian militaries were even more advanced in this regard. Although U.S. servicemen kept records of their engagements for official purposes, these were usually in the form of battle reports or logs of transmissions between different military posts.[125] Guided diary writing was not broadly systematized by the U.S. military as a training exercise as it was in East Asia, even though it was taken quite seriously by the highest military authorities. Military historian Louis Morton noted that supposedly "private" diaries among officers were often products of collective discipline; in the case of A. C. Tisdelle's account of the fall of the Philippines, Morton pointed out that Tisdelle also used the diary to make entries on behalf of his superior officer, Edward P. King, so that, in some respects, "the diary may be considered as General King's."[126] Military diary writing shows many similarities across the world at this time; like Tisdelle and King, Chinese diarists often had clerks make copies, take down dictated entries, or share their accounts. In the Soviet Union, private accounts were also compromised: invasive technologies of self-discipline were already over a decade old by 1941, dating back to self-criticisms when Stalinism emerged in the Soviet Union; these were mirrored in the armed forces.[127] It is widely known that Chiang Kai-shek invited Soviet advisors to the Huangpu Military Academy and adopted their program of political education in the military, even as he renounced communism as an ideology and greatly distrusted the Soviets.[128] Predating all of these socialist techniques, the Japanese military already had a system of military diary review in the nineteenth century, which Chiang Kai-shek greatly admired. In any event, diary writing as a form of state-sponsored indoctrination (one that penetrated down to the deepest levels) was a transnational phenomenon characteristic of modernity.

How effective was self-discipline in the U.S. military? Despite Americans' putative dedication to privacy and rugged individualism, they were able to imbibe the language of the state, mass media, and military at least as effectively as their counterparts in the USSR, China, and Japan. As Stanley Rich observed before the landing on Guadalcanal, "The men are all in high spirits—no need to wave a flag or give them a pep talk."[129] Conversely, in societies with an extremely intrusive state apparatus, such as the Soviet Union, grumblers and antiwar gripers were not in short supply. Army translator Vladimir Stezhenskii, for example, being already familiar with the army, an educated man, and part of a family victimized by Stalin's regime, was suspicious of official rhetoric and drew his language more from his studies in Moscow. His rich prose was often acerbic and biting; when drafted he quickly wrote, "Once again I'm a small cog in the enormous, creaking, unoiled machine that is called 'the Army.' "[130] Sometimes it appears that societies where an inviolable "private sphere" was believed to exist had even more effective state mobilization campaigns than their more "hands-on" correlates in other countries. In the end, however, all states relied heavily on the self-discipline of both citizen and soldier during the Second World War.

This finding has broad implications not only for how we understand the course and consequences of the war but also for the notions and theories of subjectivity in the modern era altogether. As this exploration in self-discipline has shown, state mechanisms in Nationalist China, Japan, and the United States not only enforced the content for subjectivity but also gave soldiers the tools to create it. It may seem foolish for the state to have given servicemen so much control, but we must consider the needs of nations engaged in total war, whose servicemen had to be dedicated and flexible. In the continual mobilization for total war, the state needed to harness a soldier's creative energies to realize its own program—a necessity that goes to the very heart of modernization programs.[131] No one could have foreseen the radical shifts many servicemen took when engaged in the perilous practice of self-discipline. In the postwar era, the consequences of these acts would be difficult to ignore.

CHAPTER FIVE

The Physics of Writing War

Recording the Destruction of the Japanese Empire

LANGUAGE IS NOT only defined by what it says but also by what is does not, and even cannot, articulate. In many cases, soldiers openly acknowledged this fact, rejecting the ability of writing to truly represent the war that they were experiencing. M. O'Neil began his diary account with the following disclaimer:

> No one has been able to capture the real feeling of what combat is like. Many books have been written, hundreds of feet of film have been made, thousands of words have been spoken, all of these means have failed to give the true horrible picture, the awful noise, the smell, and the fear that makes one stand up and scream out the horror that is pent up inside of you. And yet, under all this there is really something beautiful about combat.[1]

Writers of war diaries described combat experience by tinkering with various forms and genres; whether accurate or not, soldiers tried their best to shape the written language around what they experienced on the battlefield. When diarists have left out material from their self-narratives, this can, in part, be explained by the fact that whatever we wanted to hear from them—information about atrocities, confessions about sexual experiences, or reflections about the role of gender during war—was not part of the genre they chose to use. Nevertheless, the silent and dark cavities within these diaries still exercised some influence over whatever form finally came to light, much like how the immense gravity of a dark star affects visible matter all around it. We cannot fully know what it means to be a soldier in the Second World War or totally grasp the experience of trauma throughout these passages. Precisely because soldiers endeavored to write about them, however, these powerful moments twisted and transformed the language in war diaries. Forces that wield such power over us, such as trauma, fear, and love, while perhaps ultimately beyond representation, cannot be ignored. Furthermore, to avoid them in historical research because they cannot be adequately described is irresponsible, precisely because they influenced the language diarists used. How, then, should historians, whose work is entirely consumed by language, approach the unspeakable? This chapter will look at how the ineffable experiences of soldiers during the collapse of the Japanese Empire affected their writing, even if the act of writing itself ultimately could not capture those experiences, and how that writing was, in turn, a foundation for their subjectivity.

In addition to this, the role of the diary in developing a view of oneself as part of a "victorious," "failing," and historically significant military force will be examined. The remarkable similarities between the Japanese, Chinese, and Americans outlined earlier continued even as the Japanese became the losers of the war, adopting many of the same rhetorical strategies as had the Chinese Nationalists and American colonial forces when they faced total defeat. American servicemen, for their part, developed a sense of superiority over the enemy—similar to Japanese troops in 1937 and 1941—as they struggled with the conflicted morality of modern warfare. Although some of the Pacific Command leadership had been saved from capture in the Philippines, the troops themselves were largely fresh recruits, and certainly very few of them had seen action against Japan. Americans accepted a vision of themselves as cogs in a victorious military machine of historic significance, whereas the Japanese would have to reconcile the implications of their total defeat.

RETAKING THE PACIFIC: LEARNING FROM THE JAPANESE

Ralph Noonan, in one of his most observant moments, wrote that Carlson's Marine Raiders "are more like the American Indian than human beings." Drawing on an image of brutality created in the American imagination— the Native American "savage" that was popular in film, literature, and historiography before 1941—he had admitted that the U.S. troops were becoming like the Japanese as the two forces came into close contact. Since Mayne Reid's bildungsroman *The Boy Hunters,* a generation of American men were exposed to tales of boys acquiring masculine power by vanquishing the primal Other (the Native Americans) and in the process becoming, they believed, more like them.[2] Inexperienced servicemen such as Noonan, however, were initially more aghast than impressed with Americans' transformation. "Marines have reached the stage where they are absolutely bloodthirsty," Noonan wrote, "have run across evidence (plenty of it) which would indicate that the Japs are torturing their prisoners and the Marines are out to even up the score. . . . Have found [Japanese] men cut to pieces with bayonets."[3] Eventually even Noonan, who was a deeply committed family man and an observant Christian horrified by extreme violence, would effectively condone their actions as necessary for fighting a barbaric foe; this was perceived to be, as Gerald Linderman put it, a situation wherein "the Japanese imposed on their enemies the war they intended to fight."[4] Particularly after U.S. troops experienced warfare or suffered some trauma, servicemen were inclined to see their more rough-edged comrades as survivors, and many thus struggled to emulate them. To the enemy, however, it was a sign that the Americans were the moral hypocrites that the Japanese had always claimed them to be; as a Japanese propaganda pamphlet proclaimed: "America's highly polished, apparently attractive exterior has cracked, showing the ugly veins of brutality, the shoddy cheapness of its soul. America has abandoned the thin veneer of civilization and openly adopted the methods of barbarians."[5]

The first force that the U.S. deployed, in offense, against the Empire of Japan was the navy, because it was absolutely necessary to secure shipping lanes between the United States and its Commonwealth allies in the Pacific. Initially, most U.S. forces merely patrolled Pearl Harbor out of fear of another attack. The U.S. Navy had been hurt by the attack on Pearl Harbor, but fatally for Japan, its aircraft carriers survived. Still, from the soldier's perspective, preparation for war was slow and frustrating. U.S. sailors and naval officers responded much as their comrades in the marines and army would, namely, by self-mobilization, even if the armed forces were not ready yet to launch large attacks. In many ways, being a sailor waiting for battle was worse than serving in any other branch, because sailors were subject to far stricter security protocols and often trapped on board their ships. Nearly a month after Pearl Harbor, Cash wrote in his diary that the men on the USS Hopkins were "all getting restless and irritable. Some mail + liberty would be a great help."[6] Others were less eager to go to the battlefield: Guy Landers complained about being stuck on base, "sitting here blue and wonting [*sic*] to go home."[7] As the ships crossed the Pacific toward the Japanese Empire, the men on board recorded their seasickness, loneliness, and anxiety. Composing his diary in the midst of a storm, F. J. George wrote: "[r]ather an unpleasant feeling to be tearing along blindly thru unfamiliar waters." Officers like George felt a tremendous pressure to safely and successfully command their expensive (and vulnerable) charges in dangerous waters; when he was moved to a new command on a larger vessel, he stared out over the ship, isolated from his fellow officers and men, and wrote, "gawd how lonely I felt. . . . [O]ne of these days, I'm liable to bite off more than I can chew."[8] U.S. Marine Corps officers, such as Captain Harry Findley, were deeply anxious prior to the invasion of Guadalcanal: "As to my feelings—they are quite mixed; a jumble of strong emotions. The other officers, like myself, are laughing and talking but if you watch them you will see each one every now and then stop talking and gaze off into space—his face becoming quite serious."[9] Despite their anxiety, the United States achieved its crucial first victory against Japan in the Battle of Midway. This secured the shipping lanes across the Pacific and linked the United States with Australia and New Zealand, whose support would be critical in the "island hopping" campaigns that followed.

American commanders desperately needed to establish a foothold in the Solomon Islands, with an eye to taking the Japanese headquarters at Rabaul. Even though Midway was a major victory (now generally accepted as the turning point), the course of the war was far from definite in August 1942; in fact, the initial U.S. marine invasion force, led primarily by Alexender Vandergrift's First Division, may have survived this action only due to the Japanese army's grievous error in thinking that the marines were a reconnaissance force, not a full-scale invasion.[10] The marines who secured the initial victories for the United States were frightened of and horrified by the intensity of their foes—in their first diary entries they struggled to find words to express their terror. Consequently, many felt it necessary to respond in kind, and those that decided to fight like the Japanese often committed atrocities in the process. How had Japanese and American servicemen become so ferocious? Was one merely reacting to the other, or was it that, as John Dower argued, "racial and racist ways of thinking" had contributed to the ferociousness of the war?[11] Although racism supported by state propaganda certainly played a role, U.S. and Japanese servicemen's "barbaric" behavior was overall a product of their personal rationales (which could, of course, include the racist views that Dower described) rather than the machinations of the state or the power of wartime ideology.[12] As with the Japanese and Chinese during the Second Sino-Japanese War, U.S. and Japanese servicemen were self-disciplined, and this discipline was often rooted in the intensity of combat experience.

As the American armed forces mobilized to pierce the outside rim of the Japanese Empire, U.S. servicemen felt compelled to chronicle their aches and pains, even when they were victorious. First, the Pacific was a foreign environment for the vast majority of Americans. The ocean itself was a terrifying terra incognita for soldiers like William Sharpe:

> My God, doesn't the ocean look big—and endless! It stretches out to the horizon in every direction; what chance would a man have [of] being located if he were forced down out here and had to retire to the little yellow life rafts. It's a most unpleasant thing to even think about.[13]

Furthermore, despite media portrayals of cheerful camaraderie, theft among the men was unrelenting and often audacious, at times creating a decidedly hostile atmosphere.[14] The tropical jungle, however, was the space that few Americans would have known, and they came to write about it in a hateful manner. Stanley Rich described the strange new world in unflattering terms: "hacked our way into the worst jungle I have ever seen. Almost unpenetrable without a machete. Prickly vines all over and long creepers . . . The climate is damp, hot, and very humid. You live in sweat and dirt."[15] Most of the complaints would be familiar to servicemen from any war, such as vermin and insect infestation, terrible food, and disease, including cholera, beriberi, scabies, jaundice, dysentery, fungal infections of the skin, STDs, and, most feared of them all, malaria. George Dunn, who was arriving to replace exhausted marines from the First Division, noted that the men

> have all sorts of tropical skin diseases in various degrees. Some have open sores about the size of a large boil. They call it "jungle rot." Others have ringworm, fungus, or rashes. A lot of the men have pure white blotches on their bodies. It's as if they lost the pigment in these spots on their heavily tanned skin. Others are yellow from the Atabrin. I guess I look the same to them.[16]

Although they had been there longer, the Japanese too were unaccustomed to the jungle and consequently suffered in the same way: their feet were covered in burning fungal infections, and tainted water gave rise to many virulent diseases. Army doctor Omi Masao, in his "memo" from the Philippines, provided a short list of the problems afflicting Japanese troops on the run from American invaders: "Because there are so few of us, we turned back into the thick jungle. Then, malaria, malnutrition, starvation, exhaustion, total physical enervation [*zenshin suijaku*], and diarrhea produced many deaths."[17] Unrelenting U.S. attacks from the air required that the Japanese move at night, which resulted in injury, fear, and constant disruptions in communications.[18] Creeping along the coast and avoiding the jungle brush, Watanabe, who had moved from Indonesia to Guadalcanal with the Ichiki Detachment, wrote that the forest "smelled of rotting corpses." The constant rain and sand fleas left the Japanese army "utterly exhausted" and made starting fires to cook food extremely difficult.[19]

Second, the reality of war itself was a source of much frustration and anxiety. Even before he saw any action, Stanley Rich described the war as "a monotonous, detailed job that doesn't yet seem productive of victory."[20] No man is born a soldier, and getting used to combat had to involve a steep learning curve. William Sharpe described his first Japanese artillery bombardment, writing, "it seemed like a year before it hit, but the three of us just stood there, petrified, couldn't do a thing." He and the others quickly learned to drop flat to the ground, however, and revealed that camaraderie was crucial to learning survival skills on the battlefield:

> Once we got [back to the airfield], we were surrounded by inquisitive friends, asking about the shelling. It was only then that we could unburden

ourselves to sympathetic listeners. We regained our self-confidence, forgot how we had shoved our noses into the dirt in an ostrich-like attempt to be safe, forgot how scared we had been—we were suave and nonchalant now, emphasizing how close the shells had hit. We were the heroes of the moment, but only a moment, for soon a bomber came in with its co-pilot and radioman dead. Our appreciative audience moved away to take in new horrors—and we returned to camp.[21]

Rather than rely on inarticulate grunts and meaningless expletives (although those were surely not in short supply), U.S. servicemen used their diaries as a space to develop coherent thoughts about these hardships and put them into their personal record. Aviation radio operator Robert Muse went with the navy to Guadalcanal, scribbling his thoughts and personal records into a tiny, handheld diary that closely resembled those used by servicemen in East Asia. Two days after arriving at Guadalcanal, his unit was bombed by the Japanese and, as Bunker had found in the Philippines, Japanese air attacks were fierce and unrelenting: "Never knew how much I really wanted to live until today." Despite the brief encouragement inspired by a shipment of fighter planes, Muse's disgust increased as he was exposed more and more to the war in the Pacific:

> We lost five planes and our camp was destroyed. Don't feel so good now. Whoever said War is Hell sure told the truth. . . . We have been sleeping on the ground all this time. I lost all my equipment in a bombing attack. Most of us now are wearing the clothes that have been taken off of dead marines. Everybody is very hungry. One day we only had one meal. . . . You sure are miserable when you're really hungry. . . . No American ship has brought us any supplies yet.[22]

The confusion that emerged from the war conditions made the experience even more frightening; friendly fire, ghost ships, and even stories of gremlins proliferated.[23] In sum, as Americans reacted to the reality of what combat was actually like, they found that the language they arrived with was inadequate and began to experiment with their writing.

Third, as Muse pointed out, even after the United States finally took the fight to Japan in the Pacific, their performance was still frequently problematic, leading U.S. servicemen to record many frustrations.[24] Despite the U.S. Marines Corps report that the Guadalcanal landing proceeded with "the smoothness and precision of a well-rehearsed peace-time drill," as Richard B. Frank described, there was considerable bungling and misman-agement.[25] Henry Miller, a VMF pilot, lamented, "So many things went wrong today—no gas trucks, number 30's flat tire, traffic in the circuit, etc., that I came back limp."[26] These were not solely because the U.S. Armed Forces were negotiating tricky amphibious landings. Harry Findley cap-tured the chaos of the first stage of the U.S. counterattack by describing the scene in Auckland, New Zealand:

> When I say things are in a mess—it's really a masterpiece of understatement. All ships are just throwing their cargos on the docks. There are big piles as high as a house, all over the place. While all the unloading is going on, the company commanders are all running around trying to find their company property. . . . Two men were knocked down and killed by a streetcar the other day just by getting mixed up in traffic.[27]

Supplies for one company, for example, could be dispatched from as many as three different ports in the United States (for Findley, these included San Francisco, Norfolk, and New Orleans, on multiple ships from each harbor), creating a logistical nightmare. F. J. George watched with extreme frustra-tion as a brand new ship hit an American mine by mistake and sank in the harbor.[28] Junior officers and grunts alike turned on their superiors as soon as the armed forces' performance did not live up to expectations: Joseph Griffith referred to his lieutenant colonel as a "great lunkhead," "completely uninformed," and "powerless."[29] Officers like Findley also criticized their subordinates: when he discovered that no one had bothered to calculate the weight of their supplies for transport ships, he wrote, "even my own staff let me down." The anger that subordinates felt for their superiors, however, could reach dangerous levels when combined with combat anxiety:

> Cpl. Rose, the 50 cal[iber] machine gun instructor, brought this man, Pvt.——, to me saying he refused to go to school on the 50 cal. I called him over and asked him what the trouble was. He started to get smart so I told him to watch his step ending by asking him if he was afraid of his job—if so, I'd change him. He got mad saying no one was going to call him yellow, and started threatening me, his platoon leader Lt. Horton, and Cpl. Rose; he said when he got on the beach he was going to take care of us all. I told him when he shot at me he had better not miss because he wouldn't have time for

a second—and threw him in the ship's brig on five days' bread and water. . . .
If I take him ashore, I'm going to keep him with me and the first move he
makes I'll shoot him myself.[30]

In early August, officers like Findley were merely butting heads with increasingly tense subordinates, and the conflicts seemed local and personal.
By mid-September, however, this irritation on the part of U.S. troops could
come to include the entirety of the armed forces. Muse watched B-17s return from a sortie against the Japanese and sneered, "It was probably a failure because we were bombed. Our Army is really lousy. They stink."[31] Even
tough "leathernecks" like William Heggy described his experiences breaking through at Guadalcanal in less than heroic terms. He evidently felt
compelled to admit that most of the marines' initial kills were not combat
units but hapless workers for the Japanese Empire. The marines had no
tents, so they slept "in the water" and had to rely on coconut juice to keep
from passing out because of a poor canteen.[32]

Sometimes these feelings transformed into frustration with war altogether, and so soldiers, while in the midst of creating their language community, began to define the conflict in new ways. Miller felt uninhibited
commiserating with his friends about the "discouraging aspects of the
war."[33] Diarists also began noticing widespread avoidance of service. When
F. J. George organized a work detail for marines on Guadalcanal—loading
heavy equipment on and off ships—ninety-two men turned up to get away
from the front line:

> [T]o get away from the island on board a ship for a few hours is a welcome
> divirtisment [*sic*]. And another reason—they only get two meals a day on
> shore and most of them are ravenous. We served them cafeteria style and one
> boy when thru the line four times.[34]

Even Guy Landers, who was comparatively further from the front line in
1945, had his share of privation, writing that his ship was "still firing on
[Okinawa] and the Japs are firing back at us. I can't sleep at night for the
noise from the big guns."[35] Clumsy supply and a tenacious foe were bad
enough, but homesickness could feel worse. Noonan's love and longing for
his family, originally a source of resolve to fight, quickly turned into resent-

ment when he was on the battlefield: "I pray every night that we won't be separated too long. I don't want Timmy to go through his entire childhood without being with him. This war sure has raised hell with the finer things of life—my family."[36] Whether army or marine, Japanese or American, many would have recognized Heggy's frustration when he wrote, "Well, it is hard to sit here + think that World War I was to end all wars. What am I doing here?"[37] Often soldiers responded to these frustrations by engaging in car- nivalesque acts of defiance against authority. One of Sharpe's friends de- signed his own medals, which covered his chest, including one for "beating Doug-out [dugout] Doug [MacArthur] to a dug-out during a raid."[38] Ser- vicemen came to dislike the armed forces, war, and their superiors, which they reinforced through the self-disciplinary act of diary writing, just as they had used these tools to enthusiastically accept their mission at the be- ginning of the conflict. Even in situations where extreme pressure was placed on them by the government, the military, society, their comrades, and even the necessity for survival, they were clearly able to think for themselves.

The Japanese too had to deal with poor troop performance, contrary to myths circulating at the time of the fanatical, unthinking Japanese soldier. Watanabe complained that, following a bombardment by American de- stroyers off Guadalcanal, part of the Kuma Detachment dispersed and fled without fighting. "Especially the new recruits," Watanabe lamented, "arrive with no equipment, having thrown away their weapons." Watanabe's unit was soon ordered to abandon their post and much of their ammunition, but they were not resupplied. He found himself living on one ration of rice and hardtack a day, simply writing, "My stomach hurts." Soon he was surviving on hardtack only and moving into what he called "a real jungle," which re- quired more time and energy for performing even the most basic functions. His final entry described his unit's struggle to climb the rugged jungle hills and valleys, full of thick grass and brush.[39] Also contrary to American pro- paganda at the time, Japanese servicemen did not solely perceive the com- bat death of a comrade to be honorable or desirable. A Japanese naval officer wrote of his friend Kaneyama's combat death only as "very sad." More re- vealing is the Buddhist prayer included in the back of his diary. He had copied a special section of the Lotus Sutra that legendarily invoked the Kan- non Bodhisattva's powers during a time of war so that one's life might be spared. He had the proper phonetic pronunciation written out beside the

Chinese characters so that he could chant it repeatedly.[40] For Americans, however, Japanese fanaticism became a kind of "truth" that they would use to justify their own behavior, even if this truth was not strictly accurate.

It was American authors' acceptance of their personal accounts as truth that forced servicemen such as Noonan, Bunker, Rich, and Muse to acknowledge the agony of warfare and lament America's poor performance. American servicemen worked hard to join strict chronicle of fact to more descriptive language, and this often resulted in statements about experiences of the body and mind. Noonan was part of the first land army forces to support the marines' seizure of Guadalcanal. By January 1943, he was confident that the troops at Guadalcanal were equipped sufficiently to "give the Japs a fine reception." Nevertheless, that night, a heavy bombardment hit, and he felt forced to admit feeling some "strain setting in the dugout with all these bombs dropping and the AA's [anti-aircraft guns] blazing away. Absolutely helpless."[41] As a result of such conditions, men like Muse resorted to the dispassionate recording of the losses of ships, planes, and even men trying to capture, as realistically as possible, the sights and sounds of the battlefield:

> Four Jap tin cans [destroyers] + one cruiser shelled us last night. The shells were hitting so close and threw 72in spotlights all along the beach. So many shells came in you could read a newspaper from their flashes. The shelling lasted for 6 hours + 3 min. . . . You could really see the red hot lead flying.[42]

In imitation of official U.S. war diaries, even low-ranking sailors such as Jack Muecke recorded his ship's movements and battles alongside his personal reflections: "Proceeded North patrolled off Buka. Sunrise February 4, 1944 bombarded Regime Plantation. Clapton was hit bad. Enemy had the range. February 3, 1944 Moonlit night went through heavy air attack. Scared the hell out of me. Very close miss on Starboard beam and Port Quarter."[43] Muecke's and Muse's combination of precise time estimates, tactical information, and vivid, sometimes colloquial battlefield description flowed seamlessly together in what was often a painful admission of vulnerability. It was a technique, in fact, not far removed from what GMD servicemen were forced to do during the first stage of the war in East Asia. Indeed, sometimes the language used by American servicemen sounds like a direct translation

of similar sources, both "public" and "private," in China and Japan; Rich's
description of aerial bombardment—"the ground shook and the trees quiv-
ered and I felt sure I heard them whistling down"—mirrors descriptions in
Chinese of the Japanese bombardment of Shanghai in 1937.[44] By linking a
record of "true" events and narrating their fear, anger, and disgust, servicemen bound themselves to these sentiments, and these men were thus at
risk of losing their resolve to carry on fighting a "heroic" war.

The fact that servicemen decided to record the aggravations of war suggests that it was not the exigencies of the battlefield alone that turned them
into vicious fighters; these men thought a great deal about what was happening to them and what they were doing. In this way, they were more like their
enemies than perhaps they realized. Japanese servicemen who suffered from
malaria, beriberi, and dengue kept detailed personal and public records of
their own sickness and the illnesses of their subordinates and superiors.[45]
Some men even made brief mention of atrocities on the battlefield.[46] Americans who were drawn into the worst fighting struggled to explain all kinds
of distasteful experiences—their accounts were often as surreal as Japanese
diaries from the war in China—and in doing so they were going through
the process of deciding how best to behave. Like Yamamoto Kenji, who
wrote at length about the bodies he saw and touched in China, William
Heggy also recorded a disturbing encounter with an enemy's corpse, but it
was only going to get worse for him; after a major Japanese counteroffensive
on 21 August, he wrote at length about a scene even more gut-wrenching:

> Went through where battle was to bring back one of our boys who was
> killed. Never saw such horrible stinking mess. Dead japs all over, some
> blown all apart, arms, legs off, head off some, arms and legs laying around
> guts + brains hanging out of some. It was terrible. Hope I never see anything
> like that again. [Then] shot sniper out of tree + it was a woman, she was tied
> in + had food + water. I hope we don't have any more of that.

Despite orders that marine grunts on the front line were supposed to temporarily surrender their diaries, Heggy's dedication to recording these troubling experiences is striking. The fact that Heggy does not formulate any
overt explanation for why he and his fellow marines fought so ferociously,
however, does not mean that their actions were merely illogical reactions to
the demands of the battlefield. One must read deeper to see how soldiers

decided to behave—even in extreme circumstances. Heggy recounted a story of how a Japanese prisoner tried to use "Jiu-jitsu" on a military police-man on Guadalcanal. The MP "gave him one on the jaw with his bare hand + then choked him to death."[47] Was it necessary to kill the prisoner? Perhaps, but the MP was presumably armed with a pistol, so it is unclear why he hit the prisoner with his "bare hand" and then choked him—a closer and more personal way to kill. More important, why did Heggy take the time to describe this event, even in the middle of the battle for Guadalcanal and under the threat of punishment for keeping a diary on the front line?[48] At the same time, Heggy was turning to the rhetoric of revenge to justify brutal acts such as stabbing Japanese wounded to death, especially after searches of Japanese bodies revealed mementos from dead U.S. servicemen. Heggy and others busily collected their own souvenirs. His diary, like many others, was a space for formulating the rationale behind action, and these stories and events were mobilized to be evidence for implicit claims.

Even dubious rumors could be treated as evidence and then a compo-nent of subjectivity as U.S. servicemen channeled their anger toward posi-tive action. After he arrived with the army on Guadalcanal, Noonan encoun-tered marines in his office coming to sell souvenirs taken from Japanese prisoners—seventy or so—all of whom the marines had butchered. Souve-nirs included gold teeth, which were extracted from a Japanese officer while he was choked, "so he wouldn't swallow his teeth when the Marines knocked them out." Noonan gave several reasons for why these Americans had be-come so "bloodthirsty," including tall tales and unsubstantiated claims:

> 1st, they have found on dead Japs items that the Japs evidently took off Americans on Wake Island and the Philippines. [I heard a] Story that one Marine found his brother's pocketbook and diary on a Jap. . . . 2nd cause now being investigated: have reason to believe that the Japs are going can-nibalistic. Once definite case of an American body being found with the flesh on the thigh cut away. Second case where the Japs were driven out of an area, a patrol found a stew cooking and the meat base was definitely human flesh!

Although the Japanese would certainly later resort to cannibalism in order to survive, even Noonan acknowledges that, at this time, the information was mostly hearsay. Nevertheless, these very reasons made him sympathetic to the American atrocities. When writing them down in his diary, he came to accept them as real events—as if he had witnessed them himself—and by doing so, he was defining the possibilities and limits of future action. It is troubling to read this entry and particularly so when he concluded, "The Army fellows are just as bitter as the Marines."[49] U.S. soldiers used diary writing to channel their frustrations with military life into their hatred of the Japanese; this too was an act of self-discipline, as it had been for the "victorious" Japanese who invaded China in 1937.

The fate of Japanese servicemen, under considerably more difficult conditions, once again reveals the consequences of complete collapse. Despite the U.S. military's early problems, Japanese servicemen such as Nakamura Kan, a young officer in the Japanese land forces on Guadalcanal, were eventually cut off and starved out by a pugnacious U.S. attack. Initially, all seemed well: bound for Guadalcanal via Rabaul, Nakamura had been reassured that the "Imperial Navy is the best in the world." Indeed, once on the ship, he was impressed at the efficiency and the technological power of the navy: "I awoke at 0500 but the Naval men had been up since 0330. . . . The armaments on our destroyers are the best in the world and the speed so great that I couldn't stand on the deck." Once assigned to his post, however, he had to acknowledge that even that peerless Japanese military had its flaws.

After landing, Nakamura wrote that "for the first time I felt as though I was actually on a battlefield." A chronic lack of ammunition and rations meant that Japanese men holding the front line could not fire back at American forces. As he had found on Rabaul, U.S. fighter pilots constantly strafed their position, which made him "boil with anger"—recording feelings of rage and impotence similar to those described by Chinese Nationalists who suffered Japanese bombardment just a few years before.[50] One Japanese serviceman noted that, as they became "pessimistic about the war situation," some Japanese officers were "going insane."[51] Suffering under similar circumstances, officers such as Nakamura tried to keep themselves disciplined, writing, "this is my first campaign, so I have to be calm."[52] Nevertheless, Takagi Yoshito could not but admit that even the normally stoic officers were showing signs of collapse: "[I] heard an argument about food going on in the leading squad—probably between Sgt. Inoue and Sgt. Maj. Mori. I was surprised to find out that there were such NCOs. Morale among NCOs should be better."[53] Conditions rapidly worsened as Nakamura approached the front line; he even found himself forced to keep his diary in pencil. His self-discipline seemed to be driving him toward madness: he suggested that his personal will could keep him from contracting the myriad ailments that incapacitated those around him: "We must have a strong mind and not get sick."[54] As experiences of the body, however ultimately inexpressible, pressed on their minds, Japanese soldiers tried to put them to record. Takagi tried to use his diary to discipline his hunger, but it was a constant companion, even in his subconscious: "I am very hungry. . . . Rice cakes and candies appear in my dreams. I must train myself to suppress these desires."[55]

Not all Japanese servicemen, however, were susceptible to the myth of mind over matter—especially when certain illusions regarding the Japanese army were unexpectedly dispelled. One recently promoted Japanese junior officer, who initially dismissed starvation and disease casualties as "weak will," discovered the brutal truth behind their weakened states at one of his first officers' meetings:

> Certain things were revealed that are not known under ordinary conditions, such as the true nature of human beings. In a certain Company it is said that the NCOs ate twice as much and the officers three times as much as the men. A certain Battalion Commander received 100 cigarettes to divide among his men but only gave one or two to his Company Commander and he lost almost all of his usual prestige. Thanks to my more egalitarian actions, like an ordinary soldier, the NCOs of the company have thanked me, and as the supplies started to come in, they brought me various extra things. . . . An officer died of illness; because he usually does office work he was not physically strong. This makes thirty-nine and, as Company Commander, I am deeply struck.[56]

The diarist could not expand on how he "felt" seeing his comrades treated with such disregard, but he takes care to note that it affected him. The end of 1942 was a terrible time in the Pacific, with shortages in rations and brutal battles on land, sea, and air. When Nakamura ate a banquet of yams and rice on a clear day without any U.S. air attacks, he wrote, "I didn't even dream that we could eat things like these on Guadalcanal. I guess I can die any day now."[57] Days later, his diary fell into the hands of U.S. forces, after Nakamura had made use of it to guide himself toward a more "graceful" death. Although the reader cannot know through the text how the author felt, the diary shows instances where Nakamura is "deeply struck" by these experiences and how he responded to them.

How much influence did these experiences have, and to what extent did individuals have the power to change themselves as a result? One might be tempted to believe that only men with a predisposition to act violently were able to convince themselves in their diaries that such behavior was acceptable, but this was certainly not the case. Even as U.S. forces gained momentum and the Japanese cause appeared increasingly hopeless, many Americans whom we might consider less tempted to commit violent acts were surprisingly ruthless in their persecution of the war. Army Chaplain Charles V. Trent, though a Christian spiritual guide, had no apparent mercy for the lives of his enemies, just as many Buddhist priests told Japanese servicemen that their heroic deaths would catapult them into the Pure Land.[58] Using the language of war reportage in his diary, Trent valorized those who maximized the unit's killings. He faithfully marked the number of "good (meaning 'dead') Japs" in his diary of the Admiralty Islands campaign (beginning February 1944) and took particular relish in imagining the Japanese "scattered, ineffective remnants [living] like animals in an inhospitable tropical jungle."[59] Despite postwar historical narratives that attempt to write out extreme violence on the part of Americans, servicemen and veterans recorded these acts constantly. "This was combat," one veteran recalled:

> Man killing man. A Nightmare that I still can't believe really happened. Bearded boys turning into animals, carrying dried Japanese soldiers' ears around in their gear. Jap fingers jammed into spent .45 ammunition casings (hung around their necks). American marines strapped to palm tree trunks slashed to ribbons by Jap officers . . . even hoping that by some stroke of luck, we may even be photographed standing over a few dead Japanese with our rifles held in the crook of one arm—with the satisfied smile of the big game hunter.[60]

Servicemen embraced extreme violence as a response to war without any clear correlation to class, religion, region, education, or prewar occupation, and they even came to inflict it on their friends. Reports of beatings and killings among "allies" and "comrades" were as common in the U.S. Armed Forces as they were in the Japanese.[61] Still, the worst violence was saved for the enemy, and they justified this behavior in their diaries. John Gaitha

Browning, an artist and a former Boy Scout, wrote of a U.S. infantryman who decapitated with one blow a "stubborn and smart" Japanese prisoner. Was this shocking for him?

> Not at all. It is done often, as I saw with my own eyes, so I have no reason to doubt a word of the story. The irony of the whole thing was that just the same day I had read a memorandum on our bulletin board that gave a hair-raising account of an American soldier having his head cut off with a samurai sword. It had been taken from the diary of a Japanese sergeant killed near Hollandia and said in part: "... My only humiliation was that I had to take two strokes." My, my! You should have practiced with a machete, Mr. Moto. ... War is war, and the Geneva Red Cross Convention ... is a long, long way from the front line. There is but one law here, KILL, KILL, KILL![62]

Such vehemence could surprise even their comrades, as Sharpe recalled hearing a fighter pilot growl over the airwaves, "Burn you bastard, burn" and wrote that it was "one of the grimmest things I've ever heard."[63] From chronicle to narrative, narrative to coherent subject position, and then to resolve and action, U.S. servicemen were shaping themselves according to the cruel demands of the battlefield and the self-disciplinary action of diary writing. In this regard, as Browning realized, Americans were no different than their counterparts in East Asia.

Not surprisingly, servicemen's descriptions of brutal battlefield reality were often deemed by the U.S. military to be injurious to public views of the heroic armed forces. The savagery of the marines, in particular, almost never reached American ears during the war; this was a conscious act among those responsible for censoring correspondence. Lieutenant (later Captain) Meeks Vaughn, of Tennessee, however, felt compelled to keep a personal record of all the things he saw and heard that never made it back to the United States. Fiji scouts serving with the marines, on one occasion, found their men strangled and stabbed to death by Japanese forces so, when they captured three Japanese, they skinned them alive. Initially, Vaughn did not believe a lecture he heard, in which an intelligence officer attributed Japanese refusal to surrender to U.S. brutality: "Jap soldiers' failure to surrender is due *largely* to fear of torture following surrender. And it is his belief that this has taken place—principally by marines although Army has done so as well. Army has taken steps to stop this, but marines have not. *None of this is supported by any evidence.*" News of U.S. Marines' brutality eventually reached Japanese forces, and even Vaughn reported that two to three thousand Japanese servicemen offered to surrender to the army under the condition that marines were removed from the island. This offer was refused, and many marines took prisoners from GIs in order to shoot them.[64] Despite the "strategy of truth" that the Office of War Information adopted, then, the message from the state was, as Susan Brewer put it, a blend of "facts with inspiring and reassuring cultural beliefs, blurring what was true with what people wanted to believe was true."[65] The victorious American army felt compelled to shield citizens at home from its conduct abroad in a manner similar to that of the Japanese army in China.

Once the United States had its foothold in the Pacific, the massive war machine that had been building since Pearl Harbor pumped unprecedented force into the region. Even though Japanese soldiers fought well and with good equipment, their case was becoming hopeless. Sharpe described how Japanese troops were abandoned by their naval support and "unmercifully machine-gunned and torpedoed by our planes."[66] By the time the United States forced a final confrontation at Iwo Jima and Okinawa, the result of the war was a foregone conclusion and the Japanese home islands were being subjected to ruthless strategic bombing. Nevertheless, marines recalled that Japanese soldiers "begged to be shot. They begged to be killed,"[67] because of the potential consequences for family members back home if they were listed as POWs. Japanese resistance was fierce, and even in the face of defeat, troops were torturing Allied prisoners on the battlefield. Yet, as Gerald Linderman pointed out, even in this close-quarter infantry combat, the enemy was rarely seen: one soldier wrote that, whenever spotting Japanese prisoners, American servicemen would "stop and gawk. It was the first time [that some] had seen a live Japanese since landing on Iwo Jima."[68] The putatively inscrutable, mysterious foe attacked blindly, which struck terror in the minds of U.S. servicemen, particularly when it came in the form of the Special Attack pilots, or kamikaze. Behind this façade of uniformity, as Emiko Ohnuki-Tierney demonstrated, was a plethora of complex rationales that Japanese pilots had developed, in their diaries, for going on suicide missions:

> [T]he power of old capitalism is something we cannot get rid of easily but if it can be crushed by *defeat in war, we are turning the disaster into a fortunate event.* We are now searching for something like *a phoenix which rises out of*

ashes. Even if Japan gets defeated once or twice, as long as the Japanese survive, Japan will not be destroyed.[69]

Indeed, Samuel Yamashita demonstrated through close reading of wartime
diaries that political views were changing in 1944, with support for the government eroding, even among soldiers.[70] Through a combination of outright
state repression, skilled manipulation of neighborhood committees, and the
impossible situation in which the Japanese government placed its own people,
wherein they could not end the war, many soldiers felt that commitment
was the easiest option.

Nevertheless, like Ohnuki-Tierney's Special Attack pilot, Japanese war
diarists felt the need to justify their support for a losing war, as did Americans
who were suffering their way to victory. Servicemen used the tools of self-
discipline to adapt to battlefield experience, and they felt these acts of justification were important. Many of the unpleasant experiences of warfare can be
found in any diary from either side of any modern war: shellshock, disease,
nightmares, and madness.[71] There is a fundamental commonality of experience when it comes to war, particularly modern wars in which the tools and
technology are very similar. Unfortunately, this experience cannot be perfectly
or totally translated into written language. This, of course, raises troubling issues surrounding how much historians can know about "what really happened" during the war. At the very least, however, we can see servicemen's
efforts to capture experience in writing, what it meant for them as individuals, and the attendant consequences in behavior. Perhaps in reaction to servicemen's individual efforts to voice their experience, the military, state, and
mass media tried to shape discourse during the war and discipline its fighting
men. Mired in the chaos of the battlefield, however, soldiers continued to
discipline themselves in order to survive and be "truthful" about what they
experienced. In such an environment, we should not be surprised to find that
such bitter enemies, persistently emphasizing their insurmountable, essential
differences in propaganda and personal record, became so much alike.

CHINA: DEFINING THE SELF AT THE EDGES OF EMPIRE

While the U.S. forces penetrated the outer rim of the Japanese Empire,
their allies, the Chinese, continued to tie down a million Japanese soldiers
on the Asian mainland. Increasingly, however, the GMD turned its atten-

tion on "traitors," "collaborators," and "bandits" (or, in many cases, CCP units). For example, on 18 April 1941, a group of Chinese Nationalist officials from various provinces met and agreed to commit one hundred million Chinese yuan for clandestine actions against Japanese collaborators in China. The "treasonous" activities included manipulating the market and driving up commodity prices, accumulating goods, and destroying the social economy. The "traitors" created hardship for the people in their daily life, despised the war, and took various measures to oppose it. As one operative put it, "The purpose of their thought is to destroy the Party's ability to carry out the War of Resistance and national construction."[72] For the GMD, then, disciplining the Chinese people was as important, if not more so, than fighting the Japanese once the Americans had entered the war. This was because, among other factors, the eight long years of the War of Resistance had so exhausted the Chinese people that many were collaborating, fleeing, or giving up hope altogether. Wang Wenrong observed sadly in his diary that, while the Chinese Nationalist government was on the winning side, it was losing its legitimacy:

> Our leaders have asked, on this fortuitous Chinese New Year's Day, to carry out a memorial of life during the War of Resistance. I thought, after eight years of war, we ought to stamp out the flourishing corruption of [their] sort of lifestyle. Everyone knows it's a hypocritical failure, and that the corruption in the rear areas is quickly surpassing the prewar era.

Prior to this, the Japanese and GMD forces on mainland China maintained an uneasy stalemate during the three years between the fall of Wuhan at the end of 1938 and the bombing of Pearl Harbor at the end of 1941. Between the eastern urban centers controlled by Japan and the western, increasingly isolated cities controlled by the GMD lay a vast, culturally diverse stretch of land full of bandits, Communist cells, and a barely functioning state apparatus. Within this liminal political space, Japanese servicemen on excruciatingly long tours of duty fought inconclusive battles with Chinese units that maintained tenuous contact (and allegiance) to Chiang's government in Chongqing. During these desperate three years, when the Chinese capital at Chongqing was ruthlessly bombed by Japanese forces, the Chinese learned how to conduct a passive campaign of resistance while suffering general demoralization. Meanwhile, the Japanese learned just how difficult China was to govern. Within these massive armies, there were thousands of stories that were written, printed, and verbally recounted.[73] After the United States entered the war in 1941, Japan's best troops poured into the Pacific Theater, often with green conscripts taking their place, and the GMD also began to contend more with domestic Chinese rivals. On both sides, servicemen found the unresolved war increasingly tiresome, costly, and distinctly inglorious.

More and more Japanese poured into the new China, and thousands of men adapted to assuming multiple personalities: occupiers or warriors, for example, or reverting back to whomever they were before they had donned the mantle of a "Holy War" hero. While they attempted to "clear" or "pacify" small towns and villages in China's hinterland, they quickly antagonized local administrators by seizing resources, threatening officials, and firing on civilians.[74] Meanwhile, Chinese still loyal to the Nationalist regime struggled to preserve the legitimacy of independent government outside of the Japanese Empire, but the increased reliance on indirect and guerrilla tactics seemed to sap Nationalist élan. Germany's invasion of Poland registered only weakly in diaries recording the quotidian back-and-forth of the massive war in East Asia, even as this event inspired leaders in the United States to take proactive steps against "fascism." Content to own all of China's richest and most developed areas, it appeared that the Japanese armed forces' basic strategy was that, as one historian put it, "the Chinese government could be allowed to rot in the mountainous and backward southwest forever."[75] By the end of July, however, the United States began tightening an economic noose around Japan that hamstrung its forces on the mainland.

The Nationalists still claimed that the War of Resistance would be inevitably won *(bisheng)* by the Chinese people, but many Chinese soldiers no longer used their diaries to record great acts of heroism. GMD officers, such as He Shaozhou, focused their efforts on rooting out "bandits" *(tufei)* and traitors in order to secure the stability of rear areas.[76] Field diaries of Chinese air units allowed airfields to slip out of their purview without comment, only occasionally drafting reports on lost or destroyed airstrips and air sorties against superior Japanese forces.[77] Early in the war, Gao Zhihang's Fourth Flight Corps had fled to Nanzhou, in Gansu Province, to receive training from the Soviets on how to use their new Polikarpov (E16) aircraft, but their commanders were constantly giving ground to the enemy, which made mounting air attacks difficult. Particularly after Gao's death, the unit diary became more and more formulaic, no longer a chronicle of bravery as it had been in the past. If the Chinese could not record their heroism, it seems, they were now tempted to record nothing.[78]

Even though Japan's situation was becoming dire, most men who had not experienced the bitter fighting in the early stages of the war were still delighted to be part of a heroic adventure. Shipping out with a brand new "War Diary" *(jūgun nisshi)* in hand, private Kogawa Hideo, from Wakayama Prefecture, wrote of his new and interesting experiences in Guangdong, such as eating papaya for the first time. He drew a triumphant Japanese flag paired with the new flag of Japanese-occupied China when Guangdong and Wuhan fell in quick succession. Nevertheless, his duties quickly became onerous: moving heavy goods, rounding up coolies, and, most troublesome, chasing after "scattered partisans" *(haisanhei)*. Hidden beneath his victory flags, his diary entry for the day carefully noted the losses in his unit due to attacks from regrouped Nationalist troops. Kogawa was thus both a patriot and a grim chronicler of death.[79] Chinese Nationalist officers meanwhile doubled their efforts to promote "the development of a spirit of loyalty [*yangcheng zhongyong*], national defense, fierce fighting [*fendou*], and sacrifice," as well as to "raise feelings for the War of Resistance in order to revitalize the destiny of our people."[80] Their continued resistance stretched Japan's national resources more and more thinly. Indeed, as life became increasingly complex in the empire (and, surely, writing materials increasingly difficult to acquire), palimpsest diaries became more common. Hirano Seiji, from Nagasaki, initially kept simple pencil entries in each of the neat, confined spaces for each day in his diary. As the war dragged on, he learned to draw in his own dates, and wrote with fountain pen over his initial record in tiny, nearly indiscernible script.[81] Japanese servicemen's life of material scarcity only made more immediately visible a process of identity formation that occurred constantly—to look at their diaries, it was as if all the written records of their life at war, piled into an impossibly high column, melted and blended into one text.

Despite some servicemen's attempts to write a life more thrilling for themselves, working in Japanese-controlled China was only occasionally hazardous, and for many troops it was dull and uncomfortable in the extreme. Transport Corps officer Ōshita Toshirō scribbled into a long notepad that was long exposed to the elements in humid southern China. His writing has since become blurred and nearly indecipherable—a physical representation of his dreary days in the service. Like Kogawa, Ōshita was incessantly harassed by guerilla forces: "Coming back around 4pm, everyone was worried. Talk of an enemy attack. In my battalion as well there were two or three incidents, and one man was stabbed with a spear." Besides the threat of being killed, Ōshita's life at the edge of the Japanese Empire was mostly characterized by disease, hard labor, and longing:

> The transport corps never has a moment's rest. Every single day, we're night marching while diagnosing patients, watching them get admitted and dying; is there anyone who would take part in this nonstop, piston-driving labor [*kono taema nai, pisuton rōdō*]? We waited for the fall of Hengyang. . . . [My CO] had no pity for my diarrhea or my bloated stomach, just sat there watching its progress. Home has become so dear to me. I miss my mother so.[82]

Even after the establishment of Wang Jingwei's government in 1940, U.S.-supported Chinese air raids continued to frustrate the Japanese army. Despite the impasse on either side, hundreds of thousands of servicemen would continue to die for the remainder of the war. Japanese diarists did not try to conceal the aimlessness of this conflict. Even Japanese officers were alarmed and disheartened by the declining morale of servicemen in China. By the end of 1942, Shirakawa Kiyoshi, during the seesaw battles for Changsha, complained of the declining troop performance and lack of "faith" (*shinki*) in the Japanese army. Like a man suffering from a gambling addiction, Shirakawa wanted to put even more of Japan's manpower and money into the flagging fortunes of the armed forces of China in order to secure "victory," suggesting "more training, more fighting."[83] Still, Chinese Nationalist officers remained unconvinced of Japanese military superiority and, despite their deteriorating condition, vowed to fight on.[84]

To make matters worse, Japanese servicemen, many of whom were captured and reeducated, were producing propaganda for the Chinese in a GMD-run prison camp in Guilin called the "Peace Village" (Jp. *waheison*, Ch. *hepingcun*). Talented propagandists, the GMD used the discourse of the Japanese military and servicemen's own resentments, penned by Japanese captives, to conduct their campaign of psychological warfare against Japanese troops. One Japanese POW wrote the following tirade against the use of men's adoration of their mothers in Japanese military discourse:

> Comrades! We need to think more about the phrase "for mother." How many people have, because of these words, gone to bed weeping having lost

their sons, husbands, and brothers? Whenever a soldier [*heitai*] dies, the
military says, "It was for [his] mother, something to be congratulated for,"
but think about the parents who have lost their child, or the wife who has
lost her husband. After you lose your own child or brother "for [their]
mother," how much happiness, do you think, does their death really give to
the Japanese people?[85]

Japanese captives composed various texts like this piece of propaganda under Chinese observation; the GMD attempted to use guided diary writing
to mold the Japanese prisoners as they had in their own military. Nevertheless, even prison diaries monitored by the Chinese painted a grim picture of
life behind the lines. Uchimura Akira, another captive of the Chinese, kept
a diary in which he complained of the corruption that suffused the camp:
Chinese officers confiscated goods from foreign aid organizations, did not
give them food adequate to sustain their health, "collected Japanese materials (progressive literature)" from the Communist sympathizer and antiwar activist Kaji Wataru, and limited Kaji's meetings with the "enlightened
captives" *(furyo kakusei bunshi)*.[86] While many of the "awakened" rejected
their nation's war, the newly minted radicals chafed under the Chinese Nationalists and desired to learn more about leftist thought—clearly not what
the GMD had intended for their project at the Peace Village.

Chinese living at the edge of the Japanese Empire often found it difficult
to preserve hope for final victory. Shi Fangbai, an old party member, kept
detailed records of the international community's discussion of the war in
East Asia, but he did not seem to be expecting help any time soon. He collected newspaper clippings of GMD victories against the Japanese and delighted in the spectacular air engagements in late 1939 China, writing, "On
the 30th, our air force was surrounded on all sides. The enemy planes
attacked fiercely. That was the most savage air battle of 1939!" Yet his personal account also revealed the drudgery of supporting a broken political
party in enemy-occupied territory. He attended primary school gradua-
tions, dined with military commanders, and struggled to get his car to
work. All around him, it seemed, former local officials were defecting to the
enemy, and no one was making a serious effort to drive the Japanese out of
China.[87] It would not have been unusual for GMD soldiers and officials to
see Japanese military parades on Chinese soil, "comfort stations," and boys
forcibly conscripted by their enemies to perform grueling manual labor.[88]

Nevertheless, life in Japan's puppet armies was increasingly unpleasant to-ward the end of the war,[89] and high officials such as Shi undoubtedly kept a positive outlook in front of others—a faith in "absolute victory" *(bisheng)* that Chiang Kai-shek demanded. Meanwhile, Japan's "New China" was full of willing turncoats and those who had simply tired of warfare. Many others worked for the Japanese out of fear of beatings, imprisonment, or even death. Forced labor (Jp. *kyōsei renkō*, Ch. *qiangzhi lianxing*) was wide-spread after the beginning of the Pacific War, with frightened Chinese cap-tives turning up in Japanese units stationed as far as Guadalcanal.[90]

Engagements with the Japanese armed forces continued, but the sense of inevitable and imminent victory seemed to have dissipated from the diary accounts. It was clear, after the fall of Wuhan, that this was not just a larger version of the 1931–1933 conflicts with Japan. Cao Tiange spent the first few months of 1944 simply trying to figure out what the Japanese were do-ing in eastern Zhejiang, even going so far as to organize a plainclothes unit to seize Japanese soldiers for intelligence purposes (unsuccessfully). He was also preoccupied with training his men for actual combat, particularly in "new battle tactics," but also by enhancing their political education and "self-training" *(ziwo xunlian)*. He even managed to hold his ground against Japanese attacks, however lackluster and minor they may have been:

> The enemy, in order to exact revenge on our men, using a combined force of infantry, artillery, and cavalry exceeding five hundred, invaded and sur-rounded our Tangxi Seventy-Seventh Battalion at their defensive position. Following our concentrated counterattack, they were deeply terrified and disordered [*shen gan konghuang wankuang*], which is how we discovered that their strategy is basically defensive.[91]

The Japanese could be fierce opponents, however, whenever the Chinese attempted to challenge them directly, as they learned early on during the 1939 Winter Offensive. Although Chinese units could occasionally be ef-fective in defense, offense could bring unwanted attention from a techno-logically superior (and thus terrifying) enemy force. For example, while Tan Heyi and his allies claimed some minor early victories in Anhui Prov-ince, 1942, the reprisals were severe:

> Critical points along the perimeter of Taishan and Shizishan had been sur-rounded and seized by the Zhao battalion, but these two hills, because of

the strength of our defenses, are being attacked with poison gas by the Japanese, and are now being subjected to a fierce encirclement and assault. . . . We're investigating how many of our men have been captured, as well as losses in materiel and casualties. The enemy at Anqing has not been reinforced, and plans on defending it to the death; we expect that the conflict is about to drag out, and have ordered each unit to make it a point to get results. . . . [The Japanese] have sent three hundred men with artillery to counterattack us, and although we resisted with great strength, we were not reinforced and lost too many men. Our positions at Taishan are lost.[92]

More important, diarists during this period did not employ the fierce rhetoric so common to earlier accounts. When Chinese Nationalist troops flooded Shanghai in 1937, they declared the imminent eradication of Japanese forces in China and national rejuvenation. From 1940, they were focused on survival.

Chinese Nationalist troops were also spread even more thinly across increasingly foreign and undeveloped regions of Asia. GMD officer Yu Shao, who operated along the long road linking "free China" to its Anglo-American allies in northern India, led his men through utterly foreign and inhospitable climates. Yu's men, exhausted by the hundreds of miles of travel from one remote town to another, collapsed on the roadside to rest; they were lying pell-mell near the jungle, only to be assaulted by large Burmese leeches that left bloody lacerations all over their bodies. "We cannot use verbal commands to make contact with the locals, especially since we cannot understand these savages' [*yeren*] language." Looking into the jungle ahead, Yu wrote:

It's all overgrown. Where is the path? It worries me to death. . . . Besides the grass and trees, you don't see anyone or anything. Looking up at the sky, you can only see one unbroken horizon. Sometimes there are packs of wild monkeys screaming out in the jungle. . . . Outside of the yellow line that is the road ahead, it's just lots of greenery, as if one is standing in front of a jade wall. Monkey cries sometimes erupt in the woods, and the leeches are numerous. All is grass, tree, and plant. Every person has been bitten all over their bodies in a thousand places, and is bleeding. Those who sit and rest near the trees and grass after a few minutes are covered with leeches.[93]

Strictly ordered to maintain radio silence through much of the journey, Yu often had only a vague idea of what was happening elsewhere in the war.

The Nationalists still claimed that the War of Resistance would be inevitably won by the Chinese people, but many Chinese soldiers no longer used their diaries to record great acts of heroism. Particularly after the death of heroes such as Gao Zhihang, the field diaries of the Chinese air forces became formulaic. IJA forces often gave Chinese units little incentive to engage them: sitting a short distance west of the Japanese headquarters at Jinhua, Zhejiang Province, Wang Kejun wrote, "Outside of a few minor encounters, they don't seem to have any proactive strategy in mind." After months of "passive" Japanese occupation, Wang stopped collecting intelligence on them altogether. Then he wrote that "bandits have begun to run amok in the Jiangshan area. . . . Some are hiding in the Baishi village area and harming local villagers and merchants." While he did not dare directly engage with Japanese occupation forces, turning his guns on Chinese "bandits" *(tufei)* was easy enough.[94] There were, of course, many engagements throughout the 1940s, including the massive Ichigō Offensive at the end of the war, but the "front line" in China expanded across the entire country from north to south; for most soldiers in the Sino-Japanese Theater, the war was characterized by inactivity when compared with the climactic engagements of the late 1930s.

In fact, for the Chinese leadership in both the Chinese Communist and Chinese Nationalist Parties, the entry of the United States into the war spelled doom for Japan. The most troubling development, perhaps, within the Chinese resistance, was the small but rapidly proliferating conflicts behind the front lines between supposedly united Chinese forces.[95] Gregor Benton demonstrated that these events were an indication that both political organizations were preparing for the Civil War that would inevitably follow Japan's defeat.[96] Even before the attack on Pearl Harbor, GMD forces had attacked the Communist New Fourth Army for alleged "insubordination," turning the Second United Front into a "convenient fiction" for the rest of the war.[97] Following the attack, Mao Zedong warned CCP-allied armed forces that, at some point, Chiang Kai-shek would begin issuing orders to punish *(taofa)* those deemed guilty of "treason" *(panni)*, which was a term often used for Communists. Even in remote southwestern provinces like Yunnan, where Chiang Kai-shek had little power prior to the war, the attacks against the left were growing. The independent (and comparatively tolerant) warlord Long Yun had tried to check GMD anticommunist activities but ultimately failed due to the influx of men loyal to Chiang's mission. GMD troops not under the direct command of Chiang joined the movement to suppress Chinese Communism as well, suggesting that this was not merely a preoccupation of Chiang and his clique. After the flight of CCP organizations from Kunming, Cao Guozhong (who was loyal to Yan Xishan) began clearing nearby villages of "treasonous forces." These "small armed cells" *(wuzhuang xiaozu)* had been appearing in the area bearing small arms and running organized markets for sundry goods.[98] Communist guerrilla units typically skirmished with Cao's forces until they were dispersed by his field artillery, but this was still serious business: "When on the move, in order to defend against the traitors' sneak attacks, soldiers must always have bayonets fixed and ready their hand grenades."[99] Despite proclamations by the CCP that the Nationalists refused to fight Japan, Communist forces were on the offensive against the Nationalists as well, looking ahead to a future revolution.[100]

In the 1940s, when Chinese commanders kept records of their activities, they often revealed the empty rituals that came to consume their daily lives. The author of the field diary for the Fifth Flight Corps insisted on the all mechanics and service people being properly uniformed in "Sun Yatsen Military Caps" *(Zhongshan-zhuang junbo)* and spent nearly an entire month trying to lay down rules for using the unit's automobile.[101] By the 1940s, Chinese Nationalist officers wrote more about "political self-cultivation" *(zhengzhi zixiu)* and singing songs *(changge zixiu)* than fighting a war with Japan.[102] The GMD became a hollow organization, and its members' diaries reflected this emptiness. Shu Jiwu, who was close to the Japanese Fifteenth Division in 1940–1941, watched the Japanese overrun China, only barely escaping Japanese assaults on his own force. He observed, "Based on [what I've seen], the enemy troops are swarming like a cloud of insects." His lack of effort to mount a serious counterattack on the Japanese was similar to his lack of interest in creating a heroic narrative. He kept an analysis of Japanese defenses in a separate book, which he claimed was "terribly detailed." In the same tired tone, Shu wrote, "In order to conserve ink, I won't write excessively [here]—anyone who wants to review [my analysis] can check [the other book]. As for attacks, as well as the organization of our division, its battle experience and equipment, see below." He was able to summarize six months of activity in just two pages.[103] Shu's and Shi Fangbai's diaries indicate an organization operating mainly on routine procedures and empty rhetoric, going through the motions of maintaining their existence just beyond the reach of the Japanese.

Thus, China and Japan found themselves in an uneasy standoff. Nationalist China, as it existed tenuously at the edge of the Japanese Empire during the 1940s, gave rise to most foreigners' enduring image of the entire regime: corrupt, inefficient, and ineffective. The GMD churned out propaganda pieces for foreign audiences such as *China at War,* but many commanding officers were reluctant to train their barely literate men.[104] Some of these problems were rooted in the history of the party's rise to power, but these issues had never so thoroughly harmed both the efficacy and prestige of the regime. Even though some officers and their men carried the torch for the party, this, the final and most malignant incarnation of its internal problems, directly resulted from the brutality of the Japanese invasion. The "hollowing out" of the party that arose from the unimaginable casualties and stinging betrayals of the war was reflected in the transformation of servicemen's heroic narratives into an increasingly empty, formulaic process. Put bluntly, for many Nationalist soldiers, the heroes became bureaucrats. When the United States entered the war at the end of 1941, foreign dependency within the GMD increased, with the organization dependent on massive shipments of gold simply to sustain the worth of their currency. Wartime writer Lin Yutang recalled the severity of inflation in the wartime capital of Chongqing, describing how prices had increased two hundred times their 1937 levels—in 1943, purchasing an automobile tire required $100,000.[105] Unfortunately, this was the "Revolutionary Army" that was witnessed and recorded by harsh critics such as Joseph Stilwell and Theodore White, creating a misconception in foreign eyes that the GMD was always, and everywhere, a failure.[106]

One should not forget, however, that the GMD fought in the Second World War longer than any other force in the world and, despite all odds, survived. As mentioned above, some Nationalist soldiers tried to carry forward the army's tradition of revolutionary subjectivity and win the war effort in East Asia. Becoming one of the Allied powers after 1941 elevated the status of the GMD, especially in the eyes of its own officers, but even more important, the collapse of British and American forces in Asia and the Pacific at the hands of the Japanese was, ironically, a form of consolation as well: Chinese Nationalist troops were not the only ones unable to check the advance of the Japanese Empire. Yu Shao, watching the remnants of the British Empire in Burma flee Japanese invasion, described the scene:

> Every day we see Indian workers who run away from us, some women also carrying children. Sometimes British, twelve or thirteen at a time . . . The men lug baggage on their backs, or balance them on their heads as they walk. . . . Because their noses are so close to their lips, it must be easy for their food and drink to spill into their head. I don't know how they can carry food or search for vegetables in the fields. There must be considerable starvation. There are corpses on the side of the road that died from starvation. They're covered in gold jewelry but no one takes it. Some beg me for food and cigarettes, but I tell them that I've not smoked for three days. One asked a soldier to trade him a bowl of rice for gold jewelry, and the soldier said, "I need to save my own life, too [*wo ye yao jiu ming*]!" Ah! Gold is useless! I wonder when they'll make it to India. I feel terrible for them!

Yu saw European women struggling to move through the deep jungle and noted that "their whiteness was covered by the muck." Burmese, Indian, and European women implored Yu's unit to take them along: "Once again, a woman grabbed me by the shirt and begged me on her knees. It was like I was being grabbed by a leech. I felt . . ."[107] Yu was unable to finish his sentence.

Furthermore, the Chinese Nationalists mounted considerable efforts to hang onto their lifeline from, primarily, the United States, as well as to demonstrate their continued commitment to the Allies' cause. Particularly, for example, during the fighting in the southwest, around the city of Changde, the GMD tried to "show their stuff." As Zhang Liepu's troops pursued scattered Japanese forces in southwestern Hunan, one of his regimental commanders, Xie Zhongqu, was killed by the enemy: "Because he always went in before the men [*shen xian shizu*], attacking fiercely, he fell in battle due to heavy wounds from a grenade blast." Zhang's men, as did other units in the GMD Army, continued to record the transgressions of enemy soldiers against the Chinese people: rape, theft, murder, and other crimes. As fighting intensified around the key city of Changde, he delivered a speech to men increasingly demoralized by Japanese airpower and poison gas attacks:

We've investigated this operation at Changde, and the Japanese pirates have stolen and burned much. Every time the enemy sets his foot down somewhere, that place is scarred in every corner, every house is wrecked. In light of this savagery, when the pirates have run off, the merchants will slowly return.

He also warned his men that any attempt to "requisition" goods from merchants or commoners would be dealt with using "the strictest military discipline in our forces."[108] Even in the midst of the GMD's continual decline, officers were attempting to set a stern example, through self-discipline, for new recruits.

Still, there was some resistance within the GMD to the process of reforming the military. Chiang chastised his officers and officials and even attempted to extend the disciplinary gaze of the party by ordering all ranking members to keep "work diaries" subject to review.[109] This policy seemed only to encourage the proliferation of paperwork, however, as it trickled down the ranks.[110] Although Chiang often complained about subordinates failing to meet his high standards, other Chinese officers, such as Wang Wenrong, also noted a marked decline in the Chinese army by the end of the war: "These days our 109th Division stationed near Xi'an has incessantly experienced unfortunate incidents, and now I hear that platoon and battalion commanders are creating some problems." Previously, Wang had complained about the proclivity of officers and their men to indulge in theater and gambling, as well as a general lack of physical fitness in the ranks. Although he admitted that he did not know whether Chinese soldiers "paled in comparison to those before," he speculated that the GMD's removal from its urban bases of power separated ordinary soldiers from "knowing truly excellent officers" *(zhi lihai de changguan)* while being billeted in the countryside. Additionally, he noted that "8 or 9 out of 10 men don't have enough to eat, lack sufficient clothing, but amongst the commanding officer class 8 or 9 out of 10 are rich [in these]—is this considered investment in our troops?" On paper, he asserted, the Chinese looked great, "but is that proper preparation for war?"[111]

Hans van de Ven, in *War and Nationalism in China,* criticized what had become a fixture of the history of the war in China, namely, the persistence of incompetent leadership and corruption in the Nationalist Party.[112] Despite China's many problems, including endemic warlordism and foreign invasion, the GMD marshaled an impressive defense of the country that certainly exceeded the initial efforts of Westerners in Asia and the Pacific.

As van de Ven noted, it was most likely the losses toward the end of the war, particularly the Ichigō Offensive in 1944, that sealed the fate for the Nationalist regime—a time when the CCP was gathering strength. Nevertheless, the GMD created many problems for themselves as well, particularly in the eyes of the Chinese people. For much of the 1940s, top leaders in the GMD put primacy on ensuring the survival of their political supporters in Chongqing and suppressing the Chinese Communist Party. Whether the GMD was finished by 1939, 1941, or 1944 may, in the end, be a comparatively minor point to argue; as van de Ven noted, the war changed the course of Chinese history, ultimately in favor of the CCP.

Meanwhile, the Japanese military and its allies in the Japanese state and mass media tried desperately to perpetuate the illusion that Japan had already decisively conquered China, even as it mobilized for war against the Western imperial powers. Japanese and Chinese servicemen were trapped in the middle, in a miasma of incomplete political space, and they either abandoned their identities as heroes or advanced into new ones that they created on their own. Either way, many of them had played a role in developing a new sense of self, and their diaries remain as evidence of this process.

A NEW ORDER IN ASIA:
THE COLLAPSE OF THE JAPANESE EMPIRE

During the last two years of the war, the Japanese refusal to surrender, and their decision to instead engage in a foolhardy and desperate defense of the empire, has continually puzzled historians. There are, of course, explanations that focus on the minutiae of foreign relations and Japan's political leadership, such as the (baseless) hope that the Soviet Union might assist Japan in negotiating some of the terms of surrender to the United States. It is more important, I argue, to understand why ordinary Japanese people, especially soldiers, continued to support the war effort. Indeed, many who were lacking in resolve at the outset of the war turned quickly toward dismay as the fighting in Okinawa turned decisively against Japan, but still the war carried on. American servicemen were already assuming their position as conquerors before the war was over, so the mystery behind Japan's bitter defense is perplexing. What becomes clear from reading servicemen's diaries is that the actions the Japanese took at the end of the war tended to correspond to the ideas they had embraced about the world and their place in it during the war. In each individual case one can ask: did a soldier's subjectivity make it impossible for him to imagine surrender as a possibility? Or, for the American serviceman, could he have possibly accepted anything except unconditional surrender?

By the end of 1943, things were not as bad for the U.S. military in the Pacific as they had been a year prior; to begin with, the United States stopped treating the Pacific Theater as a sideshow to the conflict in Europe, and by December 1943, the Pacific and Europe finally received equal support. Air power was critical, with the "Zero," Japan's main fighter plane, pitted primarily against the US P-38 (and, eventually, P-51s). The Japanese had failed to fix some of the Zero's most serious engineering problems—a chronically leaky fuel tank and overlight armor—and P-38s were swarming in the Pacific with engineering innovations that solved these very problems. Even the normally pessimistic Robert Muse noted the Zero's weakness: "They really do burn easily and in a hurry."[113] The Japanese navy was unable to replace their losses in the Pacific, leaving their land forces isolated and unsupplied. Japanese propaganda, which did much to dampen U.S. spirits in Guadalcanal, seemed to have little impact now: Meeks Vaughn wrote, "Heard a talk over radio Tokyo in which the commentator said that U.S. losses at Saipan were being concealed from American people. . . . Also promised that U.S. forces on Saipan were only five air hours from Japan and that they would be annihilated. Actually, our progress seems satisfactory."[114] U.S. military mobilization was hitting its peak of productivity, flooding the Pacific with men and materiel never seen before—or, arguably, since. On the way to Okinawa, George Dunn marveled at it all:

> [T]he sight to be seen are the ships that are congregated here. I counted twenty four carriers. There are all types of combat vessels plus transports, cargo ships, tankers, hospital ships, ships of every size and description. The horizon all around us is a solid mass of ships as far as the eye can see. At home I used to see this in the newsreels and now here it is in front of me but so much more massive. The stage is indeed being set for the acts to follow.[115]

From 1943 to 1945, Allied aircraft were bombing the Japanese home islands, so even soldiers who were stationed in or near Japan were now on "the battlefield." Noguchi Fumio, who had been able to correspond with friends and family, as well as eat better than soldiers trapped in the Pacific, was regularly having to flee to air raid shelters in 1945. "At 3:30 the air raid came," he wrote, "and I could feel the vibrations of the explosion—it was as if it was shattering my ears." Over an hour later, he returned to the barracks, finding it destroyed and three soldiers from his unit dead.[116]

In contrast to the extreme privations of the first stage of the war, by 1944 most American servicemen were enjoying the fruits of the height of U.S. economic mobilization. Throughout the campaigns of 1944 and 1945, Tennessee sailor Guy Landers was able to regularly send and receive mail from loved ones at home, get three meals per day, and even listen to broadcasts of the Grand Ole Opry, noting, "It sure sounds good."[117] The logistical system of the U.S. Armed Forces was superior to any military in world history. While Japanese troops were starving, George Dunn and his friends were being distributed beer and sandwiches, attending nightly movies, and passing out cartons of cigarettes.[118] Many American men who had seen the war through its extraordinary first stage were shocked at the new levels of comfort, now discovering that they had copious free time and fewer concerns. Henry Miller noticed radical changes by May 1944:

> Our impression of this spot is totally different from our previous visit—it is greatly relieving to have no duties but to swim, eat good food, etc. . . . We all gobbled a lunch including real butter and excellent bread, and headed for the beach. . . . [We went] for an excellent movie—"A Yank at Eton," with a newsreel and a short—and all on a bench with a real back! The whole layout, for us, with no responsibilities, is excellent.[119]

The United States' ability to consistently supply its troops was a decisive factor in the Pacific War. Tellingly, the biggest concern among Miller and his men was the spread of sexually transmitted infections. Certainly, their situation was far better than the Japanese, who often suffered from a lack of all war materiel and necessities, including food and medicine. After weeks of drinking and cavorting in Fiji, F. J. George was ordered to ship off to a more remote location, and he subsequently lamented, "For better or for worse, it looks like [I] will be leading a clean and pure life for some time to come." Indeed, George enjoyed pointing out the "horrors of war" that he had to endure, including an overladen aircraft that was "forced to leave behind the eight cases of whiskey they were carrying" in care of his unit.[120]

For some troops the war seemed like an exotic holiday, much as the invasion of China had been for some Japanese: Americans often mixed with the "natives" in the Pacific, who would play local songs for them; diarists frequently commented on the natural beauty of the Pacific Islands and their fondness for swimming in the ocean; and they delighted in the fresh fruits and seafood that they could not enjoy at home. White American combat troops arrived with many of the racial views that had evolved in the continental United States, but once out of that context (and into an "exotic" one), their relations with nonwhites became complicated. From the start, servicemen were confused and intrigued by the diversity of peoples they encountered outside of North America. William Sharpe, after encountering Indians brought to the Pacific as laborers for the British on Fiji, admitted that "I realize my eye is not too used [to] discerning one Indian from the other, as they all look exactly like Sabu the Elephant Boy to me."[121] Because of the foreign environment, perhaps, Americans were preoccupied with where the various Pacific Islanders and Asians they encountered fit in the racial cartography of the world. Soldiers like Thomas Serier were consistently interested in whether indigenous peoples are "black" or more "like Hawaiians." In one of Serier's letters to his mother, which was published in a newspaper, he wrote that Okinawans "are mostly of Jap blood, but . . . [the] natives are looked down on by the Japs."[122] He went on to express a paternalistic sympathy for their plight. William Heggy described the indigenous peoples of Tulagi that he met as "murderous looking black buggers" but added that he did not mind, because "they were on our side."[123] Perhaps more than any theory of racial superiority itself, then, narratives of an exoticized Other were more predominant. Images of nonwhite, pretty women were vulnerable to influences from eroticized discourses. Griffith wrote: "I must, in all fairness, mention the local breasts. They are, true to narrative, wondrous to behold in their unrestrained nearly natural state. They would, aside from their color, make many an American woman green with envy."[124] The "romances" of the South Seas were not merely the product of a history of erotic fantasy; even those servicemen who arrived with an expressed disinterest in interracial relationships could change those views in time. F. J. George, describing the beauty of the South Pacific islands, wrote, "what a spot for romance this is. But who wants to be romantic with a black, bushy haired Fiji femme?" A little over two weeks later, however, on 6 July, he had a date with a "local girl, born and raised," which he "enjoyed very much."[125]

Soon after important strategic victories such as Guadalcanal and Midway, U.S. bombing campaigns of the Japanese home islands began. By the account of a U.S. Navy bomber pilot, by 1945 the defense of the home islands—even key points such as Yokosuka and Tokyo—was weak.[126] The Japanese, who had dealt a "historic" blow to the Western powers, were now facing the specter of national defeat in a way they never had even during the worst fighting in China. Their guilt was a heavy burden, often immersed in patriotic language: in 1943 a captured Japanese serviceman admitted, "I wanted to die in the action of the battle. I cannot apologize to my fellow soldiers who have died in action, when I am captured and nursed here. I do not feel like living now."[127] Many Americans engaged in vigorous acts of self-transformation after Pearl Harbor: previously they were hesitant to involve themselves in foreign wars, but now they had mobilized themselves and been mobilized, often whipping themselves into a fury. Their personal chronicles of "Jap atrocities" and "Nip treachery" made a simple cease-fire unthinkable, and U.S. authorities, eager to remake Asia according to their own desires, embraced this phenomenon. The presumption of victory made accepting any conditional surrender impossible and thus paved the road for both the atomic bomb and postwar democratic reforms.

Nevertheless, by 1944, the Japanese Empire was showing signs of serious weakness, and Japanese servicemen were increasingly aware of it. Shipping lanes between islands in the South Pacific were made impassable by constant U.S. aerial bombardment, and though it was a costly victory, American sea power was slowly proving superior. Noguchi Fumio, a sailor in the Japanese navy, quickly noted that bombing raids were being conducted over Taiwan, Okinawa, and the islands between them.[128] Imperial subjects conscripted into the armed forces showed the same lackluster loyalty to the brutal regime as Filipinos had under the Americans. George Gallion, who docked in Taiwan's southern port Gaoxiong on a prison ship, saw local "coolies" laboring miserably throughout the night in cold rain to load Japanese military vessels, and William Owen wrote: "Don't forget the Tiwanees guard who said 'Americans are kind' 'They give each other cigarettes. I have one and the Japs and Tianees do not give me any but Americans do. I pray every night the American will come here soon.' "[129] Obara Fukuzō recorded the increased activity of Filipino guerrillas with considerable venom. His personal account of the empire's collapse was like that of so many others who had naively arrogated themselves to the role of liberators: "Filipino bastards! Forgetting all gratitude [*shigi*] for the gift of independence, they yearn only for the soft pleasures of American-style hedonism!"[130] It is unlikely that the Filipinos were pining for something so abstract as "American-style hedonism" during the war; when the Americans fled the Philippines, they promised the Filipinos independence, so the latter, more than yearning for the return of the U.S. Army, were betting on the side most likely to leave the islands completely. The Japanese had learned little from their American predecessors, as the Americans had inadequately studied the errors of the Spanish before them.

Americans were still quick to embrace their new role as members of the ever-victorious army, scripting the historical memory of battles and events in literary language as soon as these concluded. The more tightly servicemen tied themselves to the seemingly inevitable course of history, the less they actually seemed to be agents and the more they appeared like faceless cogs in a history machine. As U.S. marine Stanley Rich observed en route to Guadalcanal, "This must mean the opening of the second front in the Pacific and we are to be in on the ground floor."[131] Many servicemen kept personal records as a testament to their contributions to the burgeoning victory. Muecke was careful to note all of the salient details when recording his own contribution to America's victory:

> In the afternoon at 16:35, I, Jack Muecke, sighted smoke. Reported same to bridge and immediately headed for smoke. Turned out to be an enemy destroyer. Had running gun battle with enemy destroyer. Sunk same and after all action was over, Captain Richards called me down and congratulated me on my efficiency. Commodore Brown also congratulated me. Commodore and Captain gave me next highest rate and since I was striking for Yeoman, I was immediately moved to Yeoman 3rd Class. We fired six 15.5 inch Projectors at enemy destroyer before she sunk. When I sighted the smoke we were 35 miles off Tingroon Island and New Ireland Group and he put in his action report that I picked up said target 33 miles. Since I have been in the Navy, this was the most important thing that ever happened to me. I was really Proud.

Commanding officers vigorously encouraged this sort of thinking: Muecke recorded notes circulated by officers on the importance and significance of their achievements.[132] Religious chaplains reinforced these views as well:

Trent composed his "diary" of the Admiralty Islands campaign two months following its conclusion, basing his lyrical narrative on battle reports and other records. Servicemen described their participation in "historic" events in a manner remarkably similar to that of Wang Qingguo, who claimed his battle to be the "most shining page in the military history of the Second War Zone." Though six years apart and supposedly divided by irreconcilably different cultures, Trent's division commander used nearly the same words for the Fifth Cavalry: "Your courageous, victorious conquest . . . adds a luminous page to the regimental history." Trent described the opening of the campaign thus:

> The stage was set; the actors, impatient, fidgety, were pacing the wings. And, on the morning of February 29th the curtain was rent asunder by a devastating naval and aerial bombardment. The troops, startled by this clanging of the shield of Mars, hastened to their task. . . . Thus the 1st Cavalry Division received its baptism of fire in what the Associated Press calls "one of the most brilliant maneuvers of the war." . . . The severance of the only remaining line of supply to Rabaul and Kavieng left in these two much-heralded, impenetrable bastions of the enemy's defensive system, 50,000 Sons of Heaven to starve, die and rot.[133]

Trent wrote of the "theater" of war sincerely, tying its nobility to the sacred cause of the American mission in East Asia during the war—much in the same way that the budding script writer Yamanaka Sadao had done in his first entries. Nevertheless, in the personal narratives of Yamanaka and Trent, although the history of the war could be scripted, it was also perilously real for them as servicemen.

The Japanese government still made many efforts to shield green servicemen from the terrible realities of total war before shipping off, even during the bombing of the home islands. The rituals that insinuated the language of mobilization into personal documents, such as "Farewell Letters," continued unabated. Matsuda Atsumu recorded in his 1945 diary how "orders came down stating, 'All nonofficers must prepare their Last Testaments [*isho*] and locks of hair. Place [the letter and hair] into an envelope marked with your name and turn them in within four days.'" This caught Matsuda's attention, and he remarked, "I am reminded that the end is approaching."[134] One diarist, who was stationed in the Philippines, began a 1943 diary by declaring that anyone who "does not rejoice in the road to war is terrible." Even after the privations of the war, as Japan's supply system collapsed over the year, the diarist still found considerable pride in self-discipline: "Military training is the real training. . . . Truly soldiers are great [*erai*]!"[135] As pressure on the mechanisms of the state, mass media, and military mounted, these systems showed remarkable resilience and a continued capacity for reproduction. Even Okinawans, who were consistently treated as second-class citizens by the Japanese, militarized their lives and prepared to die for the empire. Although those who did not could be summarily punished as potential "spies," as Tomiyama Ichirō showed, Okinawans also felt that their sacrifice might finally purchase proper citizenship and secure their place as "Japanese" against other subjects, including Taiwanese and Koreans;[136] the desire for non-Japanese imperial subjects to "prove their worth" through combat mirrored the issues of racism that plagued African, Mexican, and Japanese American soldiers in the United States.[137]

Japanese servicemen's self-mobilization efforts were so considerable that the Americans found that, wherever they faced the Japanese directly, the latter were extremely difficult to dislodge. Even as late as the summer of 1944, during the invasion of Guam and the last year of the war, only six of M. O'Neill's marine unit, comprising fifty-six men, survived the attack. Following a naval barrage so intense that he could not even manage roll call, O'Neill's amphibious tractor,[138] which held only twenty-five men, moved slowly over the notoriously shallow reefs surrounding Guam. Above him, U.S. Navy dive-bombers exploded in midair from Japanese antiartillery fire. O'Neill looked out and saw six amtracks burning in the water, still loaded with men. O'Neill described the unsettling experience of facing fierce Japanese resistance head on:

> There was a sudden explosion, a searing blast of heat. I had lost all count of time although I couldn't have been out for more than a second. The heat and acid smell of black powder was still in the air. We had taken the hit on the port bow. . . . I ordered everyone over the side. We were sitting ducks. . . . Either the driver or the assist driver stumbled out of the compartment. He looked as if he'd been hit bad. Wallup grabbed him, inflated his belt and pushed him over the side. . . . Like the beaches of other operations we found a bedlam of confusion. The beaches were under heavy fire. All hands were digging in or seeking cover of some sort. . . . One amphtract of the Battalion

Headquarters Company took a direct hit, killing all hands including the Battalion Executive.

Tenacious Japanese forces created an environment in which even the "victors" were transformed. O'Neill's narrative frequently emphasized the experience of lost time and being mesmerized by horrible sights, much as had the Japanese diarists. "I was looking in the direction where Mike Rooney stood when he was hit," he wrote, "I stood frozen to the ground and watched the burst take the top of his head off. It seemed like I stood there a lifetime before I could take my eyes from the horrid sight before me."[139] Japanese mobilization intensified so much so that, in the homeland and the battlefront (which quickly became inseparable), it seemed to reach a ludicrous degree even in personal narratives. Guidance over servicemen's narratives, which, among other things, aimed to control servicemen's experiences, became increasingly feckless. Japanese censors mediating the relations between servicemen and homeland intensified their efforts as the war turned against Japan. Noguchi recalled that relatives could not even ask servicemen innocuous questions such as "How are you doing [*ogenki desu ka*]?"[140] The Japanese military even pulled forces away from the sensitive Soviet border with Manchukuo in order to serve against the more aggressive American foe, because especially committed and able men were needed desperately.

Obara Fukuzō was such a man. An officer who had served in Manchukuo, a graduate of Sendai's Military Academy, he had served on the field and in the army headquarters in Tokyo. He was, quite simply, the ideal Japanese officer, who not only had imbibed propaganda but bonded easily with his comrades and subordinates, cracked jokes, and composed Japanese poetry. He managed to use his considerable skills to control and even harness anxieties common to all servicemen. While sailing through submarine-infested waters, he composed the following poem: "Soldiers afloat in the perilous thin hull of a ship . . . / Yet the thought that we guard our country brings serenity." Familial valedictions were safely corralled: "Even [my mother], over seven decades upon her, / urged, 'Go to the wars, my youngest child.' / Bravely she spoke, though the sweat showed between her shoulders, / 'Quickly go forth and turn back the hostile wave.'" Even though he never faced British forces, Obara never failed to follow the language of Japanese propagandists and refer to his "foe" as the "Anglo-Americans." As he and his men began to lose themselves, "falling into a strange kind of confusion,"

Obara's diary demonstrates the increasing tension between the unrealistic promise of victory and the daily experience of hardship:

> Now we must live the lessons [*senkun*] of "Saipan" and "Guadalcanal." We must take those bastards [*yatsura*] and kill them all like grinding them to pieces. Every grain of rice is for this purpose—a grain that is part of the Divine Will [*shin'i*]. Yet, when I think about the physical strength and tribulations of the soldiers sweating and hauling over many dozens of *ri* over the mountains every day . . . And what of the women and children at home with empty stomachs? I want that, even for one day, they might once be able to eat their fill. But, this, this is for victory!

Obara was so dedicated to "correctly" memorializing the war, in fact, that he rewrote his entire diary after the general retreat to the mountain jungles of Luzon. His rewriting, however, could not completely obscure the instability of his personal narrative, and his increasingly strident tone—anger at the unwilling colonial subjects, pain over the loss of his comrades, and stress as a result of painful skin infections, hunger, and constant strafing by U.S. Grumman fighters—only made the power he exercised over these experiences through narrative seem even more brittle. Was Obara's increasingly inflexible tone overcompensation for his fear, anger, and anxiety? Why else would he feel so compelled to rewrite his entire wartime experience? When Obara did so, he was living in the jungles of the Philippines with little food, his feet covered with jungle rot, fleeing from the tip of the American spear, mere weeks from his eventual death.[141] Even while American forces in the Philippines were surrounding Japanese positions, taking a toll on both officers and infantrymen, many Japanese soldiers were continually able to remobilize themselves for further conflict.[142]

Nevertheless, the Japanese Empire was collapsing back into the core. On the Philippine Islands, Japanese officers were fending off not only the American invasion but also increasingly Filipino guerrilla activity.[143] Even during the tough fighting on Okinawa, soldiers like Nomura Masaki began praying for death: "I've been living in a trench for a day, and Hasehira and I have been getting heat rash all over our bodies. If we get pummeled by artillery, that's fine. I want the freedom of being outside. It is excruciating, as if I can't breathe."[144] In 1945, U.S. naval commanders were regularly ordering strikes against military installations and civilian targets in Japan but also the old colonies such as Taiwan and meeting little opposition.[145] In Japan, new recruits were either older (over thirty-five) or very young (under eighteen), and even they were suffering for lack of food.[146] Not every soldier followed Obara's example: some would surrender and spend the war in Allied POW camps. Staring down the collapse of the empire, many of them reflected on the "burden" that fighting men had borne for Japan, and they desired to live.[147] When the emperor announced Japan's acceptance of the Potsdam Declaration, assembled military men could be seen openly weeping. The day after, however, citizens and soldiers alike were taking off their uniforms and "total war" attire, such as air raid gear and gas masks, and tossing them away.

Hours before he died of his wounds on Guadalcanal, Harry Findley struggled to describe the "strong emotions" inside him. Watching the "serious" faces of his fellow officers, he wrote, "Life has become very simple these last few hours. It's an emotion no one will ever feel unless they are on the verge of battle." Possessing an almost preternatural presentiment of his imminent demise, Findley's writing took on a tone that was unsettlingly resigned. "Somehow I just don't feel like writing tonight," he wrote, "Perhaps whoever reads this will understand."[148] Because the history of the war is so far behind us now, and most of us in the modern world, thankfully, are not engaged in combat, it is more likely that we do not understand what Findley was feeling. More important, we are not Findley, and because he died at Guadalcanal, we cannot inquire further as to what he was thinking in those final moments. This is one of the primary dilemmas of the historian: we are not mind readers, time travelers, or even psychologists. All that remains of the terrible war between Japan and the United States are these diaries, so we must decide on how they can and cannot be used to produce historical knowledge.

First, we must ask why anyone would bother to write a diary in the middle of a war. Scholars are, above all, skeptics—we frequently cannot believe that servicemen would write diaries under duress, or if they did, we doubt that their authors wrote them for the noble purposes they proclaim. Many servicemen from the Second World War would agree with such a sentiment. Frank Allen, a bomber pilot, wrote, "no one can conscientiously keep a diary in time of war."[149] Nevertheless, servicemen wrote at a furious pace. Some, like Japanese officer Furukawa Kanzō, simply "loved writing diaries since my youth,"[150] and Harry Findley recalled that he had "always wanted to keep a record of daily happenings. . . . We all have at some time or other I imagine. I remember that I kept my first diary in code."[151] Such a curious, noncommittal view of the diary, which soldiers had slaved over and protected from harm, persisted into the postwar era. When I interviewed Azuma Shirō, arguably Japan's most famous war diarist, in 2003, he stated that diary writing was "just an old habit of mine." Perhaps the diaries are not unique to the war experience at all or even to modernity; they are simply textual practices nearly as old as human civilization itself. It is possible that the soldier's casual view of the text exemplifies Foucault's definition of power, which operates silently and almost invisibly in the acts and thoughts of the subject.

Still, these "old habits" were the products of historically specific social and cultural influences, and in the modern era, such practices were heavily influenced by state and media forces seeking to build support for total war; this was something very new. Also, as I have argued here, most diarists wrote about the war in order to control their experiences and, finally, in an attempt to define the "truth" of past events for themselves—and sometimes for others as well. Chaplain Trent moved from reading reports, witnessing the war, writing notes, composing his diary, and, finally, publishing an edited, narrativized version of it for the First Cavalry Division. In so doing, he completed the process of controlling his experience, establishing a subjective position for himself, and, finally, defining the historical memory of long-gone events for himself and others. His unit diary, which was modeled after wartime reportage, was published in Tokyo, 1945, as the United States concluded the war.[152] This may inspire some skepticism regarding his account: was Trent's diary already tending toward this "public" narrative and therefore less reliable than secret, private accounts? "Why write a war diary" seemed to be the question on Trent's mind when he wrote:

> Through these preceding days all of them anxious, many harrowing written words and recorded messages give only bare, stark, unlifelike facts. A far more gifted pen than writers of messages or the humble compilers of facts possess would be required to portray honestly, vividly the actions and reactions of men in battle.

This mirrors the claims of leftist reportage writers from the turn of the century, who aimed to sway the public through such "truthful" representation.

It would seem, then, that whoever controls language and its subjectifying power could freely define the identities of people in the modern world. What of, then, the destabilizing effects of combat experience? Whither the self-discipline of the battlefield?

The servicemen described in this book confronted physical and psychological challenges that they could not have foreseen. Intense experiences that ultimately lay beyond language nevertheless exercised considerable influence over what could be expressed. Trent seems to have been somewhat aware of this ever-present danger to the lyrical truths of war narratives when he later added: "Life, reduced to a common denominator by just the whir of a hostile bullet is singularly unimpressed, unmoved by words or promises."[153] Thus, even Trent's taut, lyrical account, intended to be shared with his comrades, had been inescapably affected by experiences he could not put into words. In the opinion of servicemen, the most important aspects of combat cannot be explained, and thus, as Wittgenstein claimed, the ineffable occupies a higher plane of "truth" than anything language can express. Still, servicemen wrote and, by writing, used these experiences to change the way they behaved and used language. Indeed, they were driven by compulsion to chronicle their experiences, even if the war made this a challenging task. As Sharpe reflected after a long period of traumatic shelling by the Japanese, "So much happened in those two days that I can't remember to tell it all.—Maybe I can write it up more later."[154] This desire to capture the experience in text carried on into the postwar years, particularly as veterans became more reflective.

Servicemen's linguistic adaptations, however, were to a combat environment that had, fortunately, a limited time of existence. By 1945, it was clear to both sides that the war would be inevitably won by the Allied powers in the Pacific. In Japan, the realization that the war was utterly lost became a widespread reality, certainly prior to August 1945, and even among military men. Army doctor Matsuda recorded the dreadful buzzing of the B-29s over Japan and observed:

A day doesn't go by that there aren't alarms going off. In the afternoon, we are attacked by carrier planes and, at night, B-29s. The filthy passengers riding the trains are dejected and not a single person there looks like they have any energy at all. Food problems worsen day by day—I heard one unit of canned tomatoes goes for ten yen.[155]

By the time the United States dropped the second atomic bomb, the Japanese government was already resolved to surrender due to the entrance of the Soviet Union into the war. Massive numbers of Japanese soldiers and civilians in Manchuria were captured or killed in a brutal Soviet campaign. The experience of privation at home, as well as chilling tales of Soviet and American brutality abroad, would become an important foundation for postwar victim narratives in Japan. These victim narratives would dominate the public memory of the war shared among Japanese people. For Chinese officers such as Wang Wenrong, the mass bombings of civilians in Japan by the Americans was a case of "you reap what you sow. When the war began, there wasn't a single Chinese person who didn't want to bomb Tokyo."[156] In fact, the Nationalists had long been planning for a civil war with the Chinese Communist Party. Eventually, the actions of the GMD during the war were overshadowed by the Communist Revolution, and the United States focused on preserving a heroic, victorious narrative that would persist into the postwar, while ignoring the extreme violence of American soldiers in the Pacific. Whether or not the prior years of total war, and the experiences of the servicemen who fought in it, would also be discussed depended on each country's willingness to listen to its veterans.

CHAPTER SIX

The Consequences of Self-Discipline

Postwar Historical Memory and Veterans' Narratives

READING HIS WARTIME pocket diary *(techō)* after the war, Kogura Isamu found that the text contained many errors, bad handwriting, and Chinese characters that he had written incorrectly. Kogura copied pages of the diary and taped them into a notebook. Beneath the copied pages of the wartime document, he ironed the rough edges out of his personal account and composed a smoother, more coherent tale in his new notebook. He probably went to a veterans' meeting or the local library or, like many others, made the trip to Tokyo's National Institute for Defense Studies (Bōei kenkyūjo) in order to correct factual errors such as the names of his commanders, Chinese place names, and the dates and times for certain events. He may have read published diaries, reportage, and memoirs or relied on the self-published diaries of friends to find the proper information and appropriate language for his refurbished diary. None of these tools had been available to him during the war, but in rewriting the diary, he was involved in the same project of "self-censorship" as that of the wartime diarists. In his postwar notebook, for 21 March 1941, he wrote: "I am still alive after yesterday's battle. Today we will launch an assault. I am determined to die. Father!

Brother! Yuki! I think myself fortunate to die by a machine gun's bullet." It is possible that he felt that the original entry made him look too cowardly, did not fit the mold of other diaries he had read, or simply did not make for good reading; here is what Kogura removed from his wartime diary from the same date:

> It's clearer tonight than before. Some aircraft came through the night. Our planes are firing their machine guns. It is an unspeakable [illegible] they're doing it over and over again. This morning at first light, when I was sleeping, the bullets came zipping right over my head, so they woke me up. . . . I'm so tired, so, please, from here on out, will you planes give us a break when we're sleeping?[1]

On the other side of the world, former U.S. marine George Dunn launched a very similar project of amending his war diary. In his wartime record, he sniggered at a certain Lieutenant Royce, whom he deemed a "chicken and showed favoritism." Whether Dunn's opinion of Royce changed or not is unclear, but he noted somberly in his postwar notes that Royce later "was severely wounded in the face" during action on Okinawa.[2] While on training or waiting to ship out, soldiers gossiped, argued, and passed severe judgment, especially against superiors, but later they might feel compelled to change their story when new information was available. In many cases, however, veterans were unable to adjust to the new values of the postwar "language community," and as a consequence, they could feel ostracized or simply remain silent about the war.

The language with which soldiers narrated their experiences during the war was formed in the crucible of their diaries, but it did not fit in a postwar world that wanted to move on. Veterans' battlefield language combined forms of expression from war reportage, propaganda, literature, and poetry and is often difficult for civilians to understand today. In order to be part of postwar communities in Japan, Communist China, the United States, and Taiwan, servicemen had to learn to speak in a way that they could be understood; in other words, they would have to narrate the war by using the language of those who experienced the war at home (or remain silent). Still, veterans could feel deeply frustrated by postwar society's inability to understand them. Richard Preston began his memoirs with a litany of disclaimers and proclamations:

I have never written to any editor of any newspaper magazine, or any other publication, public or private, in my entire life. Now I think it's time for me to express myself for whatever it's worth to anyone—even [if] it is perhaps only to one. I feel I have every right to make my views known, and hope someone will heed, or take note. I have absolutely no desire to gain any reward of any kind—no political office, no money, no prestige, no special job, no nothing. I say I have the right to express my views about some things, as everyone does. I may even have the right to express my views maybe a little more strongly than some.[3]

This sense of "truth telling" became powerful in the postwar period among many veterans and contributed to their feelings of isolation from a community that either did not know war or was busily trying to forget it. Also, the language used to discuss the war had changed dramatically, as one former Japanese officer pointed out:

I read about the atrocities [zangyaku gyōgi] in the Fuji Battalion. In a lot of war narratives [senkimono] published after 1945, many of the reports touch on massacres [gyakusatsu] and battlefield atrocities. As a former officer in that battalion, from the perspective of a contributor to such atrocities, as someone who actually carried them out, or oversaw them, I will defend them in place of the noble spirits [eirei] who were sentenced to death [because of them]. Regarding the psychology arising from the unusual circumstances of a battlefield, I wish to speak my mind in order that you readers may better understand those actions taken in the Philippines, now called "atrocities." . . . In times of peace, these acts would be totally unthinkable and inhuman [hidō no gyōgi], but in the strange environment of the battlefield, they are easy.[4]

Truth telling, for veterans, can be as dangerous as addressing war atrocities or as mundane as offering comparatively minor correctives to perceived imbalances in the content of public memory.[5] In any case, many servicemen held onto their wartime selves, clutching their testimonies as bearers of an unassailable truth, and consequently suffered ostracism as the postwar community tried to establish a history of the war that suited its own purposes.

Tomiyama Ichirō noted perceptively that, for some soldiers, "transitioning from soldier to businessman caused some hesitation concerning a certain continuity, and this drove [the veteran] to write his war narrative" *(senkimono)*. First, veterans noted the similarity of the prewar to the postwar—what John Dower and others refer to as the "transwar"—but then they also, as Tomiyama put it, "discovered a memory of the battlefield that cannot be retrieved into this continuity."[6] In other words, the "discovery" of the wartime self, which was inscribed in the diary, created a cognitive dissonance that "transwar" veterans found difficult to ignore. This was, I argue, a consequence of battlefield self-discipline and the individual's use of language to approximate experience in a "truthful" way. This chapter will thus examine the transformation of language from wartime to postwar, from soldier to veteran, and the remarkable persistence of wartime discourse. The analysis is drawn from a variety of genres, all of which could be referred to as "memory writing," including immediate postwar diaries (wherein servicemen and veterans would reflect on the war), court testimonies and popularly published collections of "testimonies," articles and literary works, surveys, recorded interviews, oral histories, commercially and self-published memoirs, and, finally, paratextual elements (such as forewords and afterwords) in published diaries, letters, and other texts. This examination is arranged chronologically to show that, for the most part, the "voices" of the past were audible less according to changes in the wartime generation's willingness to speak and more according to the postwar community's receptivity.

THE UNENDING WAR AND THE TENACITY OF LANGUAGE

For the first week after Emperor Hirohito announced the unconditional surrender of the Japanese Empire on 15 August 1945, servicemen seemed unsure how to react. Many were, quite simply, incredulous: Wiley Woods, a pilot, wrote on 15 August: "Today we got the news the Japs has surrendered. We went right on working on our tent. It is hard to believe and everyone is still skeptical."[7] Once the reality of the end of the war sank in, most were understandably relieved—even including many of the Special Attack pilots (kamikaze), whom Americans had believed to be utterly devoted to their emperor. Still, the reality of Japan's failure could be hard to bear; Yoshimi Yoshiaki described reactions to the end of the war thus: "They heard the news of defeat and their view of the world was broken. They were seized by feelings of despondency [*kyodatsukan*], and came to pass their days in a kind of lethargy."[8] Chinese troops on either side of the war had less room for comfort, though many lay down their weapons and celebrated anyway. Except for the unease surrounding what the future would bring, it was a time of great relief for many. By examining their diaries, one can see how men in the armed forces used it to make the transition from soldier to veteran, war to postwar.

Americans stationed abroad began celebrating fairly quickly. One soldier even interrupted a letter that he began on 10 August 1945 to his wife. Describing informational pamphlets regarding life and opportunities for veterans in the United States, he wrote: "I think that when I write to DeCaux I shall send some money and ask that he send me a bunch of them to hand out. LIKE HELL I WILL. *The Japs have offered to surrender and hell has broken loose here.* SEE YOU, STEVE."[9] These armies were full of conscripts and many more who found the war neither heroic nor noble. Walter Lee, who disparaged the politics in the armed forces, the "despotic" rule of commanding officers, and spent time watching severely injured soldiers being patched up in a "filthy" Air Corps hospital, described the end thus: "Freedom at Last! I had yet to learn the true meaning of the word, freedom."[10] The Chinese had more cause than anyone to be happy for Japan's defeat, as the entire country had endured eight years of brutal warfare and socioeconomic chaos. If the account of a pro-CCP reporter's diary can be trusted, much of wartime China looked something like this:

> Last night . . . several times I heard the village guard interrogating people in loud voices: "Who goes there?" This reminds me that it isn't safe here. I overheard some folks saying that a few days ago . . . there were about four or five hundred soldiers wandering around, turning to banditry and stealing much of the villagers' property. In Lingyun village there was even one person who was covered by the bandits in oil and burned to death. . . . A store owner said, "Normally local peaches would be sent to Tianjin and sold to foreign businesses. This is our greatest export commodity. Since those Japs took Tianjin, we can't sell them anymore. Many merchants have gone bankrupt." He also told us tales of bandits; they experienced an armed theft here once so now none of the store keepers dare to open shop; their front gardens [*menting*] are left cold and they have no customers.[11]

Thus, with the end of the war, the expectation of order included the promise of prosperity. The GMD assumed control over the country having brokered a deal with the Allied powers to put an end to the treaty port system and unequal treaties, fulfilling the Nationalists' goal of restoring Chinese sovereignty.[12] As the GMD moved from Chongqing, its wartime capital, back to Nanjing (by 1946), mimeographed copies of wartime diaries were first archived in the old capital, and the GMD began the project of narrating its heroic struggle. As one division commander told his troops on 2 September 1945 (later copied into his diary):

> Today we celebrate victory in the War of Resistance, the revitalization of our people and our nation, and world peace. China started fighting this World War, and China finished it. During our eight years and thirty-three days of bitter conflict, we sought the survival of our nation and our people, and peace for the entire world. During this protracted War of Resistance, the servicemen of our entire country struggled resolutely, made the ultimate sacrifice in order to raise the status of our nation, and finally won their glorious victory.[13]

It seemed that China's period of "national humiliation" by foreign powers such as Japan, Britain, and France was finally over, and the Nationalists, who had defined themselves as heroes of the War of Resistance, were poised to claim the victory; in fact, the abrupt collapse of Japan "came as a near disaster" for the Chinese Communists, who were unprepared for the GMD's emergence as the saviors of China in the eyes of the world.[14] As a gesture of supposed magnanimity, the Chinese Nationalists for the most part pardoned Japanese troops who surrendered on the mainland, focusing their sights on eliminating the CCP.

Initially, many Japanese troops were dismayed that their eight-year effort to control Asia had ended in failure. News reached them of the dismal end of the empire, the Soviet invasion of Manchuria, and the bombing of the Japanese mainland. Messages sent around 15 August show that servicemen abroad were panicked about their relatives—particularly those trapped in the colonies. Indeed, servicemen had trouble imagining the world without the Japanese Empire. Furukawa Kanzō had difficulty with the "arrogance" he found to be in abundance in the new world, particularly as the subjects in former colonies of Japan, such as Taiwan and Korea, were liberated.[15] Tanimura Kanzō, who had been in the Japanese army in Northern China since the early 1930s, maintained his wartime voice even as he watched the empire crumble around him. Speaking condescendingly about "nurturing" imperial subjects and the "holy work" *(tengyō)* of the Japanese army in China, he even despaired at the fate of Manchuria in the new postwar world order: "Ah, at which nation's orders will [Manchuria] be sucked dry [*kyūketsu*]?" He eventually changed his tone, however, and began to speak of self-criticism *(hansei)*. Writing during his captivity in China, he described in his notebook how he had discovered "in this environment the true significance [*igi*] of self-criticism." Using the same phrases that many diarists did during the war— *hansei,* "nurturing of public morals" *(kōtoku kyōyō),* and "unified hearts" *(tōitsu shinkyō)*—Tanimura was able to imagine a national self-criticism born out of the "reality of the war's loss" *(haisen no genjitsu).*[16] Furukawa, as well, eventually "found considerable truth" in embracing Japan's loss:

> Through the trial of this great war, upon a truly global foundation, we must encourage an acknowledgment [*jikaku*] amongst Japanese people, that every single Japanese person will seek both a new, correct path and responsibility for their behavior as part of their new subjectivity [*shutaisei*]. . . . From here on out, I think that the most important task is to educate the young people who will carry the burden of building a new Japan.[17]

Japan's "quest for autonomy" for Asia and revolution against the world order created by Western imperialism had come to an end, and a heavy burden was released from the ordinary people who had been expected to achieve this task.

Indeed, as the reality of the war's end sank in, Japanese everywhere began to feel more and more at ease, looking to the future. John Long, who arrived with the occupation force, wrote home to his wife that, although initially Japanese civilians, especially women, ran in fear from U.S. troops, eventually they "were most cooperative and made every effort to be friendly and helpful, once they assured themselves that we were not there to do them bodily harm."[18] Although some begrudged the collapse of the empire (and a few even committed ritual suicide), on the Japanese home islands, relief over the war's end came quickly. As John Dower put it, what defeat showed, "to the astonishment of many, was how quickly all the years of ultranationalistic indoctrination could be sloughed off."[19] By 17 August 1945, Nakazawa Masaki in Osaka wrote in his diary that "People are walking around in front of the Hankyū Iida Station in their wartime garb, but I see many without their helmets and boots. People passing by, going nowhere in particular, have a look of relief on their faces."[20] Similarly, army doctor Matsuda recorded the end of the war in elated tones:

> [T]his war has been going on since the China Incident for eight years. The causes of the surrender were the atomic bombings and the Soviet entry into the war. In the morning, everyone lined up in front of the barracks and listened to the Emperor's voice over the radio. There aren't words for how we feel. Many soldiers were crying. . . . Orders came down that we were to burn [documents], but the reality is that none of the troops are doing their jobs anymore.[21]

Once civilians and servicemen fully realized that they would escape the war alive and without further punishment, most embraced the end of their government's devastating conflict.

Despite their victory in the War of Resistance, the Chinese Nationalists never really stopped trying to mobilize the Chinese people. The division commander mentioned earlier continued in his diary that the victory over Japan was, "of course, a just cause for shouting and dancing" but warned that grave threats to their nation had not been eliminated. When GMD officials interrogated Japanese POWs, they quickly found many of them, especially commanding officers, to be slippery and without remorse. Despite their relief that the war was over, no Japanese serviceman wanted to be punished for Japan's actions in China. In a 1946 interview with Sakurai Tokutarō concerning his participation in the Marco Polo Bridge Incident, Song Zheyuan's officers were probably surprised to hear Sakurai bemoan the "lack of mutual understanding" that led to both sides' belligerence, but they were almost certainly displeased when he proceeded to accuse Song's forces of launching an "illegal attack" *(fuhō shageki)* on Japanese troops.[22] Chinese officers dutifully copied radio announcements from the party into their diaries, passing the following warning on to their men: "The Japanese *bushidō* spirit has not been totally destroyed, so our victory cannot be considered complete." Mobilization against the specter of potential Japanese remilitarization (however implausible at that time) was connected to the GMD's attempts to clean corruption out of its own ranks: "Our Party, state, and military men are as corrupt and degenerate as ever, completely ignorant of self-respect." The message hit Chinese Nationalist troops like a wet blanket:

after years of suffering, humiliation, and deprivation exceeding that of any participant in the war save the Soviet Union, who wanted to hear that they were depraved crooks and that the war was not over? In fact, the chaos spreading across China—former puppet government armies turning to banditry, Communist insurgents spreading throughout the north, and former GMD troops looting from the departing Japanese, selling military goods to the highest bidder—would prove to be an insurmountable challenge for the returning Nationalists.[23] To make matters worse, the government's finances were so weak that even the soldiers on whom they relied for stability were living in appalling conditions.[24] The Nationalist Party's attempts to whip even its own servicemen into a fury (as they had in Shanghai) could antagonize both soldier and civilian, and this was reflected in the diary record.

Perhaps in desperation, the GMD turned their anger and frustration against "traitors." Although the GMD began attacking Communist units as early as 1944 (in addition to the 1941 "New Fourth Army Incident"), their first step following Japanese surrender was to wrest control of civil administration from the "Chinese traitors" (hanjian) who had labored under the Japanese. "In order to satisfy the wishes of the people [yi wei min wang]," many GMD military commanders and government officials hurriedly acted on their wartime obsession with these "traitors" and zealously arrested those who were still acting as government officials in formerly occupied areas.[25] The Chinese courts indicted tens of thousands of Chinese "traitors" and oversaw the execution of hundreds.[26] The courts distributed lists of offenders, with titles such as "Record of the Names of Illegitimate Nanjing Government's Economic Traitors," encouraging local courts to round up these individuals and try them. Suspected traitors were interrogated by the courts and composed "confessions" (zibaishu). Some began their self-statements by proclaiming their humiliation and described their actions as "half-hearted," while others explained that their fear of Communist expansion in occupied areas drove them to cooperate with leaders such as Wang Jingwei.[27] For example, Liu Yushu, a graduate of the Japanese Army Officer Academy (1908), detailed his experience of the war as a member of Wang Jingwei's government. He need not have composed it himself, as it primarily listed his "offenses," but he was quick to point out that it was the overnight collapse of the GMD forces in Tianjin that left him and other officials to become captives of the Japanese. During questioning, he became more defensive and insisted on portraying himself, an accused "Chinese traitor," as a man with noble motives who faced difficult decisions.[28] Court documents from the period reveal that defendants frequently attempted to thwart the process of becoming the GMD's "traitors," a legal performance that was used after the war to legitimate Nationalist authority.

While the GMD sought out their "traitors" in China, the Americans sentenced Japanese military men in similarly contested courts. The U.S. Armed Forces occupied Japan in August 1945, with General Douglas MacArthur serving as "Supreme Commander of the Allied Powers" (SCAP). The Allies, under SCAP's direction, convened the International Military Tribunal for the Far East (popularly known as the "Tokyo Trials") on 3 May 1946, but the U.S. Armed Forces had already begun the process of removing Japanese military figures from positions of authority and imprisoning them. Japan was a signatory nation to the Geneva Convention but had not ratified it (or implemented necessary training among IJA troops), which meant that the concept of "war crimes" was foreign to most Japanese soldiers. Nevertheless, having agreed to the Kellogg-Briand Pact of 1929, Japanese military authorities were guilty of "crimes against peace," and the murder of unarmed Allied POWs was also expressly forbidden by Japanese military regulations. In such murky legal waters, the courts, like China's "traitor" trials, relied on the "instincts of the people" to guide them in establishing and applying these codes of ethical behavior in Japan.[29] Similarly, occupation authorities forced through legislation that changed the structure of Japanese governmentality: the free press was protected by law, religious organizations (such as Yasukuni Shrine, where the Japanese war dead are enshrined) were separated from the state, and women were enfranchised. Simultaneously, SCAPIN 548 "purged" the government of notorious military figures and ultranationalists. The U.S. occupation unleashed domestic discontent regarding the wartime government's abuses and destroyed the Japanese military wherever it existed in government and the state. Many veterans kept their heads low while the Allies censored, purged, and tried ex-military figures. Simultaneously, the occupation government allowed many of the civilians who functioned under the wartime state to remain at their posts. Thus, many bureaucrats who would go on to shape the state's memorialization projects were personally tied to wartime mobilization campaigns—and were hardly the kind of men who would encourage a balanced perspective on the history of the war.

There were some in immediate postwar Japan who openly defied state authorities and unleashed their anger in public.[30] Unionized teachers launched an aggressive purge of their ranks, with support from SCAP, of any staff who had supported militarism in the past.[31] Many of their students had been drafted by the wartime state and bemoaned their "lost youth";[32] in the postwar period, they engaged in further self-mobilization, but this time for a vicious counterassault against former state and military leaders. Their unbridled vitriol, often couched in the terms of Marxism, even spilled over into journals that had adopted a cooperative tone during the war. They attacked a system that had, since the beginning of the modern era, tried to teach them how to be disciplined subjects. One author lambasted military authority as systemic oppression:

> The military was an inappropriate place for realizing our will. The feudal system we saw in the villages crystallized there. Under the name of military order [*gunki*], class control permeated to the very bottom; utilizing punishment and constrictions, people's blind obedience was ensured by controlling their very hearts.[33]

Those who had lived through the war also struggled to retrieve wartime examples of members from their community (whether that be defined as "students," "radicals," or simply "youth") rejecting military values. This was a struggle between the political left and the right—a theater of the evolving Cold War—so veterans who did not align themselves with one side or the other did not feel motivated to participate in these debates.

While some public figures tried to find examples of how they were led unwillingly down the dark path of collaboration, others knew from the start that their reputations were beyond salvation. Hino Ashihei, who wrote the pro-war reportage novel *Wheat and Soldiers* (among many others), composed a complicated but ultimately self-exculpatory short story entitled "The Pursued" *(Tsuihōsha)*. In this story, a semiautobiographical account of Hino's tribulations following the conclusion of the war, the protagonist (also a writer and a "friend" of Hino Ashihei in the story) was confronted by a veteran of the South Pacific, gaunt and sickly from the war, about Hino's responsibility as a pro-war ideologue. The veteran expressed anger over the fact that Hino was not convicted as a war criminal.[34] Hino then tried to

present to his audience with an explanation for his actions through the protagonist, Onogi:

> To ask whether or not there were crimes committed by those simpletons
> [*chippoke na ningen*] manipulated by the great will of war was pure idiocy,
> but surely within the sundry, connected chains of cause and effect, it cannot
> be doubted that truth and honesty created their own crimes. There was no
> mistaking his friend Hino had already repented his own errors [*gobyū wo
> hansei*] during the war, but one might wonder if Hino thought [*jikaku*] of
> himself as a war criminal in the manner that this incensed veteran described.
> Even though he had his share of suffering from the loss of the war, as a man
> bearing a large responsibility for it, did he really have the courage to repri-
> mand himself? People make judgments based on appearances. He was not
> captured, and he didn't commit ritual suicide, and these days this meant
> that he was an irresponsible egoist. . . . However, if this was the case, and his
> friend Hino was thrown in jail and hanged as a war criminal or killed him-
> self, would the world [*seken*] really be convinced? Would they be fully satis-
> fied? Would they forgive? Onogi had experienced deeply himself the
> difficulty—the *impossibility*—of looking the truth straight in the eye amidst
> the ebb and flow of history. A phenomenon, as a thing unto itself, cannot be
> the whole truth [*genshō ha sore jitai toshite ha, shinjitsu de arienai*]; but it can
> become the seed of truth.[35]

This complex statement needs to be unpacked, for Hino's public self-
evaluation reveals several trends that would become dominant in the postwar era. First, Hino suggested that "the great will of history" may be more
responsible for an individual's personal history than his own decisions, echoing the views of many soldiers and veterans. Many defined this historical
process during the war as a kind of movement in which they were willingly
participating. It was linked to their "true" records and chronicles. Now, in
Hino's work, instead of embodying the "truth" made by men and heroes,
the historical process separates us from it. In fact, in Hino's view, the imper-
sonal machinations of history make it impossible for us to criticize him at
all. The phenomenology of history is reduced to "appearances," dividing
the world into public and private events. By making his confession in a
published work of fiction, however, Hino already cast doubt on the possibility of a separate, private world. Finally, trying to know Hino's inner state
as a prerequisite of understanding his war responsibility is a chase after the

wind (which may have been his intention all along). Nevertheless, Hino's story of himself, where the individual was a mere cog in the wheels of history, would become a dominant trope in postwar Japanese remembrance.

Meanwhile, the Chinese Nationalists, still believing themselves to be in the driver's seat of history, lost their civil war with the Communists. GMD government officials-in-training struggled to understand the appeal of the CCP; Hao Fengyi, a trainee in Hebei Province, wrote in 1947 that young people were initially attracted to the Communist cause because they were "dissatisfied with their marriages and jobs" but later acknowledged that widespread GMD corruption was also to blame.[36] One problem was that the war launched by the GMD simultaneously against the CCP and the former Japanese-controlled occupation government of Wang Jingwei was, in their eyes, the same battle. GMD servicemen thus underestimated the strength of the CCP—treating the threat as an internal affair equal to clearing their ranks of pro-Japanese turncoats. Communists complained as early as 1943 that the GMD referred to their putative allies as "bandits" and "traitors." This language found its way into the diaries of GMD officers, referring to the People's Liberation Army (PLA) as the "Traitor Army" *(jianjun)*, CCP-occupied areas as "Traitor Territory" *(jianqu)* or "Bandit Territory" *(feiqu)*, and the Communist government as the "Illegitimate Traitor Government" *(jian-wei zheng)*. Toward the end of the war, as the CCP gathered strength, the Nationalists reversed course and turned their attention to the threat in the north. After 1945, the GMD in Shanxi even used Japanese prisoners in battles against the Communists. To add insult to injury, the GMD armed forces had already lost their most capable officers and men as a result of spearheading the Chinese resistance against Japan. Thus, even as the GMD began collecting personal and official records of the war for the purposes of deifying their martyrs (and themselves) in historical memory, their nascent postwar political space was destroyed. Whenever possible, those Nationalists stuck behind CCP lines quickly burned their diaries and identification cards, for fear that they would be used against them to prove their complicity in the GMD's "barbaric history" *(yeman lishi)* of repression.[37] These veterans' self-confessions, carefully scripted and signed like field diaries, were attempts to integrate themselves in the new society and be part of its historical memory of the war. The GMD collapse led directly to a CCP-dominated narrative of the War of Resistance, despite the fact that the Communists were secondary players in the war against Japan.

Once mainland China was dominated by the CCP, the linchpin in the United States' policy for an anti-communist East Asia collapsed, and thereafter Japan bore the dubious honor of being America's flagship for democracy in the region. The beginning of conflict in Korea in 1950 only exacerbated U.S. fears of the expansion of Soviet power in Asia. By 1949, SCAPIN 548 became an effective tool for the occupation authorities and the Japanese government to suppress the political left, leading to the empowerment of conservative forces.[38] The Japan Association of War-Bereaved Families (Nihon izokukai) was formed in November 1947 to facilitate government support for those who had lost someone during the war (usually a man on whom a wife and children depended). Wives of servicemen who had died were particularly active, because their postwar lives were desperate and their social status had taken a precipitous plunge: they exercised political power through social organization and (now) through suffrage to put heavy pressure on the state.[39] Directly following the end of the occupation in 1952, stipends for dependents were granted by the Japanese government by virtue of the "Wounded Veterans and Bereaved Families Support Law" and they formed ties with Yasukuni Shrine, the religious organization responsible for conducting worship services on behalf of Japan's war dead.[40] By September 1946, even Yasukuni Shrine, which was inextricably linked to Japanese militarism since its founding in 1869, was registered as a private religious organization (shūkyō hōjin) and announced its reopening in 1952; it had previously been visited by Prime Minister Yoshida Shigeru, his cabinet, and members of the Japanese Diet.

Meanwhile, Communist Party members in China, working with Japanese veterans and leftists, launched a policy, however short-lived, to educate Japanese on the mainland so that they would help expose the Imperial Army's "war crimes" when they returned in 1956. This reeducation took place at the Fushun War Criminals Detention Center and included activities such as self-criticism, exposing one's crimes, and writing diaries or self-narratives. Like "Chinese traitors" and former Nationalist soldiers, Japanese veterans who were forced to "expose" their past faced what their guards referred to as a "True Acknowledgment of Crimes" (Jp. makoto no ninzai, Ch. zhen de renzui); veterans who were "reeducated" by the Chinese referred to these documents as "Self-Penned Testimony" (zibi gongshushu).[41] It was a cathartic moment of self-transformation—much like the one that occurred when they began their diaries. When they returned home, sometimes speaking against the crimes of the IJA, they were ostracized by a community that remembered the war chiefly through the experience of U.S. fire bombings. Rumors circulated that these "Returnees" had been "brainwashed" (Jp. *sennō*, Ch. *xinao*) by the Communist Party. When the former POW Suzuki Yoshimasa was given a similarly chilly reception, he reflected on who, if anyone, had pulled his strings:

> For the first time, I thought about this term "brainwashing." Then, I real-ized afterwards that I had been "brainwashed" from childhood by Japanese militarism, and, because of that, I had committed atrocities. For me, my studies, self-criticisms, and acknowledgment of crimes [in China] only opened the door to my *True Acknowledgment of Crimes*.[42]

Thus, veterans were thrust into a vituperative postwar debate over the war-time past, suffused with competing claims over "what really happened." In time, men like Suzuki would feel compelled to enter into this discussion with their own testimonies regarding the truth.

After a brief period of leftist politics in the late 1940s, critical analyses of the empire met heavy opposition from "patriots" and affiliated right-wing groups. To add insult to injury, the Chinese Communist Party had been complicit in sweeping the extensiveness of Japan's war crimes out of the historical narrative. In this context, many veterans chose to remain silent. It would take the death of Mao Zedong, the ascendancy of Japan's economic power, and decades of water under the bridge before postwar generations would listen in earnest to veterans. In the meantime, the debate in Japan over the "collective memory" of the war was drawn into vigorous, often violent postwar political struggles, which could determine how receptive postwar society might be to veterans' narratives.

MEMORIALIZING THE WAR IN EAST ASIA

After the Second World War, W. A. Stiles, who would later become an im-portant officer during the Vietnam War, began to cross out sections of his war diary with a black marker—or this may have been done by a relative. For better or for worse, I was able to hold the text up to a lamp and read the original text. Some of the content included salacious references to "The

Persian Room," but most of the blacked-out text involved descriptions of late-night drinking sessions and sleeping until midday—but graphic descriptions of war were left unchanged.[43] Why did Stiles (or his family) feel compelled to manage his wartime record in this way? Rituals that memorialize the Second World War are necessarily tied up with geopolitics and domestic agendas, but the concerns of relatives also play a role. All governments struggle to portray their people as helpless victims or faultless victors, and private media concerns (where they exist) are usually supportive of this endeavor because citizen consumers of media (including families of veterans and deceased soldiers) find these images comforting. Takahashi Tetsuya, often a participant in roundtable discussions on war memory, clearly demonstrated how Japan's national public broadcasting network, the NHK, edited its broadcasts to eschew content that might overly offend its conservative viewers—including the testimonies of veterans.[44] Thus, in order to understand how veterans' writings about the war have become part of the general memory (and when they have been ignored), it is first necessary to understand the development of postwar historical memory itself.

Contrary to what many outside of Japan may believe (especially in countries such as China and the United States), organizations with an obvious right-wing agenda have never controlled or dominated the way the war is remembered by ordinary citizens. From the late 1940s, antiwar activists allied with, largely, the political left to form what is commonly referred to as the peace movement *(heiwa undō),* which has had tremendous influence over the remembrance of the war and preservation of its historical documentation. As Christopher Gerteis has shown, labor unions and progressive parties such as the Japanese Communist Party (JCP) and the Japanese Socialist Party (JSP) have traditionally supported pacifism rigorously since the 1950s.[45] Like its counterparts among coal miners and railway staff, the teacher's union *(Nikkyōso)* was organized to promote pacifism—or, as Franziska Seraphim put it, "to transform teachers from passive agents of a militarist state into active agents of democratic change."[46] Their call to "never send our students to war again" was dramatized by the popular film *Twenty Four Eyes* (Nijūshi no hitomi, 1954), which helped to link education to progressive, antiwar politics—a connection that the peace movement's "patriotic" opponents have consistently failed to sever. Indeed, independent scholars and university staff, particularly in foreign (Western) literature and philosophy, gave the early postwar peace movement intellectual weight, including launching Maruyama Masao's campaign to force the state to accept his pacifist history of the Second World War as a textbook for state schools. In the 1950s, Hiroshima was, naturally, a focal point for pacifist groups such as the Hiroshima Democratic Women's Council. It also became a magnet for movements that opposed the war before 1945, most of which had been released from state suppression by the Allied occupation. Popular response was also strong: when Morito Tatsuo, Osada Arata, and other members of the Hiroshima Peace Culture Association put out a call for "poems of peace," they received over 10,000 contributions.[47] To artificially separate these groups—workers, teachers, scholars, students, and pacifists—would be misleading; the Hiroshima Youth League, which included university students who were directed by progressive scholars, was connected to the Council of Cultural Circles, which itself was based in labor union organization, and as Gerteis reminded us, the women's groups that were largely a consequence of their (forced) return to domesticity by labor union leaders. In any case, historical issues (the war experience) were never far away from the peace movement's attempt to work with international nongovernmental organizations (NGOs) and local governments in Japan to pressure the state, for example, to reject the U.S.-Japan Security Treaty *(Anpō).*[48]

Being so closely affiliated with the political left, however, did have some consequences for the peace movement. Beginning with the 1950 Stockholm Appeal, calling for a ban on nuclear weapons, and contemporaneous with the expansion of the "peace movement" across Japan, conflict over postwar politics and the wartime past reached a head with the 1959 U.S.-Japan Security Treaty crisis. The effects of the 1947 Truman Doctrine (aimed to contain communism), the growing Cold War (especially the nearby Korean War), and the 1954 Lucky Dragon Incident all exacerbated existing resentment and suspicion among unions and the pacifist community, which feared a return to militarism. During this time, the proponents of peace reached deep into Japan's imperial history to justify their views. The first collection arrived out of interviews conducted with veterans; this was Kanki Haruo's controversial *Three Alls: Japanese Confessions of Crimes in the China War* (1957). Kanki's "confessions" were quickly dismissed, however, by the conservative media as a CCP-inspired fraud, and immersed in the paranoia of the Cold War, Japanese citizens sitting on the fence were not sure whom to believe.

Furthermore, conservative forces in Japan also were attempting to speak to the wartime past. "Patriotic" organizations in opposition to the peace movement linked labor unions such as Sōhyō to violent opposition against the Security Treaty, which they claimed threatened national security; these groups used force against unions, students, and pacifists, especially when this coincided with industrial strikebreaking actions. Even after the Security Treaty was ratified, in addition to assaulting union members (particularly during the Miike coal mine strikes), right-wing organizations also burned Chinese flags in Shinbashi (Tokyo) and praised Japan's military history, continuing to conflate historical questions with both domestic and foreign political issues.[49] Amidst this struggle, a mirror universe of militaristic films, produced mainly by Tōhō Studios, challenged the pacifist cinema that was popular in the early postwar period; from *The Meiji Emperor and the Russo-Japanese War* (Meiji tennō to Nichiro sensō, 1957) to *Joint Fleet Commander Yamamoto Isoroku* (Rengō kantai shireikan Yamamoto Isoroku, 1968), these films celebrated Japan's military heroes and insisted on the value of the emperor system. Even *Japan's Longest Day* (Nihon no ichiban nagai hi, 1967), which stressed the suffering of citizens, attempted to portray the emperor's surrender decision as "being concerned only with the well-being of the people," and because the audience for these late 1960s films was composed largely of young men, this phenomenon may go some way toward explaining the growing conservatism of the 1970s and 1980s.[50]

Still, the defeats of the pacifist left had as much to do with bad leadership and internal divisions as it did with pressure from right-wing groups. Andrew Gordon showed that the decline of the JCP-directed unions in the workplace was not merely a consequence of clever management tactics but also the rigid political hierarchy that these organizations enforced.[51] In fact, Sheldon Garon argued persuasively that "many progressive groups supported the state's moral suasion campaigns," which aimed to direct citizen behavior in ways useful to government—a government that would be dominated by a newly formed conservative coalition represented by the Liberal Democratic Party (LDP).[52] The turbulent political struggle between the political right and left began to turn away members of the peace movement who did not see eye to eye with, for example, the Japanese Communist Party. During the height of the Security Treaty crisis, pacifist organizations such as the Wadatsumi Society (Wadatsumi-kai), which collected the diaries and letters of drafted university students who had died in battle, began to turn away from partisan politics:

The Society has time and again avoided deploying tremendous energy into confrontational political questions. The Society first and foremost has clearly recognized its own calling, and does not gather its own forces for the purpose of critical stances [against others]. The Society is not an activist organization.[53]

In response to the wartime generation's perceived lack of commitment to antimilitarism, students in the radical left attacked Wadatsumi-kai and, dramatically, severely damaged the Wadatsumi statue, which was a symbol of the peace movement. As Fukuma Yoshiaki explained, postwar progressives had little sympathy for the peace movement as it had been defined by those who lived through the war; for them, "praying for peace" was a sign of weakness and surrender to state authority.[54] Nevertheless, the infamous 1972 Asama-Sansō Incident, in which students in the United Red Army committed multiple murders and were subsequently besieged by police in the mountains, seemed to mark the end of serious left-wing activism in Japan.

Despite the decline of progressive politics in Japan during the 1970s and 1980s, historical memory issues came to the fore due to important surrender memorial dates (thirty years in 1975, forty in 1985) and the normalization of relations with the PRC, which resulted in the "opening" of China to foreign researchers. In 1971, Honda Katsuichi stirred the pot by publishing accounts of Japanese atrocities in one of Japan's biggest dailies, the *Asahi News,* which led to organized efforts on the part of teachers in Japan to "confront the past."[55] Going into the 1980s, Japanese society seemed more receptive, so writers, journalists, and historians reinvigorated the study of the war in Asia. Fujiwara Akira and Matsuoka Tamaki collected "testimonies" by veterans who committed war crimes.[56] Honda Katsuichi continued to play a major role in exhuming the history of Japanese aggression, describing his project as "not oral history, but the history of experience" *(taikenshi).* He often included his own explanations in testimonials in order to give them expanded descriptive power and a feeling of direct communication.

A woman gave birth to a baby in the mountains and, of course, a newborn cries very loudly. If the Japanese soldiers heard the women and went into the mountains, the young girls of the village would all be raped and murdered. (At this time, Mrs. Chen's voice fell into a hoarse whisper, as if the painful confession was stuck in her throat.) It was really terrible, but we decided to kill the baby.[57]

Honda's introduction of his own voice into the narrative of Nanjing survivors is indicative of the proactive role the Japanese intelligentsia believed they should play in historical memory debates. Participants in the new movement to unearth the wartime past, such as Honda, believed that these testimonies represented the immediate transmission of truth. In this way, popular testimonials invoked the Tokyo Trials in order to buttress their claims to historical fact and authority.

Fissures within the left during the late 1990s—particularly with the 1996 split of the JSP—seemed to herald an "end of history" moment and the triumph of conservatism, but for all of the concern in Asia over the Japanese right, the Democratic Party of Japan (DPJ) victory in 2009 demonstrated that even the LDP was having difficulty controlling government. Certainly, some parts of the Japanese bureaucracy embrace a conservative, "patriotic" outlook on historical issues and have many allies among Japanese social organizations. Nevertheless, there is a vibrant progressive movement in Japan that is promoted by powerful media interests such as *Asahi News*. Few Americans or Chinese realize that some of the most important developments in research on Japan's wartime atrocities were unearthed by Japanese journalists and scholars such as Honda Katsuichi, Fujiwara Akira, and Matsuoka Tamaki. There are many scholars who are committed to portraying the war in a way that accurately reflects the way it appears in primary source documents. Organizations rooted in conflicts over, for example, the U.S.-Japan Security Treaty, continued to support research and public education on Japan's war crimes: these included the teachers' union, social groups associated with the peace movement, and even, in some cases, the Cooperatives *(Seikatsu kyōdō kumiai)*. Gerteis, Seraphim, and Robin LeBlanc have all argued that these organizations were, and are, significantly driven by women—professional educators, part-time workers, and housewives with disposable incomes and free time.

Based on this support, many prefectural and municipal governments in Japan, beginning in the 1980s, built "peace museums" in major cities such as Osaka, Takamatsu, and Shizuoka. Soon enough, however, declining public funds forced the local governments to abandon some of these spaces, and those that are not nonprofit, nongovernment organizations are currently in peril. Still, if the museums successfully become independent of the state, this will likely be remembered as one of the Japanese government's most fatal errors. Not only would the museums survive through private donations and ticket sales, but they will also be less subject to the vicissitudes of Japanese politics. Consequently, for those museums that are recent NGOs, or looking to go in that direction, their activities and exhibits have come to approximate the more centrist stance of the peace movement, as is the case in Himeji Peace Museum and the Osaka International Peace Center. Museums most dedicated to the ideals of the peace movement are those founded not on the largesse of the state but primarily on the donations of concerned veterans, as in the case of the "Grassroots House" (Kusa no ie) in Kōchi, or the support of private universities, such as the Ritsumeikan Peace Museum. These museums organize tours of their exhibits for student groups from local primary and middle schools, for which they often (though not exclusively) rely on the cooperation of parents and teachers associated with the teachers' union. However, declining rates of enrollment in the union and conservative school principals (appointed by conservative prefectural and municipal officials, often allied with the LDP) are not the only threat to peace museums' mission to educate the public.

Members of organizations accused of portraying Japan's war crimes in a "positive light" *(bika)* do not always support a stridently "right-wing" line; for the most part, their strength lies in attaching themselves to a widespread desire in Japan to respect those who died for their country. For the most part, Yasukuni Shrine, the Bereaved Families Society, and even museums such as the Chiran Tokkōtai Memorial Museum have taken steps to enshrine Japanese servicemen as undifferentiated and heroic, erasing the differences between convicted war criminals and young men drafted against their will. In other cases, the promotion of "peace" through national victimization also threatens to distort the historical understanding of Japan's aggression in Asia. The view of the war offered by the Exhibition and Reference Library for Peace and Consolation in the Sumitomo Building (a short walk from the Tokyo municipal government) shows how conservative groups have tried to use the language of the peace movement to promote narrative that portrays Japan as victim of the war. Offering a promise of a pacifist view of the war, what the museum in fact delivers is a collection of victim narratives with no contextual exhibit on Japan's imperialist aggression. After its grand opening, between 2001 and 2004, the museum contained three main exhibits: on the firebombing of Japanese civilians (usually portrayed as women and children), the cruel treatment of Japanese POWs in Siberia, and the pitiful "returnees" *(hikiagesha)* from Japan's crumbling empire. The fact that this museum is connected to the office overseeing government support for Japan's veterans and their families (*onkyū,* or "payments of gratitude") is perhaps an indication of its political outlook. It was founded by the Public Foundation for Peace and Consolation, which is supported financially through the Ministry of Home Affairs; the fact that its financial support came directly from an LDP-controlled Diet makes it a fair representation of what kind of "pacifism" the Japanese government (at that time) preferred its citizens adopt. A pamphlet for the exhibition explains its purpose:

> In the previous World War, because it was so fierce and long, the losses were immense. Servicemen, their dependents and ordinary civilians, whether at home or abroad, with many differences in between, were indiscriminately and unavoidably victimized in some way by the war. In these conditions, casualties of war, the bereaved relatives of the war dead, and those who lost the foundation of their livelihood [in the colonies, *hikiagesha*], quite different from ordinary civilians, occupy a special place. . . . What is necessary now is to communicate their sufferings and the horrible reality of war to all citizens, including the younger generation that has not experienced war, so that it will not be forgotten, so that we will understand the solemnity of peace, so that we can express our sense of gratitude to them.

This was nothing new, of course: the focus on victimization goes as far back as the establishment of the Hiroshima Peace Memorial Museum in 1952. The comfortable middle road—showing the devastation wrought on Japanese by the nation's rampant militarism—became a founding narrative for many peace museums. As Lisa Yoneyama argued, Japan's view of itself as a victim of the war is in part dependent on its myth of national homogeneity.[58] Publications concerning how even the victims of American firebombing included colonial subjects promise to continue to problematize the Japanese people's uniform status as victims of imperialism and total war.[59]

Those on the right who were not satisfied with merely hijacking the peace movement went on to attack scholars and veterans who supported acknowledgment of Japan's war crimes. Japan's infamously strict libel laws have allowed individuals, supported by right-wing social organizations, to use civil suits to intimidate authors and their publishers. As in British libel cases, the burden to show innocence is on the defendant, so even those publishing their personal diaries may find themselves party to a suit for the crime of "damaging [the plaintiff's] good name" *(meiyo songai)* for mentioning someone by name in the text. As a result, researchers such as Ono Kenji had to draw up legal waivers (to be signed by diarists or by their families if the author is dead) in order to protect themselves from litigation when the documents are published. The surviving families of veterans and survivors, even those living in foreign countries such as Korea, can block the publication of documents for decades. They can even force government archives such as the National Institute for Defense Studies to deny access to formerly public documents.[60] Reporter Honda Katsuichi may have succeeded in 2003 over his plaintiffs regarding publications on the "hundred head competition" *(hyakunin-giri,* when two wartime Japanese officers competed against one another to see who could behead more Chinese), but Azuma Shirō's loss in a similar suit still sends chills down the spines of many researchers in Japan. The conduct of prosecuting attorneys, such as calling in "authoritative" witnesses who testify against the Nanjing Massacre, causes considerable consternation and frustration among the lawyers who defend people such as Honda and Azuma or Nanjing Massacre survivor Li Xiuying in her defamation lawsuit against those who accused her of fabricating her story.[61]

In mainland China, public discourse on the war is even more restricted in Japan, because the Chinese government continues to try to control the content of museums and access to archives. It is a testament to Chinese citizens' cooperation with state goals that, although in many cases the government does not support them financially, they engage in acts of self-censorship in order to avoid trouble. Early films in the PRC such as *Dong Cunrui,* revolutionary ballets, and pulp fiction portray the suffering of nonpolitically aligned civilians or Chinese Communist mobilization in Yan'an and other rear areas. As late as the 1980s, films concerning the War of Resistance typically featured heroic anti-Japanese resistance fighters *(kangri fenzi)* using kung fu to defeat hapless Japanese guards in occupied areas or the PLA conducting another daring guerrilla raid—with the presence of the Nationalist Army notably absent (or vilified as ineffectual). Much of the state-led memorialization campaigns eschewed any attempt to gather or feature testimonies of former Nationalist servicemen.[62] Even Nationalist monuments to the War of Resistance on the mainland were destroyed by the CCP or converted into edifices portraying Communist heroism.[63] More seriously, the Chinese state itself began attempts to use the past, particularly the Nanjing Massacre, as a form of patriotic education.[64]

By the 1980s, even though China was growing closer to Japan economically, it was becoming clear that civilian interest in the history of the war was far outstripping the state's ability to control it. For example, a 1985 text, published on the fortieth anniversary of the end of the war, took the unusual step of featuring testimonies from former Nationalist servicemen and officials. Nevertheless, even though the accounts were heavily edited (likely to remove any praise of the Nationalist Army or criticism of the Communists), the editors still exhibited signs of unease in releasing the text and attempted to head off any criticism by admitting the volume might not "fulfill both the requirements of our leaders and the desires of our readership."[65] Usually these unorthodox projects were organized in or around areas of former GMD control by local historians, not launched by the central government in Beijing. During the mid-1980s, however, when these accounts began to reappear in China, mainland historians were still supporting the CCP historical orthodoxy: "the GMD counter-revolutionaries continued to carry out their passive stance towards the war, and opposed the proactive CCP policy; a great army of 400,000 retreated [from the Japanese] without a fight, losing forty eight cities." Even within such a formulaic triumphalist portrait of the CCP, however, the complexity of veterans' experiences peek through. One veteran recalled that he would argue with his uncle endlessly about whether the CCP or the GMD were waging a better war against the Japanese; in recounting these discussions, long-suppressed GMD wartime rhetoric resurfaced:

> When a security officer for our prefecture was caught by our enemies while on patrol, he was to be buried alive in a hole. He felt it difficult to try to escape, knowing in his heart that "I can't die a pointless death. If I take someone with me, that makes it even, and if I kill two that means I'm one ahead!" When a good opportunity came while he was being searched, he grabbed a metal can with one hand and struck his enemy on the head. He sacrificed himself valiantly [zhuanglie xisheng].[66]

Many of these testimonies and oral histories were organized by local officials who were most interested in regional history. Rather than seeing them as a nationwide, top-down effort to guide historical memory, then, these sporadic compilations in the PRC represent a localized historical movement that, for political safety, tried to situate itself within the orthodox framework of historical memory.

Much of mainland China's cultural production concerning the war experience focuses on the victimization of ordinary civilians and resorts to many of the same tactics as wartime propaganda for generating anger. The publication of "survivors' testimonies" *(xingcunzhe zhengyan)* was as popular during the war as it is today.[67] The mainland government did little to stem the tide of anti-Japanese sentiment, so much so that exceptions to the rule are truly outstanding. Fang Jun's *The Devil Soldiers I Knew* (1997) displayed moments of a Chinese student in Japan genuinely attempting to reach out to Japanese veterans. Even Fang, however, resorted to what Rana Mitter referred to as "literary artifice" in order to express his own brand of postwar anti-Japanese resistance. Shaking his fist at Mount Fuji while demanding that Japan's war crimes be exposed, Fang was able to reconnect with his country and his father (an Eighth Route Army veteran) even while talking "man to man" with Japanese veterans.[68] Fan Jianchuan, in his book *One Man's War of Resistance* (Yi ge ren de kangzhan, 2000), tried to narrate the war through ordinary material objects. Fan's approach to the history of the war, including an imagined dialogue between Japanese and Chinese swords, still made use of common tropes in East Asian historical memory: "These two blades 'stand off' against one another, awakening us at dawn with this reminder: do not forget the blood on these swords, do not allow this historical tragedy to repeat itself."[69] Nevertheless, these new approaches may represent a convergence of pacifist approaches to the war that are steeped in a frank appraisal of historical documents and objects, which may signify the beginning of a decline for facile patriotism in Chinese remembrance.

Still, popular Chinese resentments over Japan's "failure" to confront the past currently drown out the voices of people like Fan and Fang, as well as most professional historians on the mainland, who increasingly adopt a more measured approach to war history. Even so, one should be careful not to regard widespread anger over Japan's recalcitrance regarding war memory as the result of a well-orchestrated Beijing government cabal—despite news reports of Chinese state funds used to bus students to protest rallies (or the well-known practice of using state resources to fund free trips to war museums). For example, the establishment of the Nanjing Massacre Memorial was perhaps the greatest watershed in PRC domestic remembrance, not because this memorial represented a change in the way the state viewed the war, but rather the exact opposite: it represented a significant departure from Beijing's leadership on this issue. Founded in 1985, the most active memorial officials were local residents, and to this day, it is supported primarily through funds from the Nanjing municipal government and donations from overseas Chinese.[70] Domestic Chinese businessmen made little to no contribution to the memorial, either because they are not philanthropic by nature or (more likely) because they are avoiding an issue about which government elites were ambivalent. Following the museum's success, of course, the central government switched to supporting it vigorously, even making it part of national education initiatives. Nevertheless, even as the Chinese state apparatus attempts to establish a postwar nationalism that is rooted in wartime history, it finds that passionate patriots can quickly endanger sensitive economic treaty negotiations with countries like Japan, so it must tread carefully.[71]

The importance of the Chinese diaspora in raising the profile of the War of Resistance became apparent with the publication of Iris Chang's 1998 book, *The Rape of Nanking: The Forgotten Holocaust of World War II*. Chang successfully drew worldwide attention to Japan's atrocities in China but did so by resurrecting the voice of wartime Nationalist propaganda, with all of its concomitant demerits. By unwittingly using doctored photos and problematic "testimonies," she made herself an easy target for Japan's conservative skeptics and put the Chinese case for acknowledgment of Japan's war crimes on unstable ground. Consequently, Daqing Yang was correct when he pointed out the danger of interlocking authenticities: to many it seems that if 300,000 Chinese were not massacred in Nanjing in the winter of 1937, then the 1946 military tribunal in Nanjing is open to criticism, as is Japan's role as an aggressor in general.[72] Nevertheless, as late as 2007, this figure remained emblazoned on the Nanjing Massacre Memorial's wall. Why do Beijing elites allow Chinese civilians and local officials to express their anger over the Japanese government's actions and admiration for Nationalist servicemen? Part of the answer is certainly attributable to their desire to use anti-Japanese sentiment to put political pressure on Japan. As James Reilly has shown, however, "patriotic" anti-Japanese activism operates well beyond the control of China's government (and beyond its apparent usefulness).[73] More important, however, is Beijing's desire to court the Chinese Nationalist Party in Taiwan for the purposes of unification.

The uneasy stalemate that exists between the Chinese Nationalists in Taiwan and the Chinese Communists on the mainland has, does, and will continue to affect the way the war is remembered on both sides of the straits. In Taiwan, historically GMD vows to "retake the mainland" were publicized more widely than the history of the War of Resistance. Taiwan scholars have shown that the war is merely part of a collection of lessons taught by the GMD to the Taiwanese, who often feel ambivalent about the period of Japanese occupation,[74] with an aim to make them embrace "Chineseness."[75] Chang Jui-te demonstrated well that Taiwanese memorial rituals that touch on the war are typically split according to views of the February 28th Incident, when Chinese Nationalists violently suppressed anti-GMD political movements in Taiwan. While moderate Democratic Progressive Party (DPP) members such as Li Jinrong could pay tribute to the spirit of resistance among all Chinese people, more radical members such as Lin Yixiong refused to participate in any rituals of remembrance, continuing to see the GMD as an oppressive, foreign regime. In any case, as Chang pointed out, polls conducted at the fiftieth anniversary of the war's end found that there were many more Taiwanese who viewed rituals of remembrance concerning the "victory" over the Japanese positively than there were those who viewed it negatively.[76] Nevertheless, democratization and the rise of the DPP in Taiwan led to irrevocable changes in war remembrance there. Most important, Taiwanese archives were previously difficult to penetrate without the proper connections, and this was particularly true of those that would hold war diaries. Since the victory of the DPP, however, and prior democratization efforts, these institutions have progressed considerably in their openness, and now new research on the war is much easier to conduct. Also, a focus on Taiwanese history, symbolized by the lavish Shihsanhang Museum dedicated to Taiwan's indigenous historical experience (opened in 1998), shed light on narratives that lie outside of those supported by the Nationalists, such as the experience of Taiwanese servicemen in the Japanese armed forces.[77] In any case, even when historians are motivated by the purest desire to uncover the "true face" of the war, political concerns can be seen subtly directing their efforts.

As Tomiyama Ichirō put it, "only when there is a *national* narrative, the boundaries of 'testimony' can be set."[78] Fortunately, supporters of the political right in Japan, try as they might, have not defined the national narrative. The struggle to establish a "master narrative" of the war influences veterans and civilians, performers and their audience. The historical memory struggle is as much a part of the changing East Asian political landscape and what it finds useful in the historical record as it is a record of "things as they actually happened." Although historians' work may be informative for current political debates, the approach adopted by historians such as John Keegan, who atomized war to the individual's experience of it, may not be recognizable or useful for political activists. Keegan was correct in that the farther down a historian digs, the less likely an all-encompassing narrative seems (with the exception of simplistic phrases such as "war is hell"). Veterans, whose experience of the war was necessarily atomized, pose similar problems for the craftsmen of "collective memory" narratives. Meanwhile, the individuals who experienced war are constantly trying to guide the articulation of its memory, but it would seem that our willingness to listen to them has been historically dependent on the changes in the political conflicts necessarily tied to historical memory. It is now necessary to investigate when veterans have been successful in affecting the composition of that tale and what they are trying to add to it.

THE TROUBLE WITH LANGUAGE COMMUNITIES: VETERANS IN POSTWAR DISCOURSE

In the early postwar period, the public seemed most preoccupied with the diaries and memoirs of famous and powerful figures,[79] but the experience of the "everyman" would eventually reemerge as the most important. As their war diaries moldered in old boxes or family sheds, veterans became increasingly preoccupied with rewriting them, but their reasons for doing so are difficult to generalize. In Kogura Isamu's case, it was no secret to his friends and family that he was doing this on their behalf. Noguchi Fumio, who later became a successful fiction writer, explained his rationale in 1982 as a corrective to the "stars" of the war's history, including kamikaze pilots and drafted university students (for example, Wadatsumi-kai). For those who aimed to communicate with a large postwar audience, like Noguchi Fumio, wartime language required translation. Noguchi simply added copious notes to help postwar civilians understand the slang, technical terms, and foreign places in his original diary; also, with the benefit of hindsight, Noguchi decided to add content describing the Japanese military's cynically poor management. Take the following example:

29 July 1945, Sunny

Up at 5:30am. Making rope baskets, then cleaning. Three air raid sirens in the morning, but we didn't take cover. Kobayashi came again. That THING I've had since yesterday is getting worse and worse, and the edema in my right foot is terrible. Received 20 "Homare" [cigarettes].

- [Postwar notes:] The first sign of scabies I had was at the top of my head. . . . Just like "inadaptable systemic exhaustion"[80] was only diagnosed in "young soldiers," scabies, outside of a few extreme cases, was never seen in anyone ranked above sergeant. . . . The lower ranks suffered badly from the spread of disease from the moment Japan was showing serious signs of defeat.[81]

It must have occurred to Noguchi that "that THING" (a swollen scabies lesion) would be meaningless to any reader except himself and that publication required explication. By contrast, Ōshita Toshirō, a former transport corps infantryman, locked himself in his study while he secretly copied his decaying field notebook. Only when he was deathly ill and the project still incomplete did he hand over the text to his brother's care. Ōshita labored to transcribe every character faithfully into a new copy—a project as unforgiving as Ōshita's honest portrayal of his suffering at the crumbling edges of Japan's empire.[82] His motives for doing this remain mysterious, as do those of the countless veterans who destroyed their documents, or whose families refused to release them; there are also numerous, unfortunate cases of personal documents that have ended up, under lock and key, in Yasukuni Shrine's secretive Yūshūkan war museum. Veterans take widely varying views on postwar testimony; Marine Stanley Rich summarized well the disdain with which some of the wartime generation viewed those who discussed the war: "Anybody who gets home and worries his family with all the talk of the horror of seeing his buddies blown apart or of hundreds of dead littering the ground etc. is in my estimation a neurotic and should see a doctor."[83]

As explained above, the availability of veterans' accounts has been greatly affected by postwar politics. For example, American servicemen, who returned as heroes in a victorious nation, were greatly encouraged to publish their stories, and consequently many did; U.S. veterans' narratives, especially memoirs, would probably be impossible to read in their entirety. More important, for the American memory, however, was the construction of myths including American unity and flawless victory that would be used to continue mobilizing men in the many anticommunist wars to come.[84] In

Japan, some servicemen decided to publish their accounts from the very beginning of the postwar period, but in most cases, the world would need to wait many decades before they would ever see these documents. After China's division into two competing states, only with the arrival of a cross-straits ethno-nationalism in the 1990s would the Chinese begin to seriously investigate their wartime past. Until then, Nationalist veterans were, compared with their counterparts in Japan, silent. Nevertheless, as rulers in exile, the Nationalist government relied on its memory as victors of the war for legitimacy, so many did offer their personal narratives as a corrective measure against CCP historical revisionism and as an explanation for their right to govern Taiwan. In the United States, China, Japan, and Taiwan, what ties veterans' narratives together is the author's belief in his record as truth, and the veteran community's monopoly over how the war should be remembered.

The content of veterans' memory writings, as well as their respective roles in crafting postwar historical memory discourse, is not determinable by dividing them into "winner" and "loser" nations. American veterans, for example, do not necessarily accept public representations of the Second World War, despite the fact that the vast majority of such representations are triumphalist. Like Japanese and Chinese veterans, they feel a need to separate postwar considerations (such as this book) and "what actually happened." Postwar writings, particularly by those who kept diaries, frequently are prefaced by an assertion of authority, but that authority is not necessarily invested in the person—it is in the "truth" value of the diary. In an introduction to his own diary, for example, veteran VMF pilot Henry Miller announced that he intended to "present a factual picture, completely unvarnished" of what it meant to be a pilot during the war; he had "resisted the very strong temptation to include facts or semi-facts from other sources, and opinions or semi-opinions from other sources, or from my own thoughts over the last 45 years."[85] As documentary films such as *Let There Be Light* show, even the "winners" found themselves at a loss when trying to communicate their experiences to postwar audiences.

Indeed, it may seem odd to historians of Okinawa, Taiwan, or Korea that I am about to describe Chinese Nationalist and Japanese veterans as "outsiders" of historical memory. After all, were they not those most in control of the events that took place from 1937 to 1945? The language that servicemen came to adopt in their diaries during this period was the result of self-

discipline—a highly individualized shaping of language used to approximate the diarist's understanding of his experiences. Even though many
would eventually want to discuss those experiences with others, they may
have lacked the language to do so in a way that would be understandable to
those who did not experience the Second World War. Their voices are in
many ways unrecognizable today and alienate those on both the political
right and the left.[86] Thus, more often than not, we use veterans' narratives
selectively or overlook them completely when we discuss the war. Veterans,
however, for the most part feel compelled to "set the record straight." Here I
will examine how memoirs and diaries came into publication or came to be
archived and how this has (or has not) affected our memory of the war.

First, it is necessary to recognize veterans' desire to be heard and to communicate with others. In Japan, memoirs of the war emerged immediately
after 1945. Even memoirs of the atomic bombing, which were watched
closely by Allied occupiers, found their way into the public sphere.[87] Nevertheless, veterans' accounts are comparatively lacking from the late 1940s,
which is attributable to a number of factors, including tight occupation censorship of mass media and the fact that most of these men were still stuck
in former theaters of war, sometimes awaiting trial or being investigated for
war crimes. Once back in Japan (the largest group returning in 1949),
many veterans began to write about their experiences, read about others'
experiences, and enlist in social and political organizations. Members of
veterans' organizations in Japan (senyūkai) came from as diverse socioeconomic backgrounds as those who participated in the war—farmers, laborers, college graduates, and professional soldiers. Veterans' organizations
were not attractive merely for those who wanted to relive positive memories
of their "glory days." For example, Takahashi Yoshinori found that 49.4
percent of veterans who responded to a survey claimed that their war experience was either "on the whole difficult to endure" or "full of hardship,"
whereas figures for those with other feelings (including nostalgia) were far
lower.[88] Membership in veterans' associations in Japan skyrocketed as this
generation began to age and material conditions for Japanese citizens improved. Japanese veterans' associations were usually organized around specific units, although they maintained a national network. Their peak came
during the early 1960s, around the same time veterans' publications spiked
for the first time.[89] One would think that the Chinese Nationalists, who
were scattered around the globe after 1949 and suffered many defeats,

would be loathe to gather for the purpose of remembering their shared past as servicemen. Many Nationalist soldiers and veterans, however, faithfully attend Huangpu Military Academy Alumni Association meetings as far away as San Francisco's Chinatown. Postwar films such as the acclaimed *Everlasting Glory (Yinglie qianqiu)* demonstrate a willingness even among the GMD in Taiwan to celebrate their war history with the general public. The explosion of postwar narratives in film and text, many of which were based on the experiences of veterans, show that we must reevaluate tired canards such as "veterans don't want to talk about the war" and "only those who didn't see any action will talk about the war." Truth be told, it is usually more difficult to get a veteran to stop talking about the war once he has begun.

Takahashi Saburō demonstrated that most veterans have read "war chronicles" (*senkimono,* a term Takahashi employed to include diaries, memoirs, letters, and war literature). These documents peaked in publication as veterans began to age, but they also coincide with major memorial events—such as the fortieth and fiftieth anniversaries of the war's end.[90] Some early accounts published by veterans' groups actively encouraged the critical examination of Japan's past, including the Nanjing Massacre.[91] This suggests that veterans publish their accounts not only at the end of their lives, when feeling reflective, but also to contribute to national debates on the history of the war. Veterans have used self-published accounts to communicate with one another and even with their own families. Some publishing houses even sponsor writing seminars to teach veterans how to compose their memoirs. Although the publishing industry was initially uninterested in texts produced by those untrained in the art of writing, these *samizdat* memoirs and diaries formed horizontal lines of communication about the war in Japanese society. Anyone who has frequented official military archives in the past has seen veterans studiously reading their "unit history" *(butaishi)* or memoirs by other members of their unit (although they may be a rare sight today due to advanced age).

In Japan, veterans' memoirs began appearing in print almost immediately after the war's end. Shimao Toshio produced a series of works from 1946 that treated his war experience in the Pacific in a highly literary and aestheticized form, but this would have been slightly dissatisfying to those seeking the "true experience" of soldiers serving abroad.[92] The first major publication of personal accounts of the Second World War was the unexpectedly popular *Listen to the Voices of the Gods* (Kike, wadatsumi no koe, 1949).[93] The book attempted to channel the anger of the youth abused by the mobilization of Japan's universities at the end of the war, mainly by publishing the letters and diary selections of students who had died. It was compiled during the release of Kurosawa Akira's acclaimed antiwar film *No Regrets for Our Youth* (Wa ga seishun ni kui nashi, 1946), which focused on the wartime state's oppression of progressive young people and inspired many others. Nakamura Tokurō subsequently published his brother's diary, *In the Far Flung Hills and Streams* (Haruka naru sanga ni, 1951), and Nakamura was in part responsible for the compilation of *Voices*. *Voices* was released by a cooperative publisher connected to Tokyo University, with an underwhelming initial run of five thousand copies. After second and third reprints sold out within days, shocking the Wadatsumi Society (Senbotsu gakusei kinen kai, or Fallen Student Soldiers Memorial Society, but commonly referred to as "Wadatsumi-kai") members who had compiled it, bookstore owners began arriving at their door with bundles of 100-yen notes to ask for more. In addition to Nakamura's text, Wadatsumi enabled others to come forward in the public sphere, resulting in publications such as *To the Ends of the Floating Clouds* (Kumo nagaruru hate ni, 1952), which focused on the "lost youth" of the Special Attack pilots. Both *Listen to the Voices* and *To the Ends* were adapted into films in the 1950s. In short, the diaries and letters of educated youth who fell in battle were an instant sensation, and this helped the Wadatsumi Society to become "Japan's first pacifist organization [*heiwa dantai*]."[94] The society, however, operating under the guidance of the Japanese Communist Party, had actively searched for writings of students who had ambivalent or oppositional feelings about the war while alive. Another problem pointed out by veterans and their families was that Tokyo University students' experience of the war was hardly representative. After all, university students were exempt from the draft for most of the war.

In response to this complaint, an unlikely group of government officials in Japan's poor, rural northeast—the Iwate Prefecture Department of Agriculture and Fishing—assembled an impressive collection of letters from a group more likely to resemble the "common soldier." The project of the Iwate Prefecture Rural Culture Preservation Society (Iwate-ken nōson bunka kondankai) to include "farmer soldiers" in the narrative of the Second World War was an attempt to prove that rural people supported the army only for their own socioeconomic advancement. To this end, they released the *Letters of Fallen Farmer-Soldiers* (Senbotsu nōmin heishi no tegami) in

1961. The appeal of the army was strong for those in rural regions, the editors believed, because it allowed them to look down on the elites of the Kantō (Tokyo) and Kansai (Osaka) regions who otherwise monopolized Japan's wealth and power. Tragically, of course, the Japanese military ultimately threw their lives away—symbolized by the government's seizure and melting of local military hero Kiso Yoshinaka's statue in Morioka for scrap metal. Other writers, such as Ōoka Shōhei, weighed in with literary accounts similar to Shimao Toshio's early work, such as the iconic *Fires on the Plain* (Nobi, 1951), using devices such as metaphor, synecdoche, and symbolism, as does Ōoka's far more autobiographical *POW Memoir* (1952).[95] Not all published memoir writers indulged in "pure literature" technique or promoted the pacifist cause: Soetake Toyoda's *The End of the Imperial Navy* (Teikaigun no saigo, 1950) tenaciously maintained the wartime language of formal diary writing. Meanwhile, veterans quietly exchanged privately published memoirs among themselves and their families (for example, Umeda Fusao self-published his account in 1970); newspapers also periodically featured stories about veterans with particularly interesting stories to tell.

When the memoirs of ordinary Japanese veterans began to appear, they demonstrated unwillingness among many authors to surrender the language of the battlefield. In his memoir, Senta Rinnosuke described action against the Chinese Nationalists in Shanxi Province in a manner strikingly similar to that of a war diary:

> Late in the evening of 8 November [1937] our unit installed our mortars and field artillery in Neiling, then proceeding to Ren County at 4am the next day. It was then decided to attack Ren, so the Fifty-Second Platoon's full strength, supported by cannon, was ordered to attack from the northwest, with the Second Battalion emplaced at Wuqiu as a reserve. . . . This day's battle did not involve all of our units, but it was the first time I had ever seen a battle. In the future, it would influence my élan. The men fought stoically. It was a good fight that gave me confidence in war.[96]

Veterans clung tenaciously to the tropes, idioms, and rhetoric of combat because it had become synonymous with the "truth" of their experiences; in fact, they perceived the discipline of the battlefield to have, more often than not, intrinsic value. Special Attack pilot Hamaniwa Kasayoshi took pride in how his military discipline allowed him to work "two or three times harder" than the average person and how he was "in seventy years, never ill." Nevertheless, this was not a valorization of war itself, as the mark of Japanese antiwar sentiment is present even here:

> So, in the end, we reached the extreme limits of humanity with the organization of the Special Attack units. It is sad. In any "dare to die" brigade, there's always some thread of hope [for survival], but not for them. They were all good men. They were full of hopes and dreams. My friends will never return. Only in my memories, in unexpected times and contexts, do they visit me. . . . If they had lived they would be grandparents, holding their grandchildren high and enjoying their golden years. As for me, as well, I had fourteen bullets from a Grumman fighter rip through my body. I was burned as well. This was so painful it felt like the world was coming apart. For four days I was deaf, and ten days blind. My face was deformed by it. There was nothing good about it at all. But, putting aside the moral quandaries, I don't regret, in the passion of youth, risking my life to battle the enemy. Surviving it was the highest form of good fortune.[97]

Whenever veterans' memoirs focused on their own suffering, which was becoming the dominant theme in civilian accounts as well, they were largely palatable to postwar readers. Japanese civilian society was adjusting to a new way of speaking about the nation and daily life, but veterans often felt unable to "embrace" these changes. As it turns out, Japanese veterans' inability to change "language communities" was a problem they shared with their former enemies.

Early publications of war memoirs in post-1949 Taiwan reveal that GMD narratives about the war had changed little since their Pyrrhic victory in 1945. Liu Ziqing's 1954 memoir showed how the discursive path selected by many servicemen was nearly inescapable, even in the face of utter defeat. Resurrecting the language of the Northern Expedition, he described how the Chinese people "rose up" (*qilai*), "awakened" (*juexing*), and "grew up" (*zhangda*) to become one of the great nations of the earth. After "smashing the shackles of imperialism, this should have been our era of great rejoicing." That the GMD's self-appointed historic mission to free China was, at its moment of victory, usurped by the CCP was a source of great frustration for Nationalist veterans like Liu:

Unfortunately, it was right in the middle of this rejoicing that another pack of traitors [*hanjian*] and thieves [*qiangdao*] snuck in, and our entire continent plunged into an iron cage of even more brutality and despair. . . . The revolution is a long-term project, so we must ride over many waves and hardships—this is law of history [*lishi faze*].

Liu's commitment to his historical role was mirrored in the military style of writing that he employed. When remembering the war, such as his time in the Thirty-Second Division in Sichuan, Liu recycled rhetoric from the war. "When the Marco Polo Bridge Incident occurred, the call for a War of Resistance echoed in every corner of China; the Japanese artillery at the Bridge shook awake all those who were fast asleep." His account also borrowed techniques from wartime reportage such as using unidentified speakers ("a soldier said . . ."). When criticizing the party's inner divisions, he was careful to attack specific individuals, such as Liu Xiang and Zhang Xueliang. What was important for veterans like Liu was to preserve the place of the Nationalist Party as the victors of the War of Resistance and the legitimate rulers of China, as designated by history itself.[98]

In some cases, the adherence to wartime writing styles was so rigid that veterans' memoirs seemed to merely be copies of field diaries. Two years after Liu's memoir appeared, Li Zhenqing, a former Thirty-First Division Reserves regiment commander (elevated to the rank of general in the postwar era), published his memoir. Relying heavily on classical Chinese grammar, Li also strictly disciplined his personal record into sections bearing the titles of his engagements, such as "The Battle at Linxin," and then into categories including date, assignment, rank (at the time), and battle experience. Even the language with which officers like Li narrated these battles had not been significantly transformed. Perhaps because the GMD was then thoroughly engaged in "retaking the mainland" from Communist "bandits," Li's memories of the War of Resistance were permeated by these considerations.

When seizing territory [from the Japanese], we used information collected by the people; they observed the enemy's movements, fed our men and horses, and ensured our victory in this engagement. In the war to exterminate the bandits [CCP], we especially need to preserve military discipline in order to harness the power of the people.

Li's memoir frequently also indulged in nostalgia for the good old days of the GMD's efficacy as a fighting force, when it could marshal the patriotism of its citizens and inspire real fighting élan among its troops. "Both times we fought despite the freezing chill, bivouacking in cold water, realizing the principle of 'being reborn from the land of the dead' [*zhi zhi sidi er housheng*]." The memoir, likely based on a field diary or log, could also serve as an unforgiving mirror for Li. Like many Nationalist officers, including Chiang Kai-shek himself, Li acknowledged GMD officers' collective responsibility for losing the mainland to the Communists. Recalling the GMD's failures at Dabieshan, Li wrote, "It is known that there are no soldiers incapable of war on this earth, but there are such officers, and this should invite thorough reproach."[99] The GMD remained adamant in its claim to sole legitimacy on the mainland and its rhetoric from the wartime era—a memory and language that became increasingly strange and obsolete in the postwar years.

In East Asia, much changed in the 1980s, when publications, exhibitions, and investigations of the Second World War began to surge. No one factor could have been the primary cause. In Japanese print media, Honda Katsuichi paved the way for a new level of discourse on the war by publishing incendiary articles in the 1970s regarding the Nanjing Massacre. This was followed by other pieces in exposé journalism, such as Morimura Seiichi's work on Unit 731, *The Devil's Gluttony* (Akki no hōshoku, 1981). These publications were released at exactly the same time the PRC was "opening up" to foreign countries and "reforming" *(gaige kaifang)*. Although some undoubtedly already were aware of the extent of Japan's war crimes, mainland Chinese were being exposed in an unprecedented manner to print media outside of the main channels of the Communist Party. Furthermore, researchers and journalists such as Honda Katsuichi were able to travel throughout China and interview those who had experienced the war firsthand—leading to even more controversial publications such as *The Road to Nanjing* (Nankin he no michi, 1987). Mainland Chinese archives were simultaneously releasing books full of typed copies of GMD documents, such as the Second Historical Archive's *Files on the Japanese Invaders' Nanjing Massacre* (Qinhua Rijun Nanjing datusha dang'an, 1987), which included statistics and official reports. In Taiwan, institutions such as the National Archives and the Modern History Institute launched their Oral History Series in the 1980s, and many issues were dedicated to figures and events from the war.[100] The reinvigoration of the historical memory of Chinese suffering at the hands of Japanese invaders quickly became the basis of a new pan-Chinese nationalism. Although the Chinese Nationalists were in the process of releasing their stranglehold on political power in Taiwan (the first alternative political party formed in 1986, and the first parliamentary elections were held in 1992), the GMD was undoubtedly relieved to see mainland Chinese embrace the historical memory of their collective suffering and resistance during the war so fervently.

It was in this context that many servicemen in Japan began publishing their wartime diaries (for example, both Noguchi Fumio and Kimura Genzaemon published diaries in 1982). Skilled researchers such as Yoshimi Yoshiaki, who would later expose the Japanese army's official support of the "comfort women" system, quickly noticed the rise in self- and commercially published diaries in a 1988 article, and Takahashi Saburō would follow with his study of diaries and memoirs just a year later.[101] Azuma Shirō then stirred up a political firestorm by publishing a heavily edited version of his war diary entitled *My Nanjing Platoon* (Wa ga Nankin puratōn, 1988), which described many of the atrocities committed by the Japanese armed forces in graphic detail. Although scholars and many veterans had known for years the extent of the armed forces' excesses, the Japanese public, who had primarily experienced the war through firebombing, atomic bombing, rationing, and evacuations, were more or less newly exposed and highly dubious. Publicity surrounding Azuma's high-profile exposure of Japan's war crimes inspired many subsequent investigations, primarily because detractors claimed Azuma's account was not a "diary." Defenders of Azuma's view of the war (even if they did not embrace his war diary as "authentic") quickly found irrefutable evidence: the most successful effort was arguably Ono Kenji's documentation of Japanese war crimes in Nanjing through servicemen's diaries, published as *Imperial Soldiers Who Recorded the Nanjing Massacre* (Nankin Daigyakusatsu wo kiroku shita kōgun heishitachi, 1996). It was solely through the efforts of Ono, a truck driver for a Japanese factory in Fukushima, that the diaries of Thirteenth Division veterans such as Ōdera Takashi, Ōuchi Toshimichi, Kindō Eijirō, Saitō Jirō, and many others were known. Ono conducted sensitive negotiations with relatives and veterans, carefully prepared legal documents (to protect himself from libel suits), and traveled far and wide for these documents, with no institutional support.[102] Shortly thereafter, Azuma responded to his critics by publishing his entire diary manuscript in 2001, but it was clear that many of his generation were already responding to this zeitgeist by publishing their wartime diaries and postwar memoirs in full.

Why did Japanese veterans choose to publish their diaries and memoirs? On the one hand, they were coming to the end of their lives in the 1980s, and many were naturally feeling reflective. This personal motivation was in many cases tied to their desire to make an impact on public discourse— "setting the record straight." Taketomi Tomio, a veteran who in 1979 used his own property for a "Soldiers' and Common People's Museum" (Heishi / shomin no sensō shiryōkan), explained to interviewer Hayashi Eidai why veterans' diaries and memoirs were so critical:

> There have been a lot of publications of military unit histories [butaishi], almost what you would call a military history "boom." Stepping outside the glorious military histories of the wartime era, a more intimate record of soldiers [heitaitachi] was born. The parts that were taboo, in piecemeal fashion, have come to the surface. What is needed is a detailed record to which only the few remaining survivors can testify. . . . If the naked facts [jijitsu] of the testimonies of these survivors are not faithfully restored [saigen] and documented, then they cannot be communicated to later generations as a valuable historical record. No matter how humiliating the content may be, the truth [shinjitsu] must be put down into the record. My gut feeling [jikkan] is that, in the diaries [nisshi] of nameless soldiers [heishi], the true [hontō] face of war emerges.[103]

Taketomi used three different Japanese words *(jujitsu, shinjitsu, hontō)* to underline the importance of the authenticity of servicemen's written records and, in the same interview, explicitly condemned media representations of war—even military history *(senshi)* itself. As irrefutable proof of the misery of servicemen's existence, Taketomi, even above his own memories of the war, held up the blurry diary of Ōshita Toshirō, whose brother had donated to the museum in 1996 (after Ōshita's passing). The diary was more than just a document for history—it would speak for veterans after they passed on, taking over for them like a doppelgänger.

Indeed, according to paratextual commentaries by veterans and their families (such as forewords and appendices), the decision to publish wartime accounts had as much to do with "pacifying the spirits" *(irei,* a term frequently used by Yasukuni officials) of comrades and loved ones as it did with telling the "true story" of the war. Kawakami Yoshinobu published the war diary of his deceased elder brother, Kawakami Yoshimitsu, in 1985. Yoshinobu described the emotional experience of reading Yoshimitsu's China war diary, mentioning in particular his brother's homesickness *(bōkyō)* and nostalgia *(kaiko)*. Yoshinobu quickly added the following caveat: "In the text, there are points that will not agree with current views [*yosō*], but in my brother's heart, he only did these things as a result of his superiors' orders." Like many relatives of Japan's war dead, Yoshinobu was unwilling to acknowledge his brother's complicity in battlefield atrocities. When reading Yoshinobu's explanation for why he decided to publish Yoshimitsu's diary, however, his reasons for this reticence become clearer:

> Up until now, because of my ancestors and society, I have been healthy and able to work. I am often overwhelmed by a sense of gratitude when considering that this is entirely due to my ancestors watching over me. . . . If I were to lock up this detailed diary, into which my brother poured his energy, it would be a waste, and I would feel sorry for my brother [*ani ni sumanai*], so I decided to publish it, have others read it, and share it with the world. . . . The fact that I was fortunate enough to live through the war was probably due to my brother's death in battle.[104]

Veterans and, especially, their relatives have thus struggled to comprehend how best to both mourn their loss and respect the "truth" that wartime diarists tried to capture. A 2004 survey conducted by the National Museum of Japanese History found that many veterans and their families visit Yasukuni Shrine to "pacify the spirits" of their fallen relatives and comrades. We should not, however, assume that their attendance or their membership in veterans' organizations equals support for the stated or implied politics of these institutions. Even Azuma Shirō, whose diary was a banner for Japan's antiwar movement, felt compelled to write that "helping people to know the true face of war and promote good Sino-Japanese relations is the highest and greatest way to pacify the spirits of my fallen comrades."[105] Regular observance of "pacification" rites does not even guarantee belief in efficacy or afterlife. One respondent to the National Museum's survey, who carried out group and private rituals, wrote, "Before I shipped out, I believed in gods and Buddhas, but I changed my mind because of the war, and now I don't believe in them at all."[106] Many veterans and their families donated self-published memoirs and diaries to Japan's Peace Museums and the National Diet Library, generating an invaluable documentary history on an entirely voluntary basis. Thus, even when the results were unclear and the risks relatively high, veterans felt compelled to testify and affect the content of Japan's historical memory.

Recent Chinese Nationalist accounts of the war adopt a similar stance of "telling the truth" when narrating the past. Historians should take care, however, because Chinese veterans are just as engaged in self-fashioning at the end of their lives as they were during and directly after the war. When scholars from the Academia Sinica interviewed former ROC naval officer Li Lianheng in 1998, his evaluation of the GMD's military capabilities was as harsh as any field diary from the war. Asked whether he believed that the military training he received in Japan had "value," he immediately replied:

> It had value—all of our studies concerned philosophies of combat and building an army, and not directed towards one's own profession or accounting. . . . [Our teacher] asked Japanese instructors to come in order to pass on [*chuanshou*] the Japanese people's spirit of building an army [*jianjun jingshen*]. . . . Because, what had we learned in the Naval Academy, after all? After eight years of the War of Resistance, we were bumpkins [*baiding*], we had no military knowledge, not even the basics. So, after coming to Taiwan, I acknowledged the fact that the army, navy, and air forces were all bumpkins.

Li's compulsion to recognize the "facts" was the result of his training and his self-discipline. Acknowledgment of the GMD's weaknesses did not mean that officers such as Li gave up the ghost when it came to their identities as soldiers—Li was still putting on a performance of self similar to a wartime diarist's. While Li admitted without hesitation that "during the eight years of the War of Resistance, I never once saw a Japanese person," he also took care to note his dedication to the cause of national defense. Li claimed that when his unit pulled out of Qingdao, trekking all the way to Taierzhuang at the end of 1937, many of the enlisted men abandoned the ranks. He spoke to the officers and men, saying, "Under no circumstances should you run—it looks bad. You're fleeing even though we're resisting Japan and fighting the Japanese. Do you think you can protect yourself if you run home?" Using such rhetoric, which could have come directly from a GMD propaganda pamphlet or field diary, Li claimed to have been able to keep men in the ranks. He also took great pride in his ability to win his men's respect and constantly pointed out how his men were faithful to him during the collapse of the GMD in 1949.[107] Li held on to this voice because it had become meaningful to him. Even though strident GMD politics were hardly in fashion in 1997 (when this interview was conducted), veterans such as Li were too thoroughly attached to the identities from their past to change.

The debate in Taiwan has been irrevocably transformed, however, by the decline of GMD power and the rise of an independently Taiwanese identity. "War veteran" therefore not only applies to former Nationalist troops who fled the CCP in 1949 but also to those who served under the Japanese. As Hui-yu Caroline Ts'ai has found, Taiwanese veterans of the Japanese army confound any simplistic assumptions about their attitudes toward serving the empire. Some, such as Hong Huozhao and Zhang Jinpo, bitterly accuse the Japanese army, as many Japanese veterans do, of wasting their youth or leaving them crippled for life. "A promising Taiwanese youth became involved in the war for no reason, to serve as a guardian spirit of Japan. There is nothing more ridiculous than this." Others, like Zheng Renchong's father, recalled with great pride his brave service, even as his son attempted to stir up anger over Japan's abuse of the Taiwanese people.[108] The confusion surrounding where to place these men—as righteous victims of Japanese aggression, apologists for the Japanese Empire, or something else—stems in part from the fact that veterans' voices cannot be easily integrated into the mercilessly specific positions of postwar political factions squabbling over how the war should be remembered.

One thing that becomes immediately evident when speaking with veterans is that, though they may not have the kind of power that politicians or nationwide organizations have to mobilize public opinion, they are by and large little affected by such forces when recounting "the truth" of their experience during the war. First, the fear of ostracism affects them less and less with age. Not only are they confident in their memory of these events and the manner in which they describe them, they are not easily persuaded by conservative authority or even right-wing intimidation. It will take quite a bit more than black trucks with tinted windows and megaphones to frighten a man who fought guerrillas in northern China during a subzero blizzard or ran through GMD machine gun nests in Shanghai.[109] Second, in many cases, such self-disciplined men have decided among themselves that recognizing their crimes in Asia is their new "duty" *(ninmu);* some veterans have understood this brutal honesty as part of the rigorous process of "self-criticism" *(hansei)* that they learned in the barracks. If the veterans of the Repatriated China Front Soldiers' Association wish to express reverence for the loss of both their comrades and the Chinese victims of Japan's war of aggression, it seems unlikely that the opinion of Tokyo University professors such as Fujioka Nobukatsu will convince them to act otherwise.[110]

VETERANS AND POSTWAR HISTORICAL MEMORY

Kimura Hisao, who would eventually be executed for war crimes in Singapore, began writing his thoughts into a volume of philosophy while awaiting sentence in an Allied prison camp in 1945; he expressed the "injustice" of having to pay for "Tokyo's crimes." Nevertheless, while invoking the wartime language of patriotic self-sacrifice, he also transitioned into the postwar political reality: "I won't die as a sacrifice for the Japanese army, but if I perish by covering myself with the crimes of the Japanese people, [in order to save them] from disaster, then I will not be angry. I will die smiling."[111] Kimura's angry articulation of self-abnegation, even in the face of certain death, shows the stubbornness of wartime language. Its persistence has often made veterans pariahs of a postwar society eager to reinvent the language we use to remember the past and create a more comforting "memory."

Tomiyama Ichirō argued that one of the fears inhibiting our engagement with veterans is that, even in the postwar, there is a strong possibility that the self will be reconstructed by revisiting memories of the battlefield, and this can occur whether one desires it or not; consequently, veterans who revisit the battlefield in the postwar present, using the language of the past, often offend, with their "violent attitude" *(bōryokuteki na taido),* those who have known only peace.[112] How does one identify a "violent" (or "aggressive") attitude as being something left over from the war, except by the language the individual uses, which is riddled with historically and culturally specific (but usually implied) hierarchies, values, bigotries, and expectations? The "language community" of the battlefield was forged in an environment of camaraderie and desperate survival, and it carries with it a worldview that is not only alien to postwar audiences but also threatening.

Veterans' stubborn adherence to the "truth" that they discovered during the war was a direct result of their self-discipline. Although the state in the PRC, Taiwan, and Japan adopted myopic or stridently orthodox understandings of the war and made efforts to promulgate this historical memory, veterans were not always receptive. Even in the case of early postwar Taiwan, where GMD veterans occupied positions of power, smaller narratives, such as the role of Taiwanese in the Japanese armed forces, went unacknowledged for decades but emerged with a vengeance in the 1980s and 1990s. In some cases, however, repression was almost successful. Most veterans who had been trapped on mainland China in 1949 died without ever having told their stories to a postwar society; in many cases, all that is left are their diaries. Periodic bursts of diary and memoir publications in Japan are often timed with ephemeral media interest in public events, such as the textbook controversy in the 1980s or anniversaries of Japan's surrender. Nevertheless, veterans in East Asia, particularly toward the end of their lives, have always made their "testimonies" available in interviews and *samizdat* publications. Whether in Taiwan, China, or Japan, the voice that they had created in their diaries was always there; the only changing element was whether anyone was listening.

Conclusion

The Peril of Self-Discipline

IN HIS 2003 work of war reportage, *Jarhead,* Anthony Swofford described his experience as a U.S. marine at the front line of Operations Desert Shield and Desert Storm. In one part of the memoir, a staff sergeant explained to the men in Swofford's unit how they should conduct interviews with the press. When one of Swofford's comrades complained that the sergeant's directives violated marines' right of freedom of speech, the officer brusquely reminded him that soldiers do not possess this right. Swofford took this as an opportunity to muse on the relationship servicemen share with language:

> I want to come to the defense of free speech, but I know it will be useless. We possess no such thing. The language we own is not ours, it is not a private language, but derived from Marine Corps history and lore and tactics. . . . When you are speaking that thing, you speak like it.[1]

Swofford used the manufactured atmosphere of the media interview to stage a humorous example of soldiers' self-degradation—a mock gang rape of one of their comrades. Like Ha Jin's 2004 fictional account of Chinese POWs during the Korean War, *War Trash*, Swofford embraced graphic descriptions of servicemen's brutality and nigh bestial behavior in order to make their heroic moments appear farcical. Swofford's technique is similar to that used in many other representations of war. Yoshida Mitsuru, author of the 1952 *Requiem for Battleship Yamato*, described Japanese survivors of the "unsinkable" warship as they were called on to fight again: "The gazes pouring in on [the officer], the gloomy silence. The fatigue from our trip to death's door is too great."[2] Yoshida, Ha, and Swofford were veterans who took up the pen to describe war—either from memory or imagination—and simultaneously took care (momentarily) to show the distance between language and experience. Indeed, as Xiaofei Tian described, Chinese men at war have expressed the impossibility of capturing experience with language as far back as 1,600 years ago: "Harboring these feelings so many ages after / I've exhausted my words, but cannot express what is on my mind."[3]

If language and experience are so far apart, then why did so many veterans write novels and memoirs, and why, moreover, did servicemen write diaries (often at great personal risk) during the war itself? Perhaps more important than the question of whether language can capture experience is whether we want it to, or when and how we want it to. Psychoanalysis posits that talk therapy uncovers some "truth" about one's past that allows emotional release, or catharsis. Subsequent studies by psychologists have shown, however, that, especially in the minds of those suffering trauma (or in children), memory can be unreliable. It may be that the tales we tell about ourselves have little bearing on "truth" and more to do with power—particularly control over experience. This book has been, to a large degree, an investigation into how people come to "know" themselves and the world around them and how they make decisions based on that "knowledge." War diaries are merely one route to examining the phenomenon of subjectivity but they are particularly useful because they are both tools for and evidence of self-discipline under extreme circumstances.

The Second World War in Asia and the Pacific transformed the region's political relations and the nature of U.S. power. The Japanese Empire's attempt to create a "New Order," including the destruction of Western colonialism and imperialism in the region, brought the United States into the war and changed world history, including that of Western Europe. Although the Japanese planners never managed to fulfill their objectives, they did strike a fatal blow to foreign empires in the region—including their own. Shortly after the war, China became the world's largest socialist country, Korea reemerged as a nation, the vast majority of European colonies in Asia would become independent, and, by the 1970s, even devastated Japan had developed into the second largest economy after the United States. This launched a process of power shifting from Western Europe to the United States and Asia, which is the world we live in today. None of this would have been possible without the tremendous sacrifices that ordinary people made, even those in support of Japan's imperialist aggression. Understanding why they did this is critical, and the diary is one of our best tools for doing so.

THE IMPORTANCE OF GENRE

In diaries, genre conventions have determined what an author believes relevant to the story he wishes to tell. Religious confessions are, naturally, concerned with the author's notions of sin and his relationship with God; ship logs detail the direction of wind, weather conditions, nautical miles traveled, the state of provisions, and the mindset of the crew; and women's diaries have been historically defined by the gendered expectations of the societies in which they live, many of which were learned by the reading of fiction— including fictionalized diaries. Genre is not determinative, however, and soldiers on the battlefield, in particular, felt pressure to experiment with language in order to make it "truly" reflect "what it was really like" to fight. The genre may have been a cage, but it was a very flexible one, particularly since soldiers were usually dissatisfied with the tools given them by disciplinary institutions to describe war. Martin Clemens put it best:

> In pre-war days, District Officers in the Solomons were required to keep diaries, and I had to keep a diary as the District Officer, Guadalcanal. These diaries were supposed to contain the dull details of usual routine Government work. As times became abnormal, so my diary suffered a considerable metamorphosis, and became a more personal story. This book is based on that diary, or rather, the personal part of it.[4]

Clemens's insight on how genre was bent, twisted, and broken for the purposes of "truth telling" is unusual. Feeling the tension between writing and self, some soldiers, like William Sharpe, made comments in passing such as: "I guess we're getting near the end of the story; I feel as though I were writing the last chapter of a book."[5] Still, most soldiers never seemed to notice that they were engaged in the transformation of self-expression. How the diarist described the war inevitably had an impact on how he saw himself, which in turn helped him make decisions in the world outside of the diary. The cycle of influence between lived experience, description in a diary, definition of self, and consequent behavior patterns is subjectivity in action. The fact that the individual exercised so much agency of the construction of the self, as evinced by the diaries in this book, means that we can have meaningful discussions of responsibility.

For this book to fully grasp the power of genre over the war diary, it was first necessary to establish its most important precedents. Chapter 1 examined some of the main influences on East Asian military diary writing before 1937. In Japan and China, peer- or superior-reviewed field diary writing introduced a system that Foucault might have compared to Jeremy Bentham's "panopticon." Field diaries were always potentially subject to review, so officers learned to produce narratives that obeyed military norms, and they practiced composing these stories about themselves on a day-to-day basis. This discipline was successful considering the similarity between "official" field diaries and "private" diaries from, for example, the Russo-Japanese War; the field diary, with its disciplined record of "facts," became a model that many servicemen emulated in their personal writings. With the introduction of war reportage aimed at a broader audience, however, the compelling language of popular accounts began to affect even the way "official" diaries were written. Chinese Nationalist field diaries frequently narrated battle in the same manner that published accounts described them. Japanese servicemen began to incorporate text and image from mass media products (newspapers, magazines, and periodicals) in their diaries. In response to this trend, the Japanese military began experimenting with guided diary writing during the mid-1930s. On the one hand, whether keeping a "personal" or "official" record of war experience, the diary allowed voices of the state and mass media to penetrate servicemen's descriptions of themselves and their world. On the other hand, soldiers also increasingly produced text and images (drawings, poems, and stories) that did not fit the model of the field diary or reportage.

Through a close reading of Chinese Nationalist and Japanese diaries from the first stage of the Sino-Japanese Theater (August to November 1937), Chapter 2 demonstrated how servicemen developed their writing styles as a result of experiences on the battlefield. First, servicemen used their diaries as tools for "self-mobilization" as they prepared themselves for the war. This included what Paul Fussell referred to as "the *versus* habit," or the creation, through rhetorical strategy, of an enemy "Other" whom the diarist could overcome.[6] Second, servicemen began to seek out unconventional writing for their diaries in order to make their accounts more closely reflect their experience. Even simple matters in official field diaries, such as recording an enemy artillery attack, could introduce "irrelevant" information such as one's personal sensations and lyrical flourishes. For example, Yang Tiejun, a company commander in Northern China, described the Japanese bombardment "blasting in the north without end, my ears ringing," and Zhong Song, after abandoning Shanghai, wrote, "Heaven feels the sacrifices of these heroes—it makes the gods cry."[7] Personal diaries also showed signs of change. Nagatani Masao began by trying to put his physical sensations into words: the sensation of dizziness when he hit the shores in central China and the incessant, uncontrollable shaking in his voice. Then, as he participated in the massacre of noncombatants in Shanghai, he drew on whatever language he felt best approximated these visions, including images of the Buddhist "living hell" *(ikite iru jigoku)*.[8] In the chaos of the initial months of the war, servicemen were separated from the voices of authority that normally provided them with a language to help control the powerful emotions that these experiences unleashed. On the battlefield, they would have to be self-disciplined. Ironically, it was the discipline of diary writing (a mechanism of military control) that helped the individual create a new self.

Chapter 3 analyzed the state, mass media, and military authorities' response to the rising chaos among servicemen in China and Japan and how these men reacted to the reintroduction of discipline "from above." Beginning with the Japanese military invasion and massacre(s) in and around Nanjing, Chapter 3 showed how many men on both sides succumbed to panic and despair. The act of recording this in their diaries demonstrated how the text served them as records of experience, regardless of whether it possessed a coherent narrative, and would later become the foundation of a new self. When authorities attempted to reconstitute political space after the fall of Nanjing, one of the primary forms of guiding servicemen's speech and behavior was to offer models through published personal narratives of the war, including diaries. The diaries of some soldiers, such as Liu Jiaqi, were thus published and distributed among servicemen as a model to emulate.

With the uncertainty of the survival of the Nationalist regime and the legitimacy of Japan's puppet government, soldiers often seemed left to their own devices when it came to writing the war and describing their role in it; some were able to reattach themselves to the voices of authority once the state and mass media reasserted themselves on the battlefield, but others were too far gone down their own paths. Published servicemen who survived, like Yamamoto Kenji, learned to censor themselves in order to produce text that was acceptable for an audience in Japan that expected victorious narratives. Even unpublished servicemen, such as Taniguchi Kazuo, were able to reconnect with centers of power and replicate patriotic discourse in their diaries. Chinese Nationalists at the edge of Japan's imperial reach in China, such as Yu Shao and Wang Wenrong, still held on to the expressions that had meaning for them. Many servicemen, however, such as Kimura Genzaemon, had already built an understanding of themselves and the war through their experiences that was irreversible. Kimura concluded that "after one and a half years of working as a human target, all burning emotions have dissipated."[9] Many Chinese Nationalists, recognizing the collapse of their armed forces in Taierzhuang and Wuhan by the end of 1938, filled their diaries with bureaucratic busy work, becoming more like officials rather than revolutionary warriors. Some servicemen, such as Azuma Shirō, had gone so far beyond the point of no return that their self-narratives became seditious. In every case, soldiers made these decisions based on their understandings of themselves and the war, which was a direct result of their self-disciplinary acts.

In order to dissolve any suspicions that Japanese and Chinese servicemen were vulnerable to a particularly East Asian penchant for authoritarianism, Chapters 4 and 5 compared Japanese servicemen's diaries with those of Americans and then Chinese, from 1941 to 1945. Both American and Japanese soldiers frequently felt themselves to be active participants in a larger "historical" process. This granted their actions special significance, but it also compelled them to keep "factual" and "true" chronicles of their victories and defeats. In the U.S. Armed Forces, this compulsion was quite at home where traditions of diary writing, detailed reporting, and record keeping had developed rapidly at the beginning of the twentieth century. In fact, an examination of social organizations in China, Japan, and the United States reveals not only many striking similarities but also that Americans were just as disciplined as East Asians. Americans such as Clayton Knight and William Heggy used their diaries to mobilize themselves as the U.S. military prepared to send them to war. Like East Asians, Clayton Knight and Ralph Noonan tied family and self-interest to the interests of the state. Self-discipline among Americans could lead to unintended consequences, however, such as the torture and murder of Japanese POWs. While Japanese troops such as Obara Fukuzō may have used their diaries to aestheticize their imminent deaths, it seems that Obara may have rewritten his diary notebook *(techō)* in order to do so. Some soldiers, even those in Japan's air forces (home to the infamous kamikaze) such as Nishimoto Masaharu, used their diaries to express doubt for and criticism of Japan's armed forces. Nevertheless, like Americans, many Japanese continued to use diaries to integrate the language of authority into their self-narratives. By the end of the war, U.S. servicemen had learned to adopt the persona of a soldier in a victorious army, which would ease their transition into a postwar world. Whether occupied with the emotional process of self-mobilization, the difficult project of chronicling traumatic events, or the unpredictable journey toward a new subjectivity, servicemen in China, the United States, and Japan were engaged in acts of self-discipline.

Chapter 6 analyzed the consequences of this self-discipline in the context of postwar East Asia. Servicemen had the tools for constituting the self, but they were bound by the conventions of language, and as modern people, they were frequently responsive to efforts by the state to rediscipline them. Many veterans, however, did not "fall back into line" during the war and were even less likely to do so in the postwar era. The U.S. occupation government in Japan initially exercised control over how the war was to be remembered. As their course "reversed" to a more stridently anticommunist position, the "white" purges ended and many of Japan's social and political conservatism from the wartime era resurfaced. Memorial acts surrounding the war, therefore, tended to ignore delicate issues, such as the crimes that Japanese armed forces had committed abroad. Meanwhile, the fall of the Nationalist regime in mainland China forced triumphalist narratives of GMD victory over Japanese imperialism to the more provincial Taiwan.

Chinese Communist narratives of the War of Resistance were largely self-congratulatory, despite their comparatively minor role in the conflict. In part to continue to insist on their relevance, Chinese Nationalists never abandoned the rhetoric of the war, but also because it was the result of their own self-disciplinary efforts to understand their experiences. Servicemen slowly reached out and made connections in their narratives and through social organizations, expressing a desire to "set the record straight." Their stories, often deeply marked with a language of the past, can be troubling to both the political left and the right in Japan, to both Chinese Communists and Nationalists. The consequences of self-discipline included ostracism, accusations of libel, and feelings of isolation.

In light of the changes that occurred in the postwar era, when veterans transformed diaries into memoirs, or even rewrote and published "war diaries" in an attempt to communicate with the world after war, it is worth revisiting how the diary, as a genre, has shaped the understanding of war experience itself. First, contrast it with letter writing. Evelyn Waugh pointed out the artificiality of war correspondence as well, noting that the "form letter" was something profoundly modern;[10] correspondence, because it presumes an audience, tailored content even more severely than the diary. William A. McClain produced a "diary" of his war experience, which was actually a collection of letters that he had written to his wife. One striking difference between McClain's account and those who wrote daily personal logs on the battlefield that were, at the time, addressed to no one, is that McClain's "diary" is far more light-hearted:

> I soaped allover and was enjoying the cool water (it had been very hot topside) when all of a sudden the buzzer buzzed my emergency signal and the general alarm went off (battle stations)—There I was—soap all over me AND I had to get to the bridge in a hurry—no robe—so I grabbed a fowl [sic] weather coat—of course the sleeves were stuck together and I couldn't get my arms in—finally I got it on and the top fastener hooked up and arrived on the bridge. The rest of the coat was flying in the wind and there I was in all my glory. My big problem now is to maintain discipline—It is hard to do when every one is laughing. What a life—you think you have problems. The worse thing is that everyone is writing home about it.[11]

Rather than attempting to read McClain's mind in order to determine an "intended audience," it is far better to recognize how this genre—personal correspondence—has shaped what he felt to be salient to describing the war. Certainly, it did not tell "the whole truth," but neither does a diary; the diary, as a genre, merely opens the door for greater experimentation with a direct line of influence over one's sense of self.

Second, the war diary brought together multiple practices and assumptions: disciplined record, adherence to truth, observation of fact, critical self-reflection, and the creative use of language. These texts thus cannot be separated from the sociopolitical order, expressed through public discourse that surrounded the authors; Jochen Hellbeck described the writers living under Stalin's terror as "preoccupied with finding out who they were in essence and how they could transform themselves."[12] This was not, however, limited to societies that had embraced a revolutionary ideology; personal transformation through self-discipline was carried out in prerevolutionary China, Japan, and even the United States. Indeed, even in the Soviet Union, diarists could not stop themselves from searching for different modes of self-expression. In analyzing Vasilii Azhaev's diary, Thomas Lahusen described how we "find 'literature' where we least expect it: in a proposal concerning the results of drilling tests," and the diarist himself, Azhaev, continually applied himself to the development of his own literary voice.[13] To view the diary genre solely as a confine, then, is wrong; it was a platform or a tool. Certainly, there were many things for which this tool was ill suited, but for creating a textual image of the self that the author would accept as truthful, its power was difficult to challenge. This was precisely why the modern state, with all of its ambitions to direct and control our notion of self, found it irresistible in the preparation of men for war.

SILENCE, EXPERIENCE, AND WRITING WAR

Ludwig Wittgenstein, who famously wrote "whereof one cannot speak, thereof one must be silent," was suspicious of language and its ability to generate knowledge, particularly any understanding concerning the most important parts of the human experience. Soldiers also seemed to be intimately aware of the paucity of language, sometimes even viewing any efforts to depict war experience as perverse or blasphemous. William Sharpe described how, during periods of intense shelling, attempts to plead to a higher power became incoherent "Oh God" utterances, repeated "over and over again, trying to make it sound like a prayer, but in your ears, it sounds like a man in pain." Four days later, Sharpe admitted he still "can think of no more to say about it."[14] These days, their denial of language's descriptive capacity is very familiar and often sounds like the passage from M. O'Neil at the beginning of Chapter 5. Even the most gregarious soldier might view writing about war with as much fear and loathing as, for example, William S. Burroughs did when he declared that language is a "virus." O'Neill also felt, however, that there was "really something beautiful about combat" and that war brought out the best in men; he vehemently contrasted this with the "smart" businessman, skilled in verbal persuasion, who "lies" and "deceives" to "put across his deal."[15] Although soldiers shared Wittgenstein's dim view of language superficially, they nevertheless made frequent use of it to describe combat. Consequently, this book has explained how their acts of writing war, whether they were accurate or not, in any case had implications for how soldiers viewed the conflict, the enemy, and themselves.

Soldiers seemed unusually preoccupied with diary writing. In fact, in the field of cognitive neuroscience, the "compulsion to chronicle" and narrativize experience is now thought to be a hardwired facet of the human brain and a product of evolutionary process.[16] Scholarship on trauma—particularly wartime psychological injury—seems, however, to state the opposite: that the brain resists the narrativization of life experience and even chops out whole sections of the past, because it is, as Allan Young put it, "an affliction through which pain and fear colonize and degrade the sufferer's life-world."[17] Nevertheless, to treat this affliction, psychologists actually emphasize talk therapy, which puts disparate memories into a structured, rational narrative in order to give comfort to trauma patients. Considering the problems with trauma and the unreliability of memory, in addition to philosophy and neuroscience's suspicion of language's ability to represent real life, one might be forgiven in seeing these diaries as being entirely separate from war experience. Still, one cannot ignore the effects of unwritten experiences on the composition of the diary, even if many of those experiences cannot be discussed directly. The "physics of writing war" shows us that experience, particularly of the traumatic kind, is encoded in textual blank spots and can be detected by the activity around them. In the observable world of written language, invisible phenomena such as trauma, guilt, emotion, desire, and other indescribable mental events must be similarly treated with a Wittgensteinian mixture of respect and relative silence.

One can, however, measure the effects of these events. Changes in writing can be reasonably ascribed to the powerful influence of experience, even if the experience itself is forever beyond us. We cannot "know what war was like," but we can see the impact that it had on individuals in their writing.

Consider, for example, the phenomenon of writing about bodily experience. As has been demonstrated many times in this book, the first signature of writing about the body, particularly in trying circumstances, is the breakdown of narrative cohesion. This usually occurred when the diarist was experiencing physical strain—regardless of whether his forces were victorious. Japanese captive D. M. Moore (see Chapter 4) experienced what he described as "difficult of concentrating [sic]" and wrote in a stuttering, staccato voice. Another signature of writing bodily experience is the author's attempt to describe physical sensations. Here language is most obviously weak, because its claim to represent physical experience is highly dependent on the reader having an analogous memory. In languages such as Japanese, Chinese, and English, turning physical sensation into text is characterized by the appearance of onomatopoeia, ideophonic language, and metaphor. One Chinese Nationalist officer described Japanese airplanes "buzz buzz buzzing" up above and then added, "but we're getting used to seeing and hearing them now. To us they're like ducks and birds in the sky."[18] Sounds of artillery bombardments, rifle reports, men's groans, and the approach of aircraft fill Chinese diaries on nearly every page; they inspired phrases such as "The sounds of the assault and killing could be heard up into the heavens" and "The enemy artillery fire is unceasing and maddening." Even authors of field diaries subject to superior review included the dramatic physicality of war in their writings. Yang Tiejun (see Chapter 2), fighting the Japanese in Northern China in 1937, wrote: "At about 10am, while on the march, I saw enemy planes blasting us incessantly, and the sounds of artillery shells thundered in our ears without end." Writing about the body came into even sharper focus when servicemen were directly wounded and languished in military hospitals. Hamabe (Chapter 2), an infantryman from Shizuoka, recorded his final days in a hospital diary. Even his short descriptions of his painful treatments, oozing leg wound, and slow physical and mental deterioration are challenging for the sensitive reader.

Although the psychological effects of physical experience on historical subjects are unknowable to us today, servicemen explicitly combined records of their body and mind. Their writing often becomes filled with strange and chaotic vignettes. Stanley Rich described heavy action on Guadalcanal thus:

> On Sept. 10, one of my boys was horribly wounded by a bomb and died 4 hrs. later. Also, two of my men were wounded so badly they had to be evacuated. That particular bomb was a 500 lb. personnel bomb and landed 25 Yds. from where I was clawing the earth in a hopeless endeavor to obtain some sort of protection. Fragments flew all about and many other bombs landed all around. It was hell. . . . The Japs were all around us. Our Artillery was giving them hell only a hundred to two hundred yards away and we could hear the Japs yelling and groaning all night. . . . About 10 men in the Company cracked up and were so shell-shocked they had to be evacuated.[19]

Thus, the exposure of the body to privation, as well as to the experience of seeing things gruesome and horrible, seems to have led servicemen to attempt to describe internal psychological states. Diarists also juxtaposed horrible visions with physical sensations. Nagatani Masao (Chapter 2) described his feelings after landing on the Shanghai front: "I feel like I'm still on the boat—rocking and swaying. Everywhere you look, the place is brutally torn apart from air raids. I'm finally able to truly understand the worth of war. This is how you know how horrible, how savage a thing it is [*makurumono*]." He often wrote of his bodily trembling and of shaking in his voice. Henry Miller, a marine corps VMF pilot, failed in fully describing the horror he experienced trying and failing to pull a living man out of a burning F4F cockpit. "The pilot I tried to pull out was unrecognizable, his arms blown bare and his face bloated," he wrote. "He was unconscious when I first arrived and just alive—there are no words to describe the feeling of abandoning a man, dead or alive, in that furnace."[20] The experience of seeing the horrible was linked to other senses such as touch and smell, and this in turn was used to underline the emergence of new thoughts and expressions.

The connection between experience and writing is critical to grasp, because it was, for soldiers in the Second World War, the foundation for transformations in their sense of self. At the center of this process was the diary, acting as a tool for the subject to transform indescribable experience into articulate subjectivity. This does not mean that the end result, the diary, perfectly reflected the "reality" of war or served as a window into the "soul" of the author. It does, however, show us how the diarist understood

the war, the enemy, and himself, even if it also revealed his errors, preju-
dices, and wishful thinking.

MODERN WAR DIARIES AND THE SELF

Focusing on the textual practices of Greco-Roman culture, Michel Foucault observed that writing about oneself constitutes "the fashioning of accepted discourses, recognized as true, into rational principles of action."[21]
In other words, there is a cycle in self-writing in which the author decides,
through some means or another, what is "true," applies it to what he believes about himself, and then uses the text as a means of determining how
to behave. This seems to have been as true for premodern people as modern—
and transnational as well. Henrietta Harrison, in her study of the compul-
sive diarist Lu Dapeng, noted the importance of the "moral frame" of self-
discipline that traditional Confucianism gave to his text; she went on to
argue, however, that this was not merely the recapitulation of some genre of
writing but "an important part of the way Lu understands himself and
what is going on around him. Thus the diary becomes part of the way in
which he makes himself into the kind of person he wants to be."[22] For
people in the premodern period, however, this was a pastime primarily for
elite men. The modern era, described by Foucault as a penetration of the
minds of ordinary people by organizations such as the state, was one in
which the "everyman" sought to use writing to define the self; this was aided
and abetted by revolutions in technology and mass politics. In an era of
"total war," in which every person, regardless of age or gender, was expected
to contribute to organized efforts against the enemy, issues of truth and
behavior became important to ordinary people as well. Ironically, it was the
state that opened the door—through mass education, management of the
media, the organization of barracks and conscription, and the use of guided
diary writing—but it was the individual who ultimately decided how the
self was to be defined.

The individuals who defined the language of the battlefield, however,
often found language itself lacking, even if it was "true." This is why, I have
argued, they sought out as many sources of expression as possible from film,
propaganda, religion, and poetry, in order to develop the best means possible to transmit their experience to others and understand themselves. As a

consequence of their efforts to capture the reality of war, they found postwar descriptions crafted for the purposes of collective memory and political mobilization to be inaccurate. Many consequently kept silent. Catherine Merridale, in her study of Soviet veterans who embraced the "Ivan myth" of heroic soldiering, argued that they did so primarily because it served their political self-interest (for the Russians, this occurred during the period of Brezhnev's leadership in the USSR).[23] Soldiers in the United States, China, Taiwan, and Japan, however, constantly tried to write about war, even while decrying the medium and warfare itself. Paul Fussell, who wrote on the importance of literature on war writing and was a veteran of the Second World War, argued strongly for the adequacy of English for writing war:

> The problem was less one of "language" than of gentility and optimism; it was less a problem of "linguistics" than of rhetoric. . . . The real reason [soldiers say language is inadequate] is that soldiers have discovered that no one is very interested in the bad news they have to report. What listener wants to be torn and shaken when he doesn't have to be? We have made *unspeakable* mean indescribable: it really means *nasty*.

To quote Fussell, however, I would say, "That can't be right." First, I also argued, in Chapter 6, that one of the many factors for many veterans eschewing writing about war was because postwar and civilian audiences found it distasteful. Nevertheless, Fussell's argument for veterans' silence rests on the assumption that writing or reading about war is also a form of trauma, because the written word can capture the event itself: "Logically, one supposes, there's no reason why a language devised by man should be inadequate to describe any of man's works."[24] This book has gone to great lengths to demonstrate, however, just how inadequate language is for capturing experience, whether it was Chinese, Japanese, or English. I have argued that the language of the battlefield is more important to determining what soldiers thought about themselves—it is an act of self-discipline, not a complete description of lived reality. In fields such as cognitive psychology and neuroscience, the relationship between language and experience has already been severely questioned. Even outside the empirical sciences, however, philosophers of language have attacked this assumption as well.

Ludwig Wittgenstein argued that the creator of a private language could not communicate with anyone, so we have no reason to expect such a language to exist; language is a public commodity that we define as a community, because its sole purpose is to enable us to communicate with each other. Consider the fact that among their many (and often changing) reasons for writing, servicemen frequently noted that they kept diaries not only for themselves but also as records for their loved ones. U.S. marine Joseph H. Griffith wrote: "My main reason for keeping any record of proceedings is so that I will have a guide for future narrative—if and when—to Mary and my family."[25] Veterans, such as in the case of Kogura Isamu (Chapter 5), used their diaries as the foundation for a memoir or book, but they also felt the need to use other sources such as unit histories or other veterans' accounts. The desire to make one's narrative part of a larger story was certainly not a peculiarly East Asian obsession with "group cohesion"—it was a transnational phenomenon. When transcribing his diary in the postwar era, Clayton Knight interspersed diary entries with passages from official military histories and his postwar memories. For example, following an entry dated 9 September 1945, he felt compelled to explain the "points" system and how the navy decided the order of release for U.S. troops. He cited the ship's "War Diary" (written by the captain) as evidence for both his observations in the diary and also for his ex post facto commentary on the diary.[26] Still, the words used by soldiers and veterans to write about war were not merely defined by their community or, indeed, disciplinary institutions. As Foucault observed concerning the importance of truth in self-writing, these diaries were run through with sincere claims of personal authenticity. This approach to self-narrative, quite at odds with the insouciant self-parody of elite I-novels and autobiographical fiction by professional writers, was determined in part by modern military traditions of record keeping, which elevated the importance of "facts." Nevertheless, the ultimate decision about what kind of language rang "true," and therefore remained in the diary, was up to the individual.

The concept of truth and authenticity in these diaries was tied to the use of language itself; as demonstrated throughout this book, soldiers were able to exercise remarkable agency when it came to experimenting with language. They felt compelled to do so precisely because of the keenly felt inadequacy of language; as Gerald Linderman pointed out, soldiers arriving on the battlefield immediately recognized how poorly their training served them—"You know nothing when you enter combat"[27]—and this was equally true when it came to the language they were provided. Consequently, diarists from Nationalist China, Japan, and the United States struggled to find the best way to capture the moment in their stories. In this sense, they were traversing the same boundary between ineffable experience and the bounded universe of language that authors of war reportage were also navigating but usually with considerably weaker writing skills. It may be true that authors of reportage and officers composing field diaries were writing only what their "intended audience" wanted to hear. If the intended audience of a truly private diary is the author, however, what makes this situation any less deceptive? In Patricia Highsmith's novel *Edith's Diary,* protagonist Edith Howland retired to the privacy of sculpture and diary writing, where she invents an exciting life for herself precisely to escape painful truths in her miserable life. In the end, Edith died through a fatal accident with a statue—a false image of her son, just as idealized as the fantasy life she created in her (supposedly reliable) private diary.

Still, the authors of war diaries rarely rejected their accounts as fabrications or works of fiction; in fact, their acceptance of the text as a reflection of "real life" made its power over them even stronger. In May 1945, Wang Wenrong, reflecting on his years of service in the war against Japan, decided that soldiering was not his calling after all:

> The purpose of one's life often changes . . . [but] everything I wanted to do, I never achieved. Whenever I got the chance, some unexpected obstacle always prevented me from getting my wish, and this must be what everybody calls "fate"! Now I'm already 30 years old, and my greatest wish is that we wipe out these Japanese bastards quickly and I can go home for my family, or go into education again as I had from 1938 to 1940. [I want] to spend the rest of my years with all of those sincere little children, so full of life.[28]

Just like Wang, soldiers used the diary to imagine a self that pleased them and took actions in accordance with that image. The soldiers in this book nearly always accepted their diaries as "true," and thus, at the very least, they reflect what the authors' believed to be true about themselves, the enemy, and the world around them. In that sense, they were both the "mirrors of truth" that reflected many aspects of soldiers' lived experience and the tools for creating the self—the lens through which these men perceived the world of war.

Charles Dickens warned: "All swindlers on the earth are nothing to the self-swindlers." In the end, we must be responsible for our actions, even if we have been "tricked" down a dark path by large organizations like the state and the mass media. In the midst of postwar debates over the emperor's war crimes, Watanabe Kiyo, a former sailor, reflected on the relationship between politics, memory, and responsibility:

> I was betrayed by the emperor. Tricked. But I think that being fooled is my weakness. . . . What was betrayed was how I [allowed] myself to believe in the emperor in *that way*. It wasn't the actual emperor—I was betrayed by the false image of the emperor that I had embraced inside of myself. So, you might say that I betrayed myself. I fooled myself.[29]

The diary became a doorway for those who enjoy control over language to exercise even more power over individuals, because the diarist believed the record to possess truth about himself. Still, to the extent that he could control the way in which this record was composed, he had power over his subjectivity. Indeed, at the end of his career, Foucault, who had previously concerned himself with the power of disciplinary institutions, increasingly focused his attention on how individuals participated in the act of defining their subjectivity.[30] Considering the immense influence the state, mass media, and military had over language in the Second World War, however, the individual faced seemingly insurmountable obstacles to maintaining some degree of self-autonomy. Ironically, although it was rarely clear to a soldier during the war, the extreme nature of the battlefield forced him to rearticulate himself when engaged in the act of diary writing, because he wanted language to more closely approximate experience. At that moment, the diary could be a gateway to greater freedom of expression and thought but also possibly a life of ostracism, guilt, isolation, or worse. Servicemen used their diaries to articulate reasons for pacifism, imperialism, and murder, but in each case the diarist arrived at those conclusions through his own logic. In a diary, his conclusions became inextricably linked with the truth the diary was supposed to hold. Thus, for these men, some of the gravest perils of self-discipline were unleashed simply by the act of writing a diary itself.

Abbreviations

ASMH	(Taipei: Academia Sinica, Modern History Institute Library, *Zhongyang yanjiuyuan jindai lishi yanjiusuo tushuguan*)
CMA	(Chongqing Municipal Archives, *Chongqing-shi lishi dang'anguan*)
FPM	(Wakamatsu: Fukushima Prefectural Museum, *Fukushima kenritsu hakubutsukan*)
HePA	(Shijiazhuang: Hebei Provincial Archives, *Hebei-sheng lishi dang'anguan*)
HuPA	(Wuhan: Hubei Provincial Archives, *Hubei-sheng lishi dang'anguan*)
ISPWM	(Iizuka: The Soldiers' and Common Peoples' War Museum, *Shomin heitai sensō shiryōkan*)
KSDFM	(Kanoya: Kanoya Self-Defense Forces Museum, *Kanoya kōkūjieitai shiryōkan*)
MDHA	(Taipei: Ministry of National Defense Historical Archives, *Guofangbu lishi xingzheng bianyisuo*)
NA	(Taipei: National Archives, *Guojia lishi dang'anguan*)
NIDS	(Tokyo: National Institute for Defense Studies, *Bōeishō bōei kenkyūjo*)

NML   (Nanjing: Nanjing Municipal Library)

NPA   (Taipei: Nationalist Party Archives, *Guomindang lishi dang'anguan*)

OIPM   (Osaka: Osaka International Peace Museum, Peace Osaka, *Osaka kokusai heiwa shiryōkan*)

OMPM   (Nagasaki: Oka Masaharu Memorial Peace Museum, *Oka Masaharu heiwa kinenkan*)

PC   (Author's) Personal collection

RIPM   (Kyoto: Ritsumeikan University International Peace Museum, *Ritsumeikan daigaku kokusai heiwa myūjiamu*)

SHM   (Atsugi: Showa History Museum, *Shōwa rekishi shiryōkan*)

SJHM   (Sendai: Sendai Japanese History Museum, *Sendai minzoku rekishi shiryōkan*)

SMA   (Shijiazhuang Municipal Archives, *Shijiazhuang-shi dang'anguan*)

SML   (Shanghai Municipal Library, Republican Era Collection, *Shanghai-shi tushuguan jindai wenxian*)

SNA   (Nanjing: Second National Archives, *Di-2 lishi dang'anguan*)

SPA   (Chengdu: Sichuan Provincial Archives, *Sichuan-sheng lishi dang'anguan*)

SPM   (Shizuoka City Peace Museum, *Shizuoka heiwa shiryōshitsu*)

SuPM   (Suita City Peace Museum, *Suita-shi heiwa kinen shiryōshitsu*)

TPM   (Takamatsu City Peace Museum, *Takamatsu-shi heiwa shiryōshitsu*)

USMCA   (Quantico, VA: United States Marine Corps Archives)

USMHI   (Carlisle, PA: United States Army Military History Institute)

US NARA   (College Park, MD: US National Archives and Records Administration)

USNHC   (Washington, DC: US Navy Historical Center)

UTL   (Knoxville: University of Tennessee, James D. Hoskins Library)

Notes

INTRODUCTION

1. For a nuanced discussion of the problem of Japanese postwar responsibility, see Noda Masaaki, *Sensō to zaiseki* (Tokyo: Iwanami Shoten, 2002, 2nd ed.).

2. Michel Foucault, *Discipline and Punish: The Birth of the Prison,* trans. Alan Sheridan (New York: Vintage Books, 1977), 170.

3. Notable histories of the "Second Sino-Japanese War" (1937–1945) include Chalmers Johnson, *Peasant Nationalism and Communist Power: The Emergence of Revolutionary China* (Stanford, CA: Stanford University Press, 1962); Hsi-sheng Chi, *Nationalist China at War: Military Defeats and Political Collapse* (Ann Arbor: University of Michigan Press, 1982); and Lloyd Eastman, *Seeds of Destruction: Nationalist China in War and Revolution, 1937–1945* (Stanford, CA: Stanford University Press, 1984). Many of these initial evaluations of the war in China have been subsequently challenged: see, for example, Hans van de Ven, *War and Nationalism in China: 1925–1945* (London: Routledge, 2003); Parks Coble, *Facing Japan: Chinese Politics and Japanese Imperialism, 1931–1937* (Cambridge, MA: Harvard University Press, 1991); Stephen MacKinnon, *Wuhan, 1938: War, Refugees, and the Making of Modern China* (Berkeley: University of California Press, 2008).

4. The Union of Soviet Socialist Republics (USSR), of course, epitomized the effort toward economic autarky, but imperial Japan came to emulate this model. For more on this phenomenon, see Nakamura Takafusa, "The Yen Bloc, 1931–1941," and Ramon H. Myers, "Creating a Modern Enclave Economy: The Economic Integration of Japan, Manchuria, and North China, 1932–1945," both in Peter Duus, Ramon Myers, and Mark Peattie, eds., *The Japanese Wartime Empire, 1931–1945* (Princeton, NJ: Princeton University Press, 1984); and Michael Barnhart, *Japan Prepares for Total War: The Search for Economic Security, 1919–1941* (Ithaca, NY: Cornell University Press, 1988).

5. Some scholars have preferred to view the conflict between the GMD and Japan as an unbroken war beginning with the "Manchurian Incident" in 1931, referring to it as the "Fifteen Years' War." Others point out that official war with China was never declared until 1941 and thus insist on referring to the period 1937–1941 as "The China Incident" (Jp. *Shina jihen*, Ch. *Zhina shibian*) and the period 1941–1945 as "The Pacific War" (Jp. *Taiheiyō sensō*, Ch. *Taipingyang zhanzheng*). Nevertheless, the total war in China was one of the major motivations for Japan's expansion into the Pacific, so I have included the period 1937–1941 as part of East Asia's experience of the Second World War. I have excluded the period 1931–1937 on the basis of the Tanggu Truce (1933), which granted both sides a respite from widespread conflict until 1937.

6. Shimada Toshihiko, "Designs on North China, 1933–1937," in James William Morley, ed., *The China Quagmire: Japan's Expansion on the Asian Continent, 1933–1941* (New York: Columbia University Press, 1983).

7. Michael R. Auslin, *Negotiating with Imperialism: The Unequal Treaties and the Culture of Japanese Diplomacy* (Cambridge, MA: Harvard University Press, 2004); and John Fitzgerald, *Awakening China: Politics, Culture, and Class in the Nationalist Revolution* (Stanford, CA: Stanford University Press, 1996). In fact, the vision of a "new world order" drove Japanese foreign policy throughout the period. As Gregory Kasza put it: "Given Japan's aggressive role in initiating the Pacific War, it would be more correct to see the war as a product of renovationist principles and goals than to view these latter as functions of the war." Kasza, *The State and Mass Media in Japan, 1918–1945* (Berkeley: University of California Press, 1988), 205.

8. Robert Eskildsen, "Of Civilization and Savages: The Mimetic Imperialism of Japan's 1874 Expedition to Taiwan," *American Historical Review* 107:2 (April 2002); and Andrew Gordon, "The Crowd and Politics in Imperial Japan, 1905–1908," *Past and Present* 121 (November 1988). English-language translations of Tokutomi Soho's works are available in William Theodore de Bary et al., eds., *Sources of Japanese Tradition*, vol. 2 (New York: Columbia University Press, 2005).

9. Richard J. Samuels, *"Rich Nation, Strong Army": National Security and the Technological Transformation of Japan* (Ithaca, NY: Cornell University Press, 1994).

10. Alvin Coox, *Nomonhan: Japan against Russia* (Stanford, CA: Stanford University Press, 1985).

11. Robert A. Kapp, "Provincial Independence vs. National Rule: A Case Study of Szechwan in the 1920's and 1930's," *Journal of Asian Studies* 30:3 (May 1971).

12. GMD-supported anthropologists, for example, attempted to eschew Japanese-style colonial assimilation for a "multicultural" approach to war mobilization. Andres Rodriguez, "Building the Nation, Serving the Frontier: Mobilising and Reconstructing China's Borderlands during the War of Resistance (1937–1945)," *Modern Asian Studies* 45:2 (March 2011).

13. See the discussion of Chiang Kai-shek's diary in Jay Taylor, *The Generalissimo: Chiang Kai-shek and the Struggle for Modern China* (Cambridge, MA: Belknap Press of Harvard University Press, 2009).

14. Rana Mitter, *A Bitter Revolution: China's Struggle with the Modern World* (Oxford: Oxford University Press, 2004).

15. Diana Lary, *The Chinese People at War: Human Suffering and Social Transformation, 1937–1945* (Cambridge: Cambridge University Press, 2010); Diana Lary and Stephen Mackinnon, eds., *Scars of War: The Impact of Warfare on Modern China* (Vancouver: University of British Columbia Press, 2011).

16. The flagship study of the GMD's "failure" as a military and political force is undoubtedly Lloyd Eastman's *The Abortive Revolution: China under Nationalist Rule, 1927–1937* (Cambridge, MA: Harvard University Press, 1974), but the history of negative views of the Nationalists can be traced back much further. For example, foreign observers such as Agnes Smedley and Joseph Stilwell did much to set the precedent for future attitudes toward the Nationalists through their impressions during the period of Nationalist rule. For critique of this position, see Chapter 5.

17. On the figures, see John Dower, *War without Mercy: Race and Power in the Pacific* (New York: Pantheon Books, 1986).

18. Paul Fussell, *The Great War and Modern Memory* (Oxford: Oxford University Press, 2000), 338.

19. Stephen Kotkin, "The State—Is It Us? Memoirs, Archives, and Kremlinologists," *Russian Review* 61 (January 2002). In fact, studies of the former Soviet Union have offered some of the most sophisticated examinations of historical subjectivity thus far: Daniel Mark Vyleta, "City of the Devil: Bulgakovian Moscow and the Search for the Stalinist Subject," *Rethinking History* 4 (Spring 2000); Jochen Hellbeck, *Revolution on My Mind* (Cambridge, MA: Harvard University Press, 2006); Igal Halfin, *Terror in My Soul: Communist Autobiographies on Trial* (Cambridge, MA: Harvard University Press, 2003); as well as the discussion in Laura Englestein, "Combined Underdevelopment: Discipline and the Law in Imperial and Soviet Russia," *American Historical Review*, 98:2 (1993); and Jochen Hellbeck's response in "Fashioning the Stalinist Soul: The Diary of Stepan

Podlubnyi (1931–1939)," in Sheila Fitzpatrick, ed., *Stalinism: New Directions* (London: Routledge, 2000), 116, endnote 29. Fitzpatrick's introduction introduces some of these new approaches, and there is a good introductory bibliography on the literature there.

20. On nationalism, the important texts include, of course, Ernest Gellner, *Nations and Nationalism* (Ithaca, NY: Cornell University Press, 1983); Benedict Anderson, *Imagined Communities: Reflections on the Origin and Spread of Nationalism* (New York: Verso, 1991); and John Breuilly, *Nationalism and the State* (Chicago: University of Chicago Press, 1994, 2nd ed.). For Japan, see Sandra Wilson, ed., *Nation and Nationalism in Japan* (London: Routledge Curzon, 2002); and for China, see Hans van de Ven, *War and Nationalism in China;* and Fitzgerald, *Awakening China.*

21. See Lloyd Eastman, *Seeds of Destruction;* and Frederic Wakeman Jr., *Policing Shanghai, 1927–1937* (Berkeley: University of California Press, 1996).

22. Dower, *War without Mercy.* Dower's main argument is that racial hatred particularly motivated the United States to conduct a brutal war against Japan.

23. Poshek Fu, *Passivity, Resistance, and Collaboration: Intellectual Choices in Occupied Shanghai, 1937–1945* (Stanford, CA: Stanford University Press, 1993); Rana Mitter, *The Manchurian Myth: Nationalism, Resistance, and Collaboration in Modern China* (Berkeley: University of California Press, 2000); Timothy Brook, *Collaboration: Japanese Agents and Local Elites in Wartime China* (Cambridge, MA: Harvard University Press, 2005).

24. SNA: Liu Chongzhe, "Di-52-shi zai Anhui Jing-xian yu wo 4-jun Tan Yunlin Bo Qiu choubu zhi zuozhan xiangbao ji zhenzhong riji," 27 July 1941.

25. SNA: Luo Zhuoying et al., "Di-18-jun silingbu zhenzhong riji ji Luodian shiri zhanji jian zongsiling Luo Zhuoying," 2 September, 28 August 1937. It is unclear whether Chinese Scouts assisted the GMD in their search for and execution of suspected "traitors." See Chapter 2 for more discussion.

26. Xiaofei Tian, *Visionary Journeys: Travel Writing from Early Medieval and Nineteenth-Century China* (Cambridge, MA: Harvard University Asia Center, 2011), 7.

27. Louis Morton's collection of diaries from the fall of the Philippines, now archived at the U.S. Army Historical Archives (Carlisle, PA), was essential to this book. His multivolume project on the war in the Pacific, including *The Fall of the Philippines: United States Army in World War II, The War in the Pacific* (Washington, DC: Office of the Chief of Army, 1953), represented the definitive military historical account. Military historians since Morton have generally followed his example. Richard B. Frank's *Guadalcanal: The Definitive Account of the Landmark Battle* (New York: Random House, 1990) similarly draws on personal accounts for a strictly military and political record. Peter Schrijvers conducted one of the best studies of diaries as texts deserving sustained critical analysis: *The GI War against*

Japan: American Soldiers in Asia and the Pacific during World War II (New York: New York University Press, 2002).

28. Yoshimi Yoshiaki, "Nicchū sensō to kokumin dōin," *Rekishi hyōron,* no. 447 (1987). Takahashi Saburō followed with *Senkimono wo yomu: Sensō taiken to sengō Nihon shakai* (Kyoto: Akademia shuppan, 1988). The National Institute for Defense Studies (NIDS) compiled its official history of Japan's wars from 1966 to 1980. The edition on the first stage of the war in China, for example, was released in 1972. Bōeichō bōei kenkyūjo senshishitsu, ed. *Senshi sōsho: Chūgoku hōmen kaigun sakusen (1): Shōwa 13-nen 3-gatsu made* (Tokyo: Asagumo shimbunsha, 1972.

29. Richard H. Kohn complained that most military history prior to 1980 "has aimed at calling to memory the patriotism or loyalty of particular individuals and groups; the sociology, at advancing social science methodology or aiding the government in recruiting its armies and using manpower efficiently." Kohn, "The Social History of the American Soldier: A Review and Prospectus for Research," *American Historical Review* 86:3 (June 1981), 554.

30. John Keegan, *The Face of Battle* (London: J. Cape, 1976).

31. Catherine Merridale, *Ivan's War: Life and Death in the Red Army, 1939–1945* (New York: Metropolitan Books, 2006).

32. Peter Schrijvers, *GI War against Japan.* In this sense, the work of Fujii Tadatoshi (see note 33) and Shcrijvers mirrors that of Thomas Mallon in his study of diary writing itself. Thomas Mallon, *A Book of One's Own: People and Their Diaries* (New York: Ticknor & Fields, 1984).

33. Fujii Tadatoshi, *Heitachi no sensō: Tegami, nikki, taikenki wo yomitoku* (Tokyo: Asahi shinbunsha, 2000), 269.

34. Some scholars argue for the "truth" of personal accounts in order to reconstitute the roles of the dispossessed and vulnerable in history: Linda Anderson, "At the Threshold of the Self: Women and Autobiography," in Moira Monteith, ed., *Women's Writing. A Challenge to Theory* (Brighton: Harvester Press, 1986); Christina Sjöblad, "From Family Notes to Diary: The Development of a Genre," *Eighteenth-Century Studies* 31:4 (1998), 521.

35. Ludwig Wittgenstein, in his critique of solipsism, offered the philosophical refutation of "private languages": it begins on paragraph 243 of *Philosophical Investigations,* trans. G. E. M. Anscombe (Oxford: B. Blackwell, 1953). My reading of Wittgenstein's theory is in part inspired by Saul Kripke's *Wittgenstein on Rules and Private Language* (Cambridge, MA: Harvard University Press, 1982).

36. Sheldon Garon, *Molding Japanese Minds: The State in Everyday Life* (Princeton, NJ: Princeton University Press, 1997).

37. Michel Foucault, "What Is an Author?" in Josué V. Harari, *Textual Strategies: Perspectives in Post-Structuralist Criticism* (Ithaca, NY: Cornell University Press, 1979).

38. Edward Fowler, *The Rhetoric of Confession: Shishōsetsu in Early Twentieth-Century Japanese Fiction* (Berkeley: University of California Press, 1988), 41.

39. Lydia Liu, *Translingual Practice: Literature, National Culture, and Translated Modernity, China, 1900–1937* (Stanford, CA: Stanford University Press, 1995), 70–71.

40. Personal interview at Okamoto's office, 1 February 2003. Many thanks to the staff at the Wadatsumi-kai Tokyo Office for arranging this interview.

41. USMCA: Thomas Serier, "Diary of a U.S. Marine of World War II," 21 January 1943.

42. SJHM: Jōji Tsutomu, "Jōji nikki," in Yoshikawa Kanezō and Fujita Yoshirō, *Kono issen: Kaijō teishin dai-14 daitai no butaishi* (self-published, 1976), 117 [10 April 1944].

43. SMA: Wang Wenrong, "Gongzuo riji," 1 February 1945.

44. USMCA: William Sharpe, "VMJ-152: Securité en nuages," 28 October 1942.

45. Personal interviews conducted on 1 February 2003 with members of the China Returnee Association (Chūgoku kikōsha renraku-kai).

46. Americans were no different: Sharpe's friend Tim saw him writing in his diary and shouted "put away the Bible and let's go to a movie." Sharpe, 3 January 1943.

47. There are accounts of soldiers destroying their diaries on orders, however: Furukawa Kanzō, "P.W. ni iku," in Yoshikawa Kanezō and Fujita Yoshirō, *Kono issen,* 256.

48. Richard H. Mitchell, *Thought Control in Prewar Japan* (Ithaca, NY: Cornell University Press, 1976); Kasza, *The State and Mass Media;* Andrew Barshay, *State and Intellectual in Imperial Japan: The Public Man in Crisis* (Berkeley: University of California Press, 1988); Barak Kushner, *The Thought War: Japanese Imperial Propaganda* (Honolulu: University of Hawai'i Press, 2006).

49. Jay Winter, *Sites of Memory, Sires of Mourning: The Great War in European Cultural History* (Cambridge: Cambridge University Press, 1999).

50. Michel Foucault, "Society Must Be Defended," in Paul Rabinow, ed., *Michel Foucault, Ethics: Essential Works of Foucault, 1954–1984,* vol. 1 (London: Penguin Books, 2000), 62.

I. TALK ABOUT HEROES

1. Suita-shi heiwa kinen shiryōshitsu: "Tamura Hideto," "Shūyōroku," 3 May 1944.

2. Michael R. Auslin, *Negotiating with Imperialism: The Unequal Treaties and the Culture of Japanese Diplomacy* (Cambridge, MA: Harvard University Press, 2004); Alexis Dudden, *Japan's Colonization of Korea: Discourse and Power* (Honolulu: University of Hawai'i Press, 2005).

3. Mark Ravina, "State-Making in a Global Context: Japan in a World of Nation-States," in Joshua Fogel, ed., *The Teleology of the Nation-State* (Philadelphia: University of Pennsylvania Press, 2005).

4. Michel Foucault, *Discipline and Punish: The Birth of the Prison,* trans. Alan Sheridan (New York: Vintage, 1995, reprint ed.), 201.

5. On China, see Marston Anderson, *Limits of Realism: Chinese Fiction in the Revolutionary Period* (Berkeley: University of California Press, 1990); and Charles A. Laughlin, *Chinese Reportage: The Aesthetics of Historical Experience* (Durham, NC: Duke University Press, 2002). In the Anglophone world, John Carey's edited *Faber Book of Reportage* (London: Faber and Faber, 2003) is a good beginner's guide.

6. Bakufu officials, however, certainly employed the *nisshi,* or official log; see, for example, Morioka-shi chūō kōminkan, "Nambu-han karō-seki nisshi."

7. Researchers at NIDS have seen references to these documents in other sources from the Meiji era, but archivists think that these documents were thrown out after a certain period had elapsed.

8. A notable exception to this statement is the Taiwan Expedition: Robert Eskildsen, "Of Civilization and Savages: The Mimetic Imperialism of Japan's 1874 Expedition to Taiwan," *American Historical Review* 107:2 (April 2002). For the early empire, see introductory articles by Marius Jansen and Mark Peattie in Peattie and Ramon Myers, eds., *The Japanese Colonial Empire, 1895–1945* (Princeton, NJ: Princeton University Press, 1984).

9. Arai Katsuhiro, "Jūgun nikki ni miru heishizō to sensō no kioku," in Arai Katsuhiro and Fujii Tadatoshi, eds., *Jinrui ni totte tatakai to ha (3): Tatakai to minshū* (Tokyo: Tōyō shorin, 2000), 126. Sometimes the diaries could be amended later and then published, as in Hamamoto Risaburō, *Nisshin sensō jūgun hiroku* (Tokyo: Seishun shppansha, 1972). On the Russo-Japanese documents, the definitive study is Naoko Shimazu, *Japanese Society at War: Death, Memory, and the Russo-Japanese War* (Cambridge: Cambridge University Press, 2009), and "The Myth of the Patriotic Soldier: Japanese Attitudes towards Death in the Russo-Japanese War," *War and Society* 19:2 (October 2001).

10. Horii Shinjirō developed the *tōshaban,* later referred to as *gariban,* to Japan after Edison's mimeograph display at the 1893 Chicago World's Fair. He had little success selling the device until the IJA adopted it in 1894–1895.

11. Other media that covered the war included novels, articles, *nishiki-e,* and illustrations. All major newspapers at the time carried Sino-Japanese War stories, written by famous authors such as Emi Suiin. Kubota Beisen was one of the few artists to travel with the army, producing an eleven-volume *Nisshin sentō gahō.*

12. "Hyŏnmumun no ichi-ban nori," *Nicchū sensō jikki,* 8 (Tokyo: Hakubunkan): 101 [7 November 1895.

13. "Hyŏnmumun," 103. These passages also reflect a time when homoerotic behavior in the Japanese military was still condoned.

14. Ōhama Tetsuya, *Shōmin no mita Nisshin / Nichiro sensō: Teikoku he no ayumi* (Tokyo: Tōsui shobō, 2003), 50.

15. "Nisshi," in *Nicchū sensō jikki,* 6 (Tokyo: Hakubunkan, 19 October 1895): 111; and "Nisshi," in *Nicchū sensō jikki,* 8, 112.

16. "Waga rikugun sekkō Zhonghe ni tatakau," in ("Honki") *Nicchū sensō jikki,* 3 (Tokyo: Hakubunkan, 19 September 1895): 4.

17. Even NIDS has few archived field diaries from the Sino-Japanese War; also see Stewart Lone, *Japan's First Modern War: Army and Society in the Conflict with China, 1894–95* (New York: St Martin's Press, 1994).

18. Richard Rubinger, "Who Can't Read and Write? Illiteracy in Meiji Japan," *Monumenta Nipponica* 55:2 (Summer 2000). See also the discussion in Shimazu, *Japanese Society at War,* 55–56. By 1905 in Japan, 95 percent of children were enrolled in school. Andrew Gordon, *Labor and Imperial Democracy in Prewar Japan* (Berkeley, CA: University of California Press, 1991), 18. In the United States, rigorous testing of literacy for conscripts began in the First World War, and chaplains still provided basic literacy education.

19. Lewis Waterman perfected the fountain pen in 1884, which was in wide circulation in Japan by the 1890s, making it a contemporary of the mimeograph. Caw's "Stylographic Pen" (a predecessor) was imported to Japan in 1884.

20. NIDS: Ijichi Hikojirō, "Gunkan Mikasa senji nisshi," 27 May 1905. I wish to thank Sergeant Satō Fukuo of KSDFM for this copy.

21. Shimazu, *Japanese Society at War,* chapter 4, "Local Patriots," 119–156.

22. Sakurai Tadatoshi, *Nikudan* (Tokyo: Teimatsu shuppansha, 15 March 1909, orig. 20 April 1906), 214–215.

23. Tamon Jirō, *Nichiro sensō nikki* (Tokyo: Saihō shobō, 1980, orig. 1912), introduction (original).

24. Tamon, *Nichiro sensō nikki,* 179.

25. Ono Kenji, PC: "Yanagawa Heihachi," "Senji nikki / Senchi nikki," 4 June 1905, 31 July.

26. RIPM: "Omoto Saburō," "Jūro shussei nisshi," 10 December 1904. Question marks in brackets indicate damaged sections of the manuscript.

27. PC: *Kinen: Hohei dai-54 rentaishi* (Okayama: Kawara shoten, 30 April 1926), 11.

28. Ichinose Toshiya, *Kindai Nihon no chōheisei to shakai* (Tokyo: Yoshikawa kōbunkan, 2004); also cited in Shimazu, *Japanese Society at War,* 57.

29. SHM: "Adachi Ei'ichi," "Nisshi," 10 December 1912. Thanks to Itagaki Sadao.

30. Gordon, *Labor and Imperial Democracy in Prewar Japan,* 24.

31. See Richard Smethurst, *A Social Basis for Prewar Japanese Militarism: The Army and the Rural Community* (Berkeley: University of California Press, 1974), especially chapter 2. Opposition mobilized as well: in 1910, Seiyūkai party leaders Matsuda Masahisa and Hara Kei celebrated growth in support for electoral politics. Tetsuo Najita, *Hara Kei and the Politics of Compromise* (Cambridge, MA: Harvard University Press, 1967), 104–105.

32. Gregory Kasza, *The State and Mass Media in Japan, 1918–1945* (Berkeley: University of California Press, 1988), 14–20.

33. Richard E. Strassberg, ed. and trans., *Inscribed Landscapes: Travel Writing from Imperial China* (Berkeley: University of California Press, 1994); Emma Jinhua Teng, *Taiwan's Imagined Geography: Chinese Colonialist Travel Writing and Pictures, 1683–1895* (Cambridge, MA: Harvard University Asia Center, 2004); Henrietta Harrison, *The Man Awakened from Dreams: One Man's Life in a North China Village, 1857–1942* (Stanford, CA: Stanford University Press, 2005). See Hilde de Weerdt's forthcoming work on premodern notebooks *(biji)*, *Information, Territory, and Elite Networks: The Crisis and Maintenance of Empire in Song China*. Also see J. D. Frodsham, trans., *The First Chinese Embassy to the West: The Journals of Kuo Sung-t'ao, Liu Hsi-hung, and Chang Te-yi* (Oxford: Clarendon Press, 1974).

34. Lu's diary has been serialized in *Wenwu chunqiu* issues 2 and 3 (1992), 1 and 3 (1993), and 3 (1994). For other diary accounts, see Ma Zhongwen, "Shiren rijizhong de Guangxu huangdi, Cixi taihou zhi si," in (Beijing: Shehui kexue wenxian chubanshe, 2007), 257–268.

35. Xiaofei Tian, *Visionary Journeys: Travel Writing from Early Medieval and Nineteenth-Century China* (Cambridge, MA: Harvard University Asia Center, 2011), 218.

36. Wu Pei-yi, *The Confucian's Progress: Autobiographical Writings in Traditional China* (Princeton, NJ: Princeton University Press, 1992), 163.

37. Susan Naquin and Evelyn S. Rawski, *Chinese Society in the Eighteenth Century* (New Haven, CT: Yale University Press, 1987), 67.

38. William C. Kirby, "Engineering China: Birth of the Developmental State, 1928–1937," in Wen-hsin Yeh, ed., *Becoming Chinese: Passages to Modernity and Beyond* (Berkeley: University of California Press, 2000).

39. Christopher A. Reed, *Gutenberg in Shanghai: Chinese Print Capitalism, 1876–1937* (Honolulu: Hawai'i University Press, 2003), 103; Barbara Mittler, *A Newspaper for China? Power, Identity, and Change in Shanghai's News Media, 1872–1912* (Cambridge, MA: Harvard University Asia Center, 2004), 97.

40. This international research project is spearheaded by Hans van de Ven (Cambridge) and Robert Bickers (Bristol). Independent Chinese efforts at modern records, in conjunction with Japan, should be part of the story as well: Andrea Eberhard-Bréard, "Robert Hart and China's Statistical Revolution," *Modern Asian Studies* 40:3 (July 2006), 624.

41. For descriptions of Japanese influence on Chinese reform, see Douglas R. Reynolds: "Training Young China Hands: Tōa Dōbun Shoin and Its Precursors, 1886–1945," in Peter Duus, Ramon Myers, and Mark Peattie, eds., *Informal Empire in China, 1895–1937* (Princeton, NJ: Princeton University Press, 1989), and *China, 1898–1912: The Xinzheng Revolution and Japan* (Cambridge, MA: Harvard University Asia Center, 2002); Stephen R. Platt, *Provincial Patriots: The Hunanese*

and Modern China (Cambridge, MA: Harvard University Press, 2007), chapter 4; Christian A. Hess, "From Colonial Port to Socialist Metropolis: Imperialist Legacies and the Making of 'New Dalian,'" *Urban History* 38:3 (2011); Marjorie Dryburgh, "Japan in Tianjin: Settlers, State, and the Tensions of Empire before 1937," *Japanese Studies* 27:1 (2007); Ruth Rogaski, *Hygienic Modernity: Meanings of Health and Disease in Treaty Port China* (Berkeley: University of California Press, 2004); David Buck, "Railway City and National Capital: Two Faces of the Modern in Changchun," in Joseph W. Esherick, ed., *Remaking the Chinese City: Modernity and National Identity, 1900–1950* (Honolulu: University of Hawai'i Press, 2000); and Lydia Liu, *Translingual Practice: Literature, National Culture, and Translated Modernity, China, 1900–1937* (Stanford, CA: Stanford University Press, 1995).

42. On warlords in Japan, see Donald G. Gillin, "Portrait of a Warlord: Yen Hsi-shan in Shansi Province, 1911–1930," *Journal of Asian Studies* 19:3 (May 1960), and *Warlord: Yen His-shan in Shansi Province, 1911–1949* (Princeton, NJ: Princeton University Press, 1967). Warlords who did not train in Japan, such as Zhang Zuolin, were also deeply affected by Japanese military practices: Gavan McCormack, *Chang Tso-lin in Northeast China, 1911–1928: China, Japan, and the Manchurian Idea* (Stanford, CA: Stanford University Press, 1977), especially the note on page 20.

43. Hans van de Ven, "Recent Studies of Modern Chinese History," *Modern Asian Studies,* 30:2 (May 1996), 266; this comes from the research of Tien Chen-ya in *Chinese Military Theory: Ancient and Modern* (New York: Mosaic Press, 1992), 125–133.

44. On the importance of newsprint, see Joan Judge, *Print and Politics: "Shibao" and the Culture of Reform in Late Qing China* (Stanford, CA: Stanford University Press, 1996).

45. Kit Siong Liew, *Struggle for Democracy: Sung Chiao-jen and the 1911 Chinese Revolution* (Berkeley: University of California Press, 1971).

46. For more on the regional origins of nationalism, see Platt, *Provincial Patriots;* and Bryna Goodman, "Improvisations on a Semi-Colonial Theme, or, How to Read a Celebration of Transnational Urban Community," *Journal of Asian Studies* 59:4 (November 2000).

47. Edward McCord, *The Power of the Gun: The Emergence of Modern Chinese Warlordism* (Berkeley: University of California Press, 1993), 48.

48. Stephen R. MacKinnon, *Power and Politics in Late Imperial China: Yuan Shi-kai in Beijing and Tianjin, 1901–1908* (Berkeley: University of California Press, 1980).

49. Huang Xing's 1911 war diary is earlier, but it is not in the modern military tradition. Wuhan: Xinhai geming bowuguan: Huang Xing, "Wuchang liang riji," 1912.

50. SNA: "Di-2-jun di-3-shi zhenzhong rijilu" ji "Di-2-jun paobingchu gongke Nanjing zhenzhong riji," August 1913.

51. Quote in McCord, *Power of the Gun,* 135.

52. See the extended treatment in McCord, *Power of the Gun;* Donald S. Sutton, *Provincial Militarism and the Chinese Republic: The Yunnan Army, 1905–25* (Ann Arbor: University of Michigan Press, 1980); and Diana Lary, *Region and Nation: The Kwangsi Clique in Chinese Politics, 1925–1937* (Cambridge: Cambridge University Press, 1974).

53. SPA: Unsigned, "Di-2 huncheng-lü zhandou riji: Xiaoqing nan'an zhenzhong riji," 28 February, 1 March, 20 May 1926.

54. On local resistance to taxation, see Huaiyin Li, *Village Governance in North China, 1875–1936* (Stanford, CA: Stanford University Press, 2005), 199–205.

55. McCormack, *Chang Tso-lin,* 101.

56. SPA: Li Hongkun, "Xiaoqing nan'an zhenzhong riji," 1926.

57. SNA: Unsigned, "Duli paobing di-1-tuan xingjun biji," probably 1928, also a handwritten document. Mimeograph technology was in use in China since the late nineteenth century, but it was not used for copying field diaries until the Nationalist era.

58. SNA: Unsigned [possibly Zhang Fakui], "Guomin gemingjun si-4-jun beifa zhenzhong riji," 24 July 1926.

59. SNA: Unsigned, "Guomin gemingjun zongsilingbu sanmouchu beifa zhenzhong riji," 1926, forward.

60. SNA: Wu Guanzhou, "Guomin gemingjun di-17-jun zi Haizhou chufa zhi gongke Linxin suijun riji," introduction [June 1928] and entry 20 April 1928.

61. Hans van de Ven, *War and Nationalism: 1925–1945* (London: Routledge, 2003), chapter 2.

62. Jochen Hellbeck, *Revolution on My Mind* (Cambridge, MA: Harvard University Press, 2006), 38.

63. NIDS: Unsigned, "Zongguo dongbei minzhong jiuguojun zhenzhong riji," 8 October 1932.

64. Mittler, *Newspaper for China?,* 89, 100–101.

65. Yoshimi Yoshiaki, *Kusa no ne no fashizumu: Nihon minshū no sensō taiken* (Tokyo: Tokyo daigaku shuppankai, 1987), chapter 1.

66. Hayama Yashiki, *Umi ni ikiru hitobito* (Tokyo: Iwanami Shoten, 1977, orig. 1926), 28, 91.

67. "Sat-Chō" refers to the regional cliques, Satsuma and Chōshū, that dominated the Japanese officer class throughout the Meiji and Taishō eras.

68. Hino Ashihei, *Mugi to heitai* in *Hino Ashihei-shū* (Tokyo: Chikuma shobō, 1952, orig. 1938), 192, 194.

69. Ikeda Hiroshi argued that Hino Ashihei did not always distinguish between himself and his narrative subjects: Ikeda, *Hino Ashihei-ron* (Tokyo: Impact Publishing, 2000).

70. Quoted in Anderson, *Limits of Realism,* 44. Echoed in Laughlin, *Chinese Reportage.*

71. "Ru he xie baogao wenxue" (6 June 1932 in *Wenyi xinwen*), in Wang Ronggang, ed. *Baogao wenxue yanjiu ziliao xuanbian* (Jinan: Shandong renmin chubanshe, 1983), 35.

72. Laughlin, *Chinese Reportage.* Also see William A. Callaghan, "National Insecurities: Humiliation, Salvation and Chinese Nationalism," *Alternatives* 29:2 (2004). For a contrasting view, see Parks M. Coble, "Writing about Atrocity: Wartime Accounts and Their Contemporary Uses," *Modern Asian Studies* 45:2 (March 2011).

73. John Fitzgerald, *Awakening China: Politics, Culture, and Class in the Nationalist Revolution* (Stanford, CA: Stanford University Press, 1996).

74. NPA: Zhongyang lujun junguan xuexiao, "Huangpu jingshen ji qi jiaoyu," 52.

75. Cub Scouts learned that, among other atrocities, the Japanese army cut the ears off of their victims in Shandong. NA: GMD zhongyang zhixing weiyanyuan-hui xunlianbu (yinxing), *Zhongguo tongzijun chuji kecheng* (1930), 39.

76. Xie Bingying, *Congjun riji* (Shanghai: Shanghai guangming shuju, 1932), 2–3, 5.

77. KSDFM: Oda Makoto, "Kimitsu: Shanghai hōmen kengaku hōkoku," 16 May 1928.

78. Donald Jordan, *China's Trial by Fire: The Shanghai War of 1932* (Ann Arbor: University of Michigan Press, 2001). Also see Parks Coble, *Facing Japan: Chinese Politics and Japanese Imperialism, 1931–1937* (Cambridge, MA: Harvard University Press, 1991).

79. Chang Jui-te, *Kangzhan shiqi de guojun renshi* (Taipei: Zhongyang yanjiuyuan jinshisuo zhuankan, 1993).

80. Chiang even promoted Japanese, Baoding, and Huangpu graduates above those trained in the United States. John Wands Sacca, "Like Strangers in a Foreign Land: Chinese Officers Prepared at American Military Colleges, 1904–1937," *Journal of Military History* 70:3 (July 2006).

81. Louise Young, *Japan's Total Empire: Manchuria and the Culture of Wartime Imperialism* (Berkeley: University of California Press, 1999); and Daqing Yang, *Technology of Empire: Telecommunications and Japanese Expansion, 1895–1945* (Cambridge, MA: Harvard University Asia Center, 2011).

82. RIPM: "Tanimura Kanzō," "Guntai nisshi," and "Rechuan [Rehe] jūgun zakki," 6 October 1932, 1933 [undated entry].

83. SNA: Unsigned, "Di-32-shi zai Guangxi Hengxian dengdi zhenzhong riji," June 1936.

84. NPA: Anonymous, *Yi wei wuming yingxiong de riji* (August 1933), 1–2. The publisher of this text is unclear from the document.

85. *Yi wei wuming yingxiong,* 16 December 1933.

86. As in Japan, the GMD split its soldiers' existence into *ban* for internal affairs and *budui* (Jp. *butai*) for combat.

87. SML: Wu Tiecheng, "Shanghai-shi xuesheng jizhongjun xuncaochang yewai shishi biji," May 1936. Also see reference in Jordan, *China's Trial by Fire.*

88. PC: These medals were originally minted by the Shanghai Municipal Federation of Trade Unions (Shanghai-shi zonggonghui) in 1936. They "Commemorated the Battle of Resistance for Songhu" and were worn by soldiers in 1937.

89. SML: Various, *Shanghai xuezhan kangriji* (1932). Publication information was missing from this copy.

90. Francis K. Pan, *One Year of Rehabilitation in the Commercial Press, Ltd.* (Shanghai: Commercial Press, 1933), 24; quoted in Reed, *Gutenberg in Shanghai,* 128.

91. SJHM: "Morita Tatsuo," "Hanseiroku," 17–18, 25 March 1936.

92. UTL: Robert Galbraith, "Civil War Diaries," 1865.

93. Stephen Conway, "The Politics of British Military and Naval Mobilization, 1775–83," *English Historical Review,* 112:449 (November 1997).

94. Joseph A. Waddell, "Diary of a Prisoner of War at Quebec, 1776," *Virginia Magazine of History and Biography* 9:2 (October 1901). By 1812, personal records came to resemble official ones: Milo M. Quaife, "A Diary of the War of 1812," *Mississippi Valley Historical Review* 1:2 (September 1914). Still, this diary did not quite contain the level of "factual" detail that would appear in later texts.

95. "Our First 'War' in China: The Diary of William Henry Powell, 1856," *American Historical Review* 53:4 (July 1948), 786.

96. UTL: Robert Galbraith, "Civil War Diaries," 1865.

97. UTL: Michael Houck, "Diary," 14 May 1864. The majority of Houck's entries concerned unit movements, tactics, and the weather.

98. James McPherson, *For Cause and Comrades: Why Men Fought in the Civil War* (Oxford: Oxford University Press, 1997).

99. The *Virginia Magazine of History and Biography* has published many Civil War diaries that demonstrate this: Robert G. Athearn, "The Civil War Diary of John Wilson Phillips," 62:1 (January 1954); Louis H. Manarin, "The Civil War Diary of Rufus J. Woolwine," 71:4 (October 1963); William M. Armstrong, "The Civil War Diary of Arthur G. Sedgwick," 71:1 (October 1963). As an exception, see Jay B. Hubbell, "The War Diary of John Esten Cooke," *Journal of Southern History* 7:4 (November 1941), 526–540.

100. "A very unpleasant day—a drisling [*sic*] rain and the most slippery mud I ever walked in—both have been so bad that they have iritated [*sic*] me so much that I dare not write much for fear of iritating [*sic*] the reader, so goodbye for to-day." Edgar L. Erickson, "Hunting for Cotton in Dixie: From the Civil War Diary of Captain Charles E Wilcox," *Journal of Southern History* 4:4 (November 1938), 498.

101. For more details, see William S. Dudley, "World War I and Federal Military History," *Public Historian* 12:4 (Autumn 1990).

102. For a good summary of American accounts of the Civil War in the 1890s and 1900s, see Will Kaufman, *The Civil War in American Culture* (Edinburgh: Edinburgh University Press, 2006).

103. Ibid., 31.

104. USMCA: Paul E. Cheney, "WWI Sergeant of the Guard Book," March 1918.

105. George A. Morrice, "Diary," 30 May 1918, http://www.oryansroughnecks .org/diary.html.

106. In East Asia, these were called "unit histories" (Jp. *Butaishi,* Ch. *buduishi*), which began to appear in print in Japan following the Russo-Japanese War and in China during the 1930s. Some examples from Britain include J. H. Boraston and Cyril E. O. Bax, *The Eight Division in War, 1915–1918* (1928) and J. W. B. Mereweather and Frederick Smith, *The Indian Corps in France* (1929).

107. Paul Fussell, *Great War and Modern Memory* (Oxford: Oxford University Press, 2000), 157.

108. Morrice, *Diary.* This was published by a private company (Chicago, IL: Stanton and VanVilet).

109. For a brief and accessible summary of pre-1939 First World War accounts published in Britain, see the "Suggestions for Further Reading" in John Ellis, *Knee-Deep in Hell: Trench Warfare in WWI* (Baltimore: Johns Hopkins University Press, 1989), 207.

110. Henry A. Kindig, "Diary," 19 July 1918, http://www.worldwaronediary .com/index.html.

111. Willard Newton, "The Battle of Bellicourt," 29 September 1918 [published 12 October 1920], http://www.cmstory.org/ww1/diary.asp.

112. Quoted in Maurer Maurer, ed., *The Air Service in World War I: The Final Report and a Tactical History,* vol. 1 (Washington, DC: Office of Air Force History, 1978), 2; and Dudley, "World War I and Federal Military History," 34.

113. US NARA: Frank Jack Fletcher, "Diary, NORPACFOR," July 1944 to September 1945.

114. US NARA: Henry L. Larsen et al., "Diary, Guam Island Commander," 30 March 1944 to 15 August 1945.

115. USNHC: Francis D. Gurll, "Diary."

116. SNA: Unsigned, "Di-16 juntuan silingbu zhenzhong riji," 1 October 1937.

117. See the discussion in Foucault, *Discipline and Punish,* "The Means of Correct Training," 170–194.

2. SELF-MOBILIZATION AND THE DISCIPLINE OF THE BATTLEFIELD

1. In the Japanese case, the "National Army had become the Imperial Army." Yoshida, *Nihon no guntai: Heishi-tachi no kindaishi* (Tokyo: Iwanami shoten, 2002), 180.

2. SNA: "Deng Huanguang," "Di-64-shi Qinan yidai zhenzhong riji," 31 July 1937.

3. SNA: Ye Tiaoquan, "Paobing di-6-lü di-17-tuan Hebei Huolu fujin zhenzhong riji," 9–10 August 1937. "White Russians" referred to escaped "counter-revolutionaries" from the Czarist regime.

4. Deng, 7–8 August 1937.

5. SNA: Huang Yong'an, "Paobing di-6-lü zai Shijiazhuang dengdi zhenzhong riji," 28–30 August 1937.

6. Deng, 14 August 1937; and SNA: Liu Binghuan, "Paobing di-6-lü 12-tuan ji qi shubu zai Hebei Huolu dengdi zhenzhong riji," 9 August 1937.

7. Ye, 12 August 1937.

8. Deng, 22 August 1937.

9. This unfortunate tendency among GMD commanders has also been noted by other scholars. Chang Jui-te, "Nationalist Army Officers, 1937–1945," *Modern Asian Studies* 30:4 (October 1996).

10. Cai Yizhong, "Zhanshi de shouji," in *Zhanshi de shouji* (Hankow: Ziqiang chubanshe, February 1938), 1–2.

11. MDHA: Unsigned, "Di-3 dadui zhenzhong riji," 21 July 1937.

12. Zhang Xianwen, *Zhongguo kangri zhanzhengshi (1931–1945)* (Nanjing: Nanjing daxue chubanshe, 2001), 229–297.

13. "Di-3 dadui zhenzhong riji," 27, 30 July 1937. The phrase "Japanese slaves" can also refer to collaborators.

14. Gregory Kasza, *The State and Mass Media in Japan, 1918–1945* (Berkeley: University of California Press, 1988), 170.

15. This account is a conglomerate of three narratives of the Ōyama Incident: Zhang Xianwen et al., *Zhongguo kangri zhanzhengshi*; Bōeichō(shō) bōei kenkyūjo senshishitsu, ed., *Senshi sōsho: Chūgoku hōmen kaigun sakusen (1): Shōwa 13-nen 3-gatsu made* (Tokyo: Asagumo shinbunsha, 1972); SNA: Author unknown, "Songhu huizhan riji," 9 August 1937.

16. SNA: Twentieth Brigade Commander Zhong Song, "Di-61shi duli 20-lü Songhu huizhan zhenzhong riji," 9 August 1937.

17. SNA: Unsigned, "Shanghai zuozhan riji," in *Songhu huizhan riji,* 9–10 August 1937.

18. Hasegawa's demand that the PPC and their defenses be removed was meant to be a deathblow to the ten-year Nationalist program of reasserting its sovereignty over Shanghai. Frederic Wakeman Jr., *Policing Shanghai, 1927–1937* (Berkeley: University of California Press, 1995), 195–196.

19. "Shanghai zuozhan riji," 11 August 1937.

20. "Di-3 dadui zhenzhong riji," 12 August 1937.

21. PC: These medals were presumably given to those who had helped resist the Japanese during the first "Shanghai Incident" in 1932. See Chapter 1.

22. Yang Huimin, *Babai zhuangshi yu wo* (Taipei: Boai chubanshe, 1970, orig. 1967), 5–6. Chen Cunren, *Kangzhan shidai shenghuoshi* (Shanghai: Renmin chubanshe, 2001), 6.

23. Zhong, 12 August 1937.

24. MDHA: Gao Zhihang, "Di-4 dadui zhenzhong riji," 13 August 1937.

25. Zhong, 13 August 1937. Gao's description of the smoke would come later, on 21 August.

26. "Shanghai zuozhan riji," 13 August 1937.

27. NPA: Ma Chaojun, "Nanjing fangkong riji," 13 August 1937.

28. "Di-3 dadui zhenzhong riji," 14 August 1937. The author here is mimicking the words of Chiang Kai-shek.

29. "Shanghai zuozhan riji," 14 August 1937. This may have been in reference to the GMD air force's mistaken bombing of the foreign concessions and the author's misinterpretation.

30. Gao, 14 August 1937.

31. Cai, 4–5.

32. Gao, 15 August 1937.

33. "Di-3 dadui zhenzhong riji," 15 August 1937.

34. Zhong, 15–16 August 1937.

35. "Di-3 dadui zhenzhong riji," 16 August 1937.

36. Ma, 16 August 1937.

37. "Shanghai zuozhan riji," 17 August 1937. As it turns out, most, if not all, of the men survived the sinking of the ship by swimming to shore.

38. "Di-3 dadui zhenzhong riji," 17–18 August 1937.

39. Zhong, 19 August 1937.

40. Ma, 19 August 1937.

41. Tian Zhongyuan, "Lujun zhuangjia bingtuan zhanche fangyupaoying zhanqing huibao," 19–21 August 1937. In this collection of Tian's daily reports, he described the consequences of the Japanese artillery's ability to exploit lack of communication among Chinese forces.

42. Zhong, 20–21 August 1937.

43. OIPM: Unsigned, "Address Book" [field diary], 19–22 August 1937. This diary does not contain the author's name or rank, but it appears that he was a lower-echelon field officer who trained and commanded infantrymen directly.

44. At this point, Chiang Kai-shek was confident, cabling his son, Chiang Ching-kuo, that he had the "means to counter" the Japanese invasion of Shanghai. Jay Taylor, *The Generalissimo: Chiang Kai-shek and the Struggle for Modern China* (Cambridge, MA: Belknap Press of Harvard University Press, 2009), 146.

45. See Hata Ikuhiko, *Rokōkyo jiken no kenkyū* (Tokyo: Tokyo daigaku shuppankai, 2001), chapter 8.

46. Umeda Fusao, *Hokushi ten senki: Umeda Fusao jūgun nikki,* ed. Umeda Toshio (self-published, 1970), quoted in Yoshimi Yoshiaki, "Nicchū sensō to kokumin dōin," *Rekishi hyōron* 447 (1987): 10.

47. OIPM: "Sōbetsu no ji" (1939).

48. OIPM: "Isho" (1939).

49. Fukushima kenritsu hakubutsukan, "Hagaki." This 2 February 1942 postcard was sent from the China front to the soldier's friends and relatives in the northeast.

50. Ibid.

51. Kōchi: Kusa no ie heiwa shiryōkan: "Yamamoto Kenji," "Jinchū nisshi," 17 August 1937.

52. SPM: "Hamabe Genbei," "Jinchū nisshi."

53. PC: "Sakaguchi Jirō," "Jinchū nisshi," 14–20 August 1937.

54. Ibid., 26 August 1937.

55. Azuma Shirō, personal interview, 28 August 2004. This was how Azuma proudly described himself.

56. Azuma Shirō, *Azuma Shirō nikki* (Kumamoto: Kumamoto shuppan bunka kaikan, 2001), 21.

57. Kimura Genzaemon, *Nicchū sensō shussei nikki* (Akita: Mumeisha shuppan, 1982), 16.

58. Ibid., 16–17.

59. TPM: "Nagatani Masao," "Techō," 24–25 August 1937.

60. Sakaguchi, 30 August–1 September 1937.

61. Azuma, 9 September 1937.

62. OIPM: Kawakami Yoshimitsu, *Ani no senki,* Kawakami Yoshinobu, ed. (Osaka: Osaka karuchā sentā, self-published, 1985).

63. OIPM: "Taniguchi Kazuo," "Yasen byōin nikki," letter dated 28 August 1937.

64. Ibid., letter dated 30 August 1937.

65. Sakaguchi, 11 September 1937.

66. SJHM: "Hagaki." In 1937 the average infantryman made five to eight yen a month.

67. RIPM: "Ueda Masaki," "Zakkichō," 8 November 1937.

68. Taniguchi, letter dated 6 September 1937. The actual date may be slightly earlier, but the original copy is damaged.

69. Azuma, 14, 20 September 1937. The Japanese army stipulated that its servicemen never hurt any foreigners in China, nor could they set foot inside foreign facilities and concessions.

70. Kimura Genzaemon, 24–30 September 1937. The remaining Chinese were brought along as coolies.

71. Kawakami, 14 September 1937.

72. Taniguchi, 3 September 1937.

73. Tokyo: National Diet Library: Ishida Gi'ichi, *Sensen no jitsuroku* (self-published, 1977), 28 September 1937.

74. NIDS: Akiyama Toyochi, "Nisshi," 19 September 1937.

75. Taniguchi, 15–16 September 1937.

76. Kawakami, 24 September 1937.

77. Taniguchi, 18 September 1937.

78. Kimura Genzaemon, 24 September 1937.

79. Azuma, 22 September 1937.

80. Sakaguchi, 23 September 1937. Sakaguchi refers to the soldiers in Baoding as "regulars" *(seikigun),* and the documents he mentions were standard military issue for GMD servicemen.

81. Sakaguchi, 24–25 September 1937.

82. Gao Jingbo, in Liu Binghuan, 22 September 1937.

83. Sakaguchi, 24 September 1937.

84. Taniguchi, 19 September 1937.

85. Kawakami, 27, 30 September 1937.

86. Akiyama, 25 September 1937.

87. Tian Yufeng, in Liu Binghuan, 25 September 1937.

88. Umeda Fusao, "Nikki," quoted in Fujii Tadatoshi, *Heitachi no sensō: Tegami, nikki, taikenki wo yomitoku* (Tokyo: Asahi Shimbunsha, 2000), 104–108; Deng, 24 August 1937. "Manchukuoan Education Brigades" *(weiman jiaodaotuan)* referred to conscripts from the northeast who drafted propaganda materials for Japan.

89. Umeda, 23–26 August 1937; and Deng, 24–26 August 1937.

90. Huang, 1 October 1937.

91. Liu Binghuan, 4–8 October 1937.

92. Kimura Genzaemon, 1–3 October 1937.

93. Kawakami, 11 October 1937.

94. Liu Binghuan, 9 October 1937.

95. Huang, 11 October 1937.

96. Kimura Genzaemon, 11 October 1937.

97. Sakaguchi, 11 October 1937.

98. Kimura Genzaemon, 12–13 October 1937.

99. Kawakami, 25–26 October 1937.

100. Sakaguchi, 4 October 1937.

101. Kimura Genzaemon, 4 October 1937.

102. See also Rana Mitter's account of Xu Wancheng's *biji* (notebook) in "Writing War: Autobiography, Modernity, and Wartime Narrative in Nationalist China, 1937–1946," *Transactions of the RHS* 18 (2008).

103. Liu Binghuan, 12 October 1937.

104. Yang Tiejun, in Liu Binghuan, 15 October 1937.

105. Ibid., 22 October 1937.

106. Kimura Genzaemon, 15–28 October 1937.

107. Kawakami, 29 October 1937. There is no evidence to suggest that the soldiers fighting Kawakami's unit were Communists.

108. Ishida, 3 November 1937.

109. Deng, 23 September 1937.

110. Umeda, 25 September 1937.

111. Deng, 24–25 September 1937.

112. Akiyama received the news in Beiping one day after the events. Akiyama, 26 September 1937.

113. Umeda, 30 September 1937.

114. Deng, September 1937, attached at the end of the month.

115. SNA: Wang Jingguo, "Lujun di-19-jun Xinkou huizhan jingguo ji riji," introduction.

116. Hao famously criticized Chiang's anticommunist policies. NML: Zhuan Ping, *Kangri de yingxiong* (Hankou: Xinzhi shudian, March 1938), 19.

117. NML: Hao Mengling, *Zhenzhong riji* (Wuhan: Zhanshi chubanshe, January 1938), 3 October 1937. *Lianzuofa* was the practice of punishing all members of a unit for a single member's transgressions. Li Fuying, who had bungled his defenses at Tianzhen-Yanggao and fled his post, was shot.

118. NML: Liu Jiaqi, *Zhenzhong riji* (Wuhan: Zhanshi chubanshe, January 1938), 6 October 1937.

119. Liu Jiaqi, 9 October 1937.

120. Hao, 10 October 1937.

121. Liu Jiaqi, 10 October 1937.

122. Hao, 11 October 1937.

123. Liu Jiaqi, 11 October 1937.

124. Hao, 12 October 1937.

125. Taniguchi, 4 November 1937.

126. Umeda, 26 October 1937; Fujii, *Heitachi no sensō,* 108.

127. "Zuozhan rizhi," in *Songhu huizhan riji,* 23 August 1937.

128. Anonymous, "Dong zhanchang de yijiao," in *Zhanshi de shouji,* 4 September 1937.

129. Gao, 23 August 1937.

130. SNA: Luo Zhuoying et al., "Di-18 jun silingbu zhenzhong riji ji Luodian shiri zhanji jian zongsiling Luo Zhuoying," 23–25 August 1937.

131. Peng, in ibid., 23 August 1937.

132. Li Weipan in ibid., 23–25 August 1937.

133. Hamabe, 5 September 1937.

134. Zhong, 2–3 September 1937.

135. Nagatani, 3 September 1937.

136. "Dong zhanchang de yijiao," 7 September 1937.

137. Luo et al., 3 September 1937; also see entry for 29 August 1937.

138. "Dong zhanchang de yijiao," 26 August 1937.

139. "Di-3 dadui zhenzhong riji," 28 August 1937.

140. Luo et al., 28 August and 2 September 1937. Peng's report to Luo also noted that many suspected *hanjian* were beaten to death by civilians.

141. It is unclear whether the Chinese Scouts actually assisted the GMD in their search for and execution of suspected "traitors," but the story presented by Yang is alarming (see *Babai zhuangshi,* 9–11).

142. "Dong zhanchang de yijiao," 5 September 1937.

143. Yu Shen, *"Juntong,* SACO, and the Nationalist Guerrilla Effort," in David P. Barrett and Larry N. Shyu, eds., *China in the Anti-Japanese War, 1937–1945* (New York: Peter Lang, 2001), 136.

144. Chinese Nationalist servicemen did not typically use the term "war crime" (*zhanzheng fanzui,* or *zhanzui*).

145. Nagatani, 4–6 September 1937.

146. Hamabe, 8 September 1937.

147. Liu Binghuan, 25 August 1937.

148. Hamabe, 16 September 1937.

149. Nagatani, 7 September 1937.

150. "Dong zhanchang de yijiao," 10 September 1937.

151. Zhong, 9 September 1937.

152. Nagatani, 9 September 1937.

153. Zhong, 10 September 1937.

154. Nagatani, 14 September 1937. The circumstances of Nagatani's death were related to the archivists when his friend donated the diary.

155. Yamamoto, 12–20 September 1937.

156. Hamabe, 18 September 1937.

157. Suzuki Hideo, *Senjin micchō: Wakaki gun'i no mita Nicchū sensō* (Sodo bunko, 1982); also quoted in Fujii, *Heitachi no sensō,* 115–116.

158. Yamamoto, 22 September 1937.

159. NIDS: Kimura Matsujirō, "Shanghai-sen jūgun nisshi," 19 October 1937.

160. Yamamoto, 23–26 September 1937.

161. "Honma Masakatsu," "Sentō nisshi," 5 October 1937, and "Itō Kihachi," "Jinchū nikki," 6 October 1937, in Ono Kenji et al., eds., *Nankin daigyakusatsu wo kiroku shita kōgun heishitachi* (Tokyo: Ōtsuki shoten, 1996). Pseudonyms are the editors'.

162. Yu Yanling, "Qianxian 10-tian," in *Zhanshi de shouji,* 9–10 October 1937.

163. SNA: Unsigned, "Di-8-shi Songhu Wuxi dengdi zhenzhong riji," 1937, introductory report up to 15 November 1937.

164. Luo, 27 September 1937.

165. Zhong, 1–6 October 1937.

166. Yamamoto, 1 October 1937.

167. Hamabe, 14 October 1937.

168. Yu, 12–18 October 1937.

169. Itō, 28–30 October 1937.

170. Hamabe, 31 October 1937.

171. Zhong, 3 November 1937.

172. On refugees, see Toby Lincoln, "Fleeing from Firestorms: Government, Cities, Native Place Associations and Refugees in the Anti-Japanese War of Resistance," *Urban History* 38:3 (November 2011); Stephen Mackinnon, *Wuhan, 1938: War, Refugees, and the Making of Modern China* (Berkeley: University of California Press, 2008); and Christian Henriot, "Shanghai and the Experience of War: The Fate of Refugees," *European Journal of East Asian Studies* 5:2 (2006); R. Keith Schoppa, *In a Sea of Bitterness: Refugees during the Sino-Japanese War* (Cambridge, MA: Harvard University Press, 2011).

173. Suzuki, 27 October 1937.

174. Hamabe, 12 November 1937.

175. Yamamoto, 14 October 1937.

176. Chang Jui-te, *Kangzhan shiqi de guojun* (Taipei: Zhongyang yanjiuyuan jinshisuo zhuankan, 1993), 20.

177. Ma, 6 November 1937.

178. Bōei kenshūsho senshishitsu, *Senshi sōsho*, 387.

3. ASSEMBLING THE "NEW ORDER"

1. NIDS: Hamazaki Tomizō, "Nisshi," 7 November 1937.

2. They exacted their revenge primarily in three ways: by (1) waylaying Japanese troops marching through Jiangsu, (2) burning crops and houses behind them, and (3) attacking the Japanese with mortars. SNA: Unsigned, "Di-8-shi Songhu Wuxi dengdi zhenzhong riji," 3 December 1937.

3. Kōchi: Kusa no ie heiwa shiryōkan: "Yamamoto Kenji," "Jinchū nisshi," 5–6 November 1937.

4. FPM: "Motojima Saburō," "Gunji yūbin," August, probably 1938. The postcard was censored by a corporal in the Japanese army.

5. As low as 7 percent of field medics, in charge of both first aid and hygiene in the unit, were qualified for their jobs. Ka-che Yip, "Wartime Anti-Epidemic Efforts," in David P. Barrett and Larry N. Shyu, eds., *China in the Anti-Japanese War: Politics, Culture, and Society* (New York: Larry Yang, 2001), 173.

6. NPA: Ma Chaojun, "Nanjing fangkong riji," 7 November 1937.

7. Hamazaki, 14, 16 November 1937.

8. Ma, 9 November 1937. The Japanese and Chinese armies used small radio transmitters in the field, and both sides employed code breakers. Xiao Zhanzhong, "Qingmo Beiyang junfa he Guomindang zhengfu jishu zhencha qingbaoshi

jianshu," *Qingbao zazhi,* 15:6 (November 1996), 74. Thanks to Doi Takashi of the Yokohama Military Radio Museum.

   9. Bob Tadashi Wakabayashi, "The Messiness of Historical Reality," in Wakabayashi, ed., *The Nanking Atrocity, 1937–8: Complicating the Picture* (New York: Berhahn Books, 2007).

   10. RIPM: "Ueda Masaki," "Zakkichō," 15–31 December 1937.

   11. "Itō Kihachi," "Nikki," in Ono Kenji et al., eds. *Nankin daigyakusatsu wo kiroku shita kōgun heishitachi* (Tokyo: Ōtsuki shoten, 1996), 8 December 1937.

   12. "Kurozu Tadanobu," "Jinchū nikki," in Ono Kenji et al., *Nankin daigyakusatsu,* 10 December 1937.

   13. Ōdera Takashi, "Jinchū nikki," in Ono Kenji et al., *Nankin daigyakusatsu,* 3 December 1937.

   14. Yamamoto, 13, 22, 27, and 31 November, 1 December 1937. Whenever inspections occurred, "requisitions" *(chōhatsu)* and "outings" *(gaishutsu)* were temporarily banned.

   15. OIPM: "Inoue Yasuji," "Techō," 3 December 1937.

   16. Ōdera, 9 December 1937.

   17. "Ōuchi Toshimichi," "Jinchū nikki," in Ono Kenji et al., *Nankin daigyakusatsu,* 7 December 1937.

   18. SML: Jiang Gonggu, *Xianjing sanyueji* (Wuhan: August 1938), 4 December 1937.

   19. Inoue, 9 December 1937. What Inoue refers to as an "identification card" *(shōmeisho)* was likely a Nationalist Party member's identification.

   20. Jiang, 8 December 1937. Hamazaki wrote about the leaders' flight: "If a nation is weak, even if it has all the wealth in the world, it isn't worth anything. They've left their noble manors and fled." Hamazaki, 8 November 1937.

   21. Jiang, 12 and 9 December 1937. Still, Ueda Masaki easily convinced Chinese to haul "ammunition to kill their own troops," which impressed upon him the "tragedy of the defeated" *(haisen no ukime).* Ueda, "Notebook / Jinchū nikki," 5 December 1937. Although massacres were widespread, it was not, as Iris Chang suggested, an attempt to exterminate the Chinese as a people; see Chang, *The Rape of Nanking: The Forgotten Holocaust of World War II* (New York: Basic Books, 1997). On cultural "extermination," see Wan-yao Chou, "The Kōminka Movement in Taiwan and Korea: Comparisons and Interpretations," in Peter Duus, Ramon Myers, and Mark Peattie, eds., *The Japanese Wartime Empire, 1931–1945* (Princeton, NJ: Princeton University Press, 1984).

   22. Hamazaki, 2, 11 December 1937.

   23. On the effects of the Japanese attack for Nanjing residents, see David Askew, "The Nanjing Incident: An Examination of the Civilian Population," *Sino-Japanese Studies* 13:2 (March 2001); Martha Lund Smalley, ed., *American Missionary Eyewitnesses to the Nanking Massacre, 1937–1938* (New Haven, CT: Yale Divinity School Library, 1997); John Rabe, *The Good Man of Nanking: The Diaries*

of John Rabe, ed. Erwin Wickert, trans. John E. Woods (New York: A. A. Knopf, 1998); and Suping Lu, ed., *Terror in Minnie Vautrin's Nanjing: Diaries and Correspondence, 1937–38* (Chicago: University of Illinois Press, 2008).

24. Jiang, 14 December 1937.

25. Uwada Hiroshi, "Nikki," 15 December 1937, in Hata Ikuhito, *Nankin jiken* (Tokyo: Chūō kōronsha, 1986), 155; this diary was published as "Ittōhei no jūgun nikki," *Asahi Shimbun,* 5 August 1984.

26. Maeda Yoshimasa, "Jinchū nikki," 15 December 1937, in Nankin senshi henshū iinkai, ed., *Nankin senshi shiryōshū 1* (1989), 358.

27. "Kindō Eijirō," "Shussei nikki," in Ono Kenji et al., *Nankin daigyakusatsu,* 14 December 1937.

28. Azuma Shirō, *Azuma Shirō nikki* (Kumamoto: Kumamoto shuppan bunka kaikan, 2001), 13 December 1937. Azuma did not understand the Chinese message. "Kindō Eijirō" went so far as to say: "You can call them enemies, but they are still pitiable [*kawaisō*]." In Ono Kenji et al., *Nankin daigyakusatsu,* 13 November 1937.

29. "Saitō Jirō," "Jinchū nikki," in Ono Kenji et al., *Nankin daigyakusatsu,* 18 December 1937.

30. Kindō, 16 December 1937. Just like Saitō, Kindō also used the Buddhist concept of "marman" (Jp. *danmatsuma,* Ch. *duanmoma*) to describe the Chinese deaths. This refers to a spot on the body that, when touched, causes instantaneous, excruciating pain and inevitable death.

31. For a similar voice from the European theater, see Victor Klemperer, *I Will Bear Witness, 1942–1945: A Diary of the Nazi Years,* trans. Martin Chalmers (New York: Random House, 2001).

32. The official Japanese government statement was made on 16 January 1938. By 18 January, Konoe had proclaimed that Japan would not "abandon the use of military and all other means to crush the Nationalist government." For good English translations, see Monica Curtis, ed., *Documents on International Affairs* (Oxford: Oxford University Press, 1942), 340–341.

33. NIDS: Kawahisa Tamomochi, "Kimitsu sakusen nisshi," 5 April 1938.

34. Stephen MacKinnon, *Wuhan, 1938: War, Refugees, and the Making of Modern China* (Berkeley: University of California Press, 2008), 18–20. See Chapter 2 for the discussion of Li Fuying.

35. He Xiuhan, in SNA: Liu Binghuan, "Paobing di-6-lü 12-tuan ji qi shubu zai Hebei Huolu dengdi zhenzhong riji,"," 23 April 1938.

36. Zhang Kuitan, in Liu Binghuan, 24 April 1938.

37. Gao Jingbo, in Liu Binghuan, 7 April 1938. Gao also reported deaths from incompetent handling of ordnance.

38. NIDS: Kawahisa Tamomochi, "Kimitsu sakusen nisshi," 14 April 1938.

39. SNA: Ye Tiaoquan, "Paobing di-6-lü di-17-tuan Hebei Huolu fujin zhenzhong riji," 25 February 1938.

40. Liu Binghuan, 17 July 1938. See also SNA: Unsigned, "Di-29 juntuan 69-jun zhenzhong riji," 5 August and 27 October 1938; SNA: Unsigned, "Di-38-jun Jinan Gaoping dengdi zhenzhong riji," 2 April 1938, regarding civilian casualties.

41. Unsigned, "Di-8-shi," 7 March 1938. Chang Jui-te has noted the disastrous effect this practice had on GMD military competence in the 1940s. Chang Jui-te, *Kangzhan shiqi de guojun* (Taipei: Zhongyang yanjiuyuan jinshisuo zhuankan, 1993).

42. SNA: Unsigned, "1-zhanqu di-196-shi zai Henan Mengci Hengchi fujin dengdi zhenzhong riji," 18 July 1938.

43. Gao, in Liu Binghuan, 11 July 1938.

44. Liu Binghuan, 20, 24 November 1938.

45. Unsigned, "69-jun zhenzhong riji," 14, 16 July 1938.

46. SNA: Zhao Xitian, "Di-3-shi zai Jiujiang yidai zuozhan zhenzhong riji," 1, 6, 25 July 1938. On 27 July, GMD commanders in Wuhan were purposefully positioning their men in mountainous areas.

47. Unsigned, "69-jun zhenzhong riji," 23 July 1938. Chinese officers were reminded to remain calm and not mistake smokescreen for poison gas. Despite calls to "risk the fire from the air" and "charge bravely forward," units "fell completely apart, moving in disorder."

48. Zhao Xitian, 8 August 1938.

49. The Sixty-Ninth Army commander reported to superiors that one of his battle diaries had been lost under fire. Unsigned, "69-jun zhenzhong riji," 12 August 1938.

50. SNA: Unsigned, "Jūgun techō," in folder "Riwo riji/zaji" (a collection of diaries by various authors), 31 October 1938. This Japanese diary was captured by the GMD for intelligence purposes, which happed often: SNA: Ai Ai, "Di-92-shi jiuhuan Changde zuozhan jimi riji zuozhan riji," 7 November 1943. Ai mimeographed his captured diary and distributed it for study.

51. Zhao Xitian, 21 August 1938.

52. "Junshi weiyuanhui weiyuanzhang tianshui hangying jimi zuozhan riji," 10 January 1939, in Zhongguo di-2 dang'anguan, ed., *Kangri zhanzheng shiqi Guomindangjun jimi zuozhan riji* (Beijing: Zhongguo dang'an chubanshe, August 1995).

53. OIPM: Unsigned, "Blue Book," 1 January to 3 October 1937. It is unclear what happened to the original Chinese author.

54. See Kenneth J. Ruoff's treatment in *Imperial Japan at Its Zenith: The Wartime Celebration of the Empire's 2,600th Anniversary* (Ithaca, NY: Cornell University Press, 2010).

55. James Morley, *The China Quagmire: Japanese Expansion on the Asian Continent, 1933–1941* (New York: Columbia University Press, 1983).

56. NIDS: "Oe Yoshikusa chūi chian kōsaku shiryō: Shinmin shōnendan taikai ni okeru Oe butaichō no kōen," September 1942. The address by Oe was composed in Japanese, and the youths' submissions were in Chinese. The group was connected to the "New Citizens Movement," which was a Wang government-sponsored program to generate loyalty for the new regime. See Chen Shaojie "Wang Jingwei xiang Ri maiguo de 'Dongya lianmeng' lilun peixi," *Kangri zhanzheng yanjiu* 3 (1994); Shi Guifang, "Shilun Riwei de dongya lianmeng yundong," *Shixue yuekan* 12 (2006); Xie Xiaopeng, "Wang-wei de 'Xinguomin yundong' saoxi," *Jiangnan daxue xuebao* 6:2 (April 2007). Japanese directors were instructed to "select the superior elements" and organize them into the "New Citizens' Crack Corps." SMA: "Shinmin kōsaku senshūtai soshiki yōryō, Shinkyō-ken (Xinxiang-xian) sōkai jimukyoku," 1943. Lists of members' names still exist in local Chinese collections such as SMA: 022–1–37.

57. RIPM: Sakurai Katsu, "Furyo nikki," 6 September 1941.

58. For example, Japanese "puppet" governments in China were often ruled locally by highly ranked officers like private fiefdoms: see summary by Parks Coble, *Chinese Capitalists in Japan's New Order: The Occupied Lower Yangzi, 1937–1945* (Berkeley: University of California Press, 2003), 67–68. The early Wang government pleaded for help from the IJA in basic state functions such as tax collection and shipping passes on the Yangzi: "Xinzhengfu chengli-qian suo jiwang yu ri-fangzhe," in Wang Mingzhe et al., eds., *Riben diguozhuyi qinhua dang'an ziliao xuanbian: Wang wei-zhengquan* (Beijing: Dang'an chubanshe, 1991), 745–747.

59. "Nanjing Wang-wei jige zuzhi ji qi paixi huodong," in Wang et al., *Riben diguozhuyi qinhua dang'an ziliao xuanbian,* 778, 780. Students engaged in group discussion and public correction of each other's diaries, which were split into "notebooks" *(biji)* and "Life Diaries" *(shenghuo riji).*

60. NA (Fatingyuan): Doc341–2701 (22 October 1938): The central government issued a directive, approved by the courts, that a committee be established to oversee the treatment of servicemen's families. Doc341–179 (4 February 1939): A local court in Sichuan requested guidance regarding the proper punishment for wives and mothers obstructing draft officers.

61. While Chinese units asked that servicemen's correspondence be sent through the prefectural government (to be censored), the GMD supported letter writing so that "the conscripts can communicate with their families and obtain information, thus strengthening their battle spirit." SNA: "Fu(shi)zhang-chu," "Di-10 jituanjun yu Zhejiang Yiwu dengdi zhenzhong riji," 5 August 1938.

62. "Chūi tsūchōan (shishin keishiki)," "Rikugun taishin yori kenpei shireikan ni tatsu" (shiryō 101) in Yoshimi Yoshiaki and Yoshida Yutaka, eds., *Shiryō: Nihon gendaishi, 10: Nicchū sensōki no kokumin dōin (1)* (Tokyo: Ōtsuki shoten, 1984), 344–345. On "antiwar thought" *(hansen shisō),* see Katō Yōko, "Hansen shisō to chōhei kihi shisō no keifu," in Aoki Tamotsu et al., eds., *Kindai Nihon bunkaron (10): Sensō to guntai* (Tokyo: Iwanami shoten, 1999).

63. This quote is from an August 1938 Criminal Affairs Bureau directive to publishers, in Gregory Kasza, *The State and Mass Media in Japan, 1918–1945* (Berkeley: University of California Press, 1988), 170. While publishers were easy to control, veterans were not: Yoshimi Yoshiaki, *Kusa no ne no fashizumu: Nihon minshū no sensō taiken* (Tokyo: Tokyo daigaku shuppansha, 1987), 34.

64. The state and mass media tried simultaneously to make the Japanese public feel close to the battlefield while suppressing the more disturbing information: see Barak Kushner, *The Thought War: Japanese Imperial Propaganda* (Honolulu: University of Hawai'i Press, 2006).

65. Japanese commanders knew that the treatment given to those who had "become spirits to defend the nation" *(hokoku no tamashi to kawashitaru mono)* and those who were the "heroic wounded" *(yūgan naru senshōsha)* would "affect élan and discipline in subsequent battles." SJHM: Morita, ed., "Mitsu: Kyōiku no sankō," June 1939. Thanks to SJHM's Satō Takuya.

66. Servicemen also recorded such activities in their diaries. For example: "Takahashi Teruo," "Jinchū nikki," in Ono Kenji et al., *Nankin daigyakusatsu,* 29 December 1937. Conducting memorial services was one of the responsibilities of the battalion commander.

67. PC/OMPM: A Japanese serviceman took a photo for his personal album around the time of the battle for Xuzhou in 1938. Many thanks to his granddaughter, who allowed me access to this collection.

68. Wang Wenrong, 20 May 1945.

69. Ai, 23, 26 December 1943.

70. Beijing dianying ziliaoguan: "Kangri zhanzheng dianying teji."

71. Yamamoto, 10 January 1938. For U.S. examples, see the field photos of John Towarnicki in the USMCA.

72. NIDS: Nyūjōshiki shashinshū, December 1937. At the comfort station, Japanese sex workers charged seven yen, Koreans five, and Soviet, German, and French two. His salary was eight yen and eight sen per month. Ishida Gi'ichi, *Sensen no jitsuroku* (Self-published, 1977), 3 December 1937.

73. Censorship policy was inconsistent: sometimes a sergeant in the *naimuhan* would read outgoing letters, but other times it was done at the battalion headquarters. Personal interviews with Chūkiren members, 27 April 2004, Tokyo. According to written regulations, "in order that all documents protect [military] secrets and every man uphold military order, the officer in command of the unit [*shozoku taichō*] can remove [any offending text] when necessary." SJHM: "Guntai naimurei," 3 September 1943.

74. According to Li Gaoshan, whom I interviewed in Nanjing in 2004, there was no system for delivering war correspondence between the front and the rear. Correspondence relied on personal contacts in mobile services such as medical units, logistics, and reporters. Chinese Nationalist officer Wang Wenrong, however,

recorded multiple instances of sending and receiving letters in rear areas: SMA: Wang Wenrong, "Gongzuo riji," 18 May 1945.

75. NA: Hai Zhong, "Yuexia zhenzhong fang zhanshi," in *Wuhan ribao,* 16 October 1938.

76. NA: "Xiao meimei de xin," in *Zhenzhong ribao,* 31 October 1937.

77. NA: Li Hong, "Yi feng weiji de jiaxin," in *Xianbing zhoukan,* 1 June 1938. The terms for affiliation in these phrases—*zong* (family), *zu* (ancestors), *gu* (clan, or hamlet of interrelated households), *zu* (people, ethnos)—suggest the importance the GMD put on the connectedness between family, clan, village, locality, and nation-state.

78. FPM: "Hagaki," 2 February 1942.

79. Li Hong, "Yi feng weiji de jiaxin."

80. See reproductions in Iwate-ken nōson bunka kondankai, ed., *Senbotsu nōminheishi no tegami* (Tokyo: Iwanami Shoten, 1961).

81. Kasza, *The State and Mass Media,* chapter 7, "The Press and the Consulta-tion System," 168–193. Other techniques included blacklisting troublesome writers, confiscating offending publications, and providing directives for news content.

82. Ueda, 12 December 1937.

83. Louise Young, *Japan's Total Empire: Manchuria and the Culture of Wartime Imperialism* (Berkeley: University of California Press, 1999). "Embedded" journal-ists at this time usually traveled with combat units at great personal risk, relying less on official reports, but expected to comply with stricter censorship laws.

84. Kingu shinnengo furoku, *Shina jihen bidan buyūdan* (Tokyo: Kingu shinnengoshi, January 1938), 242.

85. Barak Kushner, "Planes, Trains, and Games: Selling Japan's War in Asia," in Jennifer Purtle and Hans Bjarne Thomsen, eds., *Looking Modern: Taisho Japan and the Modern Era* (Chicago: University of Chicago Press, 2009).

86. RIPM: Yamana Takasa, "Kamishibai: Kibidanko," 1943. In a touching scene, several soldiers bond by sharing stories of their mothers, overseen by their platoon commander. Antiwar POWs working for the GMD and Kaji Wataru produced propaganda challenging these assumptions—see Chapter 5. On antifas-cist Japanese activists, see Eric Esselstrom, "The Life and Memory of Hasegawa Teru: Contextualizing Human Rights, Trans-Nationalism, and the Antiwar Movement in Modern Japan," *Radical History Review,* no. 101 (Spring 2008), 149. Kaji and Hasegawa were members of the same organization.

87. MacKinnon, *Wuhan, 1938,* chapter 5, "Culture and the Press."

88. NA: Yu Yanling, "Wo de shitian zhanzheng shenghuo," in *Zhenzhong ribao,* 31 October 1937.

89. Shi Hezhang, "Zhandi riji," in *Zhenzhong ribao,* 31 October 1937. The events presumably took place when Shi was briefly at the front from 28 to 29 September 1937.

90. Shi Tuo, *Shanghai Correspondence* (written between 1939 and 1940). Steven Paul Day suggested that Shi Tuo's switch from epistolary form to montage was used to question the truth that letters were supposed to convey. See Day (2009), *Heroes without a Battlefield: Nationalism, Identity, and the Aesthetics of Dissolution in Chinese Wartime Literature, 1937–1945.* Doctoral Dissertation, Chapter 3. Charles Laughlin linked also montage to reporting rural guerrilla warfare. Charles A. Laughlin, *Chinese Reportage: The Aesthetics of Historical Experience* (Durham, NC: Duke University Press, 2002); and Rana Mitter, "Writing War: Autobiography, Modernity, and Wartime Narrative in Nationalist China, 1937–1946," *Transactions of the RHS* 18 (2008).

91. Hai Zhong, "Yuexia zhenzhong fang zhanshi."

92. NA: Ze Guohua, "Wo shi junren," *Xianbing zhoukan,* 25 May 1938.

93. The term *weisheng* has many connotations in modern Chinese history: see Ruth Rogaski, *Hygienic Modernity: Meanings of Health and Disease in Treaty Port China* (Berkeley: University of California Press, 2004). In the military context, it encompassed practices both hygienic (keeping one's body clean, boiling water before drinking, washing one's hands, etc.) and medical (first aid and field medicine, treatment of STDs, etc.).

94. NA: Chen Shuxun, "Jiangnan xuezhan zhuiji," in *Qianxian ribao,* 3 October 1938. *Frontline* also consistently published "comfort letters" *(weilaoxin)* for ordinary soldiers.

95. NA: Lin Dafu, "Bingzhong riji," *Xianbing zhoukan,* 4 May 1938.

96. Hino Ashihei, *Mugi to heitai* in *Hino Ashihei-shū* (Tokyo: Chikuma shobō, 1952, orig. 1938). Also see David M. Rosenfeld, *Unhappy Soldier: Hino Ashihei and Japanese World War II Literature* (Lanham, MD: Lexington Books, 2002).

97. "Qianxian yi pie," in Ah Ying, ed., *Shanghai shibian* (Hankou: 1938), 53; quoted in Laughlin, *Chinese Reportage,* 165.

98. Xie Bingying, "Kangzhan riji xinxu" (March 1981), in *Kangzhan riji* (Taipei: Dongda tushu gongsi, 1981). Many early works, such as "Zhanshi de shou," were presumed lost for most of the postwar era.

99. Xie, "Zhandi zhongqiu" (composed 19 September 1937) from *Xincongjun riji* (Wuhan: Tianma shudian, July 1938), reprinted in *Kangzhan riji,* 19.

100. Xie, "Xuezhan sanriji," in *Kangzhan riji,* 269.

101. Yamanaka Sadao, "Jinchū nisshi," in Shōwa sensō bungakukai, ed., *Shōwa sensō bungaku zenshū: Chūgoku he no shingeki* (Tokyo: Shūeisha, 1981), 275.

102. NA: Xi Qun, "Kangzhan yu xiju," in *Qianxian ribao,* 5 October 1938.

103. Kimura Genzaemon, 6 December 1937.

104. Many thanks to Azuma Shirō and Yamauchi Sayoko for a copy of the original diary.

105. Azuma, 25 November 1937, 12–13 and 14–15 December. When Japanese servicemen used the Chinese word *gunian* (Chinese for "girl," *guniang,* but frequently mispronounced), they were often being lewd.

106. OIPM: "Kogawa Hideo," "Jūgun nikki"; the blank diary was published in early 1938.

107. OIPM: "Taniguchi Kazuo," "Yasen byōin nikki," 12 December 1937.

108. PC: Ichikawa Genkichi, "Kaigun nikki," 1943–1944. This pocket diary has preprinted commemorations of Japanese victories in mainland China.

109. Taniguchi, 13 December 1937.

110. "Sakaguchi Jirō," "Jinchū nisshi," , 11 and 28 November, 28 December 1937; 1 and 17 January (on 21 January, he seems to have visited a Chinese prostitute for the first time as well), 4–6 February 1938; 4 January 1939.

111. Kawakami Yoshimitsu, *Ani no senki,* Kawakami Yoshinobu, ed. (Osaka: Osaka karuchā sentā, self-published, 1985), 12–13 and 29–31 December 1937; 3, 1, and 10 January, 1 February 1938 (Kawakami's unit was on a punitive expedition from 12 to 16 January). Kawakami obtained permission to visit the comfort stations, staffed by Korean *(yobo)* and Chinese *(shina, chyan)* women, from his battalion commander on New Year's Eve. On 30 January, "ugly" professional Chinese prostitutes flooded Yuci—*utsukushiku nai shōnin ga hairi "piiya" ga takusan ni fueru*—and he refused to pay for their services.

112. Yamamoto, 14 (reading *Tales of the Imperial Army's Military Heroism,* or *Kōgun buyūden*), 16 (Yamamoto copied the letters into the back of his notebook) and 17 December 1937.

113. Yamamoto, 23 December 1937. The Popular Front Incident *(Jinmin sensen jikken),* also known as the "Anti-Fascist Popular Front Incident," refers to the Japanese government's suppression of a perceived threat from the political left (including the Japan Proletarian Party and the Japan Congress of Labor Unions) after the fall of Nanjing.

114. Yamamoto, 16–17 January 1938, including poetry notes (at the end of his diary) from "Taking up the Gun." Japan was part of the Anti-Comintern Pact (1936) with other "fascists" but not yet in the Axis (1940); it was also pressuring Germany to block arms shipments to China. William C. Kirby, *Germany and Republican China* (Stanford, CA: Stanford University Press, 1984).

115. Kimura Genzaemon, 24 January, 4 March, 3 January, 1 February, 1 December, 14 December 1938.

4. THE UNBEARABLE LIKENESS OF BEING

1. In 1943, Carlson story was adapted into the film *Gung Ho!* George Dunn saw it en route to Okinawa: USMCA: George M. Dunn, "A Diary," 7 and 11 March 1945.

2. See description in Michael Blankfort, *The Big Yankee: The Life of Carlson of the Raiders* (Boston: Little, Brown, 1947).

3. William R. Evans, *Soochow and the 4th Marines* (Rogue River, OR: Atwood Publications, 1987). Even unit pets moved from war-torn China to "carry on the fight" against Japan in the South Pacific.

4. Oki Seiichi, "Nikki," in Ishihara Shirō, ed., *Tsuchi no sazamegoto: Kyūsei Shizuoka kōtō gakkō senbotsusha ikōshū* (Tokyo: Kōdansha, 28 June 1968), 71.

5. KSDFM: "Arai Yasujirō," "Nikki," 15 December 1941.

6. In the Philippines, Earl Sackett was woken up at 3:35 a.m. with the news that "Japan had started hostilities." USNHC: Earl C. Sackett, "War Diary," 8 December 1941.

7. USNHC: John C. Cash, "Five Year Diary," 1 January 1942.

8. KSDFM: "Hara Kinosuke," "Tōyō nikki," 1 January 1942.

9. USMHI: D. M. Moore, Headquarters II Corps, "Diary," 14 December 1941.

10. Sackett, 30 December 1941.

11. USMCA: William Sharpe, "VMJ-152: Securité en nuages" 3 February 1943.

12. USMHI: Lt. Col. Arthur L. Shreve, "Diary," 9 December 1941.

13. USMHI: Captain Achille Carlisle Tisdelle, "Story of Bataan Collapse, 9 April, 1942," 28 December 1941, 10 January 1942, and 22 February, 1942. Tisdelle blamed the loss of the Philippines on the unwillingness of U.S. officers to supply quinine, aircraft, and modern antiaircraft guns before the invasion. Rifles issued to Filipinos were discontinued in the U.S. Army from 1903. Hara Kinosuke noted U.S. guns' inability to reach him as he attacked, writing that "we weren't worried at all." Hara, 4 March 1942.

14. Hara, 5 January 1942.

15. Tisdelle, 16 February 1942.

16. Louis Morton, *War in the Pacific: Strategy and Command, the First Two Years* (Washington, DC: Government Printing Office, 2000), 267.

17. USMHI: S/Sgt Bernard O. Hopkins, "Diary," 2 February, 11 March 1942.

18. Paul D. Bunker, *Bunker's War: The World War II Diary of Col. Paul D. Bunker,* ed. Keith Barlow (Novato, CA: Presidio Press, 1996), 26 January 1941.

19. Sackett, 7 January 1941. This entry may be referring to the Malinta Tunnel.

20. Bunker, 24 January 1942. Note the following terms: HD Exec (harbor defense executive), bancas (troop ships), and "South Harbor" (between Corregidor and Hughes). The navy's refusal to act on behalf of the army, in Bunker's opinion, violated the "Joint Army and Navy Action" agreement. As with Sackett, the "Navy Tunnel" may refer to the Malinta Tunnel. On the infamous Japanese interservice rivalry, see Koyama Shinroku, "Chūshi sensen are kore," in Sensō taiken wo kiroku suru kai, ed., *Yuki ha kaerazu: Sensō taikenki* (self-published, 1984), 238–240. Charles V. Trent also related numerous tales of Japanese troops using nearly perfect English to trick U.S. troops. USMHI: Charles V. Trent, "Diary of the Admiralty Islands Campaign (typed document dated 21 April 1944)," 3 March 1944.

21. Shreve, 26 December 1941. Transport personnel had refused to go to the front line to haul out artillery. Shreve spoke with a fellow officer, who was "a grad. of New Mexico, Mil. and had a rifle in his hand, so I told him to use it."

22. Shreve, between 31 December 1941 and 5 and 10 January 1942 (among other things, he wrote, "An extra prayer for our oldest. May he be a joy to you dearest. If I do not make it through, I'm sure he will"), and "no date" February 1942.

23. D. M. Moore, date unknown: this passage was written sometime in mid- to late April 1942.

24. D. M. Moore, 20 March 1944.

25. USMHI: Wendell W. Fertig, "Diary," 15 January 1942.

26. Bunker, 17 January 1942. Tisdelle also noted the flight of Filipino soldiers of the Seventy-First Division from the Japanese and claimed that only a minority fought hard for the colonial government: Tisdelle, 29 December 1941. Nevertheless, there was considerable concern amongst high-ranking officers about the use of heavy guns for "fear of the effect of fire on the Filipinos." Shreve, 12 December 1941.

27. Hara, 6–7 March 1942. Kendari is on the Indonesian island of Sulawesi, at that time called the "Celebes."

28. USMCA: Lieutenant Watanabe, [no title; personal diary notebook], 3 and 17 March 1942.

29. Ozaki Shirō, "Sen'ei nikki," 25 December 1941, in *Taiheiyō sensō kaisen— 12-gatsu 8-nichi: Shōwa sensō bungaku zenshū* (Tokyo: Shūeisha, 1964), 264–265.

30. Colonial subjects frequently defined their national identities while interacting with fellow countrymen on long journeys, which is reminiscent of pilgrimage: Victor and Edith Turner, *Image and Pilgrimage in Christian Culture* (New York: Columbia University Press, Classics in Religion, 1995).

31. Leocadio de Asis, *From Bataan to Tokyo: Diary of a Filipino Student in Wartime Japan, 1943–1944* (New York: Paragon Book Gallery, 1979), 3 July, 17 October (de Asis was particularly proud of crushing the Manchurian basketball team), 23 November 1943.

32. The psychological assault on captives' confidence was similar to treatment of prisoners in Soviet gulags. Susan L. Caruthers, *Cold War Captives: Imprisonment, Escape, and Brainwashing* (Berkeley: University of California Press, 2009), chapter 3.

33. Michael Adas, *Machines as the Measure of Men: Science, Technology, and Ideologies of Western Dominance* (Ithaca, NY: Cornell University Press, 1990).

34. USMHI: George F. Gallion Papers, newspaper clipping describing his imprisonment and eventual death in Japan of "heart paralysis."

35. Shreve, 18 April 1942.

36. UTL: William Miner, "Diary," 27 December 1944, 29 January 1945. Although Miner's experience was not altogether good after arriving at the camp, he was given enough food to recover and survive the war.

37. Quoted in Yoshimi Yoshiaki, *Kusa no ne no fashizumu: Nihon minshū no sensō taiken* (Tokyo: Tokyo daigaku shuppansha, 1987), 246.

38. See treatment in John Dower, *War without Mercy: Race and Power in the Pacific* (New York: Pantheon Books, 1986), "Lesser Men and Supermen," 94-117.

39. UTL: Tatsuguchi Nobu, "Diary," trans. Samuel W. Hatcher, 21, 25, 26 (note: I have changed the word "Edict" in the wartime translation to the more likely "Rescript." The original Japanese text is not available), and 29 May 1942.

40. USMHI: William H. Owen, "Diary," 2 April 1944.

41. Hopkins, 2 February 1942.

42. USMHI: Ralph T. Noonan, "Daily Desk Calendar," 22 January 1942.

43. USMCA: William Heggy, "Perpetual Date Book," 24 August 1942.

44. USMCA, Eugene Boardman Documents: 2nd Lieutenant Yokota Hiroshi, "War Diary," speech copied under entry for 11 October 1942. Maruyama should not be confused with the postwar Japanese historian.

45. Shreve, 9 April 1942.

46. On social organizations supporting mobilization, see Richard Smethurst, *A Social Basis for Prewar Japanese Militarism: The Army and the Rural Community* (Berkeley: University of California Press, 1974).

47. Frederic Wakeman Jr., *Spymaster: Dai Li and the Chinese Secret Service* (Berkeley: University of California Press, 2003), 46. The GMD military recruited directly from the Boy Scouts, and there are tales of heroism on the part of the scouts as they supported Chinese troops.

48. David I. Macleod, *Building Character in the American Boy: The Boy Scouts, YMCA, and Their Forerunners, 1870–1920* (Madison: University of Wisconsin Press, 1983). The Boy Scouts of America became particularly militaristic following the 1915 resignation of cofounder Ernest Thompson Seaton.

49. The U.S. government targeted the scouts in 1916 by prohibiting U.S. military-style uniforms. For figures for the Chinese scouts, see NA: GMD zhong-yang zhixing weiyanyuanhui xunlianbu (yinxing), *Zhongguo tongzijun chuji kecheng* (1930), 74.

50. Smethurst, *Social Basis*. As Harvey Green has shown, organizations such as the YMCA and Boy Scouts aimed to create strong men for America through sport and fitness. Harvey Green, *Fit for America: Health, Fitness, Sport, and American Society* (Baltimore: Johns Hopkins University Press, 1986).

51. Just like their counterparts in East Asia, U.S. junior officers used war diaries to write monthly reports on their historical projects. Mirroring Tamon Jirō (see Chapter 1), Admiral Nimitz declared that "the experiences of the recent past should be in the hands of officers who would be operating in the immediate future." William R. McClintock, "Clio Mobilizes: Naval Reserve Historians during the Second World War," *Public Historian* 13:1 (Winter 1991), 41.

52. Unsurprisingly, class was determinative: "What the Victorians desired was privacy for the middle classes, publicity for the working classes, and segregation for both." Donald J. Olsen, "Victorian London: Specialization, Segregation, and

Privacy," *Victorian Studies* 17:3 (March 1973), 271. In the early modern Islamic world, the experience of "privacy" was highly variable depending on "government intrusiveness, population densities, communication technology, social structure, the distribution of wealth," and other factors. Abraham Marcus, "Privacy in Eighteenth Century Aleppo: The Limits of Cultural Ideals," *International Journal of Middle East Studies* 18:2 (May 1986), 166.

53. Sharpe, 16 November 1942.

54. UTL: Sherwin Northcott, "Diary," 1945.

55. See Gerald F. Linderman, *World within War: America's Combat Experience in WWII* (New York: Free Press, 1997), 200.

56. USMCA: Stanley H. Rich, "Diary," 7 July 1942. Documents in the USMC First Division did not mention diaries but strictly prohibited correspondence in combat zones, while photographs, without writing, were permitted for officers. UTL: Ben Holt, "Jungle Warfare Manual," 1944.

57. USMCA: Henry Stuckert Miller, "Diary," 11 July 1944.

58. Heggy, 24 August 1942.

59. Miller, "Introduction," 3 (1986). Japanese servicemen also censored their diaries in this manner.

60. Cash, 10 January 1942. Cash regularly wrote about how he was hoping for new mail. On 15 February, after over a month waiting in Pearl Harbor, he wrote, "Mail is about all we have to look forward to." Sharpe also remarked on the immense volume of mail he had to censor. Sharpe, 16 November 1942.

61. Rich, "Addenda #1."

62. RIPM: "Jūgun techō" (1937); RIPM: "Jūgun techō," (1942); ISPWM: "Seisen techō" (1944). These diaries were provided free of charge from the civilian "Courageous Soldiers' Fund" and were included in "comfort packages" *(imonbu-kuro)* with cigarettes, postcards *(gunji yūbin),* and candy.

63. UTL: Preprinted "Service Diary" included "Thoughts of Service Days" (1944).

64. UTL: Alfred Tramposch, "War Area Service Corps Diary" (1945).

65. Heggy, "Operators Log" (1942–1945).

66. USMCA: Unsigned, "Second Parachute Battalion (Reinforced), War Diary," 29 October and 2 September 1943.

67. USMCA: Robert P. Neuffer, "Diary," 31 July 1944. See also UTL: Richard Dane, "Diary (1941)," kept in a personal address book but in an official style.

68. USMHI: Frances P. Cameron, "Personal Diary."

69. UTL: Jack Muecke, "Diary," 2 November 1943.

70. Dunn, 21 February 1945.

71. PC: "Nakada Saburō," untitled pocket diary, 23–24 June 1944. Many thanks to Charles Cross.

72. John Dower, *War without Mercy,* "Yellow, Red, and Black Men," 147–180. See Chapter 5 for my discussion of race.

73. In 1943, Hobart participated in the Navy V-12 officer training program, sending almost one thousand men into the navy.

74. UTL: Clayton Knight, "Memorial Book," letter dated 23 April 1942; letter to his wife, dated 15 September 1941; birthday card poem, copied into diary, 16 December 1942.

75. Heggy, 4 January 1942.

76. Rich appeared at a dance wearing his "Blues," while his girlfriend (later fiancée) wore a red dress, which he noted "made quite an impression—no other uniforms at the dance." Rich, 28 February 1942.

77. Noonan, 21 January 1942.

78. Rich, 23 July 1942.

79. See Brian Victoria, *Zen at War* (New York: Weatherhill, 1997); and Helen Hardacre, *Shinto and the State, 1868–1988* (Princeton, NJ: Princeton University Press, 1989).

80. The army and navy trained priests in different locations between 1918 and 1941. From 1942 to 1944, Harvard University accepted the responsibility. For Catholic priests, Pope Pius VII established the Archdiocese for the Military Services in 1939.

81. Heggy even sneered at one of his fellow soldiers, saying, "That boy is really screwed up. I think his religion is the cause of it all, he is a 'holy roller.'" Heggy, 12 October 1942. Stanley Rich wrote to his brother that "On the 'Canal' [Guadalcanal] the boys that cracked up first were the ones who broke out the Bible every time the condition was red while those whose nerves stood up best were the ones who sang or told dirty jokes." Rich, 31 May 1944.

82. UTL: Alfred Tramposch, sketches.

83. On Guadalcanal the military still organized an honor guard, band, and several platoons in formation for mass burials. USMCA: John Towarnicki, photographs from 5 January 1943. Heggy was put on burial detail on Guadalcanal: "I don't want that detail anymore. . . . It is very downhearting." Heggy, 24 October 1942.

84. Quoted in Gregory Kasza, *The State and Mass Media in Japan, 1918–1945* (Berkeley: University of California Press, 1988), 207.

85. Florida State University, Strozier Library WWII Collection: John Savard, "V-mail," 3 March 1944.

86. UTL: Lyle [no last name included] correspondence with wife and son, 25 February 1942. In another letter to his wife dated 29 December 1941, Lyle simply wrote, "There isn't much to say about the war as the newspapers carry an account of it and you have already seen them." His son noted some time later that this "is not like my father at all! Probably they were instructed not to discuss the attack."

87. UTL: John R. Long, Correspondence with wife, 9 September 1944.

88. Paul E. Spengler, correspondence, in Andrew Carroll, ed., *War Letters: Extraordinary Correspondence from American Wars* (New York: Scribner, 2001), 185–186, 17 December 1941.

89. As Michael S. Sweeney described in *Secrets of Victory: The Office of Censorship and the American Press and Radio in World War II* (Chapel Hill: University of North Carolina Press, 2001), however, Roosevelt had already laid the foundation of government control of information pertaining to the military by 1938. The 1942 Voluntary Censorship Code resembled the "self-censorship" procedures in Japan.

90. Edgar Rice Burroughs, for example, interviewed men on the battlefield. Sharpe, 6 February 1943. Burroughs disliked being remembered for *Tarzan.*

91. Richard Tregaskis, *Guadalcanal Diary* (New York: Random House, 1943), 9 (27 July 1942), 233 (14 September), 26 (3 August, in which Tregaskis described the marines' discovery that he was a correspondent and how they tried to "get their names in the paper"), 239 (15 September), 182 (1 September), 121 (19 August, in which Tregaskis referred to the Japanese as the prisoner's "disagreeable ilk"), 212 (7 September), 21 (1 August).

92. Paul Fussell, *The Great War and Modern Memory* (Oxford: Oxford University Press, 2000), 158.

93. Rich, 28 June 1942.

94. Ibid., letter dated 31 May 1944.

95. SuPM: "Marumoto Hideshi" hōkōsei, "Zakkichō / shūyōroku," 14 April 1942.

96. KSDFM: Unsigned, "Tokkō nikki," entry from late September or early October 1945.

97. Tsuchida Shōji, *Tokkō nisshi,* ed. Hayashi Eidai (Osaka: Tōhō shuppan, 2003), 17 October 1942, 24 February 1944.

98. USMHI: Obara Fukuzō, "Gekisen," with 1976 translation by Edward J. Rasmussen, 30 October 1944. I have made some slight changes to Rasmussen's translation.

99. Nishimura Masaharu, *Yokaren nikki* (Kumamoto: Kumamoto Nichinichi Shinbun jōhō sentā, 2003), 245 [22 July 1945].

100. Nakamura Tokurō, "Shūyōroku nisshi," in Wadatsumi-kai, ed., *Tennō heika no tame nari* (Tokyo: Komichi shobō, 1986), 44 [7 December 1942].

101. Frank Gibney, *Sensō: Japanese Remember the Pacific War* (New York: Sharpe, 1995), 52–53.

102. Oki Seiichi, "Nikki," *Tsuchi no sazamegoto* (Tokyo: Kōdansha, 1968), 72.

103. SuPM: "Ishiguro Ken," sketches, probably between 1943 and 1945.

104. William Heggy described how a man who neglected his cap was ordered to tell everyone he saw, "I don't have a hat on because I have no brains to cover." Heggy, 12 January 1942. One of the most common examples of creating community through physical abuse was how "pollywogs" were turned into "shellbacks" when soldiers crossed the equator for the first time. Joseph Griffith described the initiation rites as including "liberal use of red paint, multitudinous shocking devices, paddling, eating of soap, drinking of kerosene, drinking in the waters of

the Pacific and general bodily punishment." USMCA: Joseph Griffith, "Diary," 24 April 1942. See USNA: Earl L. Sackett Papers, Box 1: Flave J. George, "Diary," 4 June 1942, which contains an original photograph.

105. When delivering official reports, servicemen used their surname and rank: for example, "Private First Class Nakane." This did not apply to the Imperial Navy, where even the lowest-ranking sailors could refer to themselves with the polite form for "I" *(watakushi)* before superiors. Noguchi Fumio, *Kaigun nikki: Saikakyūhei no kiroku* (Tokyo: Bungei shunju, 1982), 22.

106. Wadatsumi-kai, ed. *Tennō heika no tame nari* (Tokyo: Komichi shobō, 1986), 32. This term was explained as it appeared in the diary of Nakamura Tokurō, 14 October 1942.

107. Thomas Serier, in describing life on troopships, echoed Azuma Shirō (see Chapter 2) when he wrote that "All books and reading materials are passed around until everybody has read them," and books about war were numerous. USMCA: Thomas Serier, "Diary of a U.S. Marine of World War II," 21 January 1943. Naval vessels and military command headquarters also often had a library.

108. UTL: Walter Lee, "Diary Excerpts," composed sometime between 26 September 1939 and 17 November 1944. William Heggy noted: "Rumors are called 'scuttle bug [written above:] butt' Anything you don't like is 'shit for the birds.' Anything hard is 'tough shit' Sailors are called 'swab jockies' army boys are 'dog faces.'" Heggy, 29 February 1942.

109. "Rōtarii: Heitaigo," *Shūkan asashi,* 11 December 1949, 21. These Chinese terms were printed in glossaries at the back of blank diaries for those serving in China.

110. Walter Lee, 1945.

111. Griffith had his first "date" with a "half-casce [Caucasian?] native girl" only three weeks after writing that he "missed Mary [his fiancée] terribly." Griffith, 26, 6 May 1942 ["give me hell" quote on 14 January 1943].

112. USMCA: James B. O'Leary, "Diary for One Year [O'Leary writes in "Five Years"]," 3 January 1942. O'Leary claimed that there were over one hundred prostitutes in attendance.

113. George had to "step hard on" an engineer who began a highly profitable loan shark operation, where "most of the youngsters on board were easy meat." F. J. George, 2 July 1942.

114. USMHI: George F. Gallion, "Diary," 18 March 1944.

115. William Sharpe, frontispiece.

116. Noonan, untitled document, 1 January 1943. Griffith, too, noted that he was keeping the diary for his family and his fiancée but that he would use it as a "guide for future narrative," suggesting that he would edit it for them later. Griffith, 2 July 1942.

117. RIPM: "Ichikawa Jūzō," "Memo-chō," 1940–1941. The blank document was printed in 1939 by Gotō shoten in Osaka.

118. UTL: Edward Hickman, "Diary," 19 November 1943.

119. Rich, "Addendum #2."

120. Griffith, 23 June 1942.

121. Nakamura, 8, 15 December 1942. The "hundred demon night parade" is a staple of Japanese horror fiction from the premodern era. Toriyama Sekien's version depicted a chaotic world of monsters and devils.

122. USMHI: Eugene Boardman papers, U.S. G-2 documents.

123. This private correspondence was quoted by Bozena Karwowska in "Czeslaw Milosz's Self-Representation in English-Speaking Countries," *Canadian Slavonic Papers* (Sept.–Dec. 1998).

124. Linderman, *The World within War,* 219.

125. Officers of lower rank who had good handwriting, composition, and artistic skills might be assigned the duty of keeping the official log; this would be mimeographed, as it was in the East Asian military context as well. UTL, "Log of the USS Lincoln," contains narrative sections and battle reports.

126. Louis Morton, "Bataan Diary of Major Achille C. Tisdelle," *Military Affairs* 11:3 (Autumn 1947), 131.

127. See note 19 in the Introduction for the literature on the USSR. On Soviet subjectivity, also see Stephen Kotkin, *Magnetic Mountain: Stalinism as Civilization* (Berkeley: University of California Press, 1997).

128. Chiang would later claim to have advised Sun Yat-sen and other leaders of the GMD early on about the dangers of associating with the USSR. Chiang Kai-shek, *Soviet Russia in China* (New York: Farrar, Straus and Cudahy, 1957).

129. Rich, 6 August 1942.

130. Vladimir Stezhenskii, *Soldatskii dnevnik: Voennye stranitsy* (Moscow: Argaph, 2005), 17.

131. On the importance of nonstate actors in "modernization," see Carol Gluck, *Japan's Modern Myths: Ideology in the Late Meiji Period* (Princeton, NJ: Princeton University Press, 1987); and Sheldon Garon, *Molding Japanese Minds: The State in Everyday Life* (Princeton, NJ: Princeton University Press, 1998).

5. THE PHYSICS OF WRITING WAR

1. USMCA: M. O'Neil, "A Platoon, A Battle," introduction.

2. Richard Slotkin, *Regeneration through Violence: The Mythology of the American Frontier, 1600–1860* (Middleton, CT: Wesleyan University Press, 1973). On American masculinity, see Gail Bederman, *Manliness and Civilization: A Cultural History of Gender and Race in the United States, 1880–1917* (Chicago: University of Chicago Press, 1995), 172–173. "Indian lore" also factored largely into the Boy Scouts' program.

3. USMHI: Ralph T. Noonan, "Daily Desk Calendar," 19 December 1942.

4. Linderman, *World within War,* 143.

5. USMHI: William C. Braly, "Diary." Americans regularly consumed and saved Japanese propaganda.

6. USNHC: John C. Cash, "Five Year Diary," 11 January 1942.

7. UTL: Guy F. Landers, "Day by Day Memories," 7 August 1944.

8. USNHC: F. J. George, "Diary," 13 June and 12 August 1942. By 16 September, George was wondering "why the hell I ever wanted to be a skipper anyway . . . wishing heartily I could ask somebody what-shall-we-do-next."

9. USMCA: Harry Findley, "Diary," 6 August 1942.

10. At the very beginning of the invasion, the U.S. Navy suffered a humiliating defeat at the hands of the Japanese off of Savo Island, resulting in 1,500 crewmen's deaths. Fortunately for the Allies, the Japanese kept their main forces in New Guinea. See discussion in Morton, 325–327.

11. John Dower, *War without Mercy: Race and Power in the Pacific* (New York: Pantheon Books, 1986), 13.

12. Kawano Hitoshi suggested that, in the interest of understanding the operation of subjectivity, we think of soldiers' various reasons for fighting as cumulative, so no single reason was decisive. Kawano, "Gyokusai no shisō to hakuhei totsugeki: Guadalcanal-sen ni okeru 'banzai totsugeki' no jissō," in Aoki Tamotsu et al., eds., *Kindai Nihon bunkaron (10): Sensō to guntai* (Tokyo: Iwanami shoten, 1999), 167–168.

13. USMCA: William Sharpe, "VMJ-152: Securité en nuages," 16 October 1942.

14. Miller reported having an entire jeep stolen. USMCA: Henry Stuckert Miller, "Diary," 7 March 1943.

15. USMCA: Stanley H. Rich, "Diary," 17–18 August 1942.

16. USMCA: George M. Dunn, "A Diary," 27–28 February 1945.

17. Omi Masao, "Tanaka daitai memo," 8–20 May 1945, in *Iwate-ken kyōshi shōhei no kiroku* (Morioka: Iwate Prefecture Society for the Records of Local Servicemen, 1978), 567.

18. Jōji Tsutomu, "Jōji nikki," in Fujita Yoshirō and Yoshikawa Kinzō, eds., *Kono issen* (Kigyō kōronsha, 31 October 1976), 116 [29 March 1945].

19. USMCA: Lieutenant Watanabe, [no title; personal diary notebook], 6–8 June 1942.

20. Rich, 23 July 1942.

21. Sharpe, 2 November 1942.

22. UTL: Robert Muse, "Diary," 17 August, 23 August 1942 (the previous day they received Grumman and SBD fighters, after which Muse wrote, "Thank Goodness. Feel a lot better now"). Stanley Rich referred to the experience of Japanese bombardment as being filled with "a most helpless feeling." Rich, 7 August 1942.

23. George, 19 September 1942.

24. Richard B. Frank described in detail the competitiveness and mutual distrust between naval and army officers, as well as the strained relations between the General Staff and the field commanders. Richard B. Frank, *Guadalcanal: The Definitive Account of the Landmark Battle* (New York: Penguin, 1990), especially chapter 2.

25. Quoted in Frank, *Guadalcanal,* 61; and see discussion in Chapter 3.

26. Miller, 10 March 1943.

27. Findley, 16 July 1942.

28. George, 28 October 1942.

29. USMCA: Joseph Griffith, "Diary," 2 June 1942. He went on to say: "As far as I am concerned, the Bri is breaking up. Capt. CB Cross is ruining 'B' Co, while Colonel Puller and Major Rogers, both highly incompetent, are tearing down what was once a fair Bri. I have not been overlooked in the many stupid purges and everyday sees some new sort of fight between myself and the reigning hierarchy over the disposition of my men."

30. Findley, 1 and 5 August 1942. I have removed the infantryman's name for the sake of privacy.

31. Muse, 18 September 1942.

32. Heggy landed with Vandegrift's Marine Corps First Division. He wrote in desperation entries such as "I am about done in + sometimes don't care if I get shot or not" and "Our own men are as dangerous as the Japs. . . . God I wish I was home." USMCA: William Heggy, "Perpetual Date Book," 8–9 August 1942. Even the fear of conflict could make a soldier want to reject the whole idea of the war: Cash wrote, "I guess that one of these days we'll see some real action. I'll probably wish that we were back on patrol again. I [am] tired of this whole thing. I wish I could go home." Cash, 18 January 1942. The next day, he complained that if he continued to be woken up in middle of the night, "I think I will run away. That is, if there was a place to run away to. I sure wish that I could get home some time. I am getting sick of this all."

33. Miller, 22 March 1943.

34. George, 2 November 1942.

35. Landers, 30 April 1945.

36. Noonan, 2 February 1942.

37. Heggy, 11 November 1942 (the day of the Armistice negotiations for the First World War, twenty-four years prior).

38. Sharpe, 3 February 1943.

39. Watanabe, 8–11 September 1942. Presumably Watanabe was killed by invading U.S. forces, because his diary fell into the hands of the U.S. Marine Corps.

40. USMCA: [Charles J. Henry Jr. Documents] Author unknown, "Kaigun nikki," 20 August 1944 and end. The sutra is "Kanzeon namubutsu yobutsu

yūinbutsu yūenbuppō sōsenjōraku gajōchōnen kanzeon bonen kanzeon nennen jōshinki nennen furishin." The story comes from the thirty-sixth chapter of the Southern Song *Annals of the Buddhist Patriarchs* (Ch. *Fozu tongji,* Jp. *Busso tōki,* 1269) by the monk Zhi Pan. The incompetent general Wang Xuanmo, after fleeing from his enemies, feared execution and thus chanted the sutra to invoke Guanyin (Kannon or Kanzeon in Japanese). He later heard that his life was spared and attributed this to Guanyin. The diarist was killed, like his friend, by the American air attacks, and his diary was collected by the U.S. Marine Corps.

41. Noonan, 21 January and 31 October 1942.

42. Muse, 13 September 1942.

43. UTL: Jack Muecke, "Diary," 3–4 February 1944.

44. Rich, 19 August 1942.

45. USMCA, Eugene Boardman Documents: 2nd Lieutenant Yokota Hiroshi, "War Diary," 6 October 1942. Yokota, like many Americans, wrote frankly that "the fever," which reduced his troop strength by one-third, is "more dreadful than enemy bullets."

46. Miller, for example, simply wrote, "Six Japs being hunted here yesterday. Two others came in to give up—a soldier split one's head with a bayonet before the surrender was complete." Miller, 29 March 1943.

47. Heggy, 10, 22, 16 August 1942.

48. Heggy frequently noted that keeping his diary was a dangerous act. On 3 October 1942, he deliberately disobeyed a general order for all men to turn in their diaries but consoled himself by adding "if anything happens will see that it is destroyed before falling into enemy hands."

49. Noonan, 24 January 1943.

50. UTL: Nakamura Kan, "Diary," translated by Musgrove (on 15 April 1943), 9–10, 12 November 1942.

51. USMHI: "Japanese Diary (last entries)," translated by U.S. Army, entry dated 24 December 1942. The name of the author and translator are unknown.

52. Nakamura, 21 November 1942.

53. USMHI: "Takagi Yoshito," "Excerpts from a Captured Japanese Diary," translated by U.S. Army, entry dated 13 January 1943. The author and translator are unknown, but I have appended this name for the sake of convenience.

54. Nakamura, 21 December 1942.

55. Takagi, 14 January 1943.

56. USMHI: 1st Lieutenant "Oe," "Diary," translated by U.S. Army, entry dated 9 January 1943. The author's name was unclear, and the translator's name is unknown.

57. Nakamura, 21 December 1942.

58. Jōdō shinshū chaplains were particularly guilty in this regard. Sōtō Zen priests also supported militaristic discourse: Brian Victoria, *Zen at War* (New York: Weatherhill, 1997).

59. USMHI: Charles V. Trent, "Diary of the Admiralty Islands Campaign (typed document dated 21 April 1944)," 3 March 1944.

60. USMCA: Richard Madison Preston, "Regarding His Experiences as a U.S. Marine in World War II," 2–3.

61. This tendency was most pronounced among marines who had seen action in the South Pacific. Joseph Griffith, after noting how a marine who "went out of his head" during a mission killed a comrade, wrote, "I'm afraid we can expect a lot of these things from now on. I'm keeping a damn sharp eye on my boys." Griffith, 6 June 1942. William Heggy also noted widespread abuse. Japanese accounts of physical abuse within the armed forces are almost too numerous to mention.

62. John Gaitha Browning, *An Artist at War: The Journal of John Gaitha Browning* (Denton: University of North Texas Press, 1994), 234 [21 August 1944].

63. Sharpe, 6 February 1943.

64. UTL: Meeks Vaughn, "Personal Calendar, 1944," 29 March, 23 May, 24 April 1944.

65. Susan A. Brewer, *Why America Fights: Patriotism and Propaganda from the Philippines to Iraq* (Oxford: Oxford University Press, 2009), 89.

66. Sharpe, 17 November 1942.

67. Quoted in Larry Smith, *Iwo Jima: World War II Veterans Remember the Greatest Battle of the Pacific* (New York: W. W. Norton, 2008), 53.

68. Linderman, *World within War*, 159, 172.

69. Quoted in Emiko Ohnuki-Tierney, *Kamikaze, Cherry Blossoms, and Nationalisms: The Militarization of Aesthetics in Japanese History* (Chicago: University of Chicago Press, 2002), 197.

70. Samuel Yamashita, *Leaves from an Autumn of Emergencies: Selections from the Wartime Diaries of Ordinary Japanese* (Honolulu: University of Hawai'i Press, 2009), 27.

71. There are too many examples to be listed here, but consider soldiers' nightmares: Heggy wrote of servicemen losing their minds and that he was having nightmares, including one in which his sister died by suffocation (Heggy, 26 October 1942). Private Umehara Zenmirō wrote to his family that he "occasionally has bad dreams, so I worry about home" and asked them to be careful of house fires. See Iwate-ken nōson bunka kondankai, ed. *Senbotsu nôminheishi no tegami* (Tokyo: Iwanami Shoten, 1961), 88. Nightmares displaced trauma that soldiers experienced on the battlefield. Matsunaga Shigeo explained, "Yesterday I dreamed about Hiroshi and Takiki. I also dreamt once about father. I guess I shouldn't be having these dreams. But as far as my dreams about my younger brothers go, they said they were cold and couldn't sleep so I dreamt I gave them a wool coat. I myself was cold on account of my light clothing so maybe that's why I had the dream." Wadatsumi-kai, ed., *Kike, wadatsumi no koe* (Tokyo: Iwanami shoten, 1988), 101.

72. SNA: "Junweihui dian gebu yanfang hanjian huodong," 18 April 1941.

73. For example, Horie Sadao, a commander in the Wuhan security forces *(keibitai shireikan)*, collected oral accounts of the battles up to and including the occupation of Wuhan. NIDS: Horie Sadao, "Koe naki sensen heitan monogatari," unpublished manuscript composed between 1942 and 1975. Meanwhile, the GMD collected wartime records such as diaries and battle reports for analysis: SNA: "Gedi junshi jiangling xiang Jiang Jieshi [Chiang Kai-shek] Xu Yongchang chengbao zhenzhong riji ji zhanbao de dianbao," 1940.

74. Some Chinese even bothered to complain formally: "Xing Shaoting dengzheng qing xiang-weiyuanhui chengwen" (20 August 1941) and "Li Shiqun zhi qingxiang weiyuanhui chengwen" (15 November 1941), in Wang Mingzhe et al., eds., *Riben diguozhuyi qinhua dang'an ziliao xuanbian (13): Ri-Wang de qingxiang* (Beijing: Zhonghua shudian, 1995), 420, 424–427.

75. Hsi-sheng Ch'i, *Nationalist China at War: Military Defeats and Political Collapse* (Ann Arbor: University of Michigan Press, 1982), 51.

76. SNA: He Shaozhou, "Lujun di-2-jun di-103-shi zai Chuanjin bianqu 'qingxiao' de zhenzhong riji he jimi zuozhan riji," especially January 1940, in both the "field" and "combat" diaries.

77. MDHA: "Kongjun di-1-lu silingbu zhenzhong riji," 1 September 1939.

78. MDHA: "Kongjun di-4-dadui zhenzhong riji," 1938.

79. OIPM: "Kogawa Hideo," "Jūgun nikki," 23 November, 27 October 1938.

80. SNA: Wang Jingzong, "Di-170-shi Wang Jingzong-bu Guinan huizhan zhenzhong riji," 26 June 1940.

81. OMPM: "Hirano Seiji," "Note Book," 24 September 1939. Thanks to Moriguchi Hideo.

82. Iizuka: Heitai shōmin heiwa shiryōkan, Ōshita Toshirō, "Nikki," 17, 23 July 1944. "Spear" groups sprung up across China during the war. Japanese servicemen killed members of these militia: Iwate-ken nōson bunka kondankai, ed. *Senbotsu nôminheishi no tegami*, 72.

83. NIDS: Shirakawa Kiyoshi, "Nikki," 29 December 1942, 1 January 1943.

84. SNA: Ying Hong, "Di-105-shi zuozhan zhenzhong riji (rizhi),", 30 December 1939, on Japanese planes dropping "shameless" propaganda pamphlets.

85. RIPM (Kaji Wataru documents): "Gunjin no haha to ha," undated manuscript.

86. RIPM (Kaji Wataru documents): "Uchimura Akira," "Nikki," 29 November, 1 December 1943.

87. HuPA: Shi Fangbai, "Riji," 22 November 1939.

88. SNA: Unsigned, "Di-75-jun 6-shi Changde huizhan zhenzhong riji," 1 November 1943.

89. Prisoners taken by the GMD complained that the living conditions in Japanese "puppet forces" were "extremely dire." SNA: Ai Ai, "Di-92-shi jiuhuan Changde zuozhan jimi riji zuozhan riji," 21 November 1943.

90. Evidently, a Chinese man came running to U.S. forces while shouting, "Me Hong Kong man." Noonan reported him to have been captured in Hong Kong and "put in practically slave labor by Japs." One day later, Noonan complained about the disorderliness of the "Chinks," who wanted to "visit the Japs for just a few minutes," evidently to settle a score. Noonan, 25 January 1942.

91. Cao Tiange, "Zuozhan riji," in *Kangri zhanzheng shiqi Guomindangjun jimi zuozhan riji* (Beijing: Zhongguo dang'an chubanshe, 1995), 25 March 1944 (p. 632), 6 April (p. 633), and 26 February (p. 629). Cao was a graduate of the Huangpu Military Academy (Fourth Class).

92. Tan Heyi, "Lujun di-176-shi Minguo 31-nian 4-zhi-6-yuefen zuozhan riji," in *Kangri zhanzheng shiqi Guomindangjun jimi zuozhan riji*, 26–27 May 1942 (pp. 1325–1326).

93. SNA: Yu Shao, "Yu Shao Miandian zhanyi riji," 12–18 May 1942.

94. Wang Kejun, "Lujun di-26-shi 32-niandu chunji jimi zuozhan riji," in *Kangri zhanzheng shiqi Guomindangjun jimi zuozhan riji*, 21 February 1943 (p. 590), 15 September (p. 600), 19 October (p. 601).

95. By 23 January 1943, Li Pinxian had described action against "traitors" *(jian),* "bandits" *(fei),* and "puppets" *(wei).* Li, "Di-21-jituanjun 32-nian 1, 2, 3-yuefen zuozhan jimi rizhi," in *Kangri zhanzheng shiqi Guomindangjun jimi zuozhan riji*, 28 January 1943 (pp. 1383–1385).

96. In the 1940s, Chiang's goals mostly involved clearing former Nationalist strongholds in the south of potentially dangerous Communist forces. Gregor Benton, *New Fourth Army: Communist Resistance along the Yangtze and the Huai, 1938–1941* (Berkeley: University of California, 1999), 513.

97. John Israel, *Lianda: A Chinese University at War: A Chinese University in War and Revolution* (Stanford, CA: Stanford University Press, 1998), 296.

98. In Cao Guozhong, "Lu jun zhuanbian di-48-shi Minguo 33-niandu 1-zhi-3-yuefen jimi riji," in *Kangri zhanzheng shiqi Guomindangjun jimi zuozhan riji,* for example, on 280, Cao was ordered to "liquidate" *(jianmie)* various "guerrillas" *(youjidui).* Pro-GMD factions in Yunnan were fighting local governments organized by the CCP. Israel, *Lianda,* 297.

99. Cao Tiange, 295 [26 August 1944].

100. SNA: Unsigned, "Di-31-shi zai Yu-bianjing Deng-xian zhenzhong riji," 17 January 1943, on the organization of "Red Rifles" *(hongqianghui)* by the "Traitorous New 4th Route Army."

101. MDHA: Unsigned, "Kongjun di-5-dadui zhenzhong riji," 9 January and 30 January, 9 February 1940.

102. MDHA: Unsigned, "Kongjun hongzha zongdui zhenzhong riji," 1940.

103. Shu Jiwu, "Di-108-shi Shi Jiwu-bu jimi zuozhan riji," 21 January 1941 and "zonglun" section for September 1941, in *Kangri zhanzheng shiqi Guomindangjun jimi zuozhan riji.*

104. After the retreat from Nanjing, GMD propaganda aggressively sought foreign support. See *China at War* (Chongqing: China Information Publishing Company, from 1938 to 1945).

105. Lin Yutang, *The Vigil of a Nation* (New York: John Day, 1945), 42.

106. Barbara Tuchman, *Stilwell and the American Experience in China, 1911–1945* (New York: Grove Press, 2001). Theodore White and Annalee Jacoby described the Nationalist forces "a pulp, a tired, dispirited, unorganized mass, despised by the enemy, alien to its own people, neglected by its government, ridiculed by its allies." White and Annalee Jacoby, *Thunder out of China* (New York: William Sloane Associates, 1946), 132.

107. Yu Shao, 18, 21–22 May 1942.

108. SNA: Zhang Lingpu, "Di-74-jun 58-shi Xiangnan Tiaoyuan fujin zhenzhong riji," 3, 14 December 1943. On the record of "evil acts" *(dong'e),* see Ai Ai, 29 November 1943.

109. NA (Fatingyuan): "Gongzuo riji an," 1941.

110. Tan Heyi ordered the 176th Division to regularly generate documents: "Besides delivering their daily battle reports, at the first of every month combat units must separately submit summaries of combat results and the previous month's reports (collected [from subordinates] three times per month), but special reports on combat results must be prepared as they arrive." Tan, 1320 [28 April 1942].

111. Wang Wenrong, 20 February 1945.

112. Hans van de Ven, *War and Nationalism: 1925–1945* (London: Routledge, 2003). Van de Ven appropriately referred to the myth of consistent Nationalist inefficacy as the "Stillwell-White paradigm."

113. Muse, 10 October 1942.

114. Vaughn, 23 June 1944. Also see Cash, 6 and 8 January 1942, and Braly, propaganda clippings.

115. Dunn, 18–21 March 1945.

116. Noguchi Fumio, *Kaigun nikki: Saikakyūhei no kiroku* (Tokyo: Bungei shunju, 1982), 18 July 1945.

117. Landers, 30 June 1945.

118. Dunn, 12 March 1945.

119. Miller, 16–18 May 1944.

120. George, 24 July and 26 September 1942.

121. Sharpe, 24 October 1942. *Elephant Boy* was a 1937 British film starring Sabu Dastagir, based on Kipling's *The Jungle Book.* Sabu would later volunteer for the U.S. Army Air Force and fly B-24s, eventually winning a Distinguished Flying Cross.

122. USMCA: Thomas Serier, "Diary of a U.S. Marine of World War II," 25 January, 1 February 1943 (comparing Polynesian Samoans with the Melanesians of New Caledonia), and news clipping.

123. Heggy, 12 August 1942.

124. Griffith, 6 June 1942.

125. George, 19 June 1942. Most of the officers had "girlfriends" in Fiji. See the entry for 20 July, when a fellow officer's "best girlfriend (in Suva)" was smuggled on board for his birthday party.

126. USMCA: Robert J. Snipes, "Naval War Diary," 10 July 1945 (to the end of the war).

127. USMHI: "Confidential: Statement of Prisoner of War Concerning Attitude of Japanese on Capture and Future Return Home to Japan," January 1943.

128. Noguchi, *Kaigun nikki*. The first mention of U.S. air attacks on Okinawa and the nearby islands was 12 October 1944; on Taiwan, 13 October 1944.

129. USMHI: George F. Gallion, "Diary," 29 March 1944; and USMHI: William H. Owen, "Diary," 8 April 1944. Owen also claimed that the Filipinos were "loyal but scared of Japs."

130. USMHI: Obara Fukuzō, "Gekisen," 26 December 1944.

131. Rich, 26 July 1942. The memory of the historic adventure in the Pacific, and the rise of American power, was strong and persisted into memoirs as well: "being a land-locked boy from Ohio, I thought this was the life. Here I was, 18 years old, in the U.S. Navy, fighting the largest of any confrontation the United States had ever been engaged in, on a brand new ship headed for all sorts of adventures in the Pacific Theater of Operations"; see UTL: "One person's experience in the Pacific Theater of Operations, World War II."

132. Muecke, 22 February 1944.

133. Trent, 29 February 1944.

134. RIPM: "Matsuda Atsumu," "Jūhō nikki," 14 June 1945.

135. RIPM: "Kaichū nikki," 1 January 1943.

136. Tomiyama Ichirō, *Senjō no kioku* (Tokyo: Keizai hyōronsha, 1995), 70–73.

137. John Bodnar, *The "Good War" in American Memory* (Baltimore: Johns Hopkins University Press, 2010), chapter 6, "The Outsiders."

138. Amphibious tractors, or "amtraks" (O'Neill referred to them as "amphtracts") and LVTs (Landing Vehicle Tracked), were used for islands with shallow bays.

139. USMCA: M. O'Neill, "A Platoon, a Battle," 21 July 1944.

140. Noguchi, *Kaigun nikki*, 34 (6 October 1944). Correspondence including such epistolary niceties might be considered a "letter of doubt" *(gimonbun)*.

141. Obara, "Gekisen," 23, 31 August 1944, 27 January, 13 February 1945. Dermatophyte infections, such as athlete's foot, were a serious threat for U.S. and Japanese forces. Heggy complained of one such infection in his own diary (on 17 August 1942). On 27 October 1942, yet another infection like "poison ivy" had spread all over his body and had become an epidemic in his unit. Even common dermatophyte infections can make movement very painful, which can fatally immobilize an entire unit.

142. Jōji Tsutomu, "Jōji nikki," 31 March 1944.

143. Ibid., 20 March 1944.

144. Nomura Masaki, *Okinawa-sen haihei nikki* (Tokyo: Taihei shuppansha, 1978), 122 [5 June 1945].

145. USNHC: Francis D. Gurll, "Diary," 3 January 1945.

146. Matsuda, entries for the summer of 1945.

147. SPM: "Tokuyō nikki," 28 June 1945. This diary, kept by a Japanese nurse in a POW camp, contains many poems.

148. Findley, 6 August 1942.

149. UTL: Frank Allen, "Diary of Frank Allen," or "Frank Allen Goes to War," written roughly one year after 7 December 1941, looking back on his participation in the war.

150. Furukawa Kanzō, "P.W. ni iku," in Yoshikawa Kanezō and Fujita Yoshirō, eds., *Kono issen: Kaijō teishin dai-14 daitai no butaishi* (self-published, 1976), 256.

151. Findley, 15 July 1942.

152. USMHI: Charles V. Trent, *Souvenir Battle Diary: The 1st Cavalry Division* (Tokyo: published by the division, 1945).

153. Trent, *Souvenir Battle Diary,* 2 April 1944.

154. Sharpe, 10 November 1942.

155. Matsuda, 1 August 1945.

156. Wang Wenrong, 21 February 1945.

6. THE CONSEQUENCES OF SELF-DISCIPLINE

1. RIPM: "Kogura Isamu," "Kogura nikki," 12 March 1941 (it is unclear when he composed the notebook).

2. USMCA: George M. Dunn, "A Diary," 23 February 1945, note 7.

3. USMCA: Richard Madison Preston, "Regarding His Experiences as a U.S. Marine in World War II."

4. SJHM: Yoshikawa Kanezō and Fujita Yoshirō, *Kono issen: Kaijō teishin dai-14 daitai no butaishi* (self-published, 1976), 182.

5. Some veterans stress their particular unit's contribution to the war. USMCA: Dallas R. Bennett Documents, Memoir.

6. Tomiyama Ichirō, *Senjō no kioku* (Tokyo: Keizai hyōronsha, 1995), 18. For the "transwar" approach, see Dower's *Japan in War and Peace: Selected Essays* (New York: New Press, 1995).

7. UTL: Wiley O. Woods, "Diary," 15 August 1945.

8. Yoshimi, *Kusa no ne,* 263. Also see Dower, *Embracing Defeat: Japan in the Wake of WWII* (New York: W. W. Norton, 1999), 87–120.

9. UTL: Eben A Stephenson, correspondence.

10. UTL: Walter Lee, "Excerpts from a Diary," 1945.

11. NML: Li Bo, *Zhandi riji* (Hankou: Dashi wenku, 25 June 1938), entry dated 27 December 1937.

12. Of course, Hong Kong and Macau persisted as foreign enclaves after 1946.

13. MDHA: Unsigned, "Lujun qibingshi zhenzhong riji (qi-7-shi)," 2 September 1945.

14. Odd Arne Westad, *Decisive Encounters: The Chinese Civil War, 1946–1950* (Stanford, CA: Stanford University Press, 2003), 30. Also see the discussion in Stephen Levine, *Anvil of Victory: The Communist Revolution in Manchuria, 1945–1948* (New York: Columbia University Press, 1972).

15. Furukawa Kanzō, "P.W. ni iku," in Yoshikawa Kanezō and Fujita Yoshirō, eds., *Kono issen: Kaijō teishin dai-14 daitai no butaishi* (self-published, 1976), 257.

16. RIPM: "Tanimura Kanzō," "Wasureru na, kono kurushimi," book 1 [date of entry unclear, some time after February 1946] and 28 April 1946.

17. Furukawa, "P.W. ni iku," 268.

18. USMCA: John Long, correspondence with wife, 18 September 1945.

19. Dower, *Embracing Defeat,* 122.

20. OIPM: "Nakazawa Masaki," "Shirushi," 17 August 1945.

21. RIPM: "Matsuda Atsumu," "Jūhō nikki," 15–16 August 1945.

22. NIDS: "Rokōkyo (Lugouqiao) jiken." Sakurai primarily blamed the GMD "spirit of resistance" *(kōsen no seishin).*

23 "Lujun qibingshi," 2 September, 20 November 1945. On 28 October 1945, the diarist wrote about "cries of despair from the common people [*baixing*]" due to the CCP conscription, how Communist forces were taking over Japanese territories, and that "enemy traitor armies" were cutting communication and transportation links. Liu Shaowu stated that former "Self-Defense Forces" *(ziweidui)* in the north were voluntarily incorporated into the CCP army as irregular guerrillas. MDHA: Liu Shaowu, "Lujunshi zhenzhong riji (159-shi)," 27 October, 6 November 1945. GMD troops also reported alarming numbers of PLA forces in Hebei, possibly in the thousands. HePA: Unsigned, "Shi-shi budui qingkuang, zhenzhong riji," 24 December 1945.

24. Liu Shaowu,, 2 December 1945.

25. NA (Fatingyuan): "Hanjian-an," [the phrase *yi wei min wang* appeared in a request from the Zhejiang government to the capital concerning punishment of "traitors"]. Liu Shaowu first records arrests of "traitors" on 26 October 1945.

26. Takashi Yoshida, *The Making of the "Rape of Nanking": History and Memory in Japan, China, and the United States* (Oxford: Oxford University Press, 2006), 63.

27. Nanjing-shi dang'anguan, ed., *Shenxun Wang wei hanjian bilu* (Nanjing: Jiangsu guji chubanshe, 1992), "confessions" of Luo Junqiang (10 September 1946) and Mei Siping (15 December 1945).

28. Liu Yushu, "Zibaishu," in *Shenxun Wang wei hanjian bilu,* 1324, 1344.

29. Richard H. Minear, *Victors' Justice: The Tokyo War Crimes Trial* (Ann Arbor: Center for Japanese Studies, University of Michigan, 2001, 2nd ed.), 16.

30. For more on postwar Japanese opposition, see J. Victor Koschmann, *Revolution and Subjectivity in Postwar Japan* (Chicago: University of Chicago Press, 1996).

31. Franziska Seraphim, *War Memory and Social Politics in Japan, 1945–2005* (Cambridge, MA: Harvard University Asia Center, 2006), 90.

32. SJHM: Yamakage Hiro, "Wakakimono haru ni naita 19-sai," 2 September 1989.

33. Iide Yō, "Fukuin gakuto no kansō," in *Bungei shunju* (November 1945): 18–19.

34. For more on Hino's "culture crimes," see David M. Rosenfeld, *Unhappy Soldier: Hino Ashihei and Japanese World War II Literature* (Lanham, MD: Lexington Books, 2002).

35. Hino Ashihei, "Tsuihōsha," *Kaizō* (December 1950), 201.

36. HePA: Hao Fengyi, "Di-6-qi xueyuan biji, rijiben," 12 February 1947. In preparing for government work in Hebei, trainees like Hao were also required to study the history of the Chinese Communist Party.

37. Some enlisted men, who knew that the PLA could use captured public records in Nanjing to track them down, went directly to local CCP officials to offer up a confession. This went a long way to avoiding punishment. Personal interview, Li Gaoshan, 6 June 2004.

38. Hans H. Baerwald, "Postwar Japan: A Reminiscence," in *Japan Policy Research Institute,* Occasional Papers, no. 22 (July 2002). On the connection between perceived Communist threat and historical revision, see Takashi Yoshida, *The Making of the "Rape of Nanking,"* 53.

39. For an extended analysis and history, see Seraphim, *War Memory and Social Politics in Japan,* chapter 2.

40. The organization was originally called the Japan Bereaved Families Welfare League (Nihon izoku kōsei renmei) but changed to its current name in March 1953, when it became an official nongovernmental organization *(zaidan hōjin).* Nearly all respondents in a 2004 survey (excepting veterans who were discharged in good health) received some kind of state stipend. For example, Hamaguchi Yuki of Akita Prefecture applied for support in December 1953 and began receiving an annual award beginning in March 1954. The award amounted to, per year, 10,000 yen for the loss of her husband and 4,800 yen for herself and her two children. Kokuritsu rekishi minzoku hakubutsukan, *Sensō taiken no kiroku to katari ni kan suru shiryō chōsa 1* (Sakura, Chiba: Kokuritsu rekishi minzoku hakubutsukan, 2004), 289. Many thanks to Satō Masaya.

41. Personal interviews with Chūkiren members, 27 April 2004, Tokyo. Thanks to Hoshi Tōru.

42. Hoshi Tōru, *Watashitachi ga Chūgoku de shita koto: Chūgoku kikōsha renkakukai no hitobito* (Tokyo: Rokufū shuppan, 2002), 28.

43. See USMCA: W.A. Stiles, "Diary Notebook," 17 July 1942.

44. Isolde Standish, *Myth and Masculinity in the Japanese Cinema* (London: Routledge Curzon, 2000). For a discussion of NHK's editorial politics, see chapter 2, "Nani ga chokuzen ni kesaretaka—NHK 'towareru senji seibōryoku' kaihen wo kangaeru," in Takahashi Tetsuya, *Shōgen no poritikusu* (Tokyo: Miraisha: 2004), 113.

45. Christopher Gerteis, *Gender Struggles: Wage-Earning Women and Male-Dominated Unions in Postwar Japan* (Cambridge, MA: Harvard University Asia Center, 2009), especially chapter 4.

46. Seraphim, *War Memory and Social Politics in Japan,* 86.

47. The Committee for the Compilation of Materials on Damage Caused by the Atomic Bombs in Hiroshima and Nagasaki, *Hiroshima and Nagasaki: The Physical, Medical, and Social Effects of the Atomic Bombings,* trans. Eisei Ishikawa and David L. Swain (London: Hutchinson, 1981), 572.

48. See the description in Committee for the Compilation of Materials, *Hiroshima and Nagasaki,* 575–585.

49. Kinoshita Hanji, *Nihon uyoku no kenkyū* (Tokyo: Gendai hyōronsha, 1977), 240–246.

50. Inoue Kiyoshi, *Nihon no gunkokushugi IV: Saigunbi to gunkokushugi no fukkatsu* (Tokyo: Gendai hyōronsha, 1977), 256.

51. Gordon's description of the reemergence of the pro-company Tōshiba union is a typical example: Andrew Gordon, *The Evolution of Labor Relations in Japan: Heavy Industry, 1853–1955* (Cambridge, MA: Harvard University Press, 1988), 371–372.

52. Sheldon Garon, *Molding Japanese Minds: The State in Everyday Life* (Princeton, NJ: Princeton University Press, 1995), 153.

53. Yamashita Hajime, "Kai no undō no kihon hōshin," *Wadatsumi no koe* 1 (1959), quoted in Fukuma Yoshiaki, *"Sensō taiken" no sengoshi: Sedai, kyōyō, ideorogī* (Tokyo: Chūō kōron shinsha, 2009), 96.

54. Fukuma, *"Sensō taiken" no sengoshi,* 98–99.

55. Takashi Yoshida, *The Making of the "Rape of Nanking,"* 88.

56. Matsuoka Tamaki, ed., *Nankin-sen: Tōzasareta kioku wo tazunete, motohei-shi 102-nin no shōgen* (Tokyo: Shakai hyōronsha, 2002); and Arai Toshio and Fujiwara Akira, ed., *Shinryaku no shōgen: Chūgoku ni okeru Nihonjin senpan jihitsu kyōjutsusho* (Tokyo: Iwanami shoten, 1999).

57. Honda Katsuichi, "Gonin no taikenshi," in Fujiwara Akira, ed., *Nankin daigyakusatsu no genba he* (Tokyo: Asahi Shinbunsha, 1988), 174.

58. Lisa Yoneyama, *Hiroshima Traces: Time, Space, and the Dialectics of Memory* (Berkeley: University of California Press, 1999).

59. On debates over Korean victims of the atomic bomb, see ibid. On Korean servicemen in the Japanese army, see Hayashi Eidai, [*Sengō 50-nenme no kenshō*] *Wasurareta Chōsenjin kōgun heishi: Shiberia dassōki* (Fukuoka: Kanshoin, 1996).

Taiwanese subjects are also featured in Japanese publications, such as Chen Huimei's *Taiwanjin jūgun kangofu tsuisōki: Sumire no hana ga saita koro* (Tokyo: Tentensha, 2002).

60. As Yoshimi Yoshiaki found, even public documents are not safe from the reach of Japan's libel laws. After the publication of his book on "comfort women," several documents were marked "restricted" by the NIDS archives at the demand of their original authors and their families.

61. This information came out of a series of conversations with members of the Nankin Daigyakusatsu Kenkyūkai (Research Group on the Nanjing Massacre) during a 2003 meeting.

62. The Japanese textbook controversy of the 1980s seemed to have provided the impetus for such activities. Ian Buruma, *The Wages of Guilt: Memories of War in Germany and Japan* (New York: Meridian, 1995), 126.

63. Xu Zhongmao, "Zhonggong zhengquan yu kangri qingjie," *Zhongguo shibao*, 20 September 1995, as cited in Chang Jui-te, "The Politics of Commemoration: A Comparative Analysis of the Fiftieth Anniversary Commemoration in Mainland China and Taiwan of the Victory in the Anti-Japanese War," in Diana Lary and Stephen MacKinnon, eds., *Scars of War* (Vancouver: UBC Press, 2001).

64. Takashi Yoshida, *The Making of the "Rape of Nanking,"* chapter 8.

65. ASMH: Zhengxie wenshi ziliao gongzuo zu, ed., *Kangzhan shengli 40-zhounian jinian tekan* (Nanjing: self-published, 1985), afterword.

66. Deng Lingxiang et al., eds., *Zhongqiu fenglei* (Zhengzhou: Henan renmin chubanshe, 1985), 2, 261, 181.

67. The most famous survivor's testimony is probably Zhu Chengshan, ed., *Qinhua Rijun Nanjing datusha xincunzhe zhengyan-ji* (Nanjing: Nanjing daxue chubanshe, 1994).

68. Rana Mitter, "China's 'Good War:' Voices, Locations and Generations in the Interpretation of the War of Resistance to Japan," in Sheila Jager and Rana Mitter, eds., *Ruptured Histories: War and Memory in Post-Cold War Asia* (Cambridge, MA: Harvard University Press, 2009).

69. Fan Jianchuan, *Yi ge ren de kangzhan: Cong yige ren de cangpin kan yichang quan minzu de zhanzheng* (Beijing: Zhongguo duiwai fanyi chuban gongsi, 2002), 51.

70. Personal interview, Zhu Chengshan, 12 June 2004.

71. James Reilly, "The Rebirth of *Minjian Waijiao:* China's Popular Diplomacy toward Japan," in Chiho Sawada, ed., *Public Diplomacy, Counterpublics, and the Asia Pacific* (Stanford, CA: Stanford University Press, 2009).

72. Daqing Yang, "The Challenges of the Nanjing Massacre: Reflections on Historical Memory," in Joshua Fogel, ed., *The Nanjing Massacre in History and Historiography* (Berkeley: University of California Press, 2000), 151.

73. James Reilly, "China's History Activists and Sino-Japanese Relations," *China: An International Journal* 4:2 (2006).

74. Leo T. S. Ching, "Give Me Japan and Nothing Else! Postcoloniality, Identity, and the Traces of Colonialism," *South Atlantic Quarterly* 99:4 (2000).

75. Allen Chun, "From Nationalism to Nationalizing: Cultural Imagination and State Formation in Postwar Taiwan," *Australian Journal of Chinese Affairs* 31 (1994), and "Fuck Chineseness: On the Ambiguities of Ethnicity as Culture as Identity," *boundary 2* 23:2 (Summer 1996).

76. Chang, "The Politics of Commemoration," 155.

77. Ts'ai Caroline Hui-yu, ed., *Zouguo liangge shidai de ren: Taiji Ribenbing* (Taipei: Zhongyang yanjiuyuan Taiwan-shi yanjiusuo choubeichu, 1997).

78. Tomiyama, *Senjō no kioku*, 92.

79. A brief account, in English, on memoirs of note up to 1951 is offered in Nobutaka Ike, "Japanese Memoirs—Reflections of the Recent Past," *Pacific Affairs* 24:2 (June 1951).

80. This term *(fujunkasei zenshin suijakushō)* was a navy medical euphemism for malnutrition and starvation.

81. Noguchi Fumio, *Kaigun nikki: Saikakyūhei no kiroku* (Tokyo: Bungei shunju, 1982), 242–244.

82. Iizuka: Heitai shōmin heiwa shiryōkan: Ōshita Toshirō, "Nikki," 1944–1945.

83. Rich, 11 October 1944.

84. Emily S. Rosenberg, *A Date Which Will Live: Pearl Harbor in American Memory* (Durham, NC: Duke University Press, 2003); and John Bodnar, *The "Good War" in American Memory* (Baltimore: Johns Hopkins University Press, 2010).

85. USMCA: Henry Stuckert Miller, "Introduction."

86. As stated in Chapter 4, veterans' slang and jargon make them especially difficult to understand: Fujiwara Akira, ed., *Nankinsen*, 50–54.

87. Nagai Takashi's *Bells of Nagasaki* (1946) was arguably the first important work, followed by Hara Tamiki's "Summer Flower" (1947), Ibuse Masuji's *The Crazy Iris* (1951), Ota Yōko's *Fireflies* (1953), and Hachiya Michihiko's *Hiroshima Diary* (1955). Other important collections survivors' accounts have appeared as well but not in translation: *Nagasaki—Nijūni'nin no genbaku taiken kiroku* (1949), *Genbaku taikenki* (1950), and *Genbaku ni ikite—Genbaku higaisha no shuki* (1953).

88. Takahashi Yoshinori, "Senyūkai wo tsukuru hitobito," in Kyōdō kenkyū, ed., *Senyūkai* (Tokyo: Impakuto shuppankai, 2005), 110–111.

89. Amano Masako noted the 1960s rise in veterans' associations in her book *"Tsukiai" no sengoshi: Sākuru nettowāku no hiraku jihei* (Tokyo: Yoshikawa genbunkan, 2005). Still, Takahashi Saburō's data showed that, although 1965 was the peak, veterans' groups were assembled throughout the postwar period. Takahashi Saburō, *Senkimono wo yomu: Sensō taiken to sengō Nihon shakai* (Kyoto: Akademia shuppan, 1988), shiryō 17.

90. Ibid., Takahashi.

91. Takashi Yoshida, *The Making of the "Rape of Nanking,"* 59.

92. Philip Gabriel, "The Alphabet of Trauma: Shimao Toshio and the Narrative of Dreams," *Journal of the Association of Teachers of Japanese* 30:2 (Oct. 1996).

93. Also see Seraphim, *War Memory and Social Politics in Japan,* chapter 5.

94. Hosaka Masayasu, *"Kike wadatsumi no koe" no sengoshi* (Tokyo: Bungei shunju, 1999), "Wadatsumi no koe no tanjō."

95. David Stahl's study of Ōoka also combined biography with the critical examination of his literature: *The Burdens of Survival: Ōoka Shōhei's Writings on the Pacific War* (Honolulu: Hawai'i University Press, 2003). Also see Keiko McDonald, "Ooka's Examination of the Self in *A POW's Memoirs,*" *Journal of the Association of Teachers of Japanese* 21:1 (April 1987).

96. *Iwate-ken kyōshi shōhei no kiroku* (Morioka: Iwate Prefecture Society for the Records of Local Servicemen, 1978), 116.

97. Hamaen Kasayoshi, *Suiheisen: Soromon kara Okinawa tokkō made reisen / kanbō tajōin no kiroku* (Chiran: Chiran tokkō heiwa kaikan, 12 June 1998), 72.

98. ASMH: Liu Ziqing, *Congjun sanshi-nian* (Taipei: self-published, 1954), introduction and p. 154.

99. ASMH: Li Zhenqing, *Kangri shenluan canyu zhanyi huiyi jilu* (Taipei: self-published, 1956), 13, 61.

100. Oral History Series No. 4 was an extended interview with General Bai Chongxi (2nd edition published in 1985 by the Institute of Modern History), and in 1997 the Institute published an entire issue dedicated to Taiwanese who served in the Japanese military.

101. Yoshimi Yoshiaki, "Nicchū sensō to kokumin undō," *Rekishi hyōron,* 7:447 (1987).

102. Personal interview with Ono Kenji, 15 May 2004.

103. Hayashi Eidai, *[Kikigaki] Taketomi Tomioz-den: Yakōbana: Heishi / shomin no sensō shiryōkan* (Tokyo: Shōba shuppansha, 2000), 260–261.

104. Kawakami Yoshimitsu, *Ani no senki,* ed. Kawakami Yoshinobu (Osaka: Osaka karuchā sentā, self-published, 1985), introduction, 2–3.

105. Azuma Shirō, *Waga Nankin puratōn: Hito meishūhei no taiken shita Nankin daigyakusatsu* (Tokyo: Aoki shoten, 1996, new edition), introduction, 2–3.

106. Kokuritsu rekishi minzoku hakubutsukan, *Sensō taiken,* 586.

107. Chang Li et al., interview, *Haijun renwu fangwen jilu, di-1-pian* (Zhongyang yanjiuyuan jindaishi yanjiusuo: Koushu lishi congshu 71, 1997), 59, 27, 23.

108. Hui-yu Caroline Ts'ai, "The War Never Ended: The War Compensation Movement in Taiwan," in David P. Barrett and Larry N. Shyu, eds., *China in the Anti-Japanese War: Politics, Culture, and Society* (New York: Peter Lang, 2001), 214–215.

109. During my 2004 interview, Azuma Shirō was bullied by right-wing thugs at his home after the publication of *Wa ga Nankin puratōn* (1988), but their tactics inspired in him "overblown feelings of resistance" *(yokei na teikōkan).*

110. Conservative forces routinely attempt to discredit and silence veterans. During the Fifty-Ninth Division Veterans Association's Pacification of Spirits Ceremonies *(ireisai)* from 1962 to 1967, Fujita Shigeru wrote in his Note of Veneration *(saibun)* that "we have engaged in acts of brutality [*zangyaku na gyōgi*]" and "we are also praying for the spirits of the Chinese [who died during the war]." He was heavily criticized by the Izokukai, Yasukuni Shrine, and the relatives of soldiers but not by most of his fellow veterans.

111. Kimura Hisao, notes written in the margins of Tanabe Hajime's *Tetsugaku tsūron* (1933), in Wadatsumi-kai, ed., *Heiwa e no isho / ihinten: Senbotsu seinen to no taiwa* (Tokyo: Wadatsumi-kai, 10 August 2002), 27 [probably in early 1946].

112. Tomiyama, *Senjō no kioku,* 141–146.

CONCLUSION

1. Anthony Swofford, *Jarhead: A Marine's Chronicle of the Gulf War and Other Battles* (New York: Scribner, 2003), 14.

2. Yoshida Mitsuru, *Requiem for Battleship Yamato,* trans. Richard Minear (Annapolis: Naval Institute Press, 1999), 147.

3. Xiaofei Tian, *Visionary Journeys: Travel Writing from Early Medieval and Nineteenth-Century China* (Cambridge, MA: Harvard University Asia Center, 2011), 76.

4. USMCA: Martin Clemens, "The Author's Approach"; for more information, see Clemens, *Alone on Guadalcanal: A Coastwatcher's Story* (Washington, DC: U.S. Naval Institute Press, 1998).

5. Sharpe, 23 September 1943.

6. Paul Fussell, *The Great War and Modern Memory* (Oxford: Oxford University Press, 2000), 79–90.

7. SNA: Huang Yong'an, "Paobing di-6-lü zai Shijiazhuang dengdi zhenzhong riji," 26 December 1937; SNA: Zhong Song, "Di-61shi duli 20-lü Sonhu huizhan zhenzhong riji," 3 November 1937.

8. "Nagatani Masao," "Techō" (Takamatsu: Takamatsu-shi heiwa shiryōshitsu), 6 September 1937.

9. Kimura Genzaemon, *Nicchū sensō shussei nikki* (Akita: Mumeisha shuppan, 1982), 1 December 1938.

10. See discussion in Fussell, *Great War,* 185.

11. UTL: William A. McClain, "Diary," 14 November 1944.

12. Jochen Hellbeck, *Revolution on My Mind* (Cambridge, MA: Harvard University Press, 2006), 5.

13. Thomas Lahusen, *How Life Writes the Book: Real Socialism and Socialist Realism in Stalin's Russia* (Ithaca, NY: Cornell University Press, 1997), 85.

14. USMCA: William Sharpe, "VMJ-152: Securité en nuages," 10 November 1942.

15. USMCA: M. O'Neill, "A Platoon, a Battle," 29 August 1944.

16. For an account accessible to nonspecialists, see David J. Linden, *The Accidental Mind: How the Brain Has Given Us Love, Memory, Dreams, and God* (Cambridge, MA: Belknap Press of Harvard University Press, 2007). In fact, psychologists have long argued that humans favor the construction of an articulated, coherent narrative over factual accounting of influences (many of which are, of course, subconscious). See R. E. Nisbett and T. D. Wilson, "Telling More than We Know: Verbal Reports on Mental Processes," *Psychological Review* 84 (1977); and, more recently, M. S. Gazzaniga, "Consciousness and the Cerebral Hemispheres," in M. S. Gazzaniga, ed., *The Cognitive Neurosciences* (Cambridge, MA: MIT Press, 1995).

17. Allan Young, "Suffering and the Origins of Traumatic Memory," *Daedalus* 125:1 (Winter 1996), 261. In fact, traumatic experience results in a reduction of the hippocampus, visible through functional MRI, which is responsible for much of the brain's memory functions. J. D. Bremner, P. R. Randall, T. M. Scott, R. A. Bronen, R. C. Delaney, J. P. Seibyl, S. M. Southwick, G. McCarthy, D. S. Charney, and R. B. Innis, "MRI-Based Measurement of Hippocampal Volume in Posttraumatic Stress Disorder," *American Journal of Psychiatry* 152 (1995). In this sense, experiencing psychological trauma can be compared with physical brain damage to the most important area in the creation and maintenance of memory.

18. Anonymous, "Dong zhanchang de yijiao," in Yu Yanling et al., *Zhanshi de shouji* (Hankow: Ziqiang chubanshe, February 1938), 4 September 1937.

19. USMCA: Stanley H. Rich, "Diary," 9 October 1942 (describing the previous week's action).

20. USMCA: Henry Stuckert Miller, "Diary," 13 April 1944.

21. Michel Foucault, "Self-Writing," in Paul Rabinow, ed., *Ethics: Subjectivity and Truth* (New York: New Press, 1998), 209.

22. Henrietta Harrison, *The Man Awakened from Dreams: One Man's Life in a North China Village, 1857–1942* (Stanford, CA: Stanford University Press, 2005), 12.

23. Catherine Merridale, *Ivan's War: Life and Death in the Red Army, 1939–1945* (New York: Metropolitan Books, 2006), 375.

24. Fussell, *Great War,* 170.

25. USMCA: Joseph Griffith, "Diary," 2 July 1942.

26. UTL: Clayton Knight, typed manuscript, 40–42 [9 September 1945].

27. Linderman, *World within War*, 55.

28. SMA: Wang Wenrong, "Gongzuo riji," 20 May 1945.

29. Quoted in Fukuma Yoshiaki, *"Sensō taiken" no sengoshi: Sedai, kyōyō, ideorogī* (Tokyo: Chūō kōron shinsha, 2009), 212.

30. Michel Foucault, "The Subject and Power," *Critical Inquiry* 8: 4 (Summer 1982), 777–795.

Bibliography of War Diaries

This book involved the analysis of over two hundred diaries (and many other primary documents), but not every text could be included. Only diaries cited in the text are listed here.

"Adachi Ei'ichi," "Nisshi" (SHM).

Ai Ai, "Di-92-shi jiuhuan Changde zuozhan jimi riji zuozhan riji" (SNA).

Akiyama Toyochi, "Nisshi" (NIDS).

Allen, Frank, "Diary of Frank Allen," or "Frank Allen Goes to War" (written roughly one year after 7 December 1941, UTL).

"Arai Yasujirō," "Nikki" (KSDFM).

Azuma Shirō, "Nikki" (manuscript) and *Azuma Shirō nikki* (Kumamoto: Kumamoto shuppan bunka kaikan, 2001).

Braly, William C., "Diary" (USMHI).

Browning, John Gaitha, *An Artist at War: The Journal of John Gaitha Browning* (Denton: University of North Texas Press, 1994).

Bunker, Paul D., *Bunker's War: The World War II Diary of Col. Paul D. Bunker,* ed. Keith Barlow (Novato, CA: Presidio Press, 1996).

Cai Yizhong, "Zhanshi de shouji," in Yu Yanling et al., *Zhanshi de shouji* (Hankow: Ziqiang chubanshe, February 1938).

Cameron, Frances P., "Personal Diary" (USMHI).

Cash, John C., "Five Year Diary" (USNHC).

Cheney, Paul E., "WWI Sergeant of the Guard Book" (USMCA).

De Asis, Leocadio, *From Bataan to Tokyo: Diary of a Filipino Student in Wartime Japan, 1943–1944* (New York: Paragon Book Gallery, 1979).

"Deng Huanguang," "Di-64-shi Qinan yidai zhenzhong riji" (SNA).

Dunn, George M., "A Diary" (USMCA).

Fertig, Wendell W., "Diary" (USMHI).

Fletcher, Frank Jack, "Diary, NORPACFOR" (US NARA).

Findley, Harry, "Diary" (USMCA).

Furukawa Kanzō, "P.W. ni iku," in Yoshikawa Kanezō and Fujita Yoshirō, eds., *Kono issen: Kaijō teishin dai-14 daitai no butaishi* (self-published, 1976).

"Fu(shi)zhang-chu," "Di-10 jituanjun yu Zhejiang Yiwu dengdi zhenzhong riji" (SNA).

Galbraith, Robert, "Civil War Diaries" (UTL).

Gallion, George F., "Diary" and papers (USMHI).

Gao Zhihang, "Di-4 dadui zhenzhong riji" (MDHA).

George, Flave J., "Diary," (USNA, Earl L. Sackett Papers).

Griffith, Joseph, "Diary" (USMCA).

Gurll, Francis D., "Diary" (USNHC).

"Hamabe Genbei," "Jinchū nisshi" (SPM).

Hamamoto Risaburō, *Nisshin sensō jūgun hiroku* (Tokyo: Seishun shppansha, 1972).

Hamazaki Tomizō, "Nisshi" (NIDS).

Hao Fengyi, "Di-6-qi xueyuan biji, rijiben" (HePA).

Hao Mengling, "Zhenzhong riji," in *Zhenzhong riji* (Wuhan: Zhanshi chubanshe, January 1938).

"Hara Kinosuke," "Tōyō nikki" (KSDFM).

Heggy, William, "Perpetual Date Book" (USMCA).

He Shaozhou, "Lujun di-2-jun di-103-shi zai Chuanjin bianqu 'qingxiao' de zhenzhong riji he jimi zuozhan riji" (SNA).

Hickman, Edward, "Diary" (UTL).

"Hirano Seiji," "Note Book" (OMPM).

Hopkins, Bernard O., "Diary" (USMHI).

Huang Xing, "Wuchang liang riji" (Wuhan: Xinhai geming bowuguan).

Huang Yong'an, "Paobing di-6-lü zai Shijiazhuang dengdi zhenzhong riji" (SNA).

Ichikawa Genkichi, "Kaigun nikki" (PC).

"Ichikawa Jūzō," "Memo-chō" (RIPM).

Ijichi Hikojirō, "Gunkan Mikasa senji nisshi" (NIDS).

"Inoue Yasuji," "Techō" (OIPM).

Ishida Gi'ichi, *Sensen no jitsuroku* (self-published, 1977).

Jiang Gonggu, *Xianjing sanyueji* (Wuhan: August 1938).

Jōji Tsutomu, "Jōji nikki," in Yoshikawa Kanezō and Fujita Yoshirō, eds., *Kono issen: Kaijō teishin dai-14 daitai no butaishi* (self-published, 1976).

Kawahisa Tamomochi, "Kimitsu sakusen nisshi" (NIDS).

Kawakami Yoshimitsu, *Ani no senki,* ed. Kawakami Yoshinobu (Osaka: Osaka karuchā sentā, self-published, 1985).

Kimura Genzaemon, *Nicchū sensō shussei nikki* (Akita: Mumeisha shuppan, 1982).

Kimura Matsujirō, "Shanghai-sen jūgun nisshi" (NIDS).

Kindig, Henry A., "Diary," http://www.worldwaronediary.com/index.html.

Knight, Clayton, "Memorial Book" and "Day by Day in the Army" (UTL).

"Kogawa Hideo," "Jūgun nikki" (OIPM).

"Kogura Isamu," "Kogura nikki" (RIPM).

Landers, Guy F., "Day by Day Memories" (UTL).

Larsen, Henry L., et al., "Diary, Guam Island Commander" (US NARA).

Lee, Walter, "Diary Excerpts" (UTL).

Li Bo, *Zhandi riji* (Hankou: Dashi wenku, 25 June 1938).

Li Hongkun, "Xiaoqing nan'an zhenzhong riji" (SPA).

Lin Dafu, "Bingzhong riji," in *Xianbing zhoukan* (4 May 1938).

Liu Binghuan, "Paobing di-6-lü 12-tuan ji qi shubu zai Hebei Huolu dengdi zhenzhong riji" (SNA). Liu also included the diaries of his subordinates: Gao Jingbo, He Xiuhan, Tian Yufeng, and Zhang Kuitan..

Liu Chongzhe, "Di-52-shi zai Anhui Jing-xian yu wo 4-jun Tan Yunlin Bo Qiu choubu zhi zuozhan xiangbao ji zhenzhong riji" (SNA).

Liu Jiaqi, "Zhenzhong riji," in *Zhenzhong riji* (Wuhan: Zhanshi chubanshe, January 1938).

Liu Shaowu, "Lujunshi zhenzhong riji (159-shi)" (MDHA).

Luo Zhuoying, "Di-18jun silingbu zhenzhong riji ji Luodian shiri zhanji jian zongsiling Luo Zhuoying" (SNA), including Li Weipan's and Peng Xi's diaries.

Ma Chaojun, "Nanjing fangkong riji" (NPA).

Maeda Yoshimasa, "Jinchū nikki," in Nankin senshi henshū iinkai, ed., *Nankin senshi shiryōshū 1* (Tokyo: Self-Published, 1989).

"Marumoto Hideshi" hōkōsei, "Zakkichō / shūyōroku" (Suita: Suita-shi heiwa kinen shiryōshitsu).

"Matsuda Atsumu," "Jūho nikki" (RIPM).

McClain, William A., "Diary" (UTL).

Miller, Henry Stuckert, "Diary" (USMCA).

Miner, William, "Diary" (UTL).

Moore, D. M., Headquarters II Corps, "Diary" (USMHI).

Morrice, George A., "Diary", http://www.oryansroughnecks.org/diary.html.

Muecke, Jack, "Diary" (UTL).

Muse, Robert, "Diary" (UTL).

"Nagatani Masao," "Techō" (Takamatsu: Takamatsu-shi heiwa shiryōshitsu).

"Nakada Saburō," pocket diary (PC).

Nakamura Kan, "Diary," translated by Musgrove on April 15, 1943 (UTL).

Nakamura Tokurō, "Shūyōroku nisshi," in Wadatsumi-kai, ed., *Tennō heika no tame nari* (Tokyo: Komichi shobō, 1986).

"Nakazawa Masaki," "Shirushi" (OIPM).

Neuffer, Robert P., "Diary" (USMCA).

Newton, Willard, "The Battle of Bellicourt," http://www.cmstory.org/ww1/diary.asp.

Nishimura Masaharu, *Yokaren nikki* (Kumamoto: Kumamoto Nichinichi Shinbun jōhō sentā, 2003).

Noguchi Fumio, *Kaigun nikki: Saikakyūhei no kiroku* (Tokyo: Bungei shunju, 1982).

Nomura Masaki, *Okinawa-sen haihei nikki* (Tokyo: Taihei shuppansha, 1978).

Noonan, Ralph T., "Daily Desk Calendar" (USMHI).

Northcott, Sherwin, "Diary" (UTL).

Obara Fukuzō, "Gekisen," with 1976 translation by Edward J. Rasmussen (USMHI).

Oda Makoto, "Kimitsu: Shanghai hōmen kengaku hōkoku" (KSDFM).

"Oe" (first name unknown), "Diary," trans. U.S. Army (USMHI).

O'Leary, James B., "Diary for One Year" (USMCA).

Omi Masao, "Tanaka daitai memo," in *Iwate-ken kyōshi shōhei no kiroku* (Morioka: Iwate Prefecture Society for the Records of Local Servicemen, 1978).

"Omoto Saburō," "Jūro shussei nisshi" (RIPM).

Ono Kenji et al., ed. *Nankin daigyakusatsu wo kiroku shita kōgun heishitachi* (Tokyo: Ōtsuki shoten, 1996):

    "Honma Masakatsu," "Sentō nisshi,"

    "Kindō Eijirō," "Shussei nikki,"

    "Kurozu Tadanobu," "Jinchū nikki,"

    "Itō Kihachi," "Jinchū nikki,"

    "Saitō Jirō," "Jinchū nikki,"

    "Takahashi Teruo," "Jinchū nikki,"

    Ōdera Takashi, "Jinchū nikki,"

    "Ōuchi Toshimichi," "Jinchū nikki."

Ōshita Toshirō, "Nikki" (Iizuka: Heitai shōmin heiwa shiryōkan).

Owen, William H., "Diary" (USMHI).

Ozaki Shirō, "Sen'ei nikki," in *Taiheiyō sensō kaisen—12-gatsu 8-nichi: Shōwa sensō bungaku zenshū* (Tokyo: Shūeisha, 1964).

Preston, Richard Madison, "Regarding His Experiences as a U.S. Marine in World War II" (USMCA).

Rich, Stanley H., "Diary" (USMCA).

Sackett, Earl C., "War Diary" (USNHC).

"Sakaguchi Jirō," "Jinchū nisshi" (PC).

Serier, Thomas, "Diary of a U.S. Marine of World War II" (USMCA).

Sharpe, William, "VMJ-152: Securité en nuages" (USMCA).

Shi Fangbai, "Riji" (Wuchang: Hubei-sheng dang'anguan).

Shi Hezhang, "Zhandi riji," serialized in *Zhenzhong ribao*.

Shirakawa Kiyoshi, "Nikki" (NIDS).

Shreve, Arthur L., "Diary" (USMHI).

Stiles, W.A., "Diary Notebook" (USMCA).

Suzuki Hideo, *Senjin micchō: Wakaki gun'i no mita Nicchū sensō* (Sodo bunko, 1982).

"Takagi Yoshito," "Excerpts from a Captured Japanese Diary," trans. U.S. Army (USMHI).

"Tamura Hideto," "Shūyōroku" (Suita-shi heiwa kinen shiryōshitsu).

"Taniguchi Kazuo," "Yasen byōin nikki" (OIPM).

"Tanimura Kanzō," "Guntai nisshi," and "Rechuan [Rehe] jūgun zakki" (RIPM).

Tatsuguchi Nobu, "Diary," trans. Samuel W. Hatcher (UTL).

Tisdelle, Achille Carlisle, "Story of Bataan Collapse, 9 April, 1942" (USMHI).

Tramposch, Alfred, sketches and diary (UTL).

Trent, Charles V.:
"Diary of the Admiralty Islands Campaign" (USMHI),
Souvenir Battle Diary: The 1st Cavalry Division (Tokyo: published by the division, 1945).

Tsuchida Shōji, *Tokkō nisshi*, ed. Hayashi Eidai (Osaka: Tōhō shuppan, 2003).

"Uchimura Akira," "Nikki" (RIPM, Kaji Wataru Collection).

"Ueda Masaki," "Zakkichō," and "Notebook / Jinchū nikki" (RIPM).

Umeda Fusao, *Hokushi ten senki: Umeda Fusao jūgun nikki*, ed. Umeda Toshio (self-published, 1970).

Uwada Hiroshi, "Nikki," in Hata Ikuhito, ed., *Nankin jiken* (Tokyo: Chūō kōronsha, 1986).

Vaughn, Meeks, "Personal Calendar, 1944" (UTL).

Wang Jingguo, "Lujun di-19-jun Xinkou huizhan jingguo ji riji" (SNA).

Wang Jingzong, "Di-170-shi Wang Jingzong-bu Guinan huizhan zhenzhong riji" (SNA).

Wang Wenrong, "Gongzuo riji" (SMA).

Watanabe [no given name], diary notebook (USMCA).

Woods, Wiley O., "Diary" (UTL).

Wu Guanzhou, "Guomin gemingjun di-17-jun zi Haizhou chufa zhi gongke Linxin suijun riji" (SNA).

Yamakage Hiro, "Wakakimono haru ni naita 19-sai" (SJHM).

"Yamamoto Kenji," "Jinchū nisshi" (Kōchi: Kusa no ie heiwa shiryōkan).

Yamanaka Sadao, "Jinchū nisshi," in Shōwa sensō bungakukai, ed., *Shōwa sensō bungaku zenshū: Chūgoku he no shingeki* (Tokyo: Shūeisha, 1981).

"Yanagawa Heihachi," "Senji nikki / Senchi nikki" (Ono Kenji, personal collection).

Ye Tiaoquan, "Paobing di-6-lü di-17-tuan Hebei Huolu fujin zhenzhong riji" (SNA).

Ying Hong, "Di-105-shi zuozhan zhenzhong riji (rizhi)" (SNA).

Yokota Hiroshi, "War Diary" (USMCA, Eugene Boardman Documents).

Yu Shao, "Yu Shao Miandian zhanyi riji" (SNA).

Yu Yanling:

"Qianxian 10-tian," in *Zhanshi de shouji* (1937),

"Wo de shitian zhanzheng shenghuo," serialized in *Zhenzhong ribao* (1938).

Zhang Lingpu, "Di-74-jun 58-shi Xiangnan Tiaoyuan fujin zhenzhong riji" (SNA).

"Zhao Weiguo," "Address Book" [field diary] (OIPM).

Zhao Xitian (and subcommander Hu Songshan), "Di-3-shi zai Jiujiang yidai zuozhan zhenzhong riji" (SNA).

Zhongguo di-2 dang'anguan, ed., *Kangri zhanzheng shiqi Guomindangjun jimi zuozhan riji* (Beijing: Zhongguo dang'an chubanshe, 1995):

Cao Guozhong, "Lu jun zhuanbian di-48-shi Minguo 33-niandu 1-zhi-3-yuefen jimi riji,"

Cao Tiange, "Zuozhan riji,"

"Junshi weiyuanhui weiyuanzhang tianshui hangying jimi zuozhan riji,"

Li Pinxian, "Di-21-jituanjun 32-nian 1, 2, 3-yuefen zuozhan jimi rizhi,"

Shu Jiwu, "Di-108-shi Shi Jiwu-bu jimi zuozhan riji,"

Tan Heyi, "Lujun di-176-shi Minguo 31-nian 4-zhi-6-yuefen zuozhan riji,"

Wang Kejun, "Lujun di-26-shi 32-niandu chunji jimi zuozhan riji."

Zhong Song, "Di-61shi duli 20-lü Sonhu huizhan zhenzhong riji" (SNA).

DIARIES THAT ARE UNSIGNED OR FOR WHICH THE AUTHOR IS UNCLEAR

"1-zhanqu di-196-shi zai Henan Mengci Hengchi fujin dengdi zhenzhong riji" (SNA).

"69-jun zhenzhong riji" (SNA).

Anonymous, "Dong zhanchang de yijiao," in Yu Yanling et al., *Zhanshi de shouji* (Hankow: Ziqiang chubanshe, February 1938).

Anonymous, *Yi wei wuming yingxiong de riji* (August 1933, limited circulation, NPA).

"Blue Book" (OIPM) [Two authors].

"Di-2-jun di-3-shi zhenzhong rijilu" and "Di-2-jun paobingchu gongke Nanjing zhenzhong riji" (SNA).

"Di-2 huncheng-lü zhandou riji: Xiaoqing nan'an zhenzhong riji" (SPA).

"Di-3 dadui zhenzhong riji" (MDHA).

"Di-8-shi Songhu Wuxi dengdi zhenzhong riji" (SNA).

"Di-16 juntuan silingbu zhenzhong riji" (SNA).

"Di-29 juntuan 69-jun zhenzhong riji" (SNA).

"Di-32-shi zai Guangxi Hengxian dengdi zhenzhong riji" (SNA).

"Di-38-jun Jinan Gaoping dengdi zhenzhong riji" (SNA).

"Di-75-jun 6-shi Changde huizhan zhenzhong riji" (SNA).

"Duli paobing di-1-tuan xingjun biji" (SNA).

"Guomin gemingjun si-4-jun beifa zhenzhong riji" [possibly Zhang Fakui] (SNA).

"Guomin gemingjun zongsilingbu sanmouchu beifa zhenzhong riji" (SNA).

"Japanese Diary (last entries)," trans. U.S. Army (USMHI).

"Jūgun techō," in folder "Riwo riji/zaji" (SNA).

"Kaichū nikki" (RIPM).

"Kongjun di-1-lu silingbu zhenzhong riji" (MDHA).

"Kongjun di-4-dadui zhenzhong riji" (MDHA).

"Kongjun di-5-dadui zhenzhong riji" (MDHA).

"Kongjun hongzha zongdui zhenzhong riji" (MDHA).

"Log of the USS Lincoln" (UTL).

"Lujun qibingshi zhenzhong riji (qi-7-shi)" (MDHA).

"Second Parachute Battalion (Reinforced), War Diary" (USMCA).

"Shanghai zuozhan riji," in "Songhu huizhan riji" (SNA).

"Shi-shi budui qingkuang, zhenzhong riji" (HePA).

"Tokkō nikki" (KSDFM).

"Tokuyō nikki" (SPM).

"Zongguo dongbei minzhong jiuguojun zhenzhong riji / Chūgoku tōhoku minshū kyūkokugun jinchū nikki" (NIDS).

BLANK DIARIES

"Jūgun techō," 1937 (RIPM).

"Jūgun techō," 1942 (RIPM).

"Seisen techō," 1944 (ISPWM).

"Service Diary," 1944 (UTL).

Acknowledgments

First and foremost, I received excellent support from Susan Naquin, David Howell, and Sheldon Garon at Princeton University. Shel in particular demonstrated extraordinary patience as I pitched implausible schemes. I also learned a great deal from Paul Miles, Ruth Rogaski, and Stephen Kotkin while at Princeton. Advisors at Oberlin, including Ann Sherif and Ron DiCenzo, and at the University of Michigan, such as Ken K. Ito, helped me develop the skills necessary for this project. My work has profited immensely from critical readings by Andrew Gordon, Daqing Yang, Parks Coble, Henrietta Harrison, Edward McCord, Theodore Cook, Samuel Yamashita, and Richard Smethurst. During my time at Oxford, Rana Mitter was extremely generous with his time. Anonymous reviewers at Harvard University Press provided important critical feedback, and my editor Kathleen McDermott has been exceedingly patient as I tamed this project. Micah L. Auerback responded to far too many versions of this work for me to ever be able to return the debt. Friends and colleagues who have sent me diaries, books, and articles critical to my research are simply too numerous to mention, but I shall always remember my debt to them.

Invaluable financial support came from East Asian Studies at Princeton, the Andrew J. Mellon Foundation, and the Dean's Fund. The Blakemore Foundation provided me with a one-year grant to improve my Chinese in Beijing and Taipei. PhD research was funded by the Itō Foundation and the Mrs. Giles Whiting Foundation. A postdoctoral fellowship from the Reischauer Institute of Japanese Studies at Harvard University transformed the manuscript into a book. While I was at Oxford University, the final stages of research were funded by the Leverhulme Trust, the Great Britain Sasakawa Foundation, the British Academy, the Shanghai Academy of Social Sciences, and Oxford University's Faculty of History.

It would be impossible for me to mention all of the people in East Asia who have assisted me in this challenging endeavor, but I feel obligated to mention a few outstanding individuals. Tomiyama Ichirō assisted me with my affiliation at Osaka University and proved to be a fantastic intellectual interlocutor. Yamauchi Sayoko, Hoshi Tōru, Yoshimi Yoshiaki, and Ono Kenji offered valuable information and guidance. In Taiwan, I relied on Chen Yung-fa and the staff at the Modern History Institute at the Academia Sinica, and Chang Jui-te was my guide to the complex world of the GMD military. Zhang Xianwen at Nanjing University helped with mainland archives, and Zhu Chengshan of the Nanjing Massacre Memorial secured interviews.

Many archivists went above and beyond the call of duty to help me make this book possible; this sort of project could not be conducted solely in a library or a single research institute, so I was dependent on the goodwill of colleagues in China, Taiwan, Japan, and the United States. For Japanese research, I wish to thank Yamabe Masahiko and the staff at Ritsumeikan, Tsunemoto Hajime and the staff at Peace Osaka, the staff of the Wadatsumi-kai, members of the Chūgoku Kikōsha Renrakukai, Kanoya's SDF Historical Museum director Matsunaga Shigeo, Satō Masaya of the Sendai Rekishi Minzoku Shiryōkan, the staff at the Sensō Shiryōkan (Atsugi and Itagaki Sadao), staff and friends at Kusa no Ie, the Oka Masaharu Heiwa Shiryōkan, Iwate Kenritsu Hakubutsukan, Takamatsu Heiwa Kinenkan, Kitakami Heiwa Kinen Kenjikan, Taketomi Tomoko, and many more. For work in China and Taiwan, I wish to thank the staff of the Ministry of Defense Archives (Taipei), the Chinese Nationalist Party Archives, the National Archives (Taipei), the Institute of Modern History at the Academia Sinica, Ma Zhendu and Xu Yin at the Second Historical Archives (Nanjing), and staff at the Hubei, Hebei, Sichuan, Yunnan, and Zhejiang Provincial Archives. In the United States, I was greatly assisted by Cynthia Tucker and Kurt Piehler at the University of Tennessee (Knoxville), David Keough at the US Army Military History Institute (Carlisle, PA), and the staff at the U.S. Marine Corps Archives (Quantico, VA). I am solely responsible for any flaws in this book.

Of course, I would be remiss indeed if I did not thank my family for their un-flagging support. They are the unshakeable foundation for everything that I have achieved. Researching war reminded me of my grandfather, who always stressed that understanding leads to compassion for others, even if they have wronged you. I therefore dedicate this book to his memory.

Index

Please note that Chinese places are arranged by province, with the exception of Nanjing.